UQ HOLDER!

KEN AKAMATSU

vol.19

CHARACTERS

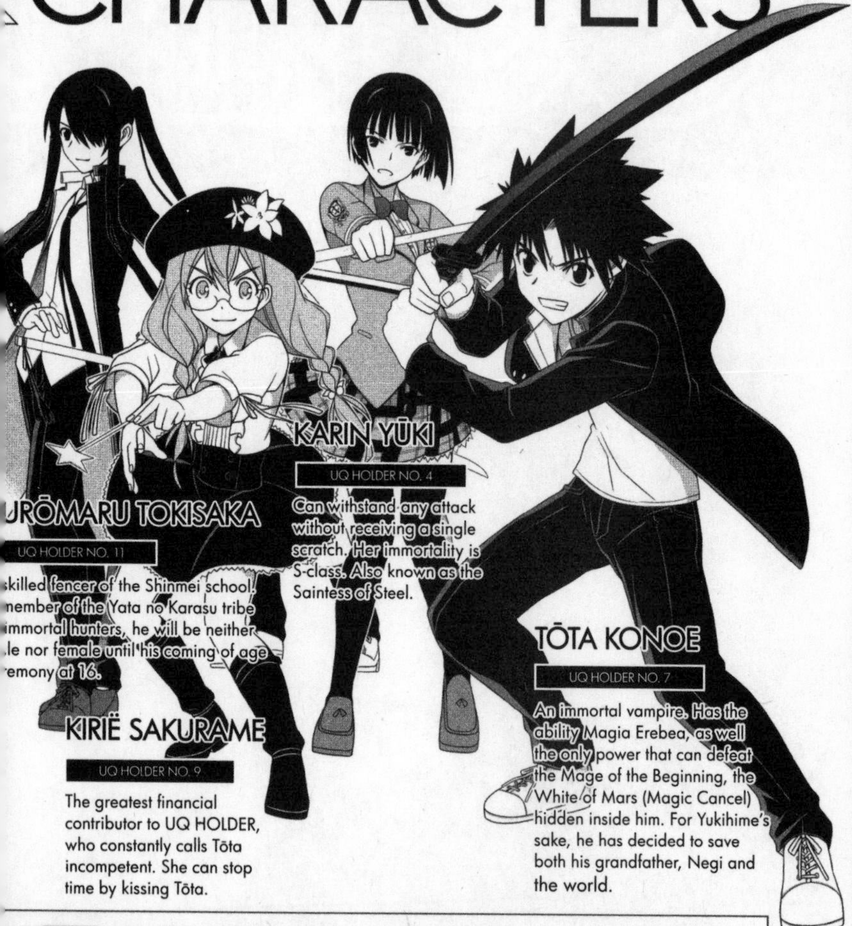

URŌMARU TOKISAKA

UQ HOLDER NO. 11

skilled fencer of the Shinmei school.
member of the Yata no Karasu tribe
immortal hunters, he will be neither
le nor female until his coming of age
emony at 16.

KIRIË SAKURAME

UQ HOLDER NO. 9

The greatest financial contributor to UQ HOLDER, who constantly calls Tōta incompetent. She can stop time by kissing Tōta.

KARIN YŪKI

UQ HOLDER NO. 4

Can withstand any attack without receiving a single scratch. Her immortality is S-class. Also known as the Saintess of Steel.

TŌTA KONOE

UQ HOLDER NO. 7

An immortal vampire. Has the ability Magia Erebea, as well the only power that can defeat the Mage of the Beginning, the White of Mars (Magic Cancel) hidden inside him. For Yukihime's sake, he has decided to save both his grandfather, Negi and the world.

UQ HOLDER IMMORTAL NUMBERS

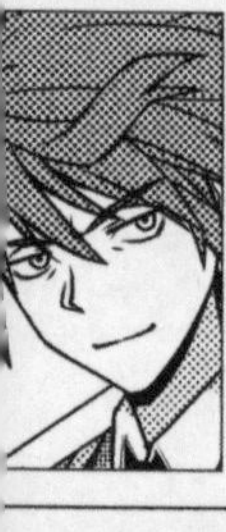

JINBEI SHISHIDO

UQ HOLDER NO. 2

UQ HOLDER's oldest member. Became an immortal in the middle ages, when he ate mermaid flesh in the Muromachi Period. Has the "Switcheroo" skill that switches the locations of physical objects.

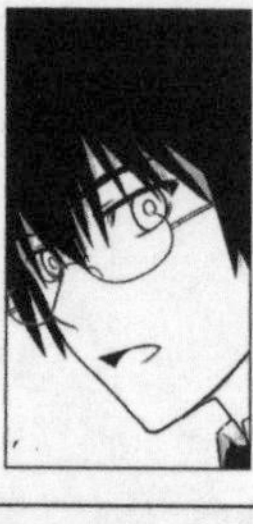

GENGORŌ MAKABE

UQ HOLDER NO. 6

Manages the business side of UQ HOLDER's hideout and inn. He has a skill known as "Multiple Lives," so when he dies, another Gengorō appears.

UQ HOLDER!

Ken Akamatsu Presents

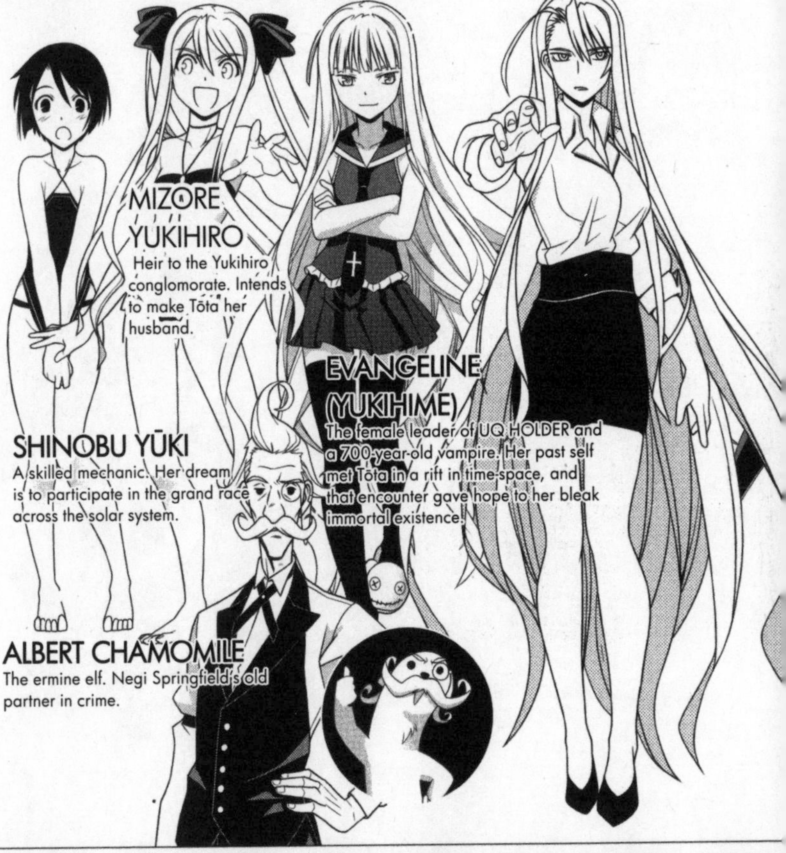

MIZORE YUKIHIRO
Heir to the Yukihiro conglomerate. Intends to make Tōta her husband.

EVANGELINE (YUKIHIME)
The female leader of UQ HOLDER and a 700-year-old vampire. Her past self met Tōta in a rift in time-space, and that encounter gave hope to her bleak immortal existence.

SHINOBU YŪKI
A skilled mechanic. Her dream is to participate in the grand race across the solar system.

ALBERT CHAMOMILE
The ermine elf. Negi Springfield's old partner in crime.

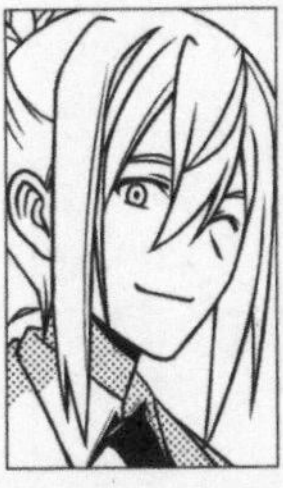

IKKŪ AMEYA

UQ HOLDER NO. 10

After falling into a coma at age 13 and lying in a hospital bed for 72 years, he became a full-body cyborg at age 85. He's very good with his hands. ♡

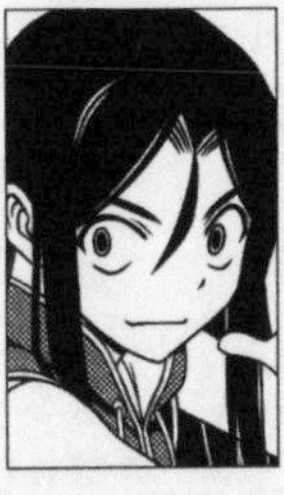

SANTA SASAKI

UQ HOLDER NO. 12

A revenant brought back to life through necromancy. He has multiple abilities, including flight, intangibility, possession telekinesis, etc.

After but a moment's rest with Evangeline...

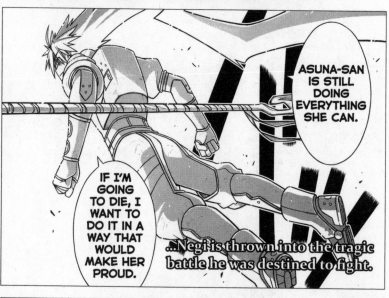

ASUNA-SAN IS STILL DOING EVERYTHING SHE CAN.

IF I'M GOING TO DIE, I WANT TO DO IT IN A WAY THAT WOULD MAKE HER PROUD.

...Negi is thrown into the tragic battle he was destined to fight.

CALL OFF THE NEGI SPRINGFIELD CLONING PROJECT.

I WILL KILL NEGI

AND PUT AN END TO ALL OF THIS.

Then, Fate and Evangeline dispatch with the Negi clone plan...

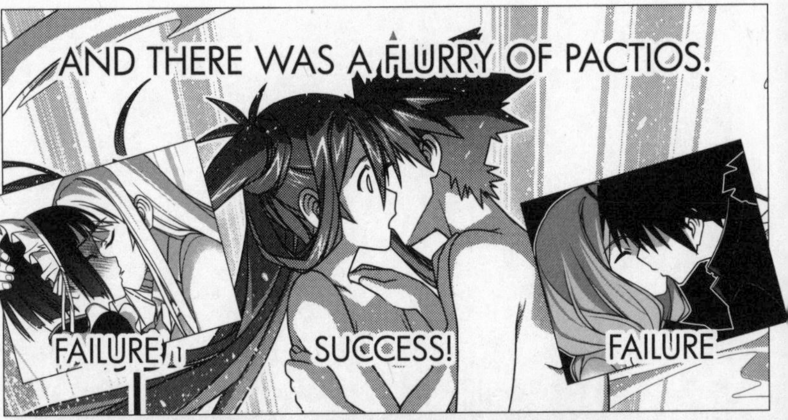
AND THERE WAS A FLURRY OF PACTIOS.
FAILURE
SUCCESS!
FAILURE

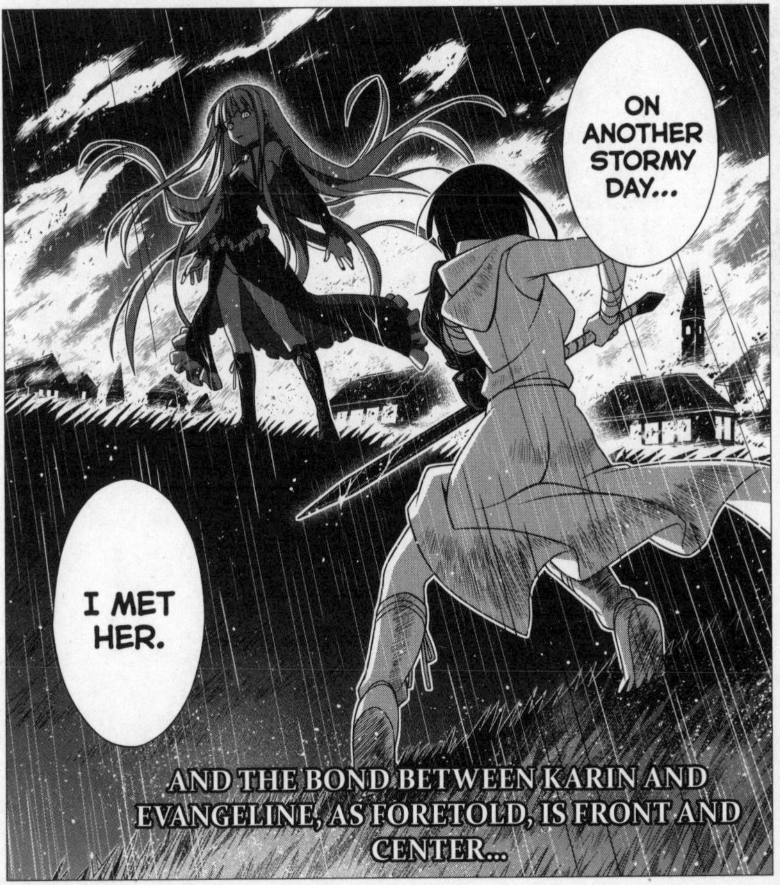
ON ANOTHER STORMY DAY...
I MET HER.
AND THE BOND BETWEEN KARIN AND EVANGELINE, AS FORETOLD, IS FRONT AND CENTER...

CONTENTS

Stage.153 THE MAGES 7

Stage.154 THE ROAD TO THE BIRTH OF THE DEMON QUEEN 47

Stage.155 THE LONG FATED BATTLE 87

Stage.156 THE LONG, LONG THREE HOURS 125

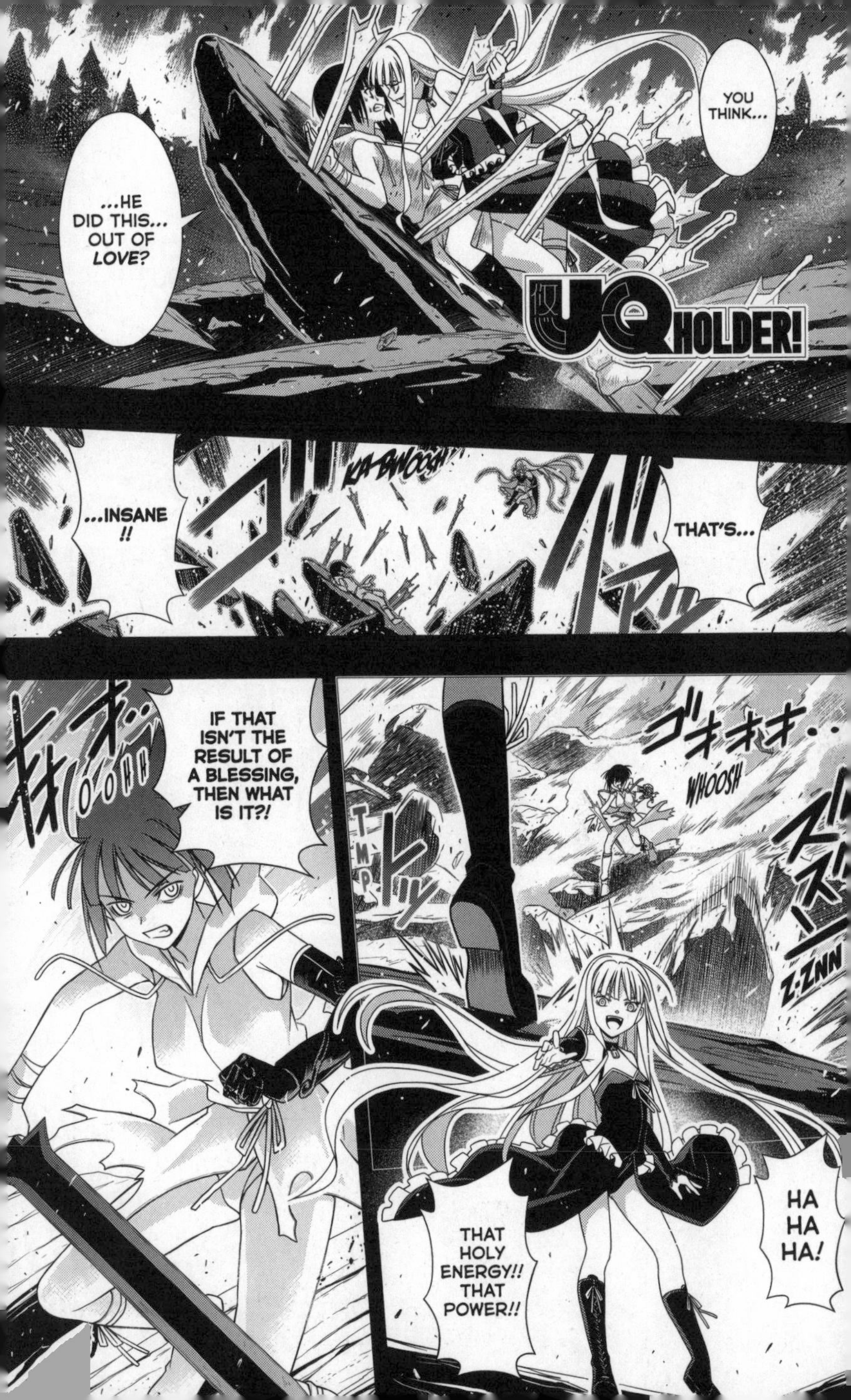
YOU THINK...
...HE DID THIS... OUT OF LOVE?
UQ HOLDER!
THAT'S...
KA-BWOOSH
...INSANE!!
WHOOSH
Z-ZNN
TMP
HA HA HA!
THAT HOLY ENERGY!! THAT POWER!!
IF THAT ISN'T THE RESULT OF A BLESSING, THEN WHAT IS IT?!
OOHH

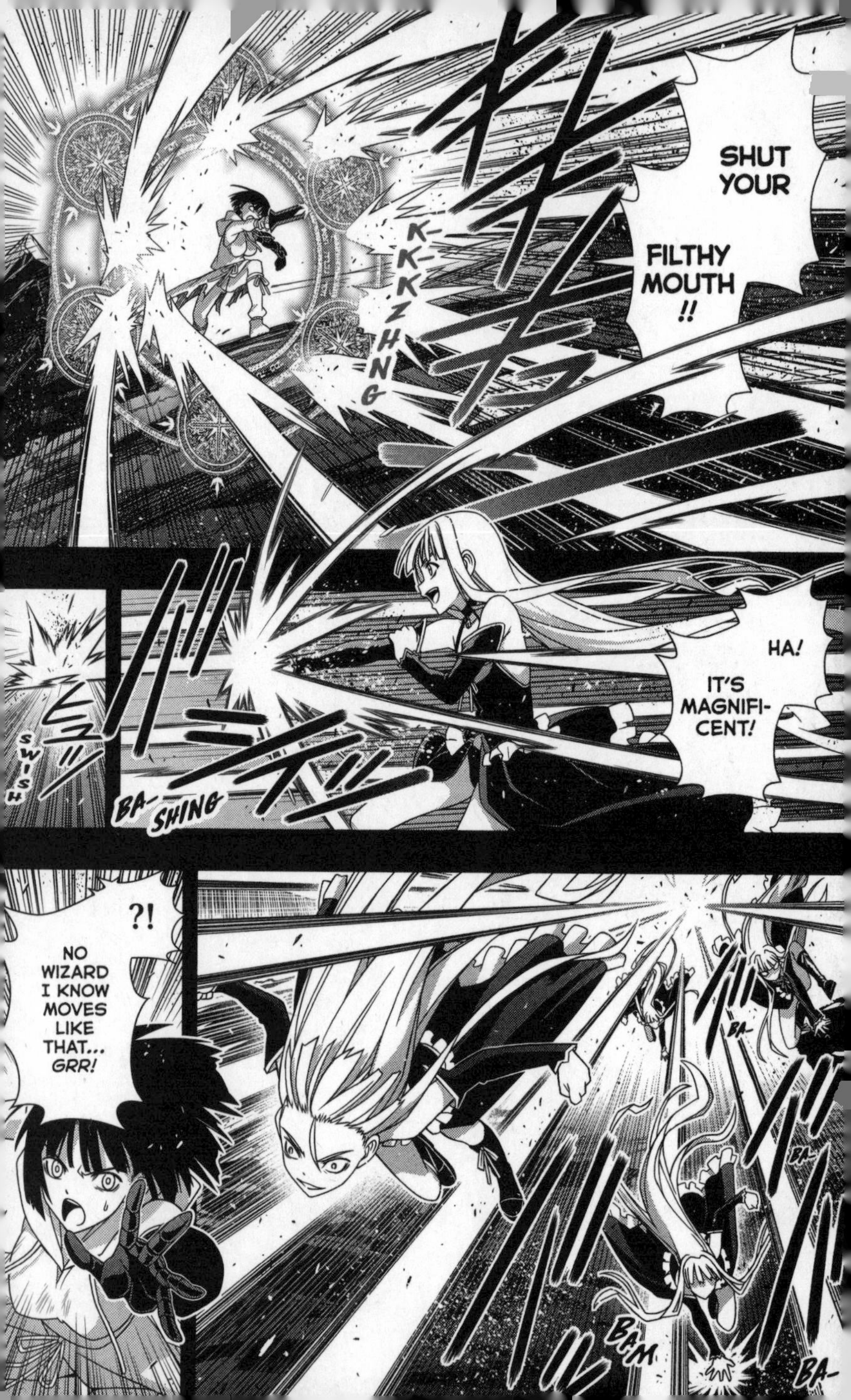
SHUT YOUR FILTHY MOUTH!!
K-K-K-K-ZHNNG
HA! IT'S MAGNIFI-CENT!
BA-SHING
SWISH
BA-
BA-
BAM
BA-
?!
NO WIZARD I KNOW MOVES LIKE THAT... GRR!

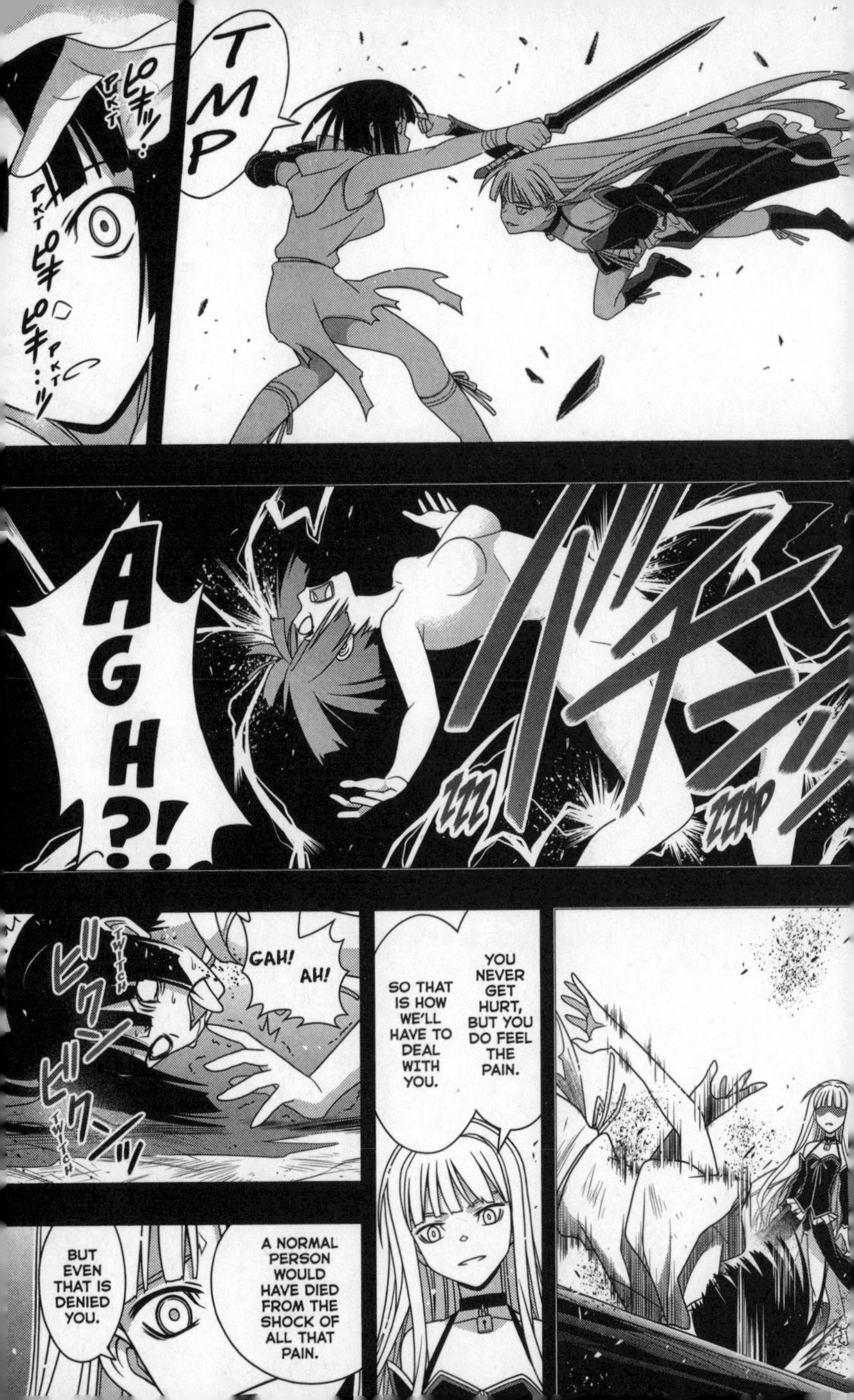
TMP
ピキッ! PKT
ピキ PKT ピキ ピキ...ッ PKT
ZZZ
ZZAP
AGH?!
YOU NEVER GET HURT, BUT YOU DO FEEL THE PAIN.
SO THAT IS HOW WE'LL HAVE TO DEAL WITH YOU.
GAH!
AH!
ビクン TWITCH
ビクン...ッ TWITCH
A NORMAL PERSON WOULD HAVE DIED FROM THE SHOCK OF ALL THAT PAIN.
BUT EVEN THAT IS DENIED YOU.

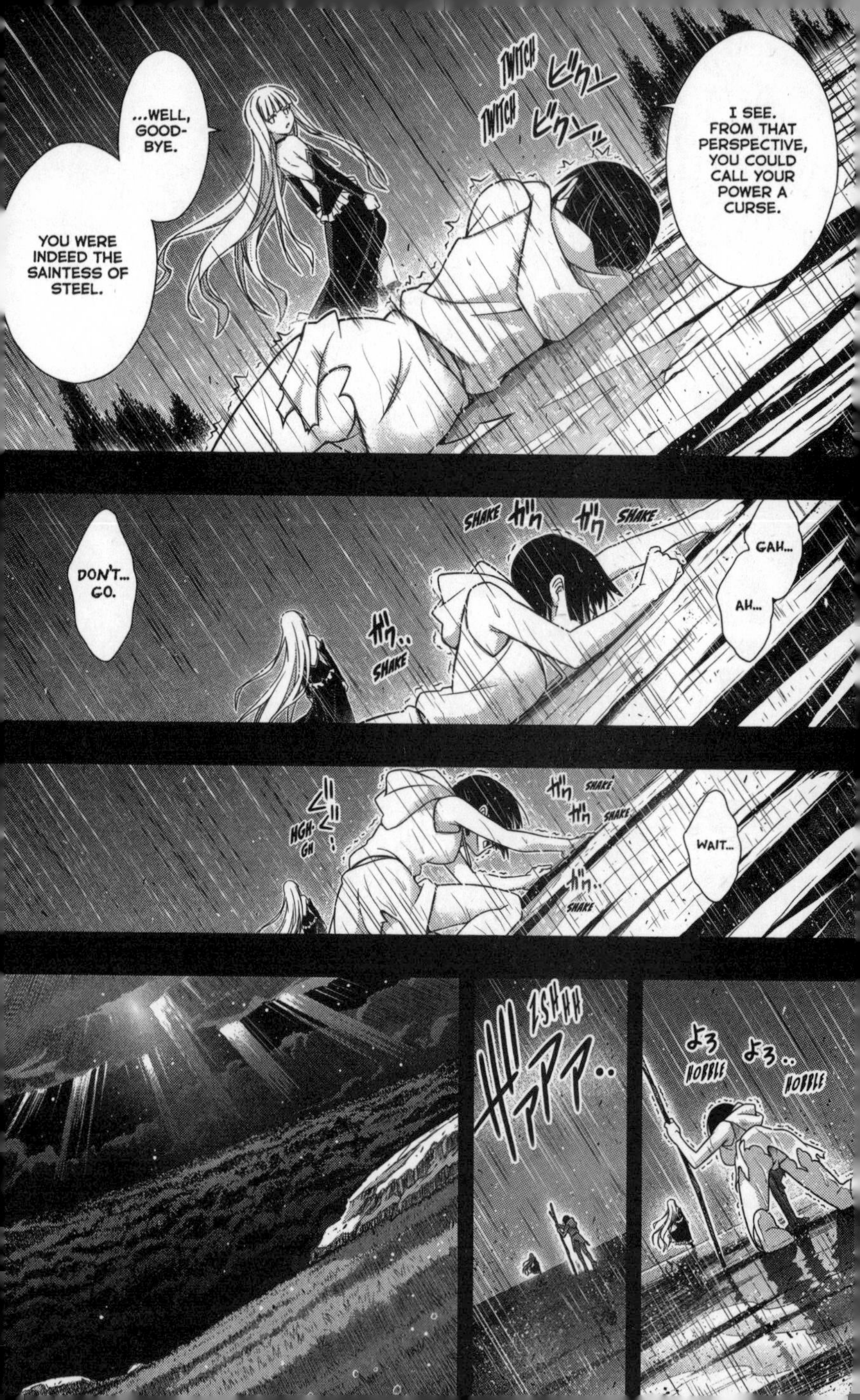
I SEE. FROM THAT PERSPECTIVE, YOU COULD CALL YOUR POWER A CURSE.
TWITCH ビクッ
TWITCH ビクンッ
...WELL, GOOD-BYE.
YOU WERE INDEED THE SAINTESS OF STEEL.
GAH...
AH...
SHAKE ガク
ガク SHAKE
ガク.. SHAKE
DON'T... GO.
WAIT...
ガク SHAKE
ガク SHAKE
ガク.. SHAKE
HGH-GH
よろ HOBBLE
よろ.. HOBBLE
ZSHHH
ザアア..

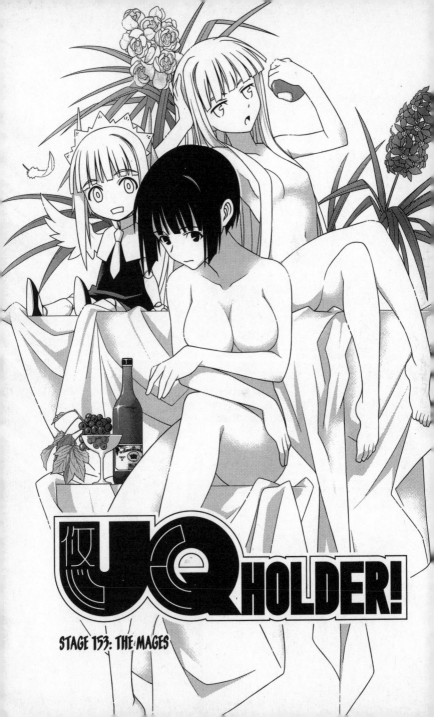

UQ HOLDER!

STAGE 153: THE MAGES

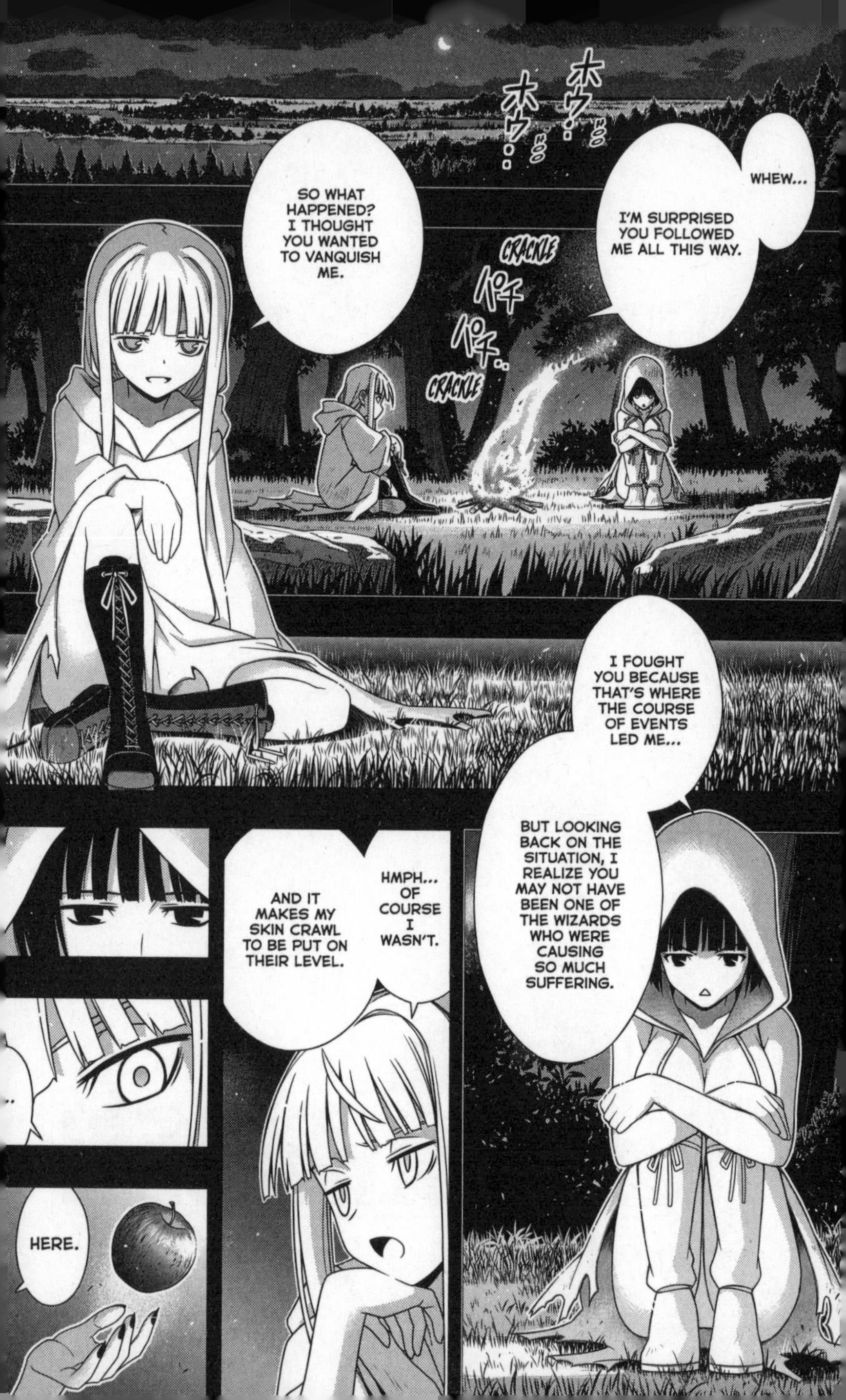

ホウ…
ホウ…
WHEW...
I'M SURPRISED YOU FOLLOWED ME ALL THIS WAY.
CRACKLE
パチ
パチ
CRACKLE
SO WHAT HAPPENED? I THOUGHT YOU WANTED TO VANQUISH ME.
I FOUGHT YOU BECAUSE THAT'S WHERE THE COURSE OF EVENTS LED ME...
BUT LOOKING BACK ON THE SITUATION, I REALIZE YOU MAY NOT HAVE BEEN ONE OF THE WIZARDS WHO WERE CAUSING SO MUCH SUFFERING.
HMPH... OF COURSE I WASN'T.
AND IT MAKES MY SKIN CRAWL TO BE PUT ON THEIR LEVEL.
..
HERE.

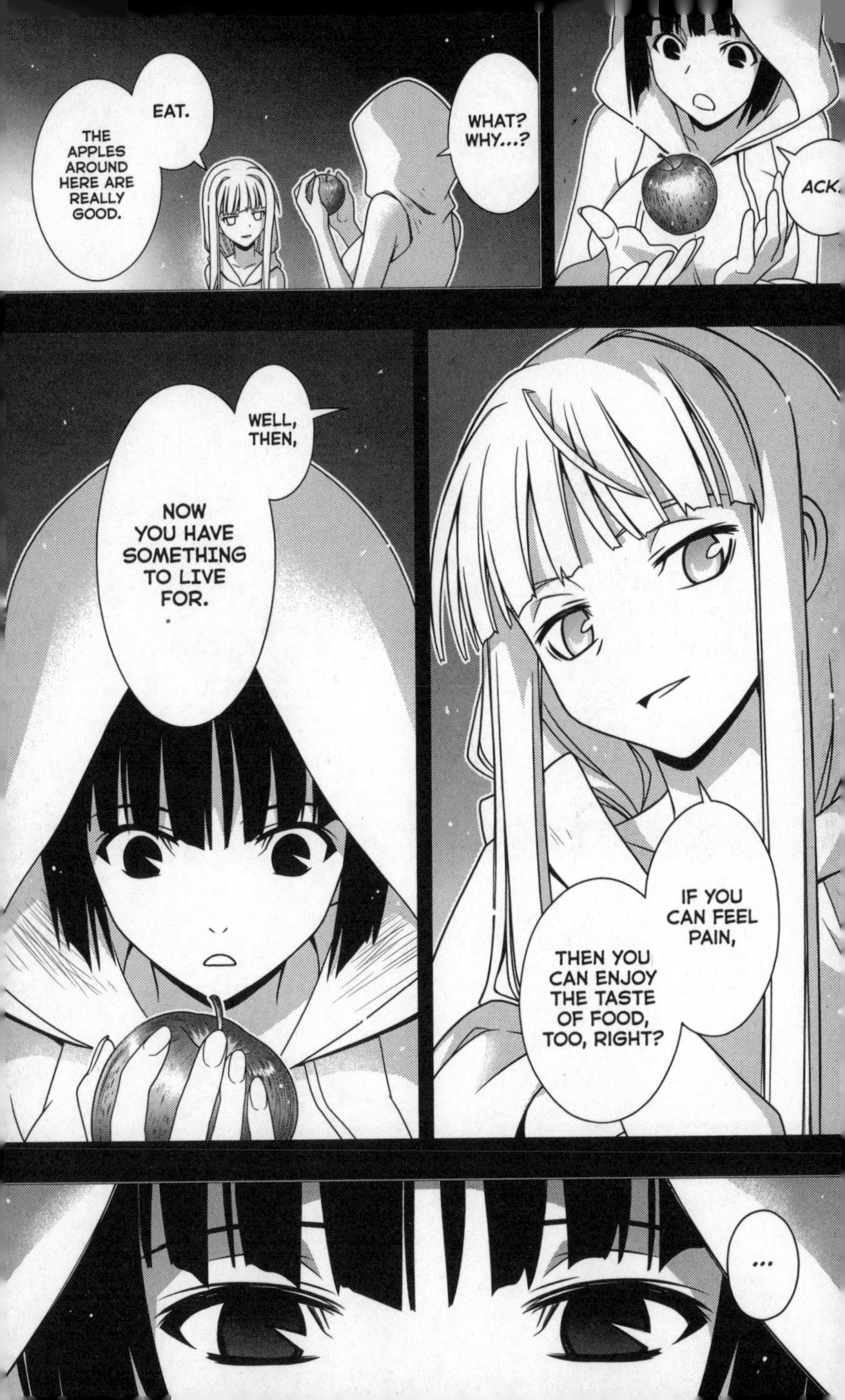
ACK.
WHAT? WHY...?
EAT.
THE APPLES AROUND HERE ARE REALLY GOOD.
IF YOU CAN FEEL PAIN,
THEN YOU CAN ENJOY THE TASTE OF FOOD, TOO, RIGHT?
WELL, THEN,
NOW YOU HAVE SOMETHING TO LIVE FOR.
...

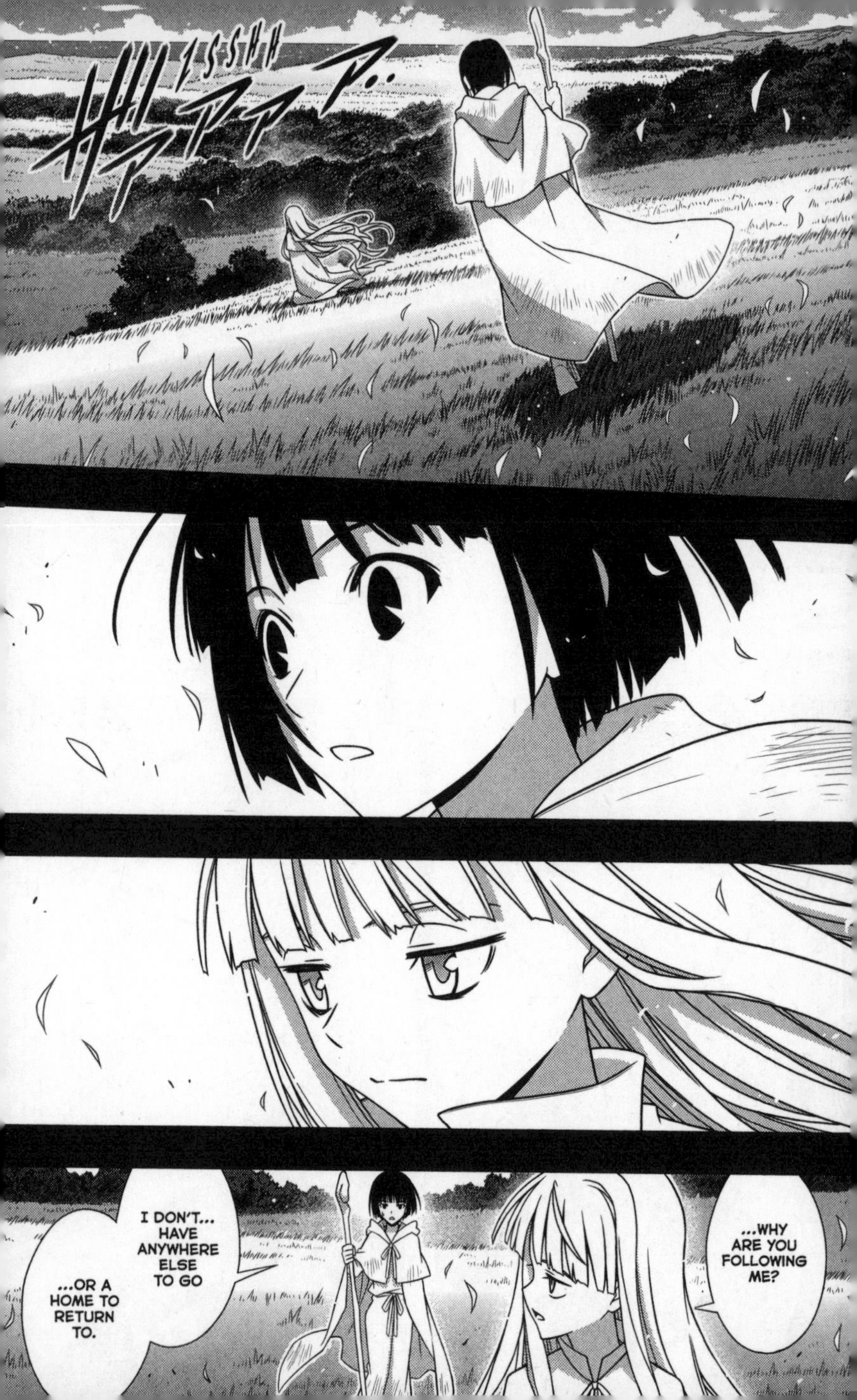
ZSSHH
ザァァァ…
...WHY ARE YOU FOLLOWING ME?
I DON'T... HAVE ANYWHERE ELSE TO GO
...OR A HOME TO RETURN TO.

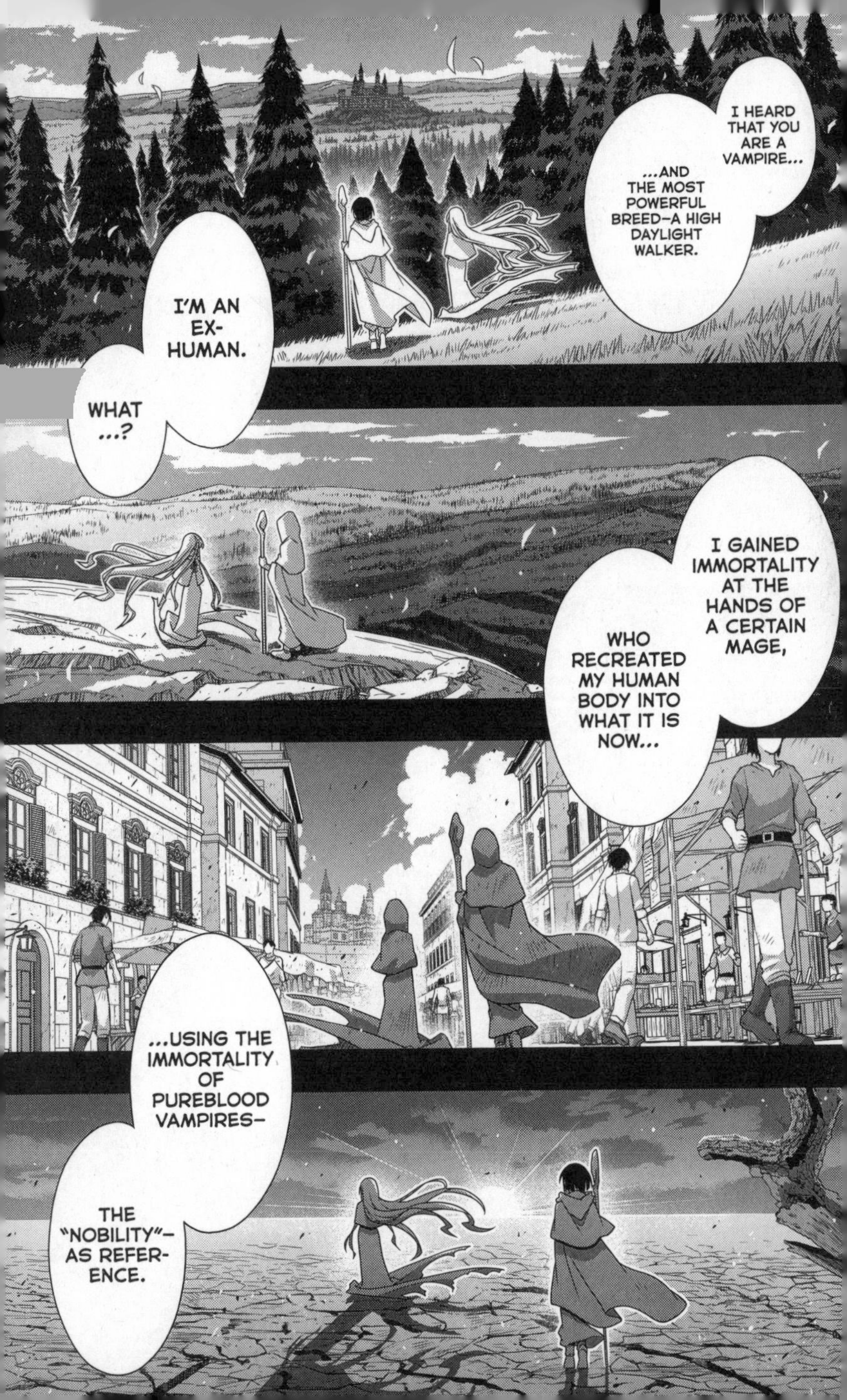
I HEARD THAT YOU ARE A VAMPIRE...
...AND THE MOST POWERFUL BREED—A HIGH DAYLIGHT WALKER.
I'M AN EX-HUMAN.
WHAT ...?
I GAINED IMMORTALITY AT THE HANDS OF A CERTAIN MAGE,
WHO RECREATED MY HUMAN BODY INTO WHAT IT IS NOW...
...USING THE IMMORTALITY OF PUREBLOOD VAMPIRES—
THE "NOBILITY"—AS REFERENCE.

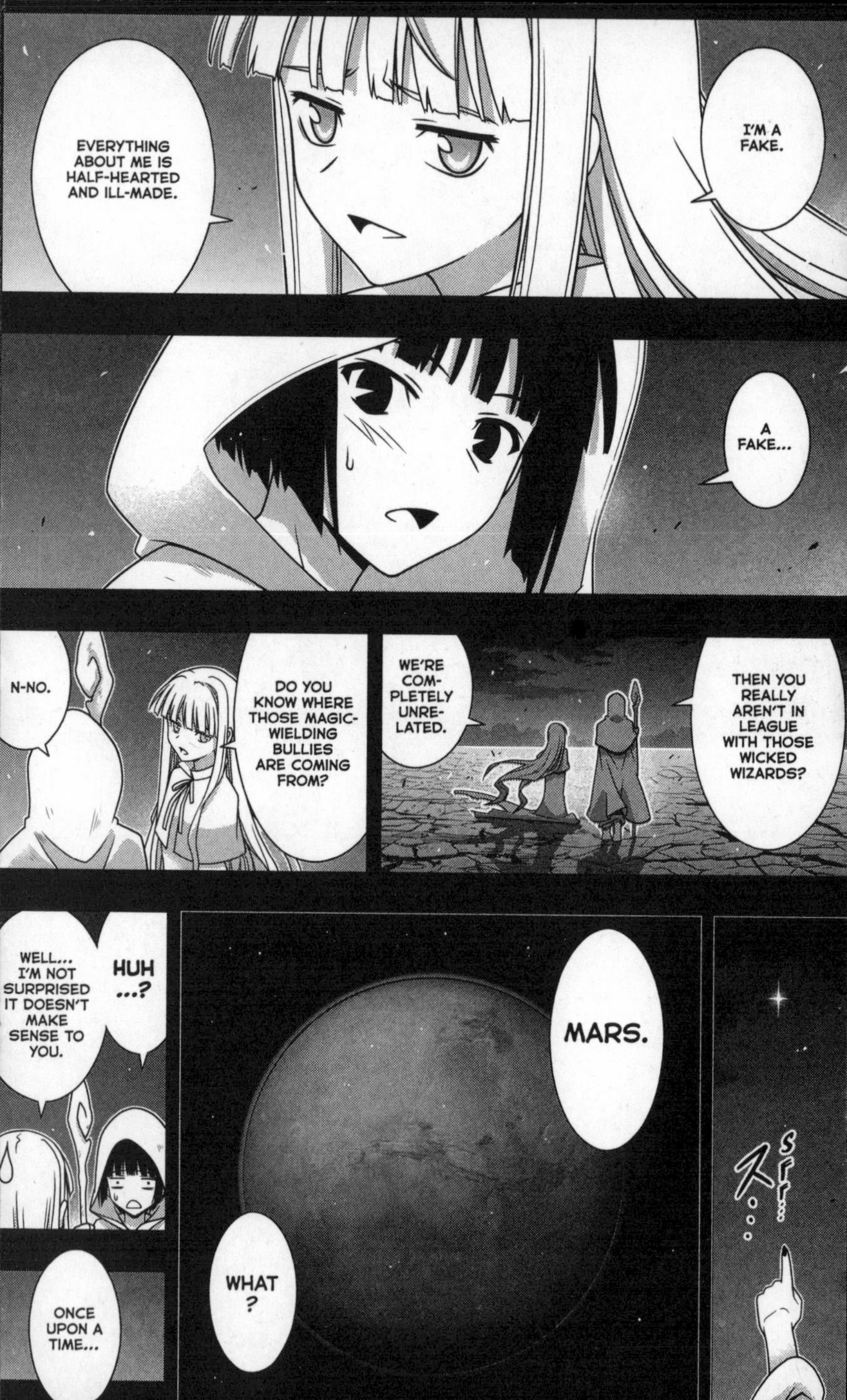
I'M A FAKE.
EVERYTHING ABOUT ME IS HALF-HEARTED AND ILL-MADE.
A FAKE...
THEN YOU REALLY AREN'T IN LEAGUE WITH THOSE WICKED WIZARDS?
WE'RE COMPLETELY UNRELATED.
DO YOU KNOW WHERE THOSE MAGIC-WIELDING BULLIES ARE COMING FROM?
N-NO.
ス
SFF...
MARS.
WHAT?
HUH...?
WELL... I'M NOT SURPRISED IT DOESN'T MAKE SENSE TO YOU.
ONCE UPON A TIME...

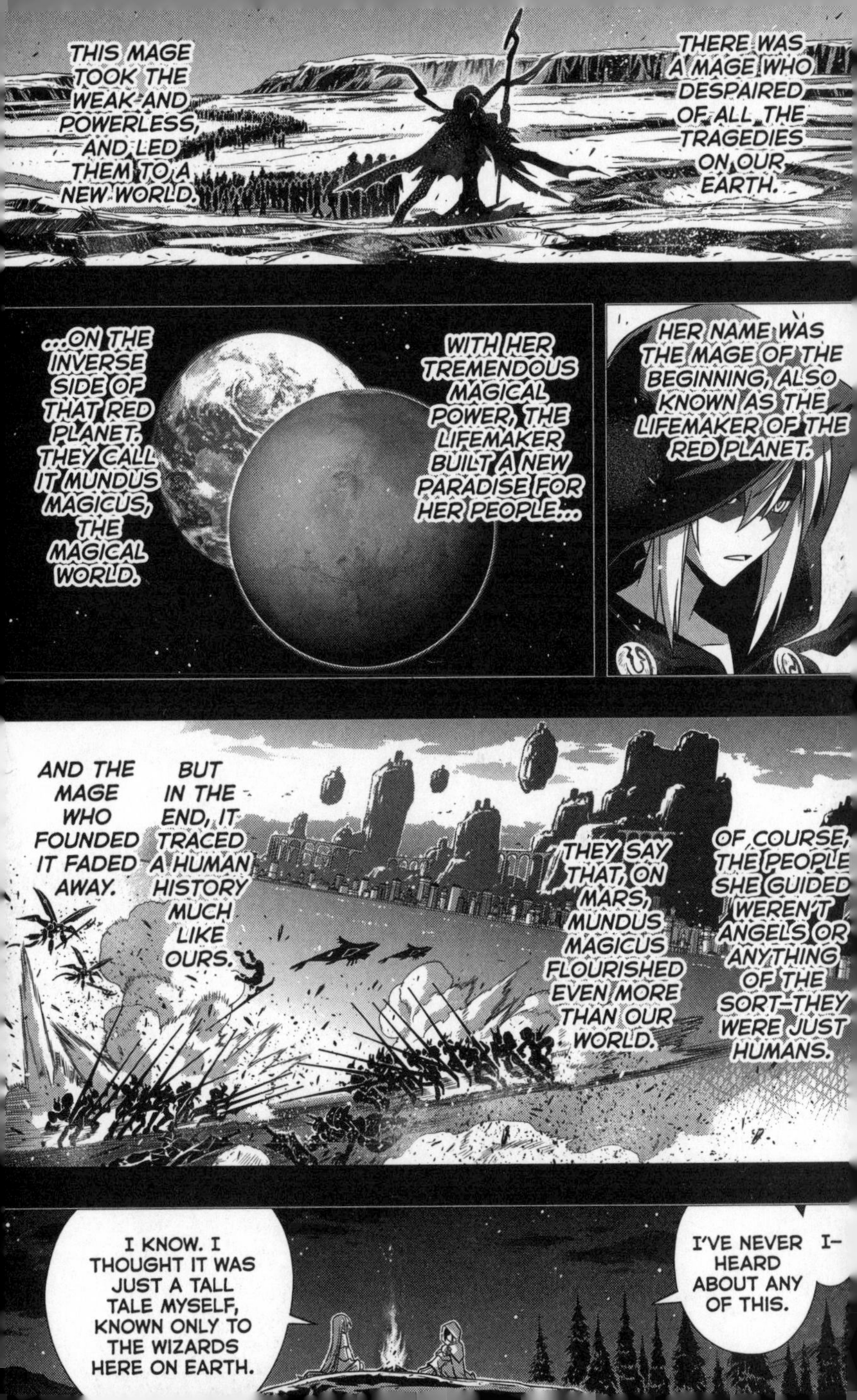
THERE WAS A MAGE WHO DESPAIRED OF ALL THE TRAGEDIES ON OUR EARTH.
THIS MAGE TOOK THE WEAK AND POWERLESS, AND LED THEM TO A NEW WORLD.
HER NAME WAS THE MAGE OF THE BEGINNING, ALSO KNOWN AS THE LIFEMAKER OF THE RED PLANET.
WITH HER TREMENDOUS MAGICAL POWER, THE LIFEMAKER BUILT A NEW PARADISE FOR HER PEOPLE...
...ON THE INVERSE SIDE OF THAT RED PLANET. THEY CALL IT MUNDUS MAGICUS, THE MAGICAL WORLD.
OF COURSE, THE PEOPLE SHE GUIDED WEREN'T ANGELS OR ANYTHING OF THE SORT—THEY WERE JUST HUMANS.
THEY SAY THAT, ON MARS, MUNDUS MAGICUS FLOURISHED EVEN MORE THAN OUR WORLD.
BUT IN THE END, IT TRACED A HUMAN HISTORY MUCH LIKE OURS.
AND THE MAGE WHO FOUNDED IT FADED AWAY.
I—
I'VE NEVER HEARD ABOUT ANY OF THIS.
I KNOW. I THOUGHT IT WAS JUST A TALL TALE MYSELF, KNOWN ONLY TO THE WIZARDS HERE ON EARTH.

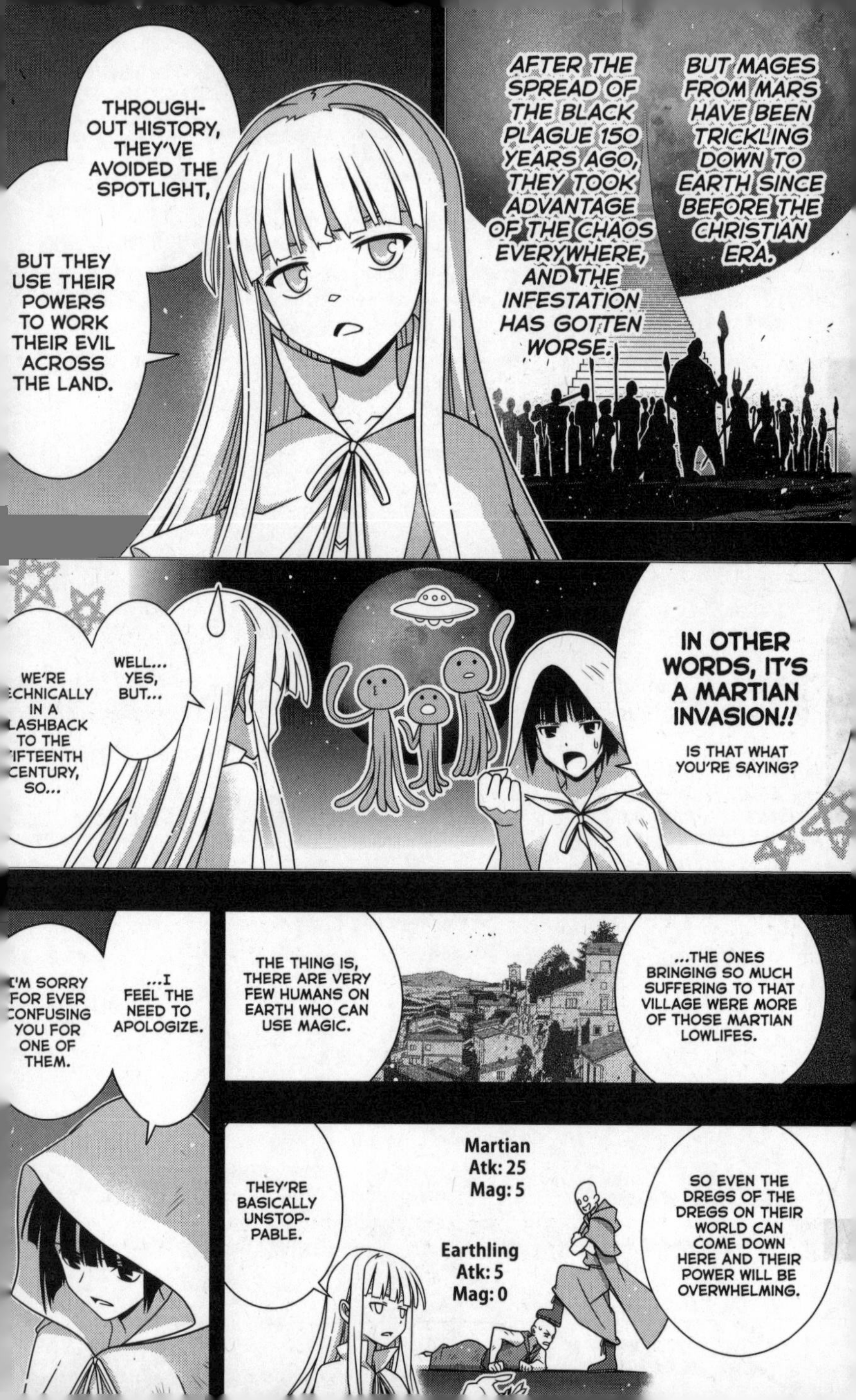
BUT MAGES FROM MARS HAVE BEEN TRICKLING DOWN TO EARTH SINCE BEFORE THE CHRISTIAN ERA.
AFTER THE SPREAD OF THE BLACK PLAGUE 150 YEARS AGO, THEY TOOK ADVANTAGE OF THE CHAOS EVERYWHERE, AND THE INFESTATION HAS GOTTEN WORSE.
THROUGH-OUT HISTORY, THEY'VE AVOIDED THE SPOTLIGHT,
BUT THEY USE THEIR POWERS TO WORK THEIR EVIL ACROSS THE LAND.
IN OTHER WORDS, IT'S A MARTIAN INVASION!!
IS THAT WHAT YOU'RE SAYING?
WELL... YES, BUT...
WE'RE ECHNICALLY IN A LASHBACK TO THE IFTEENTH CENTURY, SO...
...THE ONES BRINGING SO MUCH SUFFERING TO THAT VILLAGE WERE MORE OF THOSE MARTIAN LOWLIFES.
THE THING IS, THERE ARE VERY FEW HUMANS ON EARTH WHO CAN USE MAGIC.
SO EVEN THE DREGS OF THE DREGS ON THEIR WORLD CAN COME DOWN HERE AND THEIR POWER WILL BE OVERWHELMING.
Martian Atk: 25 Mag: 5
THEY'RE BASICALLY UNSTOP-PABLE.
Earthling Atk: 5 Mag: 0
...I FEEL THE NEED TO APOLOGIZE.
'M SORRY FOR EVER ONFUSING YOU FOR ONE OF THEM.

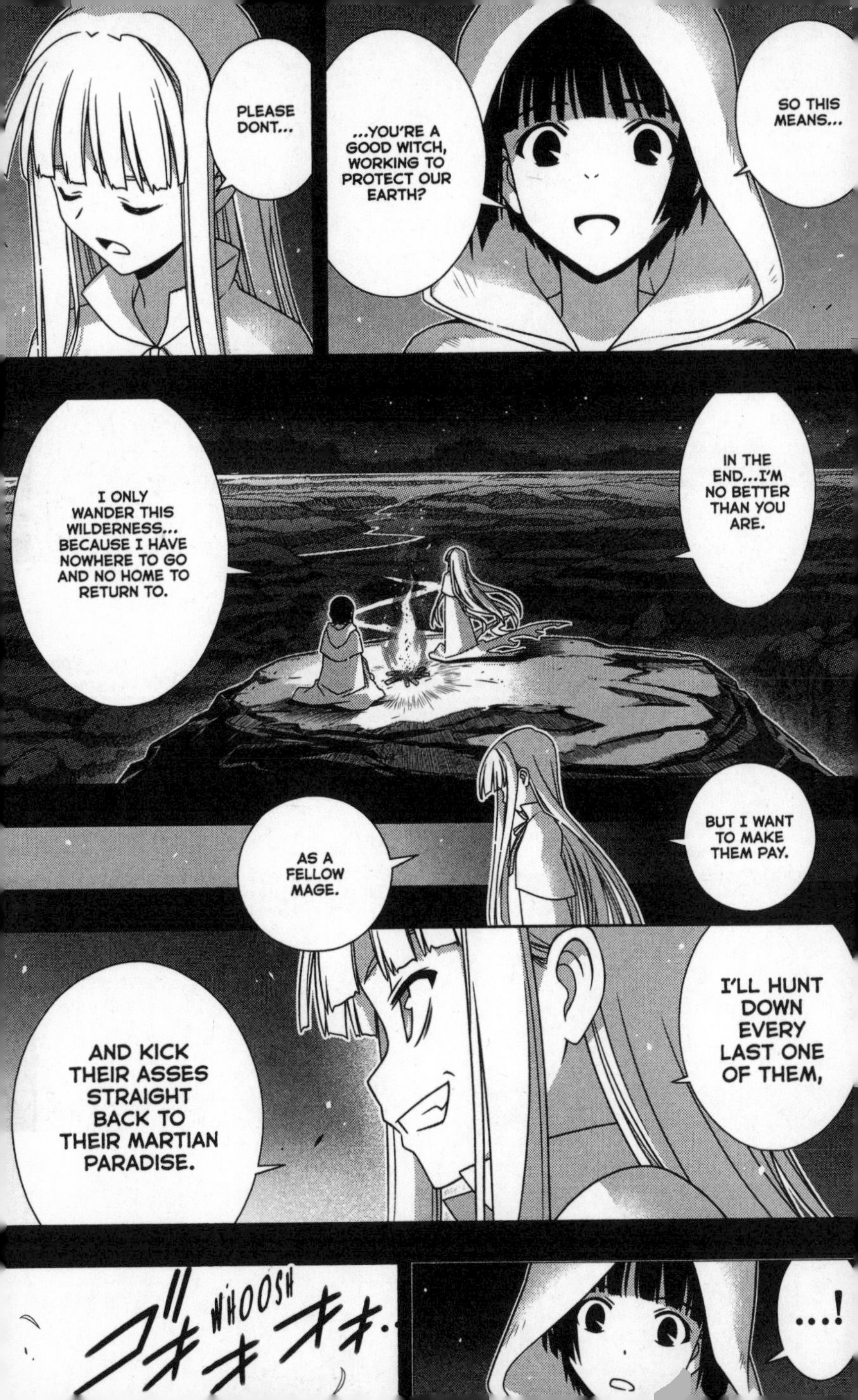
SO THIS MEANS...
...YOU'RE A GOOD WITCH, WORKING TO PROTECT OUR EARTH?
PLEASE DONT...
IN THE END...I'M NO BETTER THAN YOU ARE.
I ONLY WANDER THIS WILDERNESS... BECAUSE I HAVE NOWHERE TO GO AND NO HOME TO RETURN TO.
BUT I WANT TO MAKE THEM PAY.
AS A FELLOW MAGE.
I'LL HUNT DOWN EVERY LAST ONE OF THEM,
AND KICK THEIR ASSES STRAIGHT BACK TO THEIR MARTIAN PARADISE.
...!
WHOOSH
ゴオォォォ..

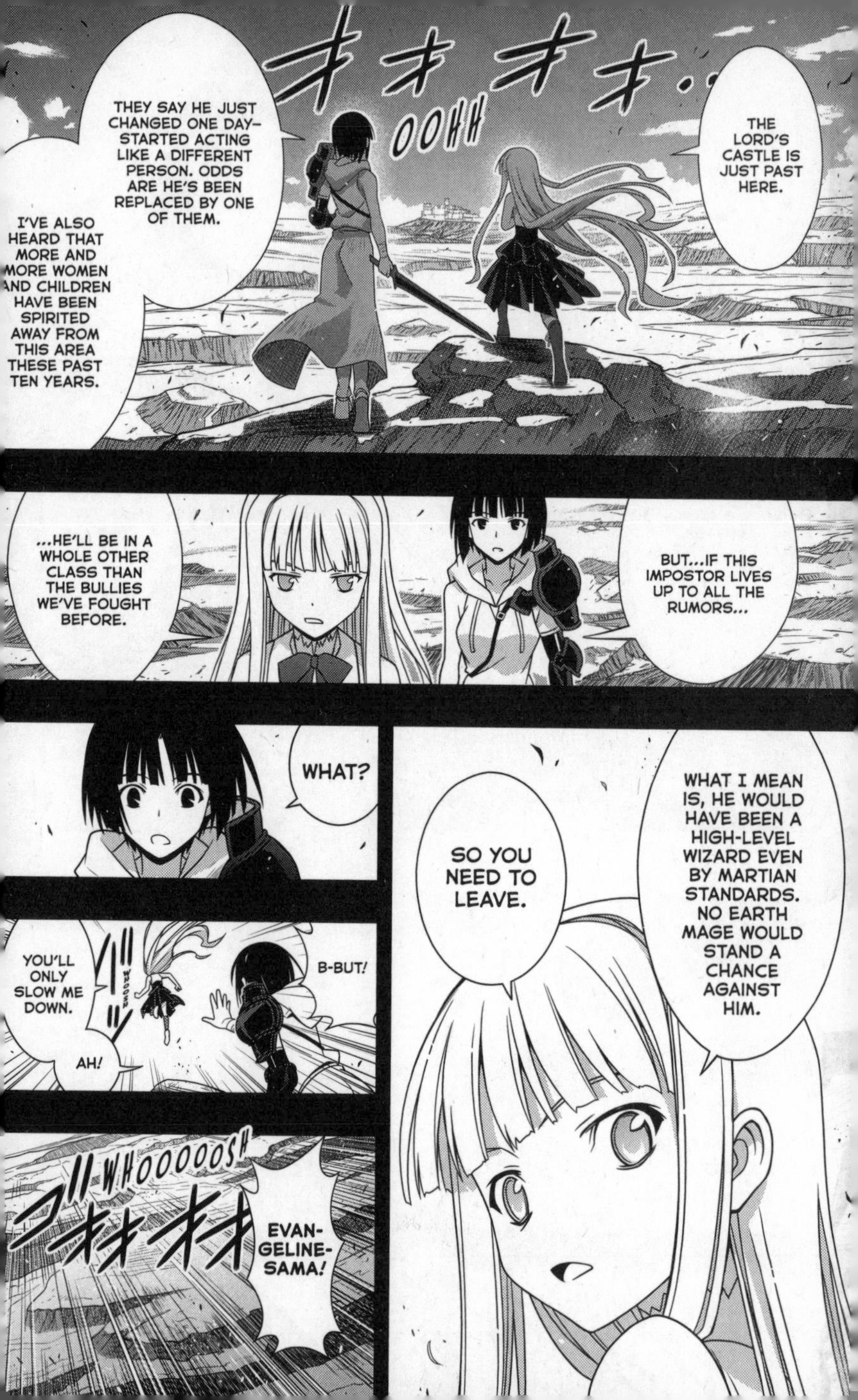
オオオオ..
OOHH
THE LORD'S CASTLE IS JUST PAST HERE.
THEY SAY HE JUST CHANGED ONE DAY–STARTED ACTING LIKE A DIFFERENT PERSON. ODDS ARE HE'S BEEN REPLACED BY ONE OF THEM.
I'VE ALSO HEARD THAT MORE AND MORE WOMEN AND CHILDREN HAVE BEEN SPIRITED AWAY FROM THIS AREA THESE PAST TEN YEARS.
BUT...IF THIS IMPOSTOR LIVES UP TO ALL THE RUMORS...
...HE'LL BE IN A WHOLE OTHER CLASS THAN THE BULLIES WE'VE FOUGHT BEFORE.
WHAT I MEAN IS, HE WOULD HAVE BEEN A HIGH-LEVEL WIZARD EVEN BY MARTIAN STANDARDS. NO EARTH MAGE WOULD STAND A CHANCE AGAINST HIM.
SO YOU NEED TO LEAVE.
WHAT?
B-BUT!
YOU'LL ONLY SLOW ME DOWN.
AH!
EVAN-GELINE-SAMA!
WHOOOOOSH

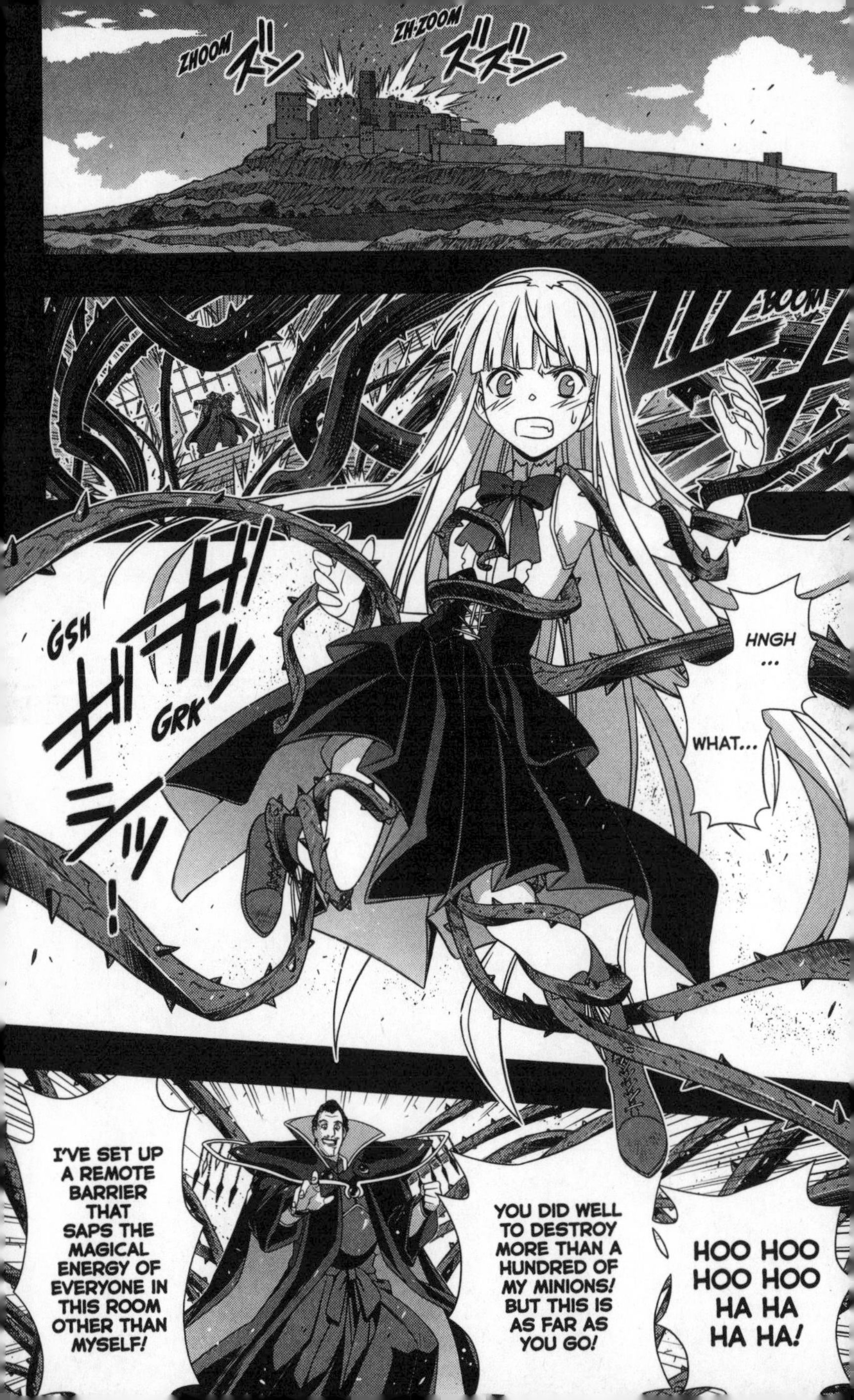
ZH·ZOOM
ズズン
ZHOOM
ズン
BOOM
HNGH ...
WHAT...
GSH
GRK
!
HOO HOO HOO HOO HA HA HA HA!
YOU DID WELL TO DESTROY MORE THAN A HUNDRED OF MY MINIONS! BUT THIS IS AS FAR AS YOU GO!
I'VE SET UP A REMOTE BARRIER THAT SAPS THE MAGICAL ENERGY OF EVERYONE IN THIS ROOM OTHER THAN MYSELF!

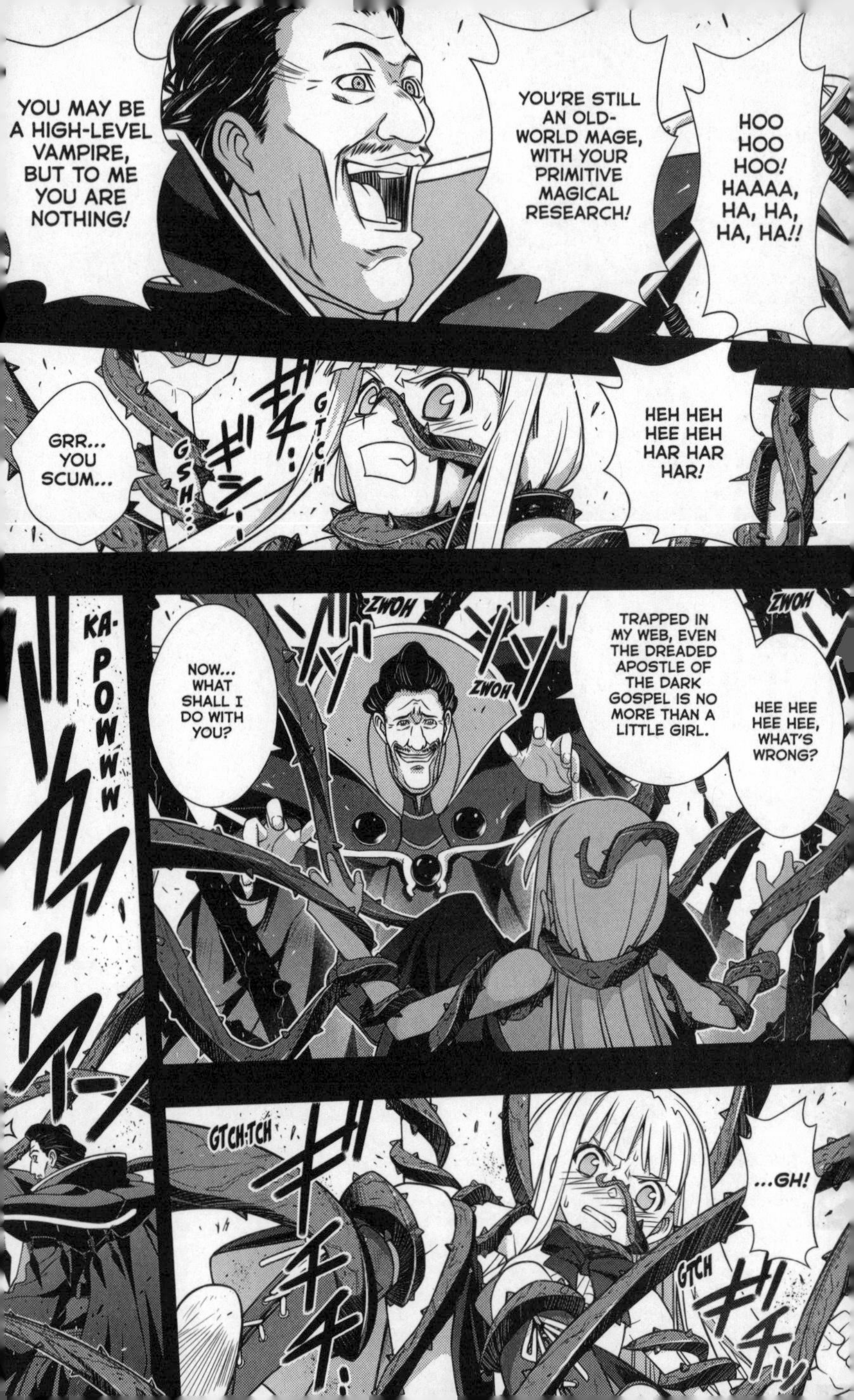
HOO HOO HOO! HAAAA, HA, HA, HA, HA!!
YOU'RE STILL AN OLD-WORLD MAGE, WITH YOUR PRIMITIVE MAGICAL RESEARCH!
YOU MAY BE A HIGH-LEVEL VAMPIRE, BUT TO ME YOU ARE NOTHING!
HEH HEH HEE HEH HAR HAR HAR!
GTCH
GSH...
GRR... YOU SCUM...
ZWOH
HEE HEE HEE HEE, WHAT'S WRONG?
TRAPPED IN MY WEB, EVEN THE DREADED APOSTLE OF THE DARK GOSPEL IS NO MORE THAN A LITTLE GIRL.
ZWOH
ZWOH
NOW... WHAT SHALL I DO WITH YOU?
...GH!
GTCH
GTCH-TCH
KA-POWWWW

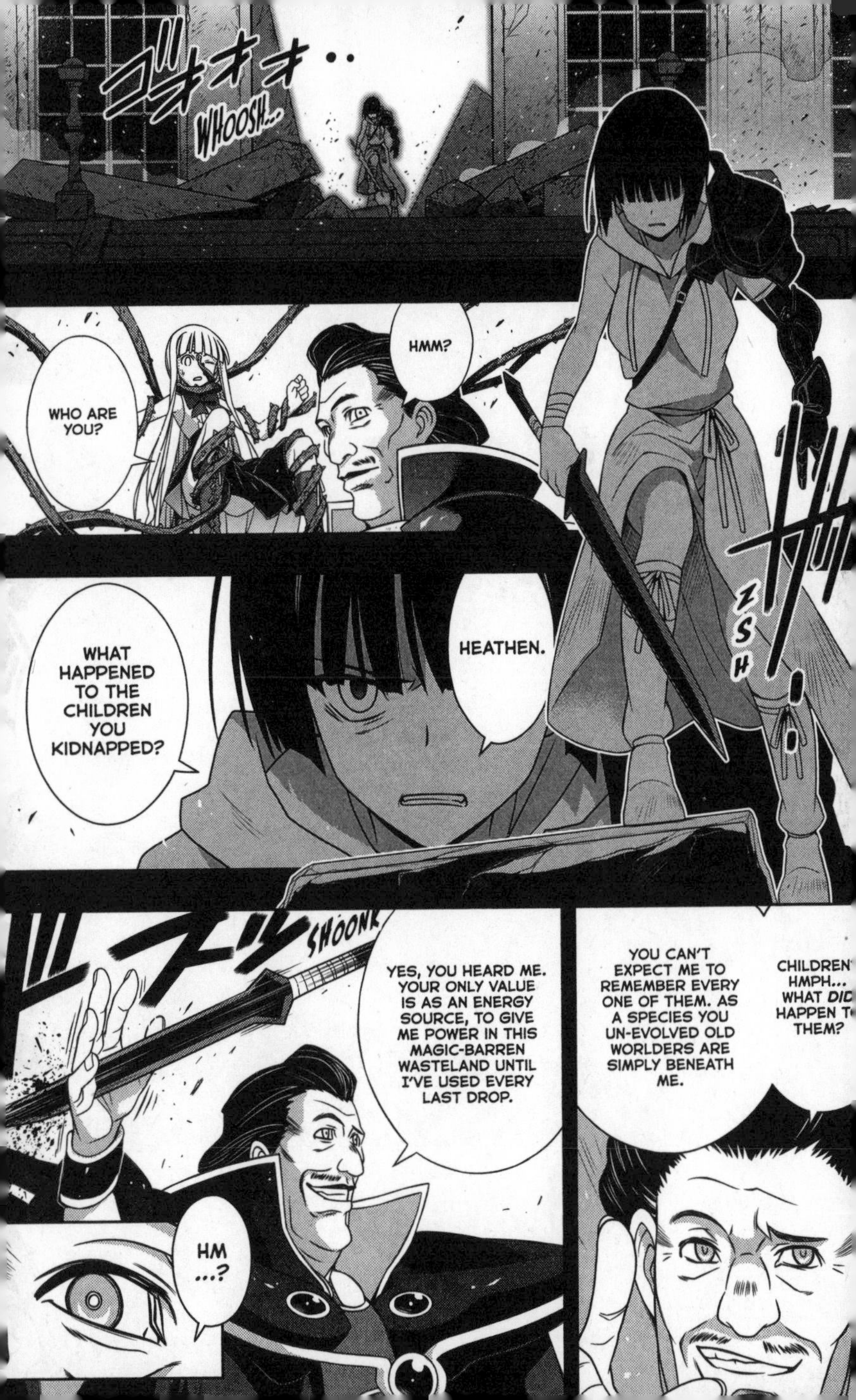
ゴオオオ..
WHOOSH...
HMM?
WHO ARE YOU?
ZSH
HEATHEN.
WHAT HAPPENED TO THE CHILDREN YOU KIDNAPPED?
CHILDREN HMPH... WHAT DID HAPPEN T THEM?
YOU CAN'T EXPECT ME TO REMEMBER EVERY ONE OF THEM. AS A SPECIES YOU UN-EVOLVED OLD WORLDERS ARE SIMPLY BENEATH ME.
SHOONK
YES, YOU HEARD ME. YOUR ONLY VALUE IS AS AN ENERGY SOURCE, TO GIVE ME POWER IN THIS MAGIC-BARREN WASTELAND UNTIL I'VE USED EVERY LAST DROP.
HM ...?

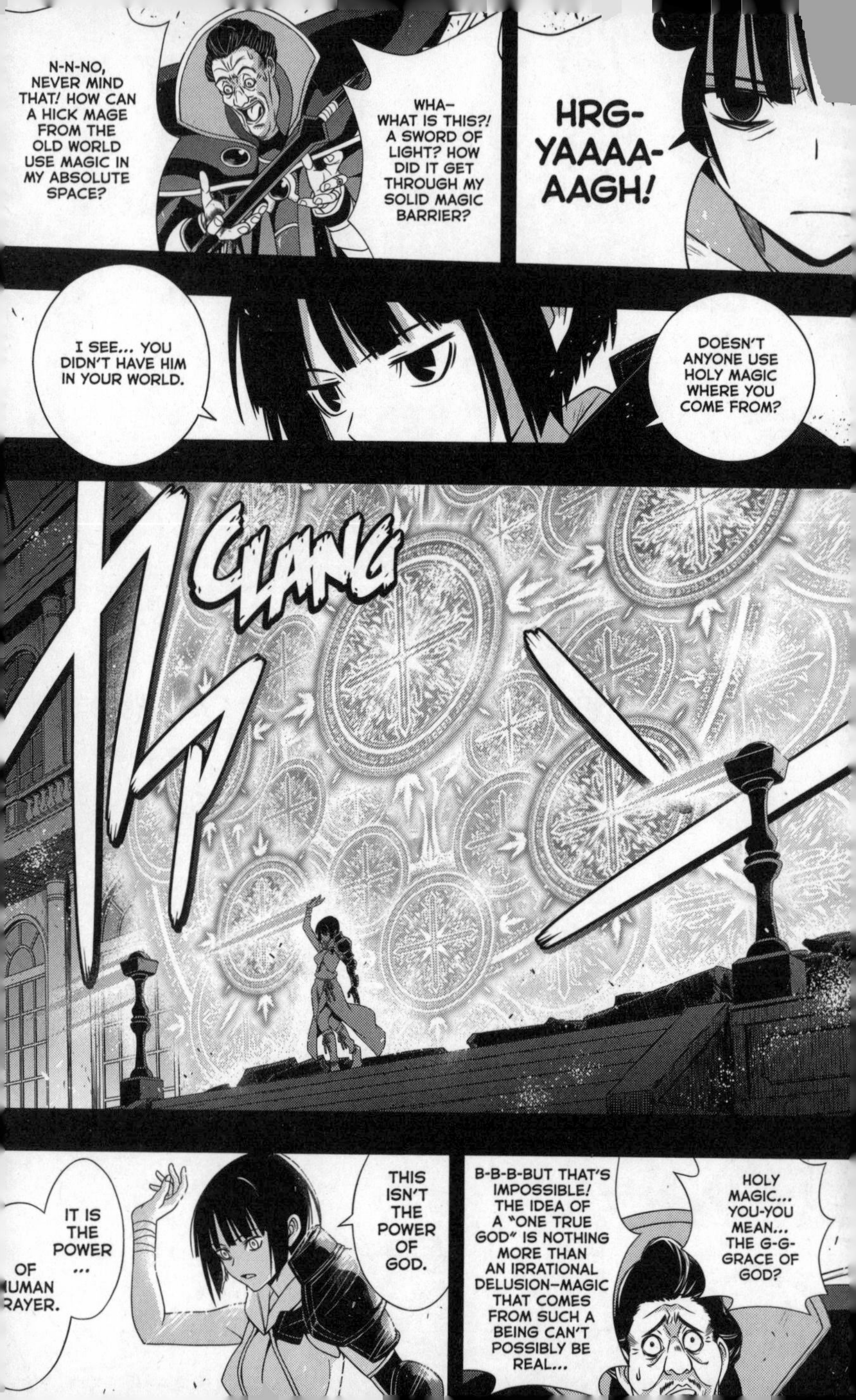

HRG-YAAAA-AAGH!
WHA— WHAT IS THIS?! A SWORD OF LIGHT? HOW DID IT GET THROUGH MY SOLID MAGIC BARRIER?
N-N-NO, NEVER MIND THAT! HOW CAN A HICK MAGE FROM THE OLD WORLD USE MAGIC IN MY ABSOLUTE SPACE?
DOESN'T ANYONE USE HOLY MAGIC WHERE YOU COME FROM?
I SEE... YOU DIDN'T HAVE HIM IN YOUR WORLD.
CLANG
HOLY MAGIC... YOU-YOU MEAN... THE G-G-GRACE OF GOD?
B-B-B-BUT THAT'S IMPOSSIBLE! THE IDEA OF A "ONE TRUE GOD" IS NOTHING MORE THAN AN IRRATIONAL DELUSION—MAGIC THAT COMES FROM SUCH A BEING CAN'T POSSIBLY BE REAL...
THIS ISN'T THE POWER OF GOD.
IT IS THE POWER ... OF UMAN RAYER.

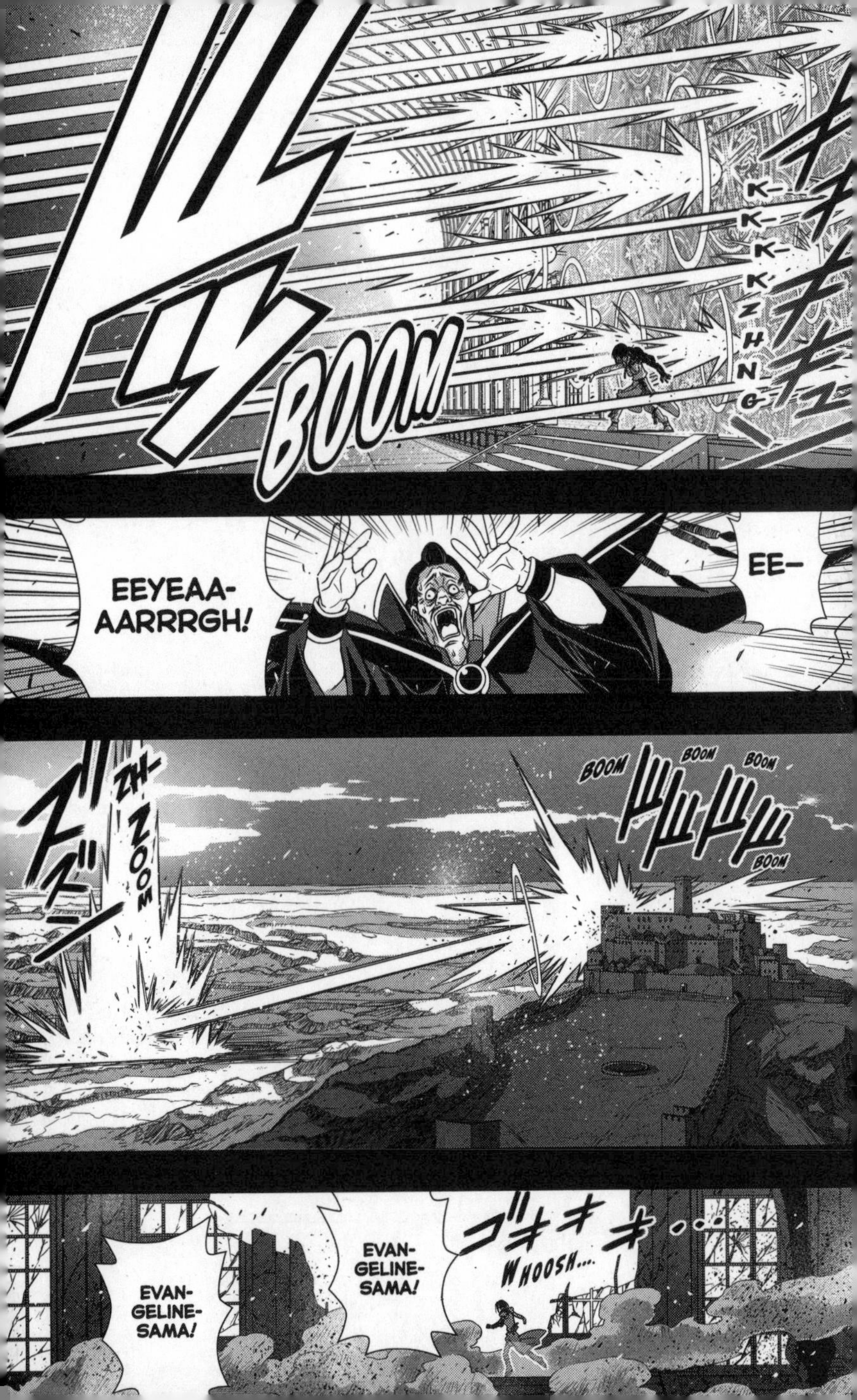
K-K-K-K-ZHHNG
BOOM
EE-
EEYEAA-AARRRGH!
BOOM BOOM BOOM BOOM
ZH-ZOOM
WHOOSH....
EVAN-GELINE-SAMA!
EVAN-GELINE-SAMA!

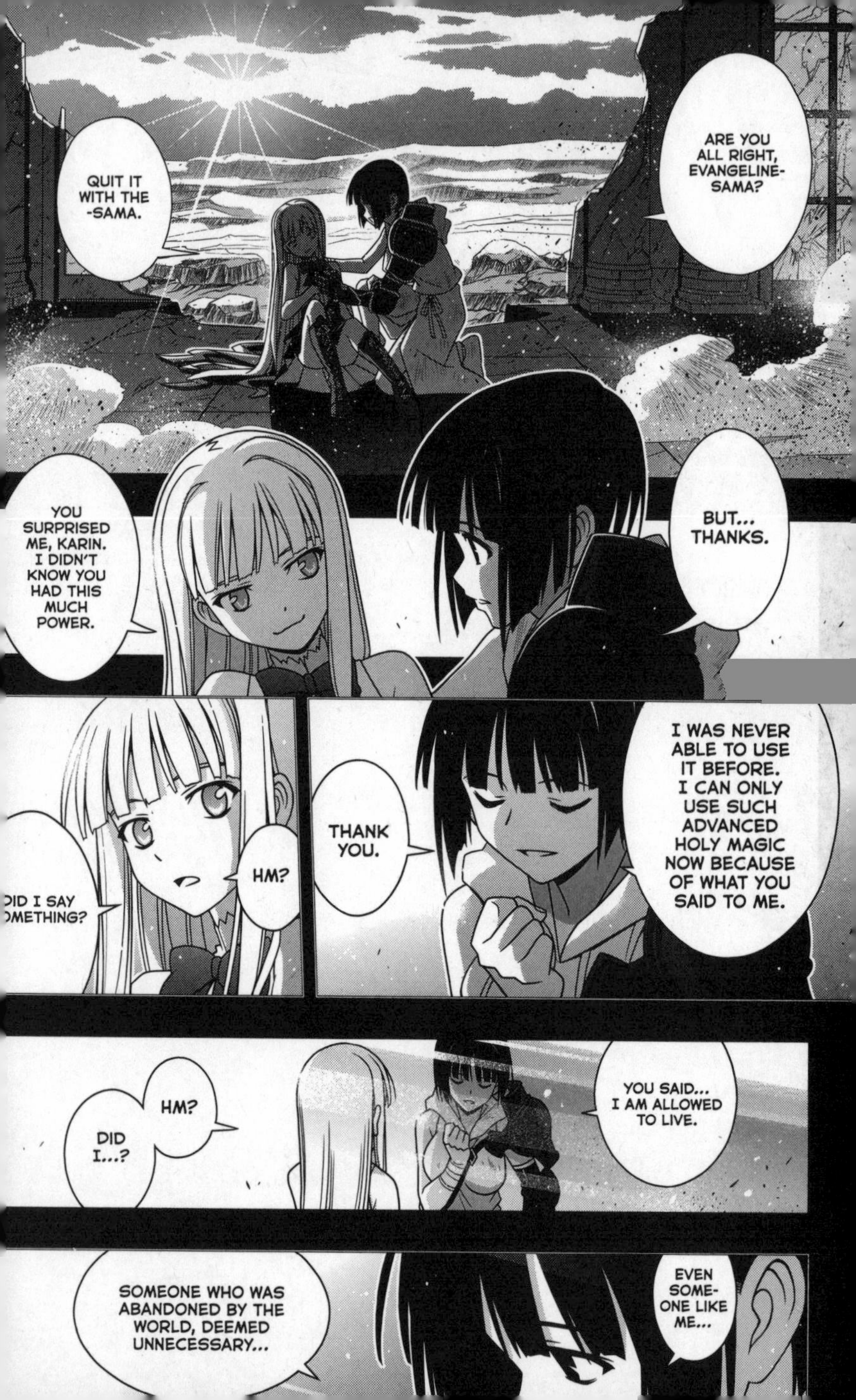

ARE YOU ALL RIGHT, EVANGELINE-SAMA?
QUIT IT WITH THE -SAMA.
YOU SURPRISED ME, KARIN. I DIDN'T KNOW YOU HAD THIS MUCH POWER.
BUT... THANKS.
I WAS NEVER ABLE TO USE IT BEFORE. I CAN ONLY USE SUCH ADVANCED HOLY MAGIC NOW BECAUSE OF WHAT YOU SAID TO ME.
THANK YOU.
HM?
DID I SAY OMETHING?
YOU SAID... I AM ALLOWED TO LIVE.
HM?
DID I...?
EVEN SOME-ONE LIKE ME...
SOMEONE WHO WAS ABANDONED BY THE WORLD, DEEMED UNNECESSARY...

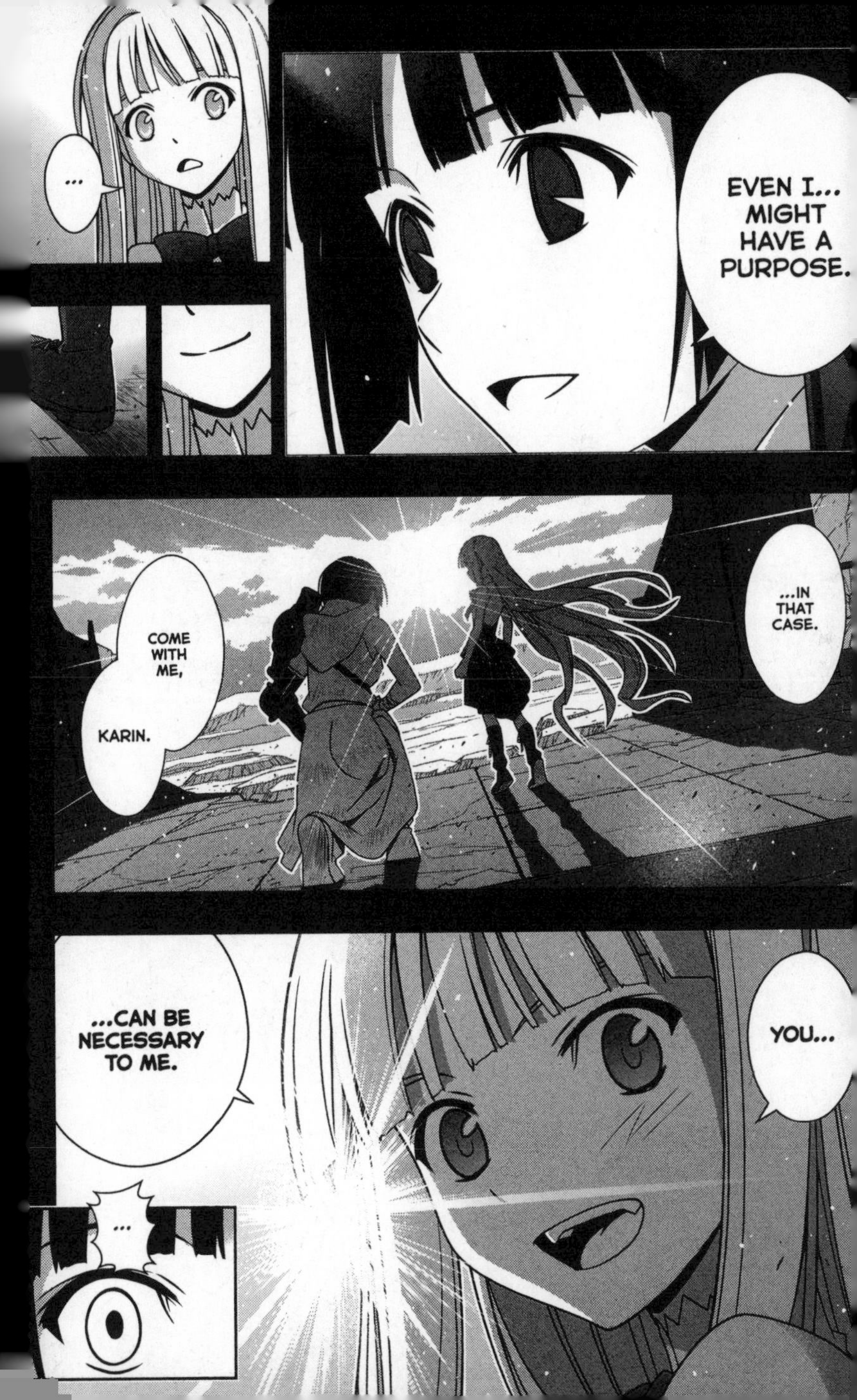
EVEN I... MIGHT HAVE A PURPOSE.
...
...IN THAT CASE.
COME WITH ME,
KARIN.
YOU...
...CAN BE NECESSARY TO ME.
...

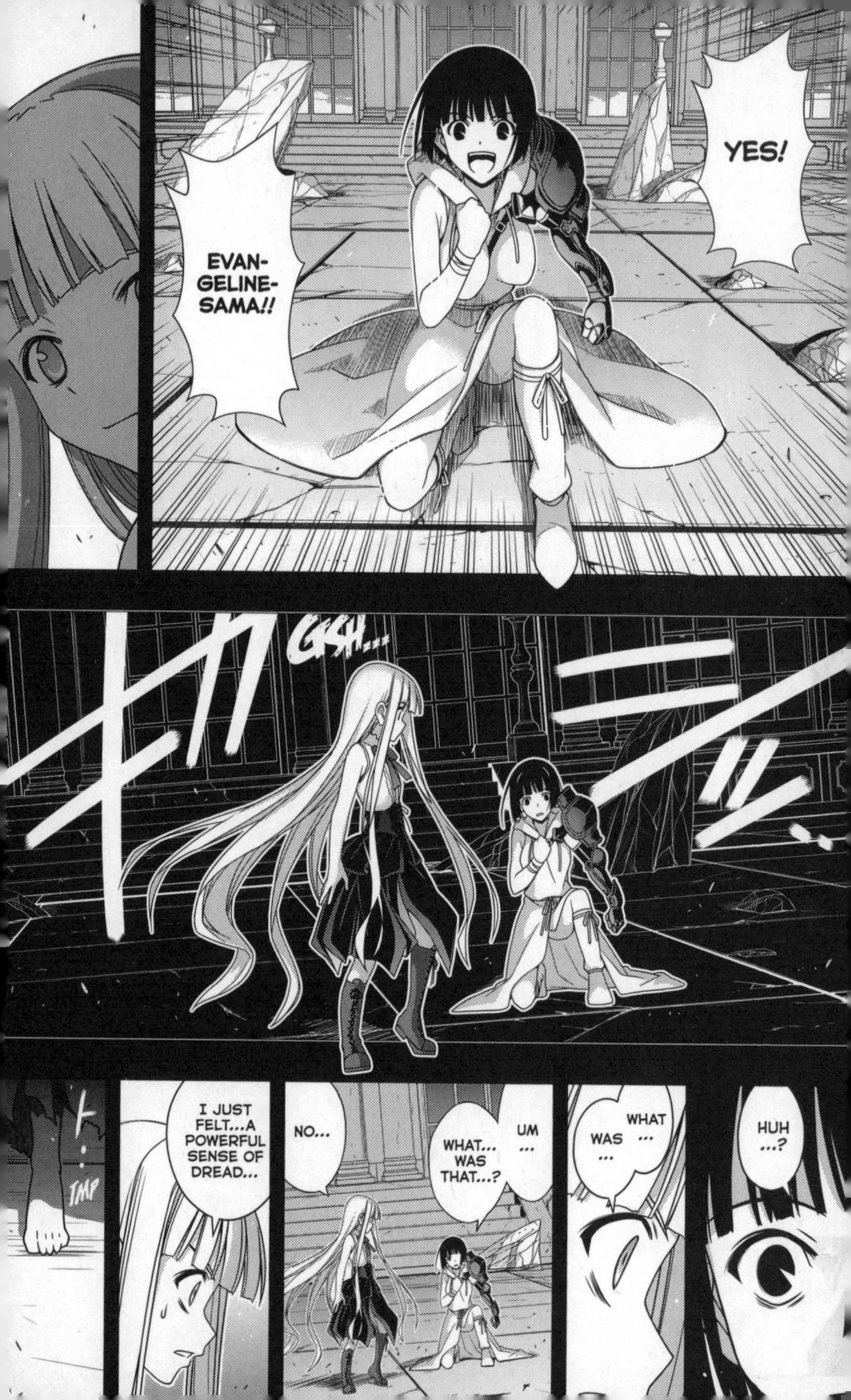
YES!
EVAN-GELINE-SAMA!!
GISH...
HUH...?
WHAT... WAS...
UM...
WHAT... WAS THAT...?
NO...
I JUST FELT...A POWERFUL SENSE OF DREAD...
TMP

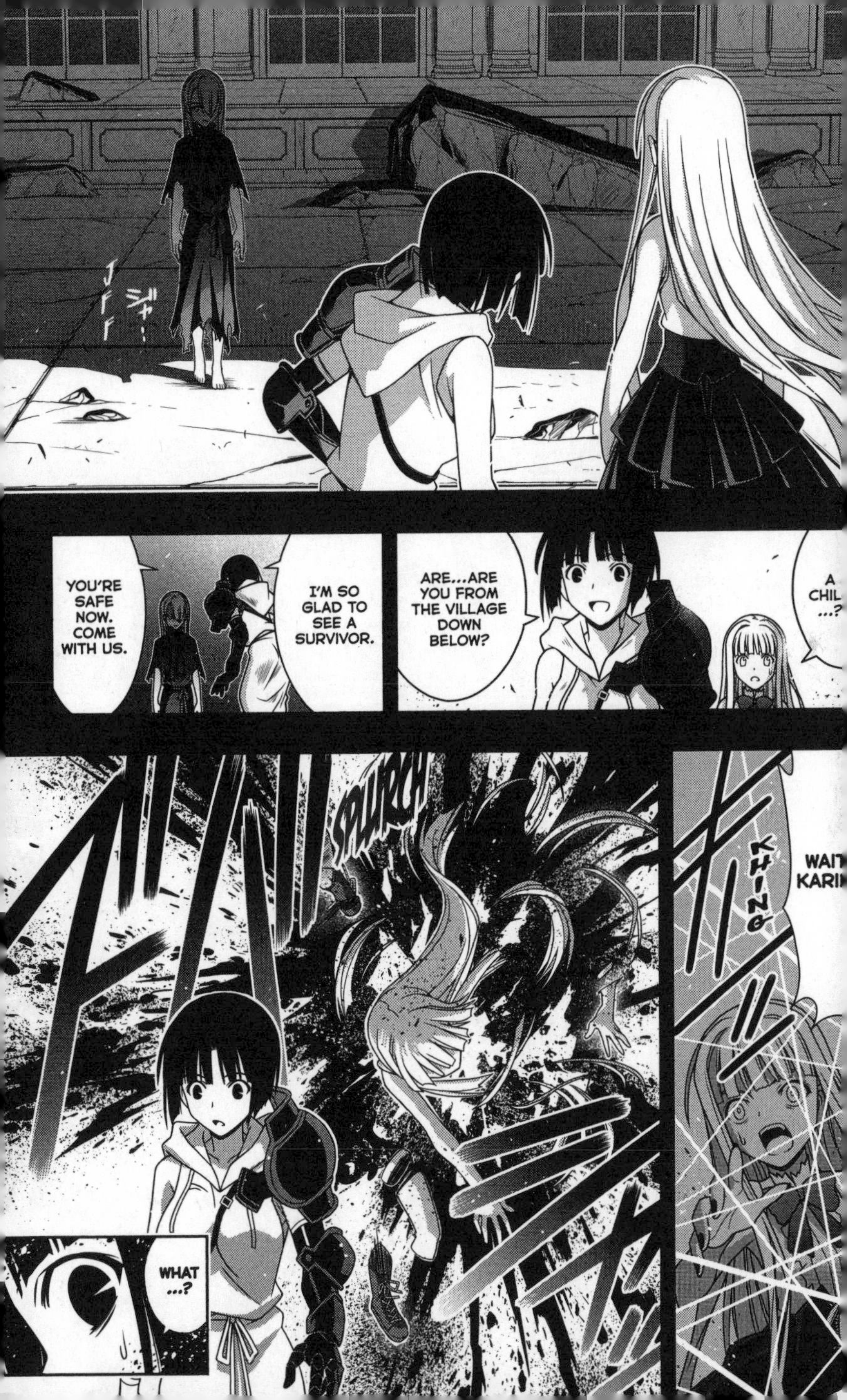
ジャ…
A CHIL ...?
ARE...ARE YOU FROM THE VILLAGE DOWN BELOW?
I'M SO GLAD TO SEE A SURVIVOR.
YOU'RE SAFE NOW. COME WITH US.
WAIT KARI
KHING
SPLURCH
WHAT ...?

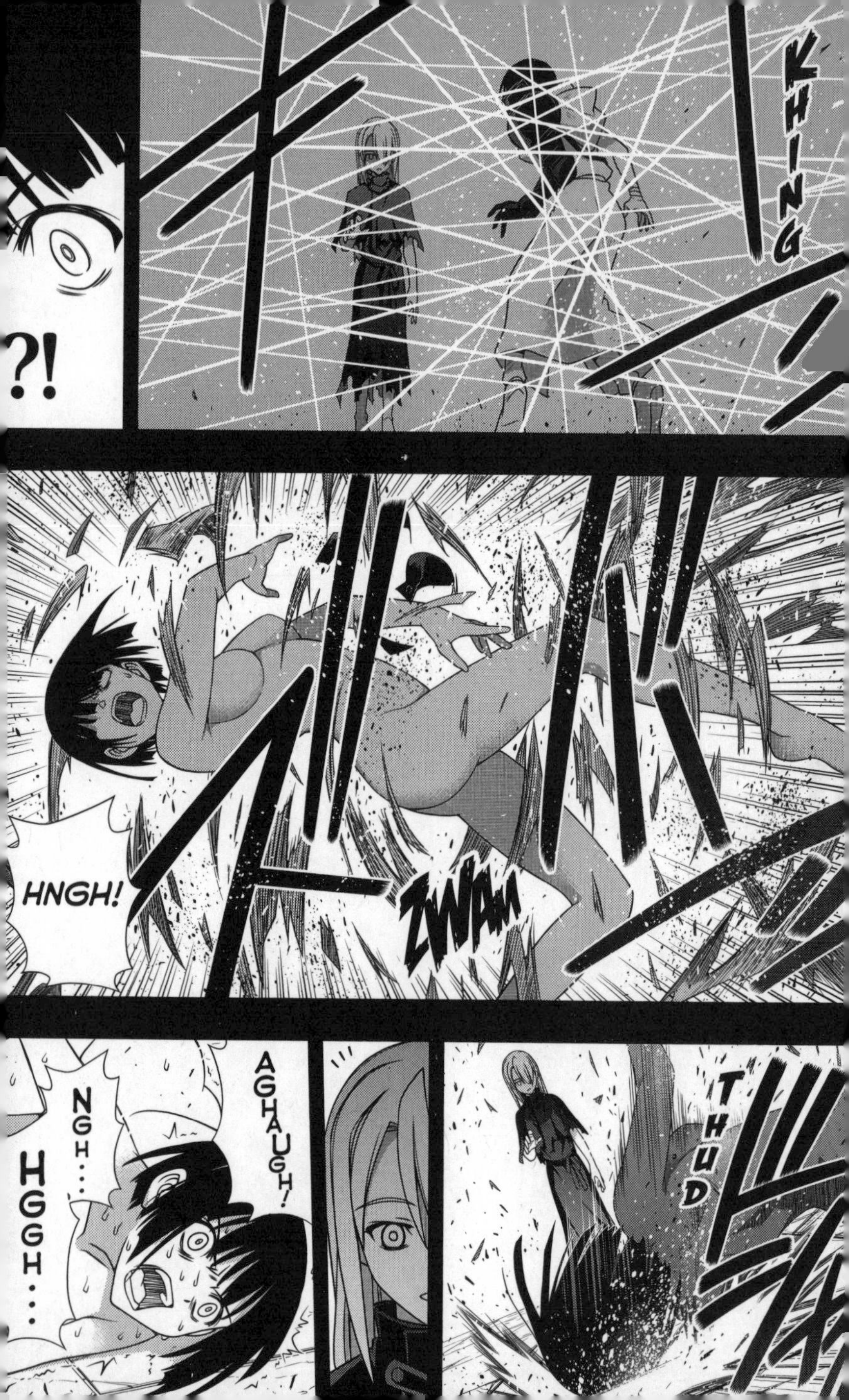
KHING
?!
ZWAM
HNGH!
THUD
AGHAUGH!
NGH...
HGGH...

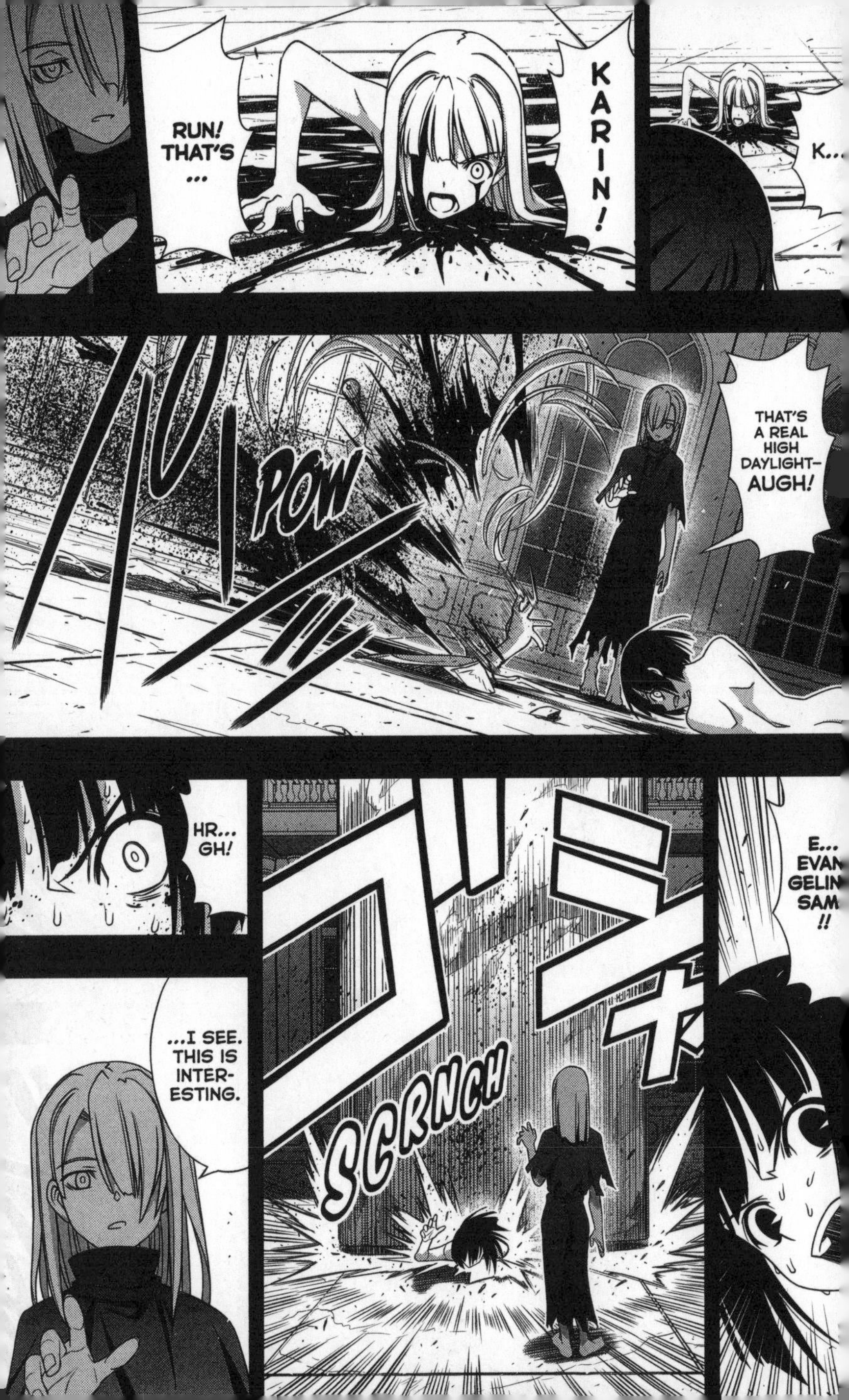
K...
KARIN!
RUN! THAT'S ...
THAT'S A REAL HIGH DAYLIGHT—AUGH!
POW
E... EVAN GELIN SAM !!
SCRNCH
HR... GH!
...I SEE. THIS IS INTER-ESTING.

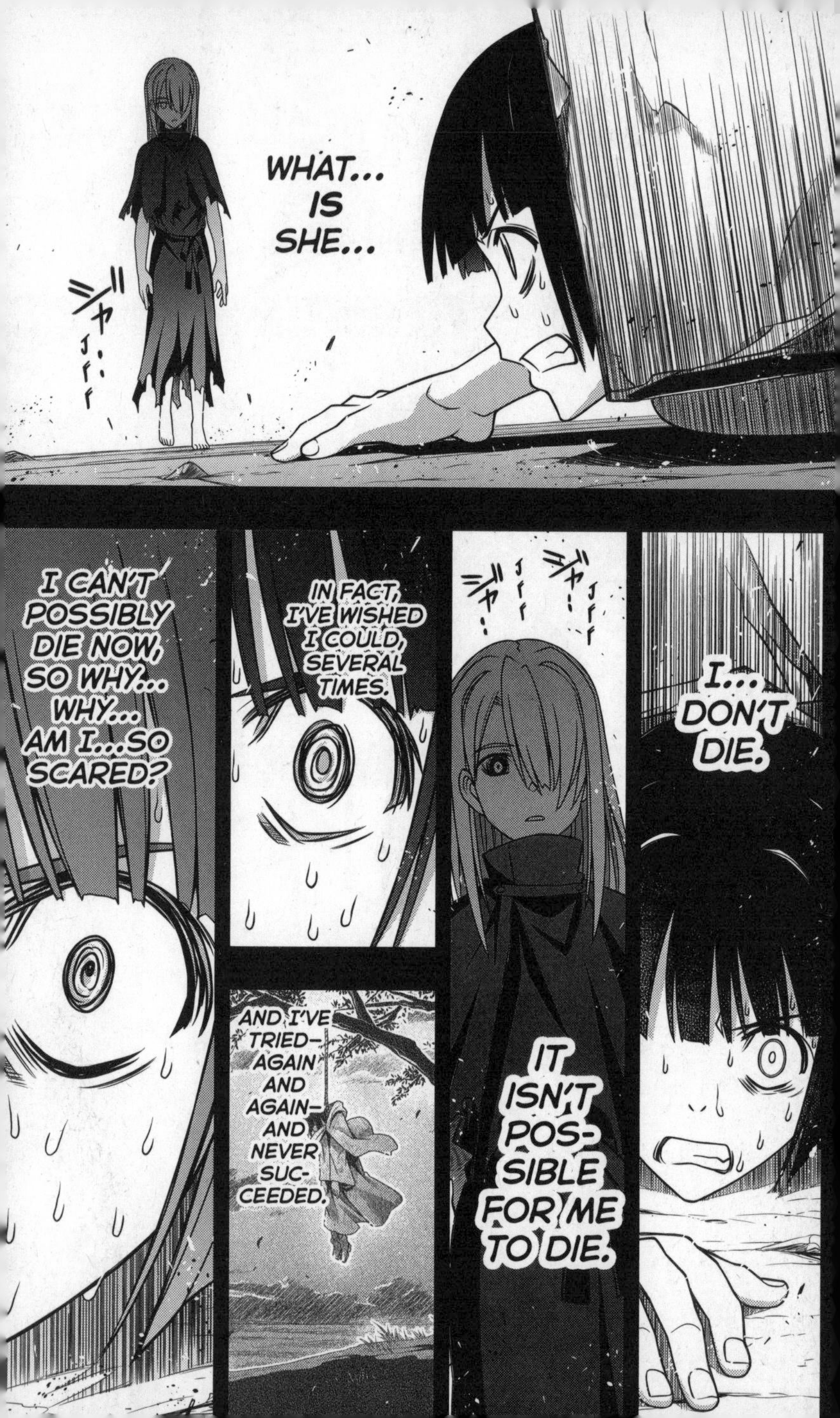
WHAT... IS SHE...
ジャ...
JFF
I... DON'T DIE.
ジャ...
JFF
ジャ...
JFF
IT ISN'T POSSIBLE FOR ME TO DIE.
IN FACT, I'VE WISHED I COULD, SEVERAL TIMES.
AND I'VE TRIED—AGAIN AND AGAIN—AND NEVER SUCCEEDED.
I CAN'T POSSIBLY DIE NOW, SO WHY... WHY... AM I...SO SCARED?

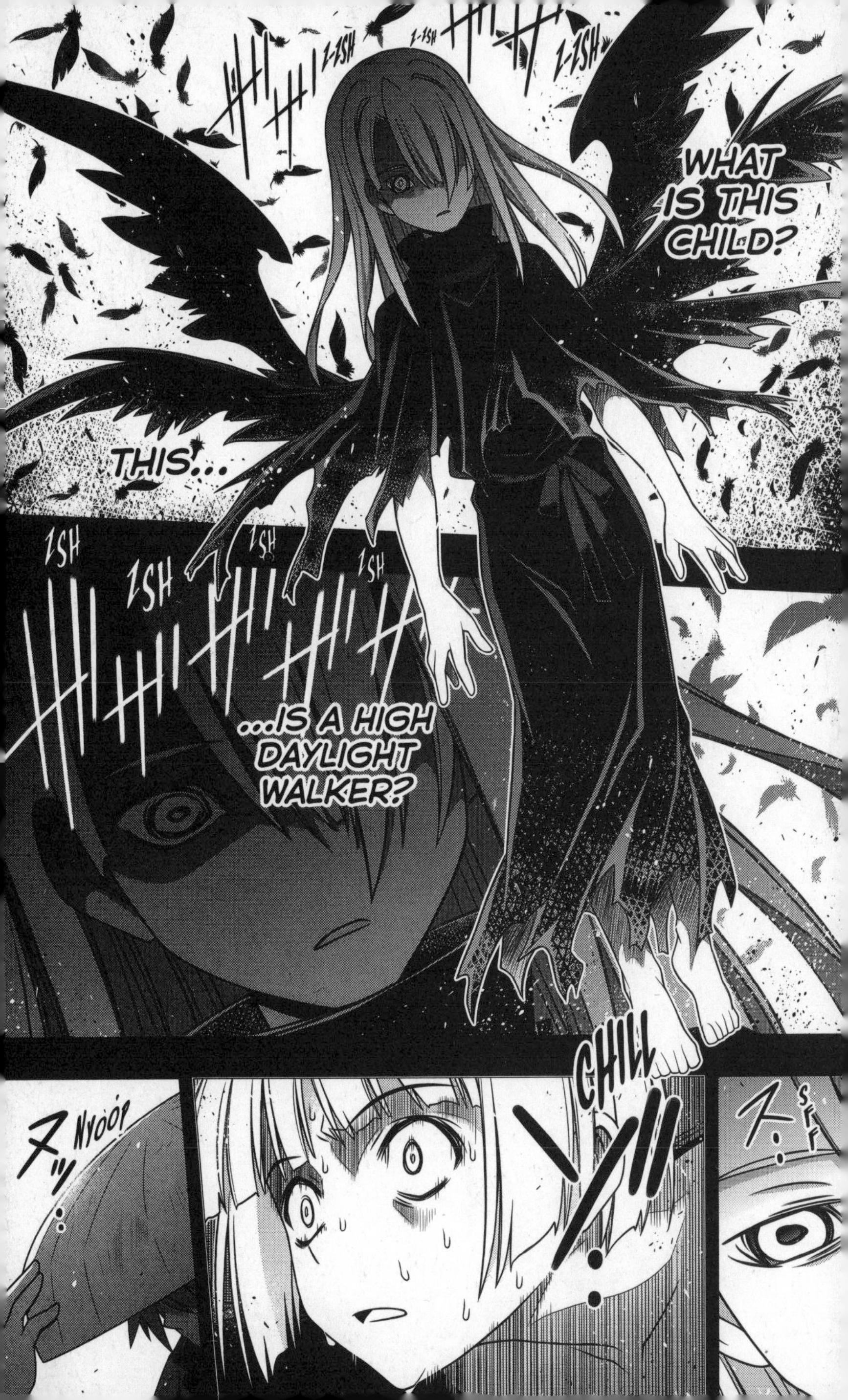
Z-ZSH
Z-ZSH
Z-ZSH
WHAT IS THIS CHILD?
THIS...
ZSH
ZSH
ZSH
ZSH
...IS A HIGH DAYLIGHT WALKER?
SFF
CHILL
NYOOP

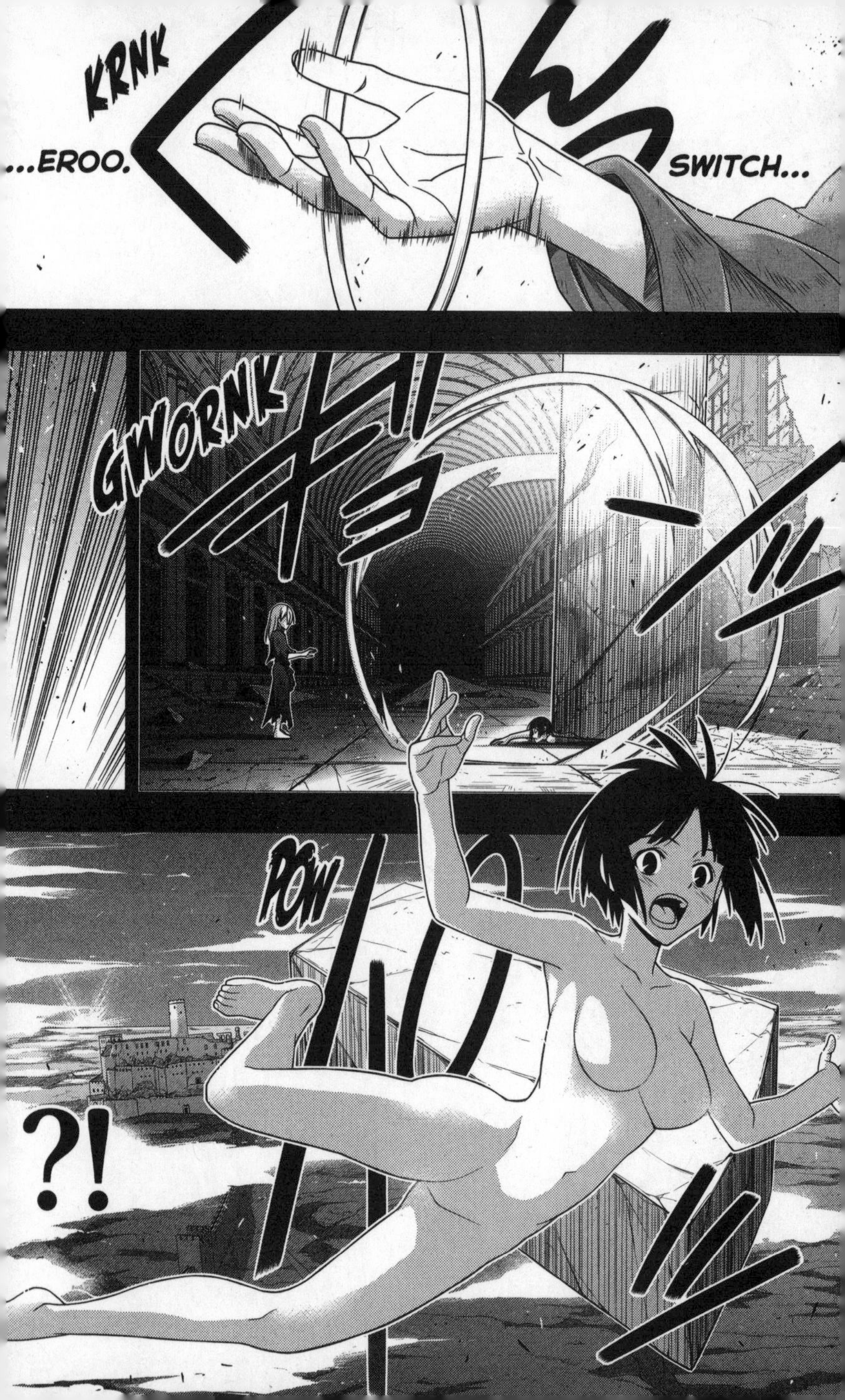
SWITCH...
KRNK
...EROO.
GWORNK
POW
?!

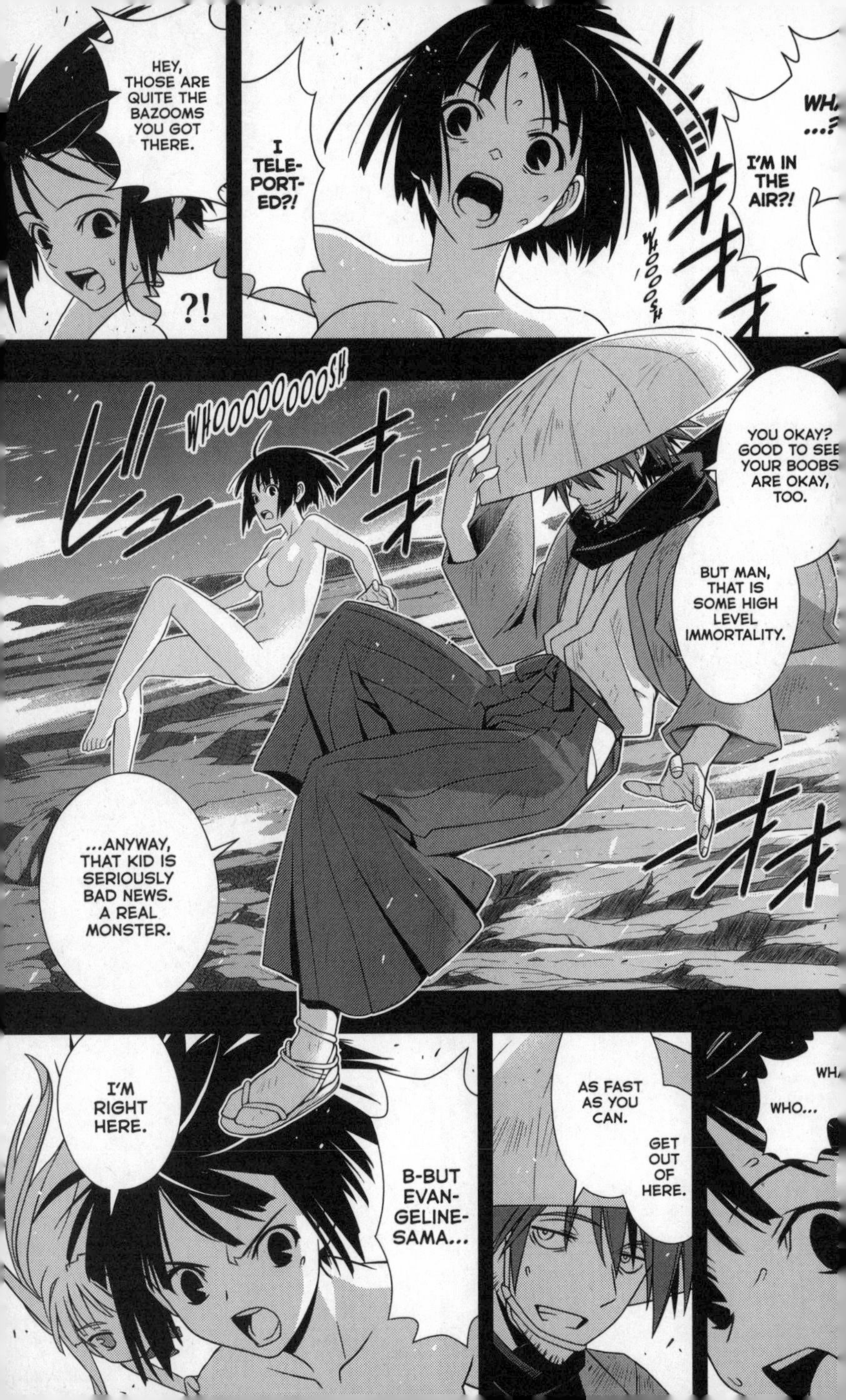
WHA ...?!
I'M IN THE AIR?!
WHOOOSH
I TELEPORTED?!
HEY, THOSE ARE QUITE THE BAZOOMS YOU GOT THERE.
?!
WHOOOOOOOOOSH
YOU OKAY? GOOD TO SEE YOUR BOOBS ARE OKAY, TOO.
BUT MAN, THAT IS SOME HIGH LEVEL IMMORTALITY.
...ANYWAY, THAT KID IS SERIOUSLY BAD NEWS. A REAL MONSTER.
WHA
WHO...
GET OUT OF HERE.
AS FAST AS YOU CAN.
B-BUT EVANGELINE-SAMA...
I'M RIGHT HERE.

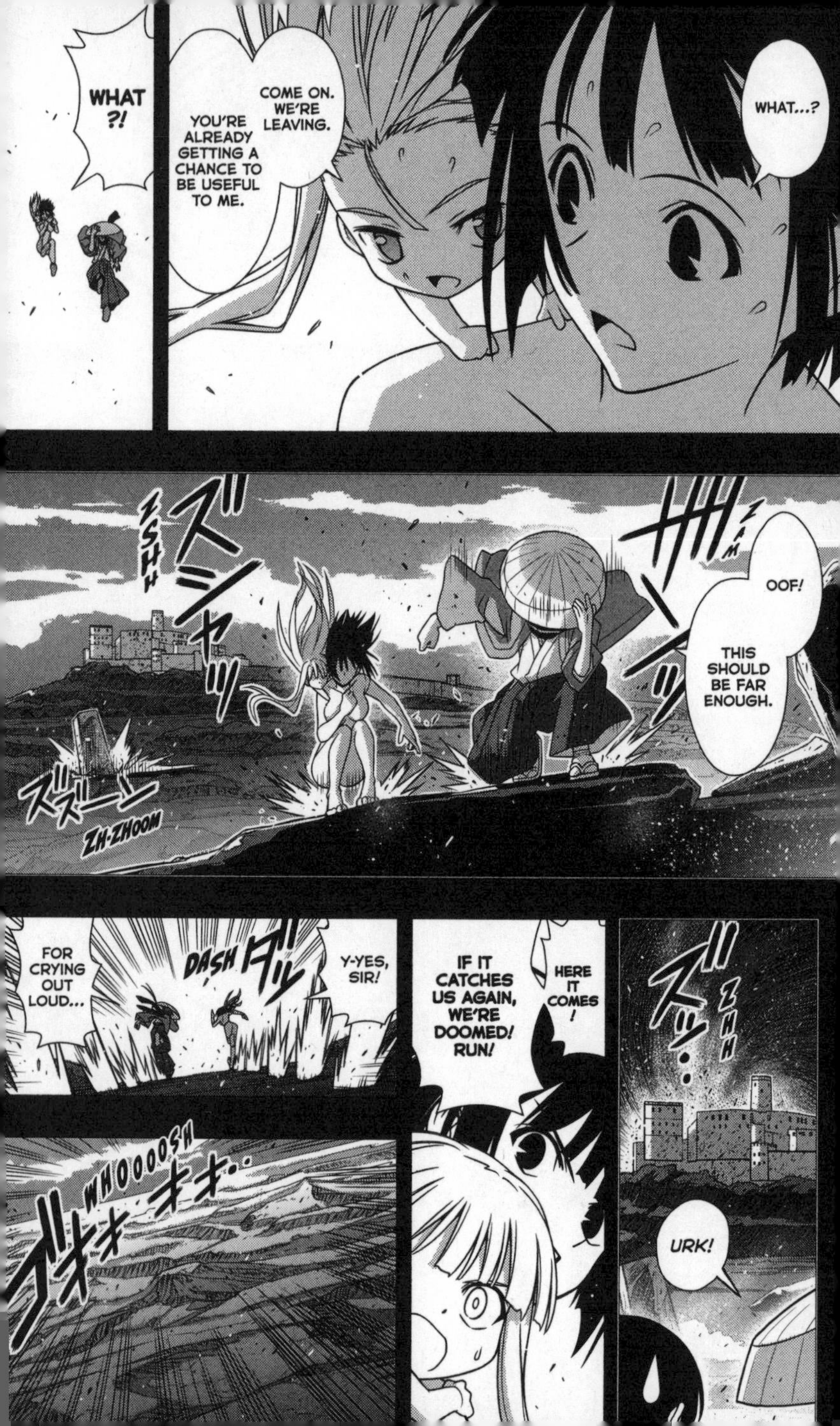
WHAT...?
COME ON. WE'RE LEAVING.
YOU'RE ALREADY GETTING A CHANCE TO BE USEFUL TO ME.
WHAT?!
ZAM
OOF!
THIS SHOULD BE FAR ENOUGH.
ZSHH
ZH-ZHOOM
ZHH
URK!
HERE IT COMES!
IF IT CATCHES US AGAIN, WE'RE DOOMED! RUN!
Y-YES, SIR!
DASH
FOR CRYING OUT LOUD...
WHOOOOSH

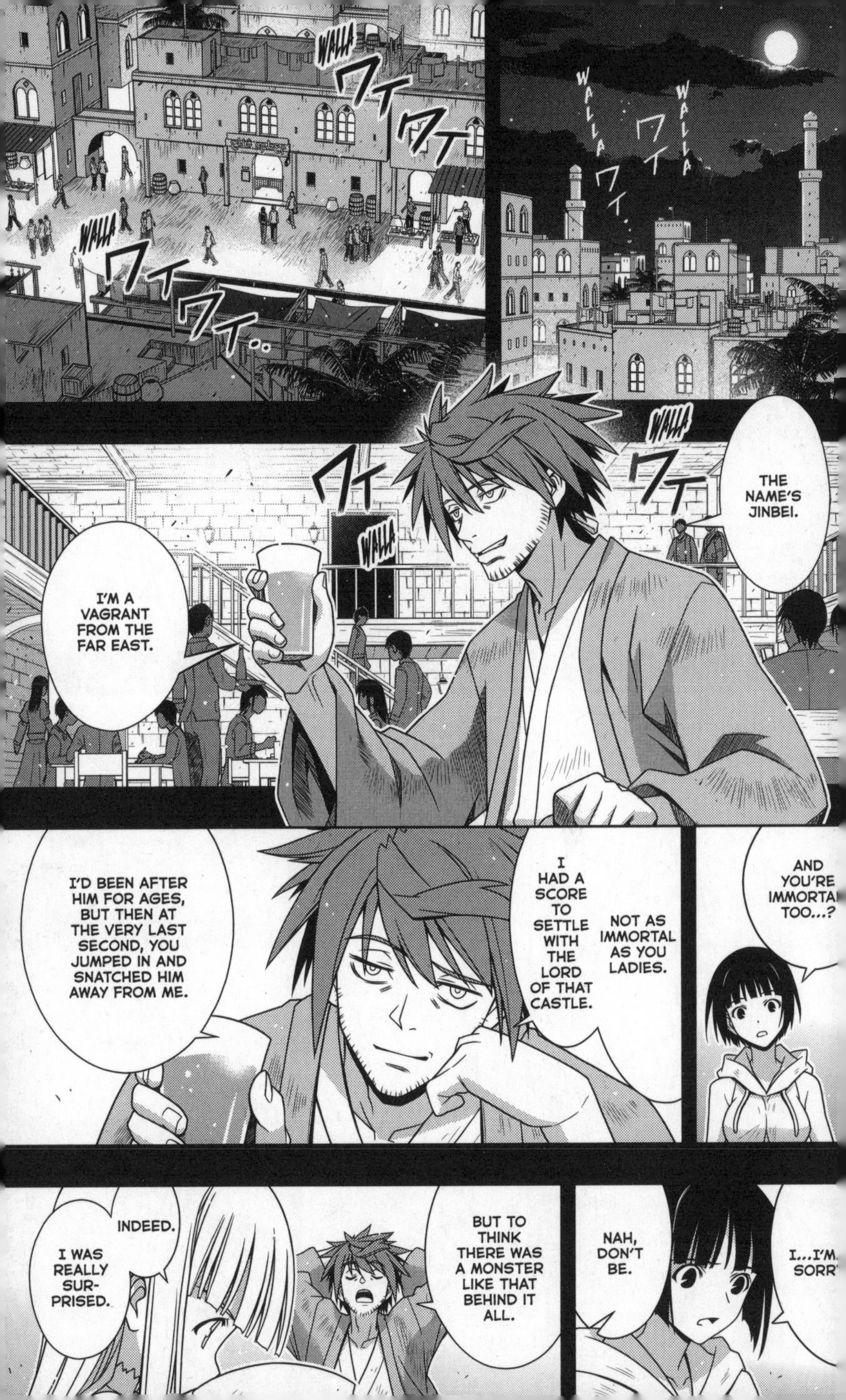
WALLA
WALLA
WALLA
WALLA
WALLA
WALLA
THE NAME'S JINBEI.
WALLA
I'M A VAGRANT FROM THE FAR EAST.
AND YOU'RE IMMORTA TOO...?
NOT AS IMMORTAL AS YOU LADIES.
I HAD A SCORE TO SETTLE WITH THE LORD OF THAT CASTLE.
I'D BEEN AFTER HIM FOR AGES, BUT THEN AT THE VERY LAST SECOND, YOU JUMPED IN AND SNATCHED HIM AWAY FROM ME.
I...I'M SORR
NAH, DON'T BE.
BUT TO THINK THERE WAS A MONSTER LIKE THAT BEHIND IT ALL.
INDEED.
I WAS REALLY SUR-PRISED.

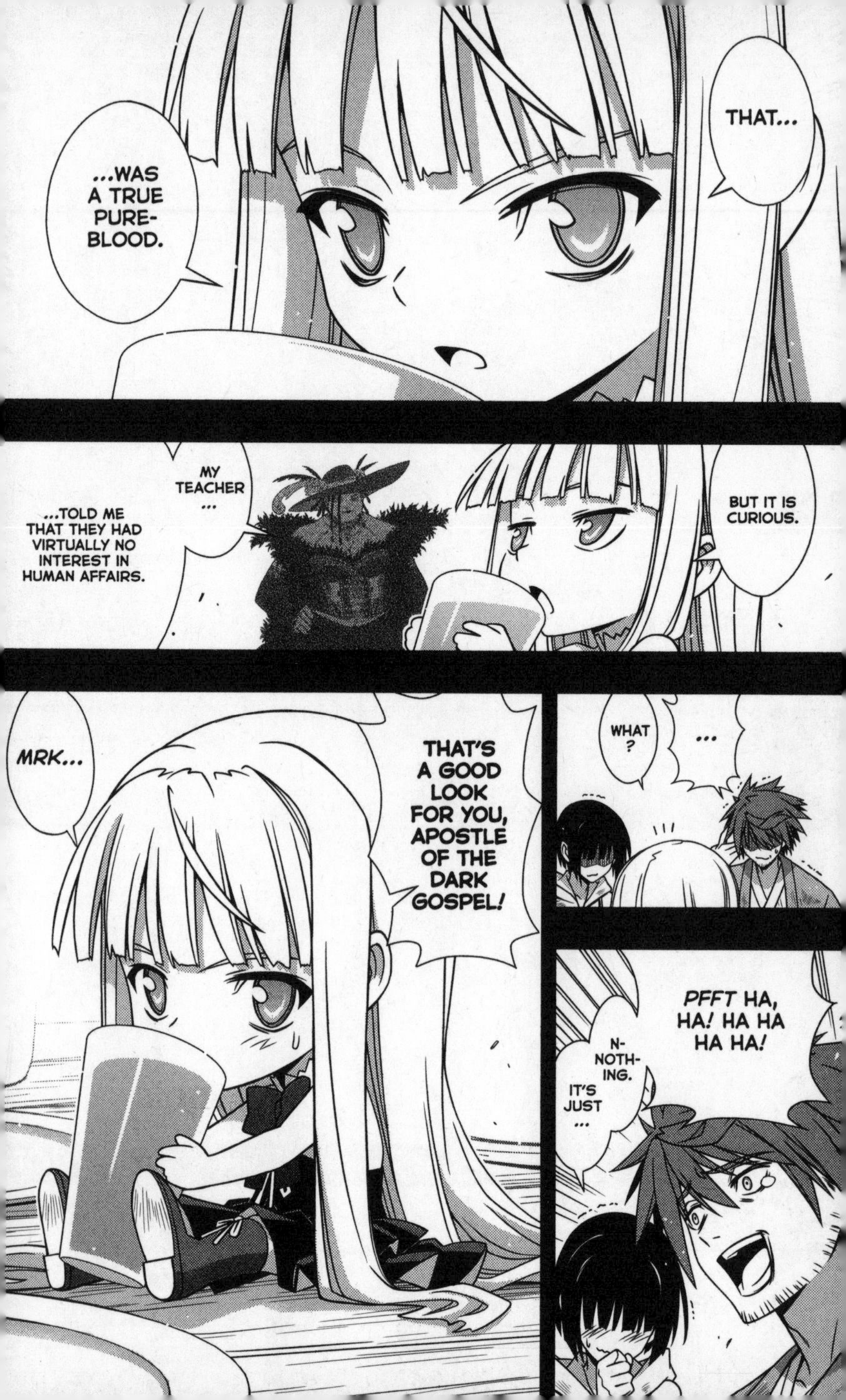
THAT...
...WAS A TRUE PURE-BLOOD.
BUT IT IS CURIOUS.
MY TEACHER ...
...TOLD ME THAT THEY HAD VIRTUALLY NO INTEREST IN HUMAN AFFAIRS.
...
WHAT?
PFFT HA, HA! HA HA HA HA!
N-NOTHING. IT'S JUST ...
THAT'S A GOOD LOOK FOR YOU, APOSTLE OF THE DARK GOSPEL!
MRK...

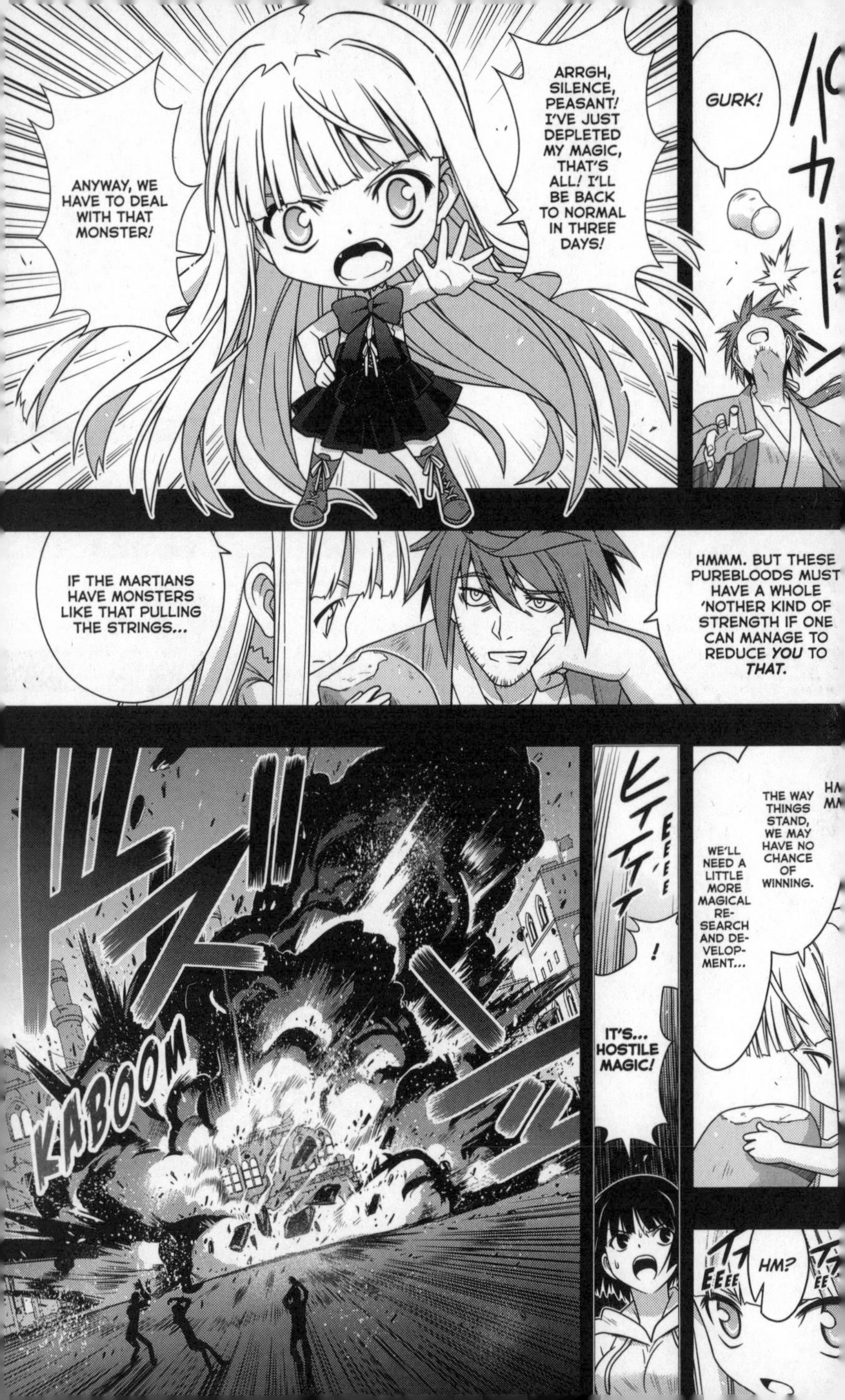
GURK!
ARRGH, SILENCE, PEASANT! I'VE JUST DEPLETED MY MAGIC, THAT'S ALL! I'LL BE BACK TO NORMAL IN THREE DAYS!
ANYWAY, WE HAVE TO DEAL WITH THAT MONSTER!
HMMM. BUT THESE PUREBLOODS MUST HAVE A WHOLE 'NOTHER KIND OF STRENGTH IF ONE CAN MANAGE TO REDUCE YOU TO THAT.
IF THE MARTIANS HAVE MONSTERS LIKE THAT PULLING THE STRINGS...
THE WAY THINGS STAND, WE MAY HAVE NO CHANCE OF WINNING.
WE'LL NEED A LITTLE MORE MAGICAL RE-SEARCH AND DE-VELOP-MENT...
HM?
!
IT'S... HOSTILE MAGIC!
KABOOM

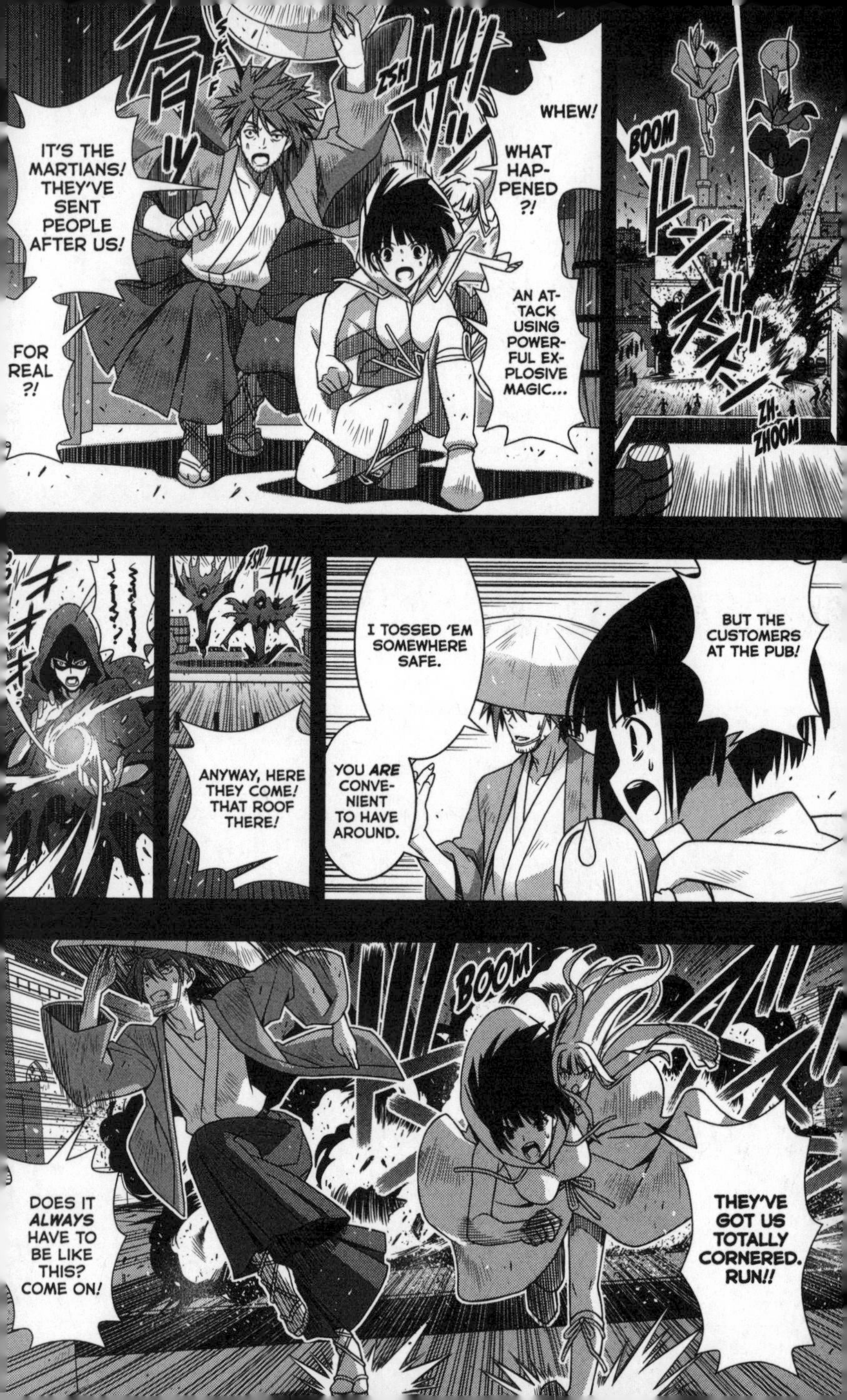
BOOM
ZH-ZHOOM
WHEW!
WHAT HAPPENED?!
AN ATTACK USING POWERFUL EXPLOSIVE MAGIC...
ZSH
SKFF
IT'S THE MARTIANS! THEY'VE SENT PEOPLE AFTER US!
FOR REAL?!
BUT THE CUSTOMERS AT THE PUB!
I TOSSED 'EM SOMEWHERE SAFE.
YOU *ARE* CONVENIENT TO HAVE AROUND.
ZSH
ANYWAY, HERE THEY COME! THAT ROOF THERE!
THEY'VE GOT US TOTALLY CORNERED. RUN!!
BOOM
DOES IT *ALWAYS* HAVE TO BE LIKE THIS? COME ON!

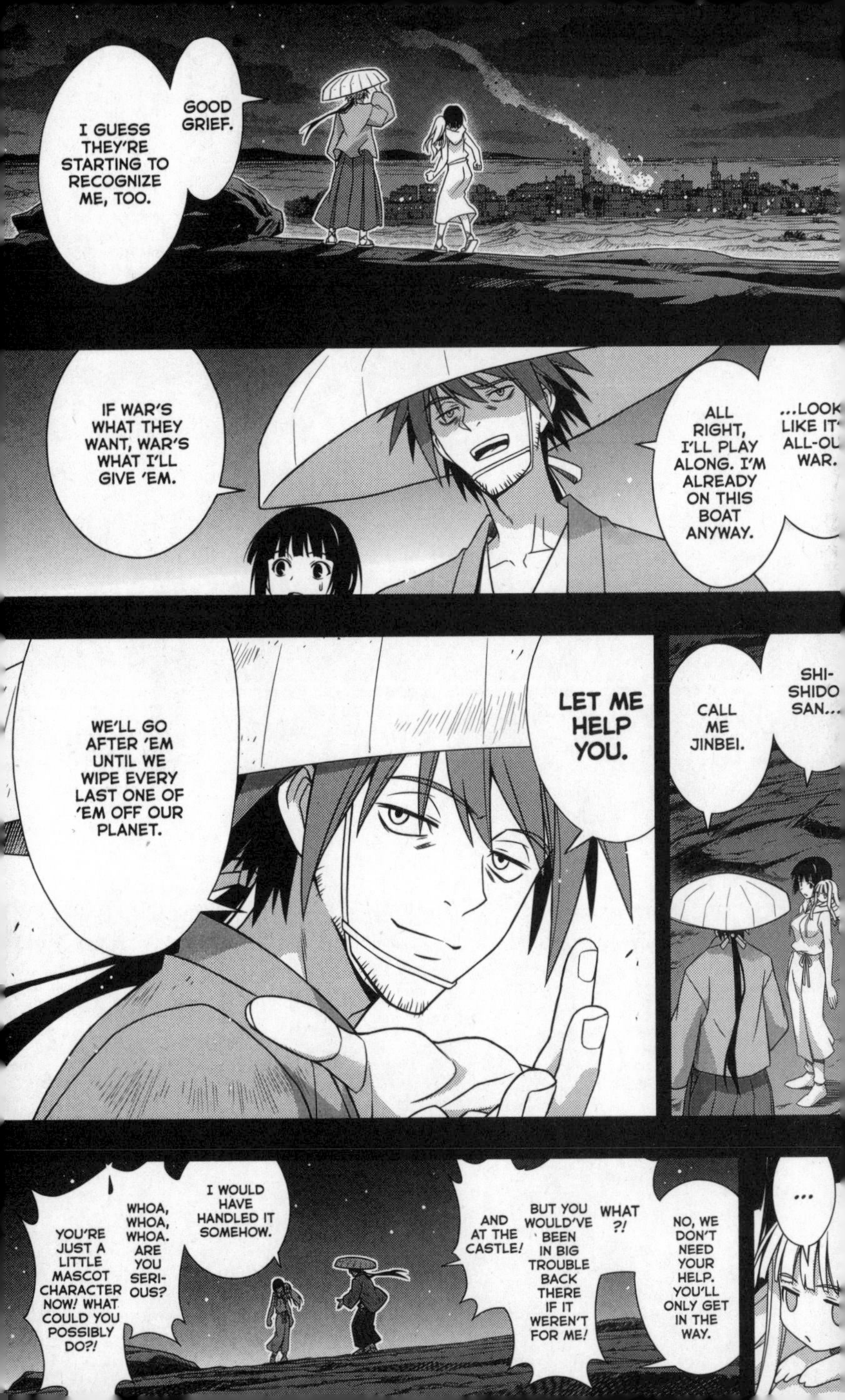
GOOD GRIEF.
I GUESS THEY'RE STARTING TO RECOGNIZE ME, TOO.
...LOOK LIKE IT ALL-OU WAR.
ALL RIGHT, I'LL PLAY ALONG. I'M ALREADY ON THIS BOAT ANYWAY.
IF WAR'S WHAT THEY WANT, WAR'S WHAT I'LL GIVE 'EM.
SHI-SHIDO SAN...
CALL ME JINBEI.
LET ME HELP YOU.
WE'LL GO AFTER 'EM UNTIL WE WIPE EVERY LAST ONE OF 'EM OFF OUR PLANET.
...
NO, WE DON'T NEED YOUR HELP. YOU'LL ONLY GET IN THE WAY.
WHAT ?!
BUT YOU WOULD'VE BEEN IN BIG TROUBLE BACK THERE IF IT WEREN'T FOR ME!
AND AT THE CASTLE!
I WOULD HAVE HANDLED IT SOMEHOW.
WHOA, WHOA, WHOA. ARE YOU SERIOUS?
YOU'RE JUST A LITTLE MASCOT CHARACTER NOW! WHAT COULD YOU POSSIBLY DO?!

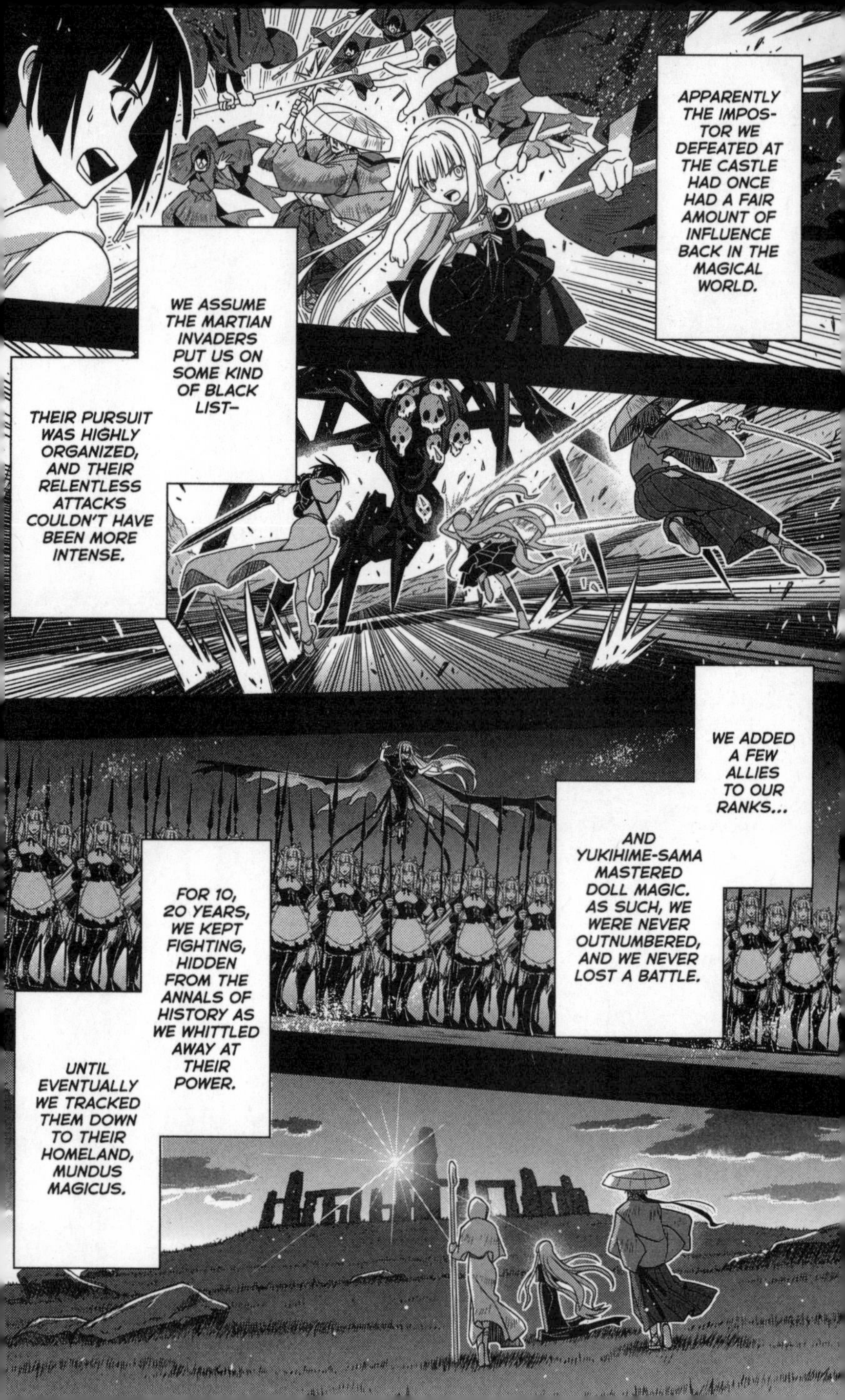
APPARENTLY THE IMPOSTOR WE DEFEATED AT THE CASTLE HAD ONCE HAD A FAIR AMOUNT OF INFLUENCE BACK IN THE MAGICAL WORLD.
WE ASSUME THE MARTIAN INVADERS PUT US ON SOME KIND OF BLACK LIST–
THEIR PURSUIT WAS HIGHLY ORGANIZED, AND THEIR RELENTLESS ATTACKS COULDN'T HAVE BEEN MORE INTENSE.
WE ADDED A FEW ALLIES TO OUR RANKS...
AND YUKIHIME-SAMA MASTERED DOLL MAGIC. AS SUCH, WE WERE NEVER OUTNUMBERED, AND WE NEVER LOST A BATTLE.
FOR 10, 20 YEARS, WE KEPT FIGHTING, HIDDEN FROM THE ANNALS OF HISTORY AS WE WHITTLED AWAY AT THEIR POWER.
UNTIL EVENTUALLY WE TRACKED THEM DOWN TO THEIR HOMELAND, MUNDUS MAGICUS.

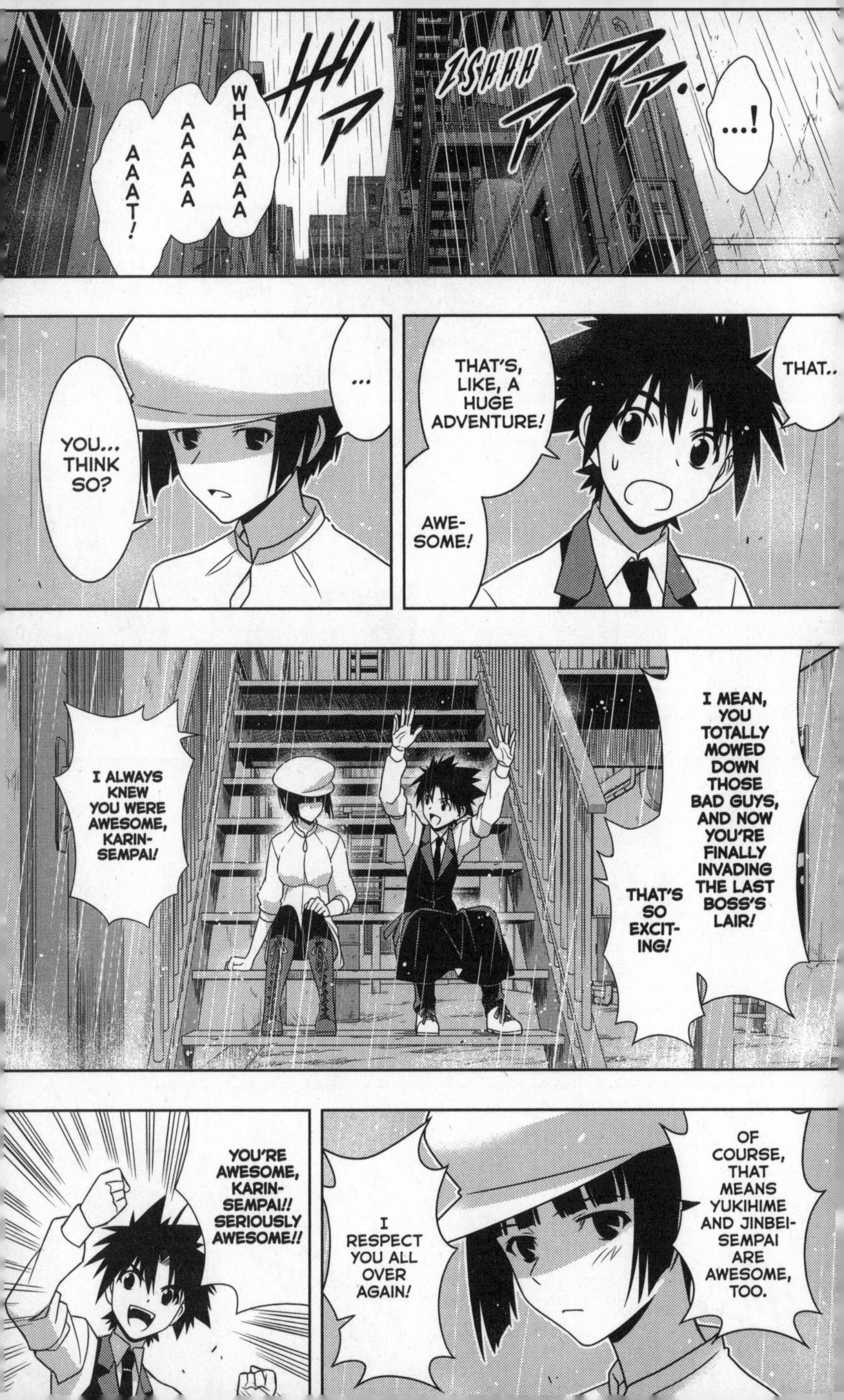
...!
ZSHHHH
WHAAAAAAAAAAAAAAAT!
THAT..
THAT'S, LIKE, A HUGE ADVENTURE!
AWE-SOME!
...
YOU... THINK SO?
I MEAN, YOU TOTALLY MOWED DOWN THOSE BAD GUYS, AND NOW YOU'RE FINALLY INVADING THE LAST BOSS'S LAIR!
THAT'S SO EXCIT-ING!
I ALWAYS KNEW YOU WERE AWESOME, KARIN-SEMPAI!
OF COURSE, THAT MEANS YUKIHIME AND JINBEI-SEMPAI ARE AWESOME, TOO.
I RESPECT YOU ALL OVER AGAIN!
YOU'RE AWESOME, KARIN-SEMPAI!! SERIOUSLY AWESOME!!

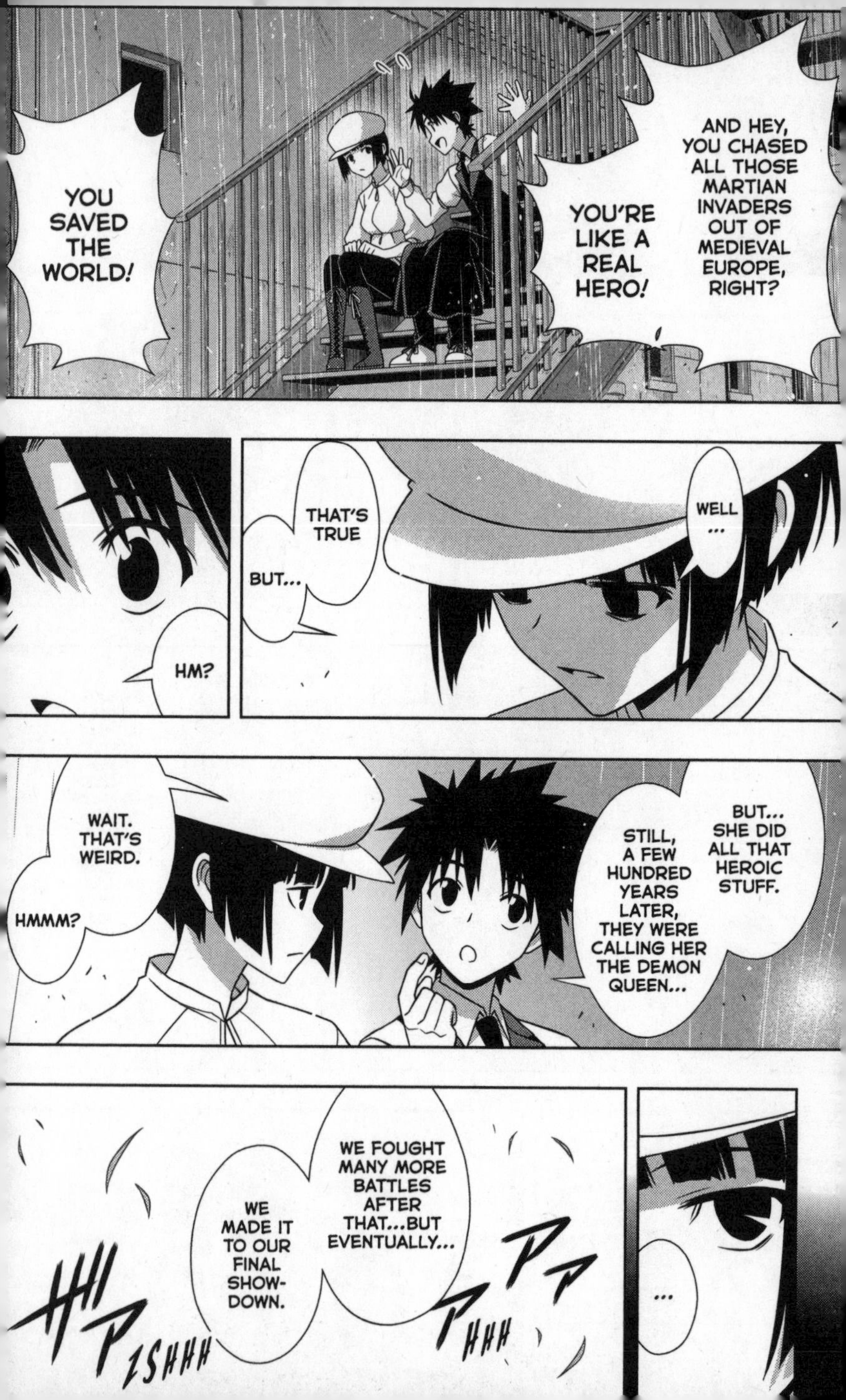
AND HEY, YOU CHASED ALL THOSE MARTIAN INVADERS OUT OF MEDIEVAL EUROPE, RIGHT?
YOU'RE LIKE A REAL HERO!
YOU SAVED THE WORLD!
WELL...
THAT'S TRUE
BUT...
HM?
BUT... SHE DID ALL THAT HEROIC STUFF.
STILL, A FEW HUNDRED YEARS LATER, THEY WERE CALLING HER THE DEMON QUEEN...
WAIT. THAT'S WEIRD.
HMMM?
...
WE FOUGHT MANY MORE BATTLES AFTER THAT...BUT EVENTUALLY...
WE MADE IT TO OUR FINAL SHOW-DOWN.

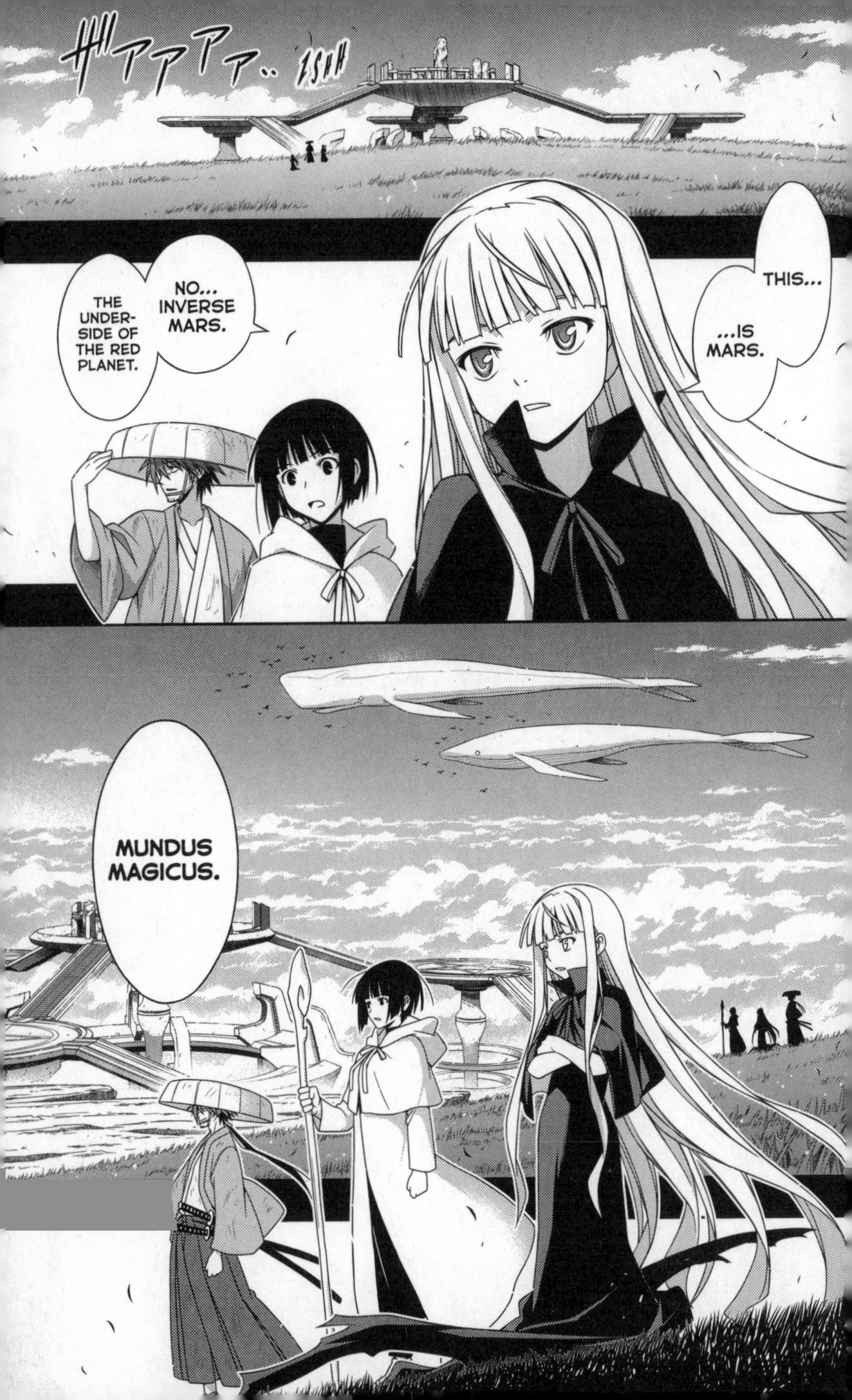
ZSHH
THIS...
...IS MARS.
NO... INVERSE MARS.
THE UNDER-SIDE OF THE RED PLANET.
MUNDUS MAGICUS.

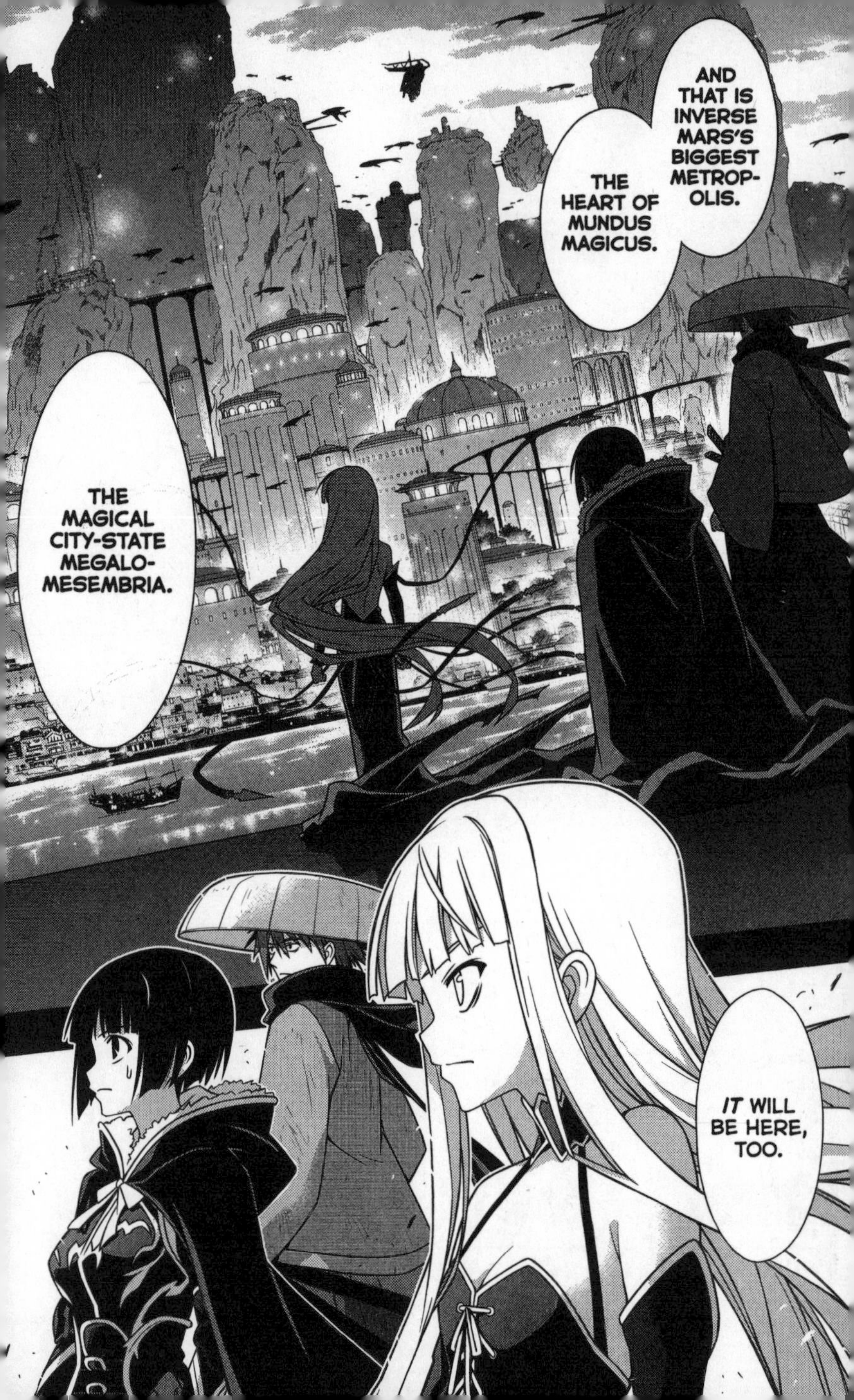
AND THAT IS INVERSE MARS'S BIGGEST METROP-OLIS.
THE HEART OF MUNDUS MAGICUS.
THE MAGICAL CITY-STATE MEGALO-MESEMBRIA.
IT WILL BE HERE, TOO.

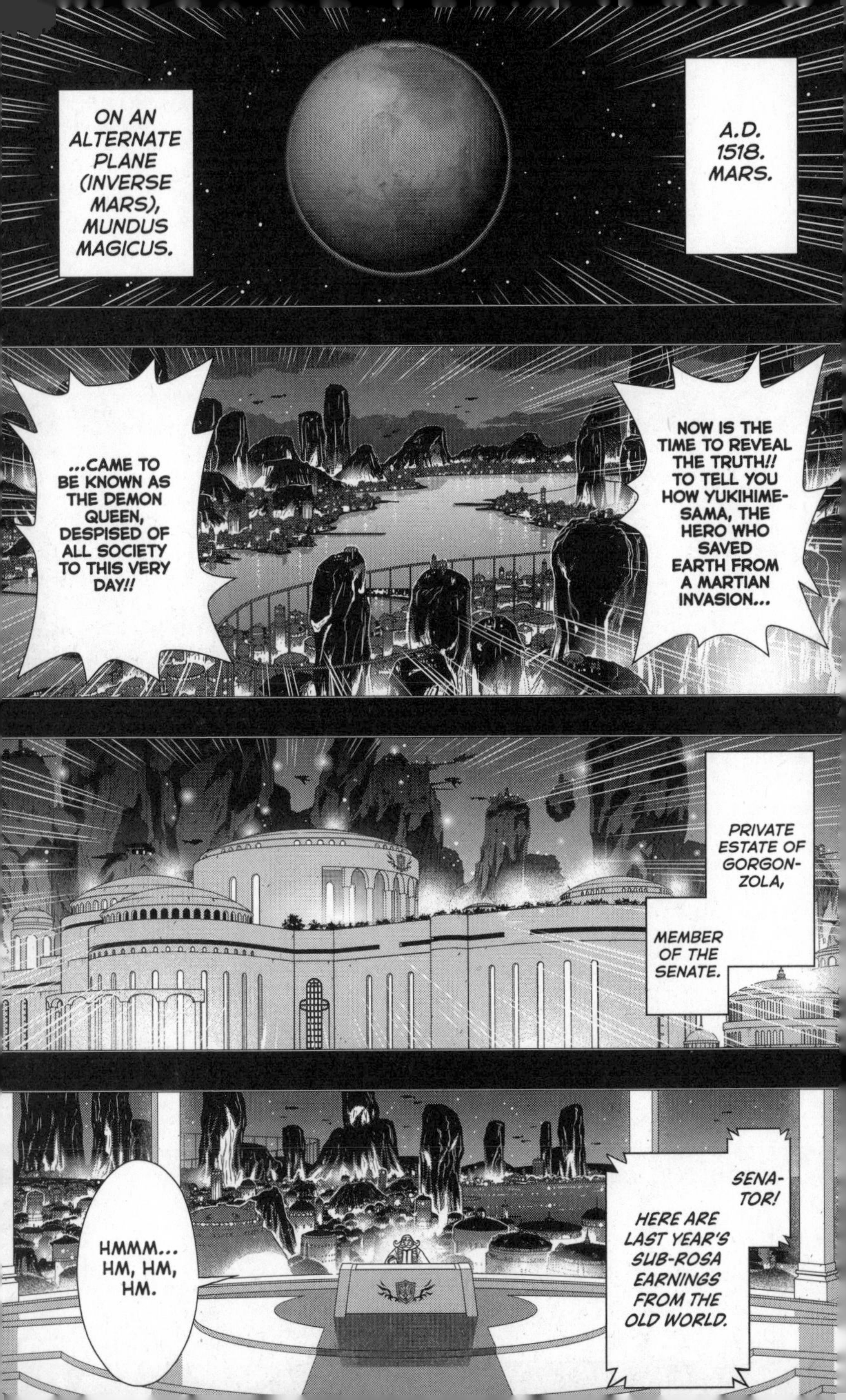
A.D. 1518. MARS.
ON AN ALTERNATE PLANE (INVERSE MARS), MUNDUS MAGICUS.
NOW IS THE TIME TO REVEAL THE TRUTH!! TO TELL YOU HOW YUKIHIME-SAMA, THE HERO WHO SAVED EARTH FROM A MARTIAN INVASION...
...CAME TO BE KNOWN AS THE DEMON QUEEN, DESPISED OF ALL SOCIETY TO THIS VERY DAY!!
PRIVATE ESTATE OF GORGON-ZOLA,
MEMBER OF THE SENATE.
SENA-TOR!
HERE ARE LAST YEAR'S SUB-ROSA EARNINGS FROM THE OLD WORLD.
HMMM... HM, HM, HM.

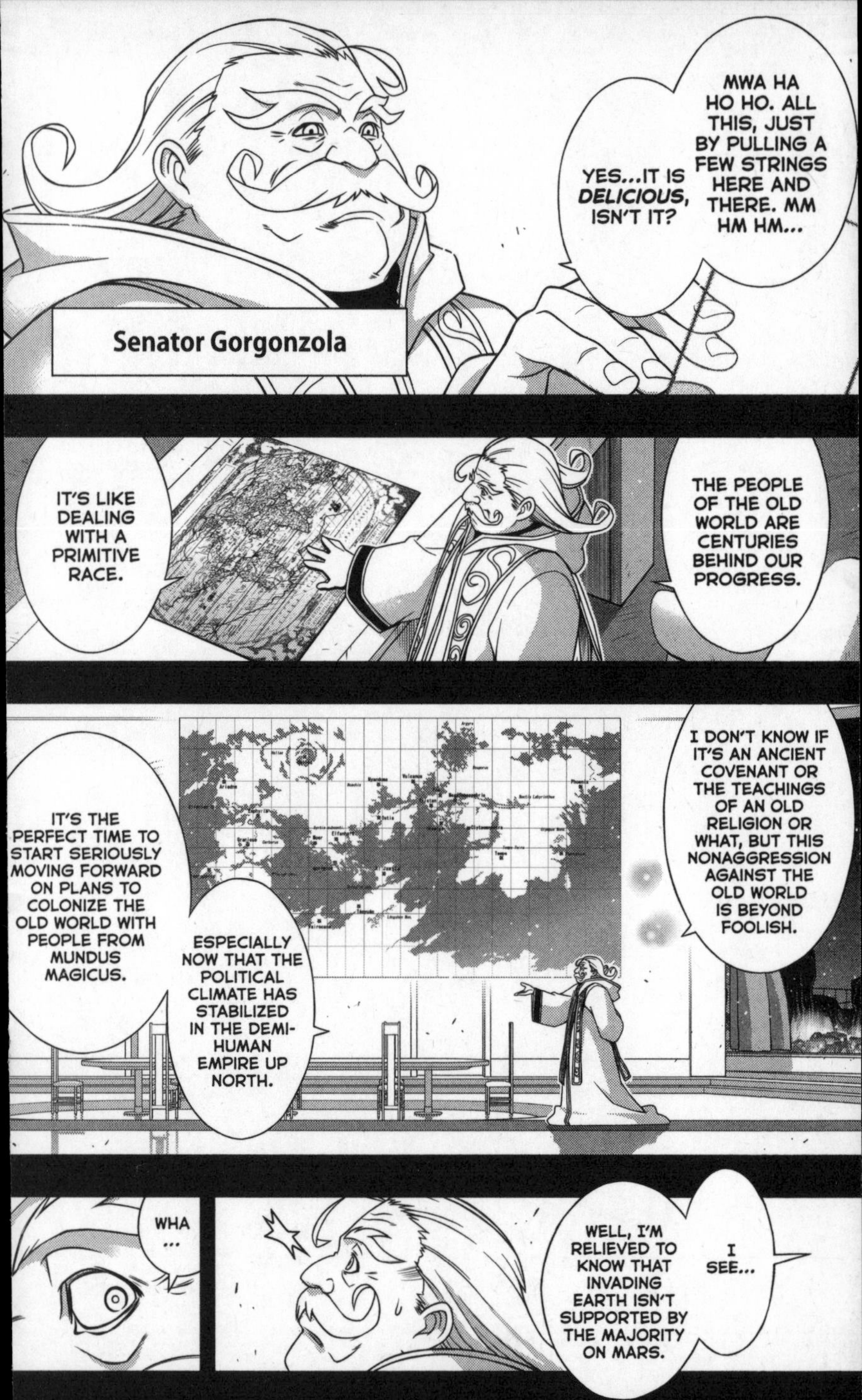
MWA HA HO HO. ALL THIS, JUST BY PULLING A FEW STRINGS HERE AND THERE. MM HM HM...
YES...IT IS *DELICIOUS*, ISN'T IT?
Senator Gorgonzola
THE PEOPLE OF THE OLD WORLD ARE CENTURIES BEHIND OUR PROGRESS.
IT'S LIKE DEALING WITH A PRIMITIVE RACE.
I DON'T KNOW IF IT'S AN ANCIENT COVENANT OR THE TEACHINGS OF AN OLD RELIGION OR WHAT, BUT THIS NONAGGRESSION AGAINST THE OLD WORLD IS BEYOND FOOLISH.
IT'S THE PERFECT TIME TO START SERIOUSLY MOVING FORWARD ON PLANS TO COLONIZE THE OLD WORLD WITH PEOPLE FROM MUNDUS MAGICUS.
ESPECIALLY NOW THAT THE POLITICAL CLIMATE HAS STABILIZED IN THE DEMI-HUMAN EMPIRE UP NORTH.
I SEE...
WELL, I'M RELIEVED TO KNOW THAT INVADING EARTH ISN'T SUPPORTED BY THE MAJORITY ON MARS.
WHA ...

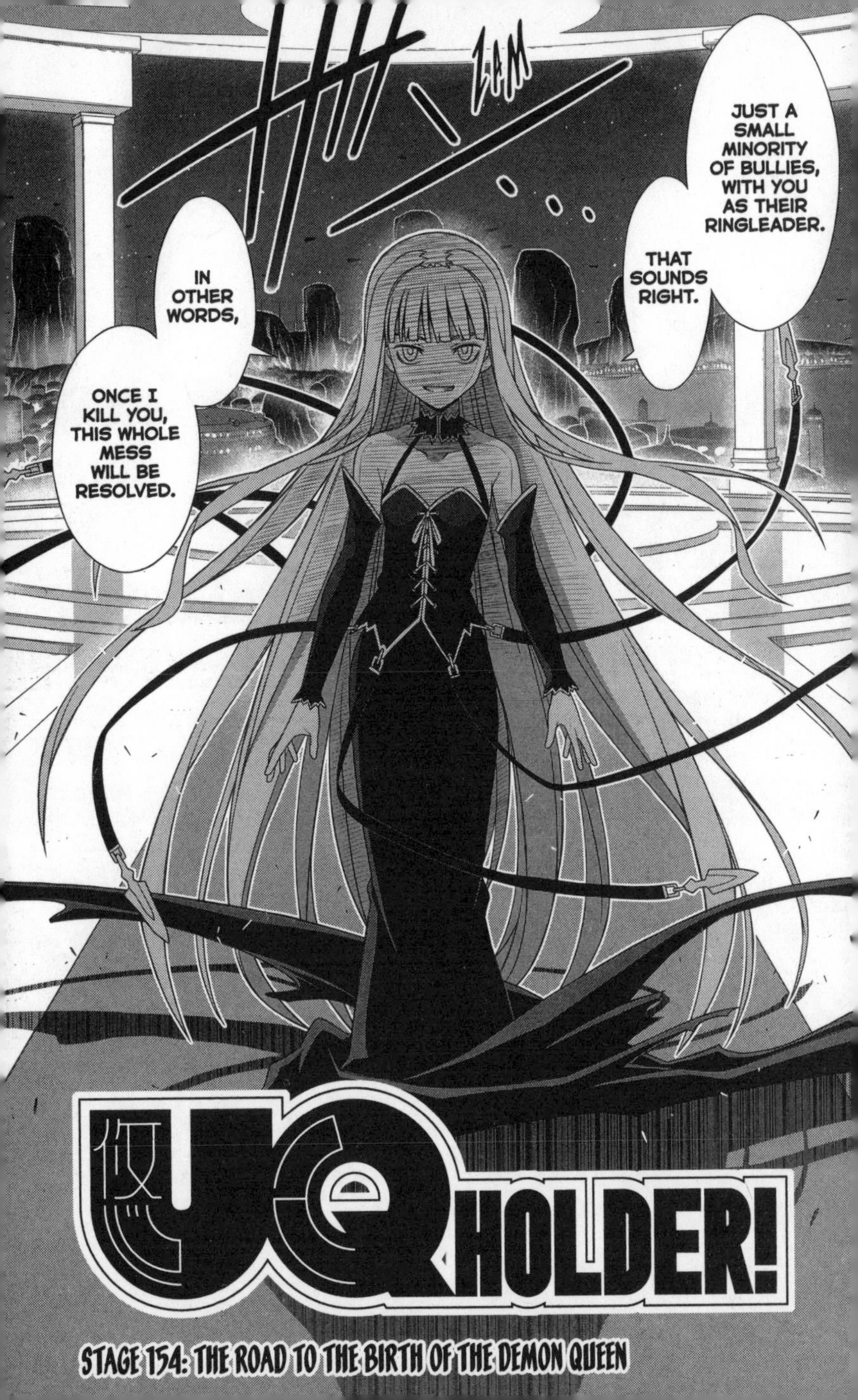
JUST A SMALL MINORITY OF BULLIES, WITH YOU AS THEIR RINGLEADER.
THAT SOUNDS RIGHT.
ZAM
...
IN OTHER WORDS,
ONCE I KILL YOU, THIS WHOLE MESS WILL BE RESOLVED.
UQ HOLDER!
STAGE 154: THE ROAD TO THE BIRTH OF THE DEMON QUEEN

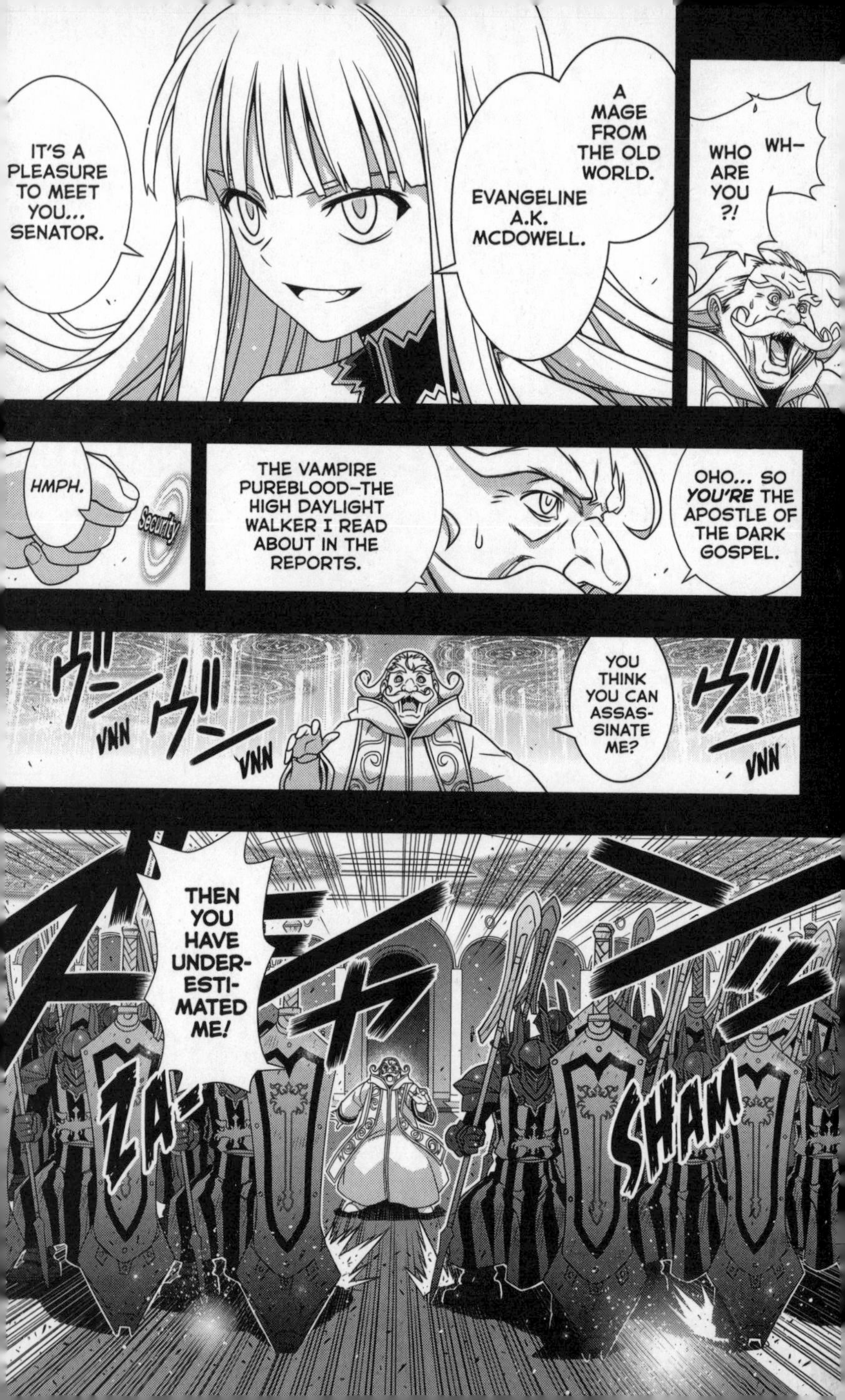

WH—
WHO ARE YOU?!
A MAGE FROM THE OLD WORLD.
EVANGELINE A.K. MCDOWELL.
IT'S A PLEASURE TO MEET YOU... SENATOR.
OHO... SO *YOU'RE* THE APOSTLE OF THE DARK GOSPEL.
THE VAMPIRE PUREBLOOD—THE HIGH DAYLIGHT WALKER I READ ABOUT IN THE REPORTS.
HMPH.
Security
VNN
YOU THINK YOU CAN ASSAS-SINATE ME?
VNN
VNN
THEN YOU HAVE UNDER-ESTI-MATED ME!
SHAM
ZA-

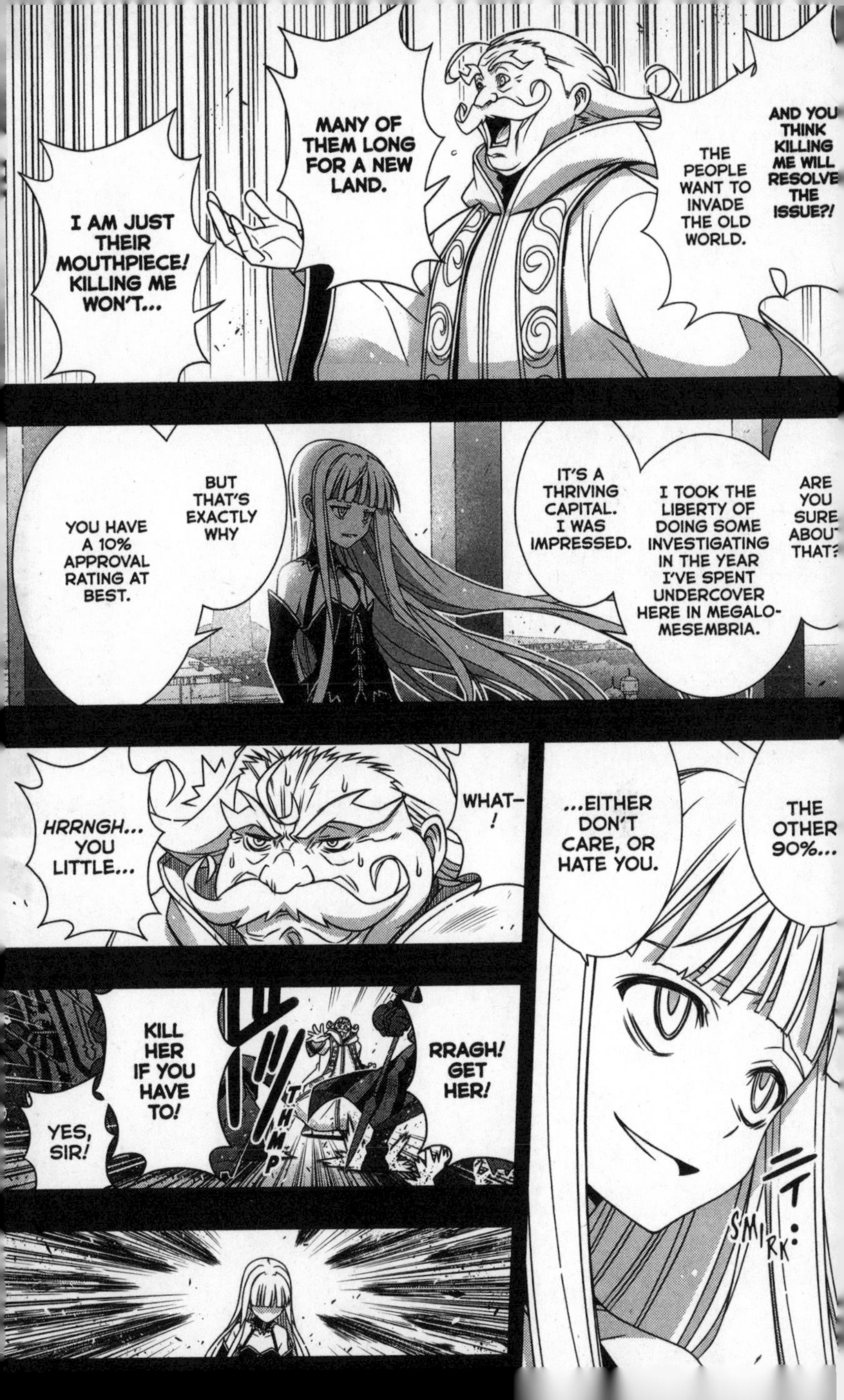
AND YOU THINK KILLING ME WILL RESOLVE THE ISSUE?!
THE PEOPLE WANT TO INVADE THE OLD WORLD.
MANY OF THEM LONG FOR A NEW LAND.
I AM JUST THEIR MOUTHPIECE! KILLING ME WON'T...
ARE YOU SURE ABOUT THAT?
I TOOK THE LIBERTY OF DOING SOME INVESTIGATING IN THE YEAR I'VE SPENT UNDERCOVER HERE IN MEGALO-MESEMBRIA.
IT'S A THRIVING CAPITAL. I WAS IMPRESSED.
BUT THAT'S EXACTLY WHY
YOU HAVE A 10% APPROVAL RATING AT BEST.
THE OTHER 90%...
...EITHER DON'T CARE, OR HATE YOU.
SMIRK
WHAT—!
HRRNGH... YOU LITTLE...
RRAGH! GET HER!
THMP
KILL HER IF YOU HAVE TO!
YES, SIR!

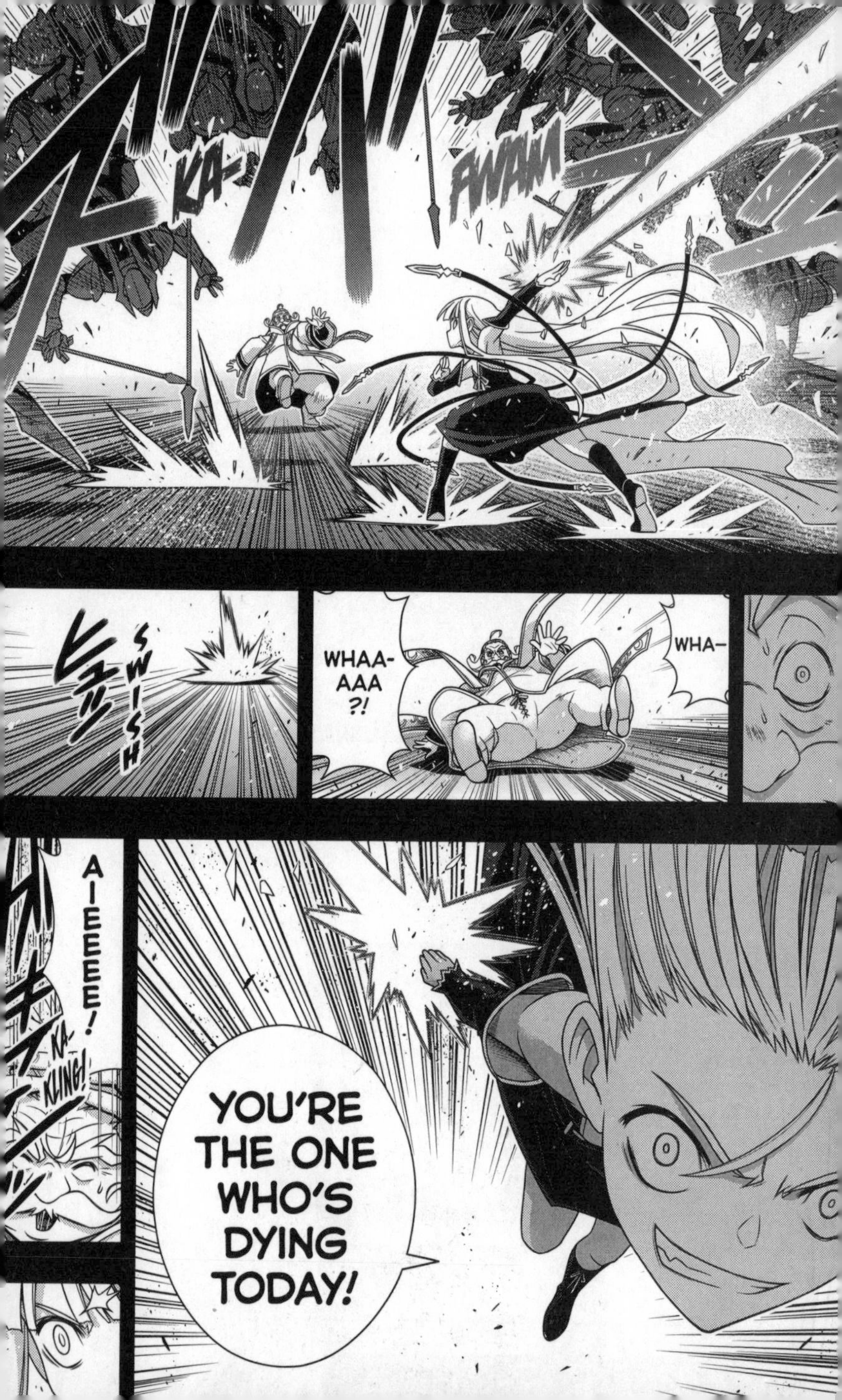
FWAM
KA-
WHA-
WHAA-AAA?!
SWISH
YOU'RE THE ONE WHO'S DYING TODAY!
AIEEEE!
KA-KLING!

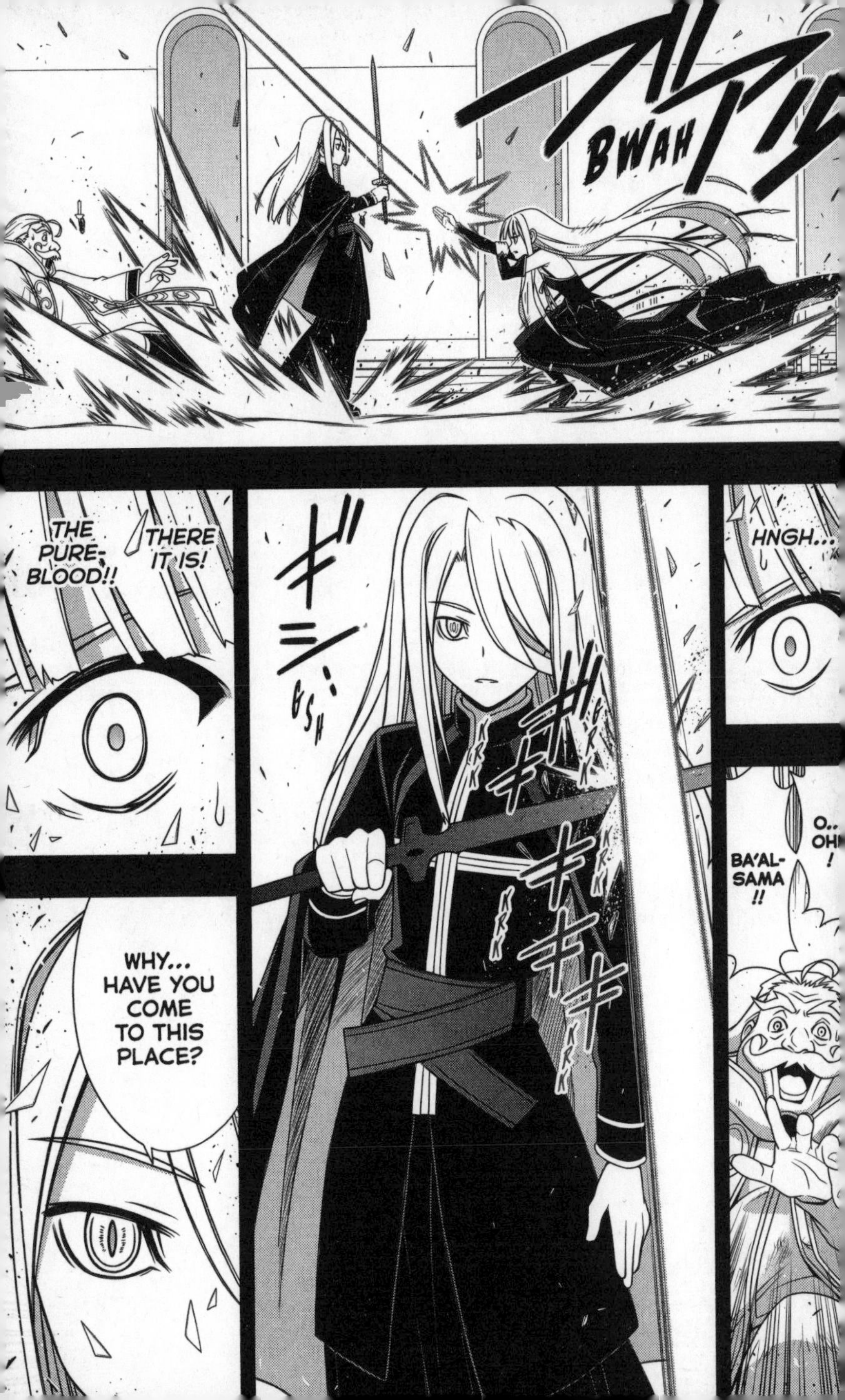
BWAH
HNGH...
O... OH!
BA'AL-SAMA!!
GSH
KRK
THERE IT IS!
THE PURE-BLOOD!!
WHY... HAVE YOU COME TO THIS PLACE?

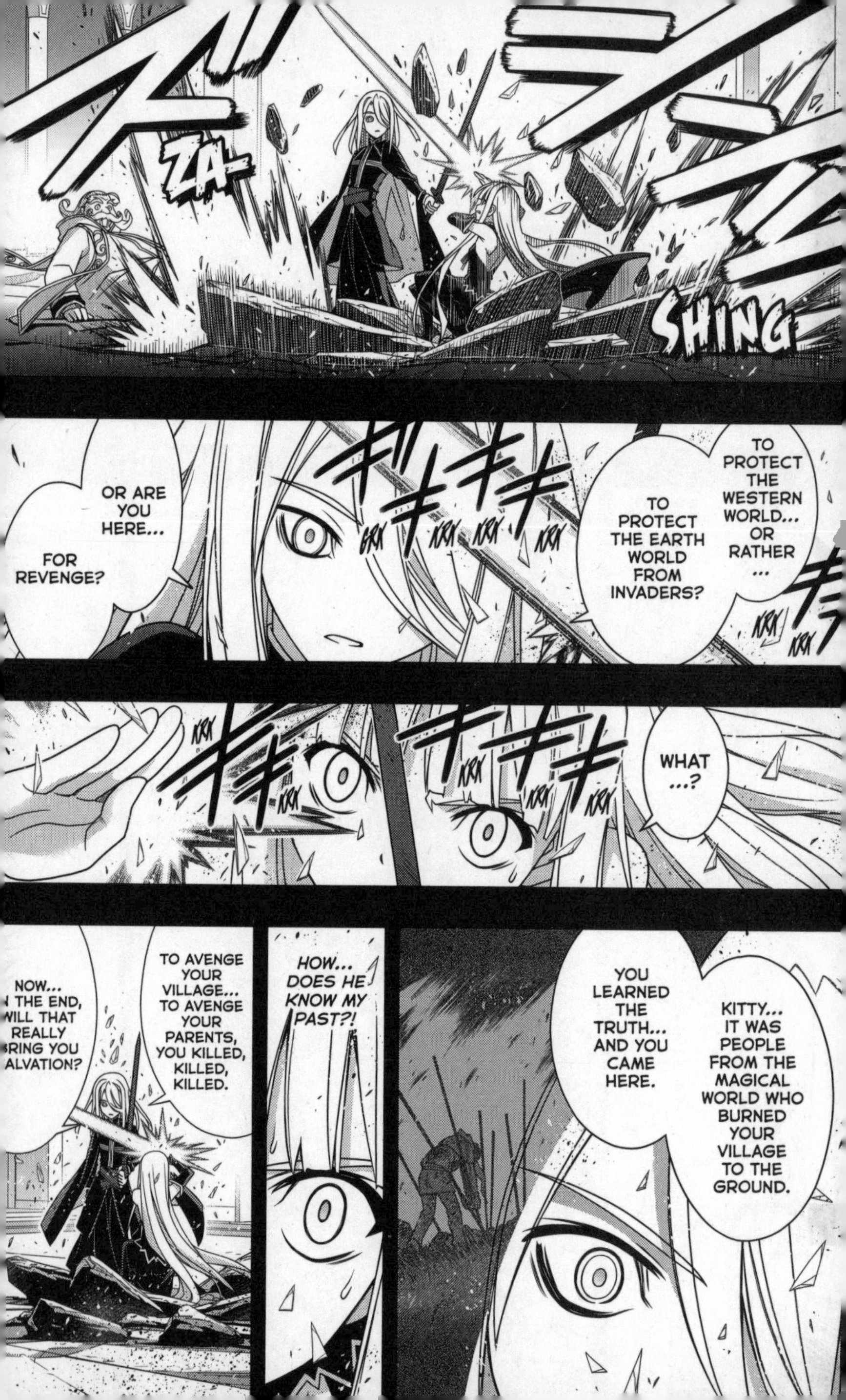
SHING
ZA
TO PROTECT THE WESTERN WORLD... OR RATHER ...
TO PROTECT THE EARTH WORLD FROM INVADERS?
KRK KRK
KRK KRK KRK GRK
OR ARE YOU HERE... FOR REVENGE?
WHAT ...?
KRK KRK KRK KRK KRK KRK
KITTY... IT WAS PEOPLE FROM THE MAGICAL WORLD WHO BURNED YOUR VILLAGE TO THE GROUND.
YOU LEARNED THE TRUTH... AND YOU CAME HERE.
HOW... DOES HE KNOW MY PAST?!
TO AVENGE YOUR VILLAGE... TO AVENGE YOUR PARENTS, YOU KILLED, KILLED, KILLED.
NOW... N THE END, WILL THAT REALLY BRING YOU ALVATION?

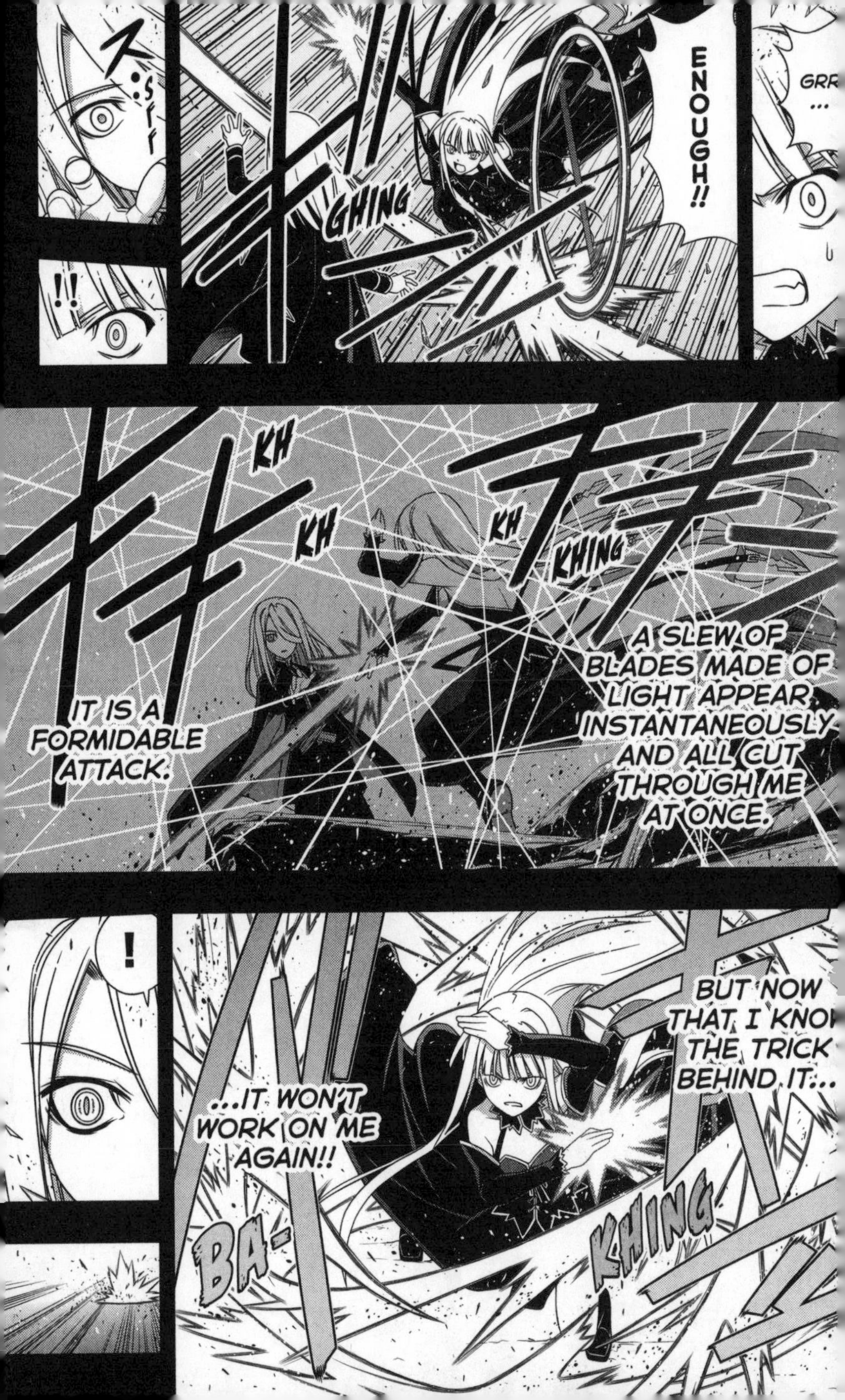

GRR...
ENOUGH!!
GHING
ス
SFF
!!
KHING
KH
KH
KH
A SLEW OF BLADES MADE OF LIGHT APPEAR INSTANTANEOUSLY AND ALL CUT THROUGH ME AT ONCE.
IT IS A FORMIDABLE ATTACK.
BUT NOW THAT I KNOW THE TRICK BEHIND IT...
...IT WON'T WORK ON ME AGAIN!!
BA-KHING
!

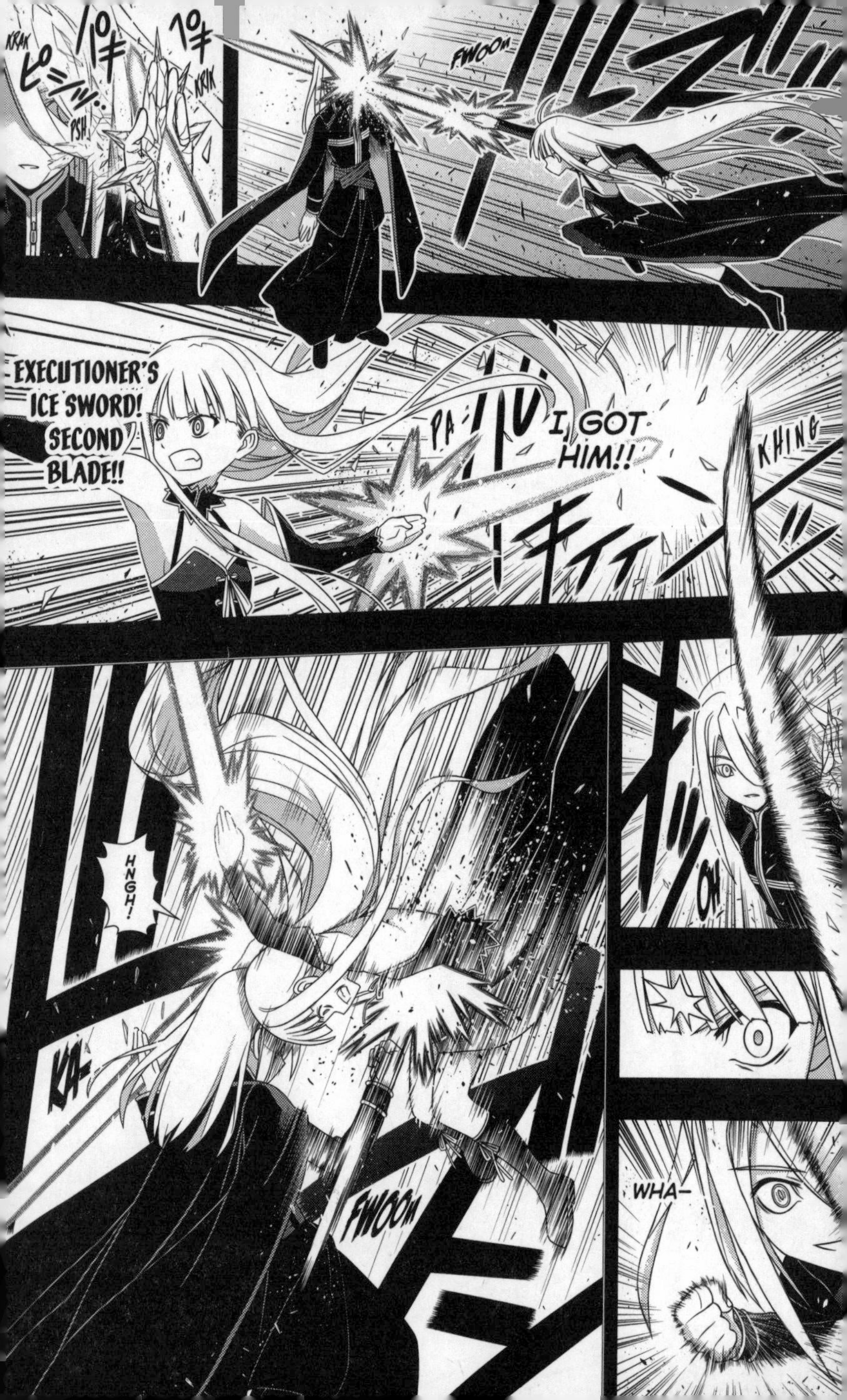
FWOOM
KRAK
KRIK
PSH
EXECUTIONER'S ICE SWORD! SECOND BLADE!!
PA
I GOT HIM!!
KHING
OH
WHA-
HNGH!
KA
FWOOM

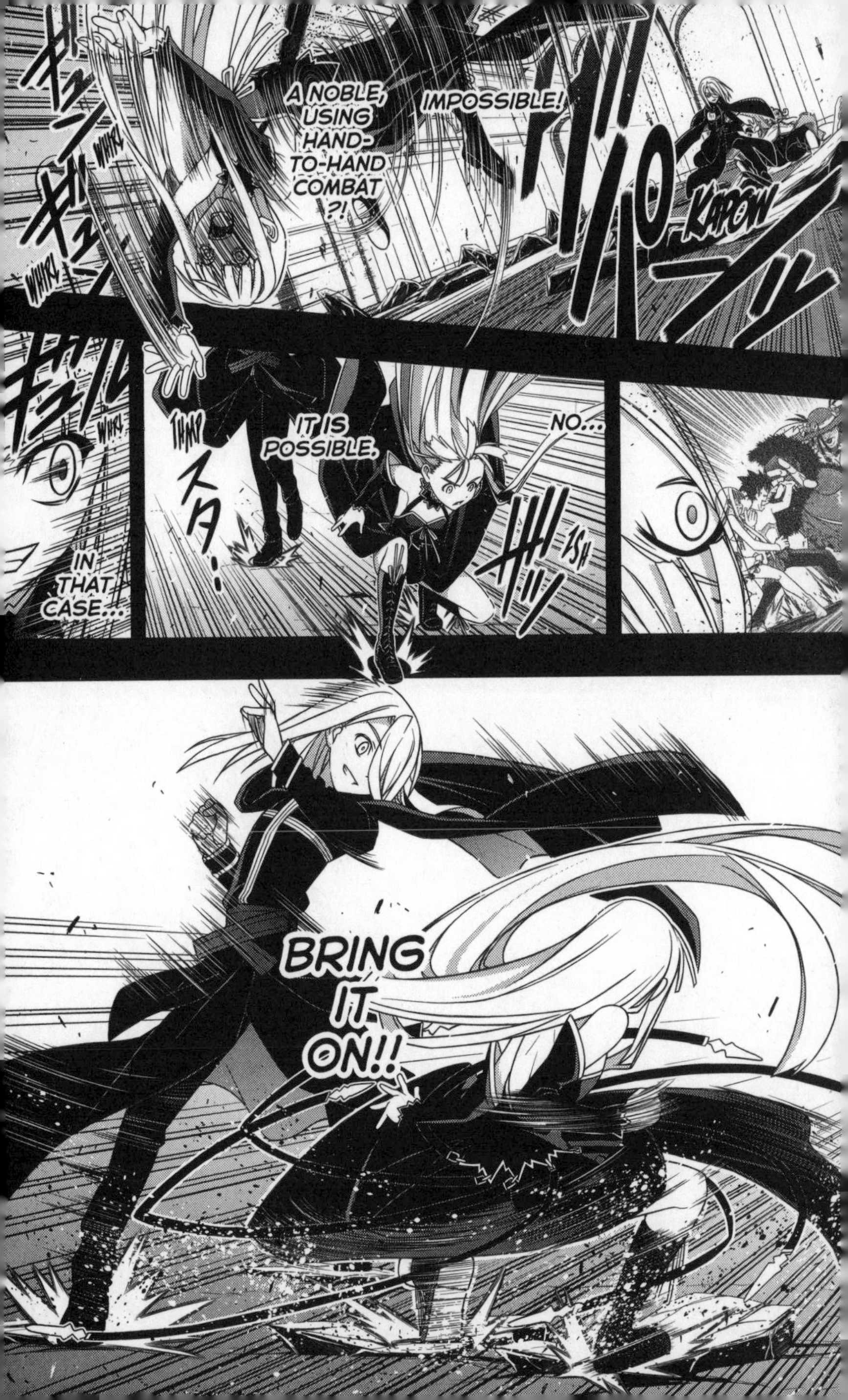
KAPOW
IMPOSSIBLE!
A NOBLE, USING HAND-TO-HAND COMBAT?!
WHIRL
WHIRL
NO...
IT IS POSSIBLE.
THMP
WHIRL
IN THAT CASE...
BRING IT ON!!

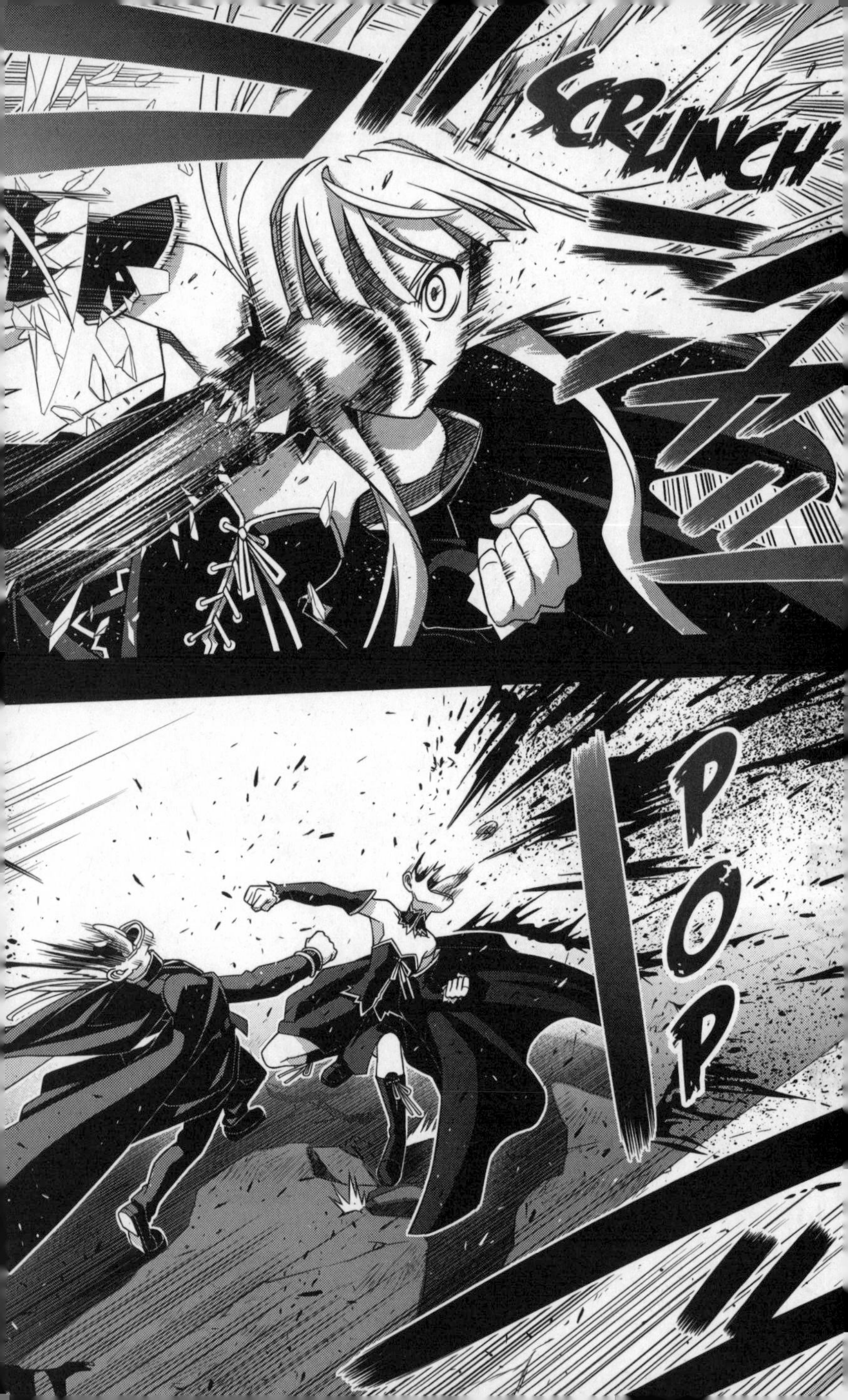
SCRUNCH
POP

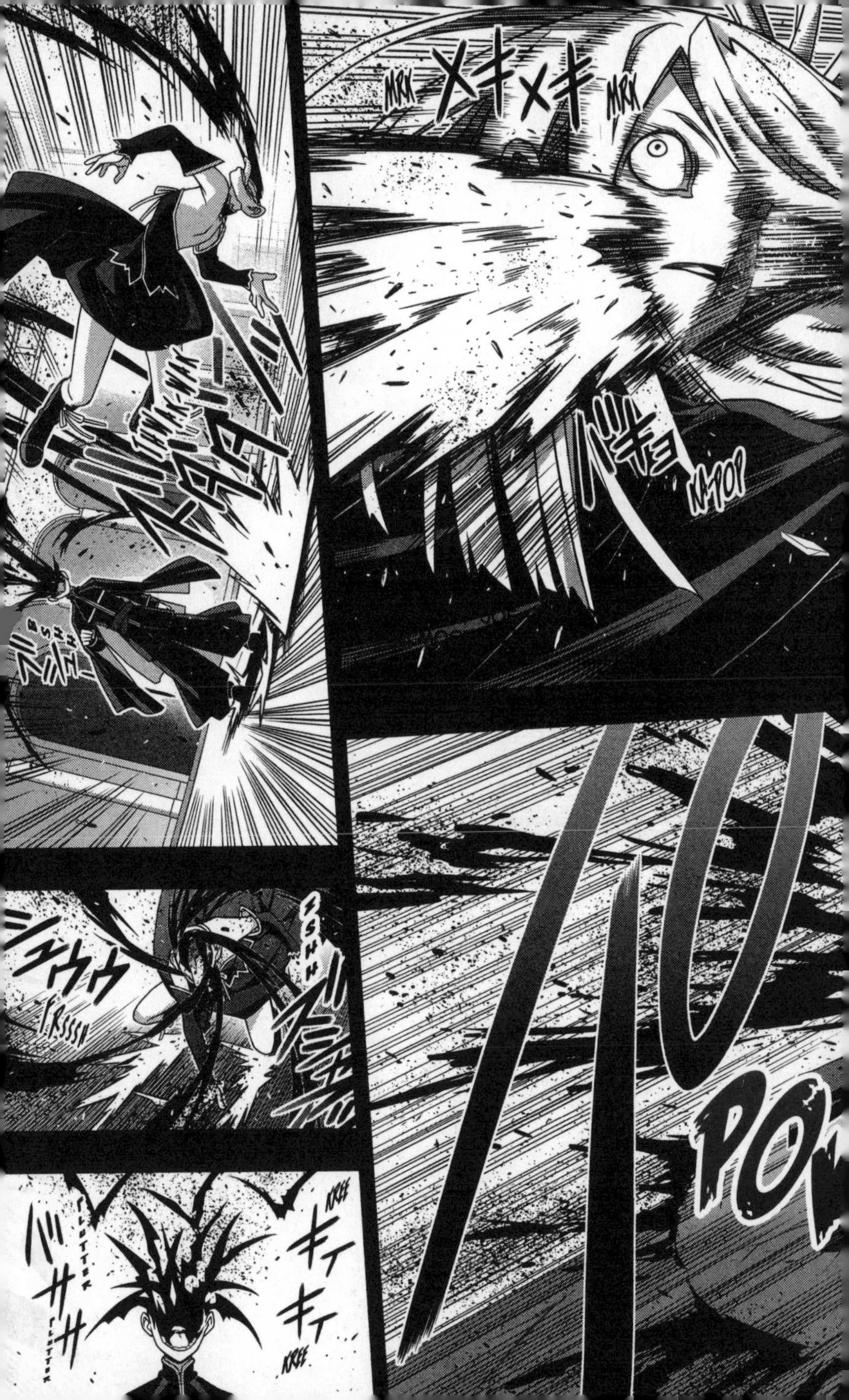
MRK
メキメキ
MRK
バキョ
NAPOP
WHAK-WHAK
ZSHH
POP
ZSHH
FRSSSH
キィ キィ
KREE
KREE
バサササ
FLUTTER
FLUTTER

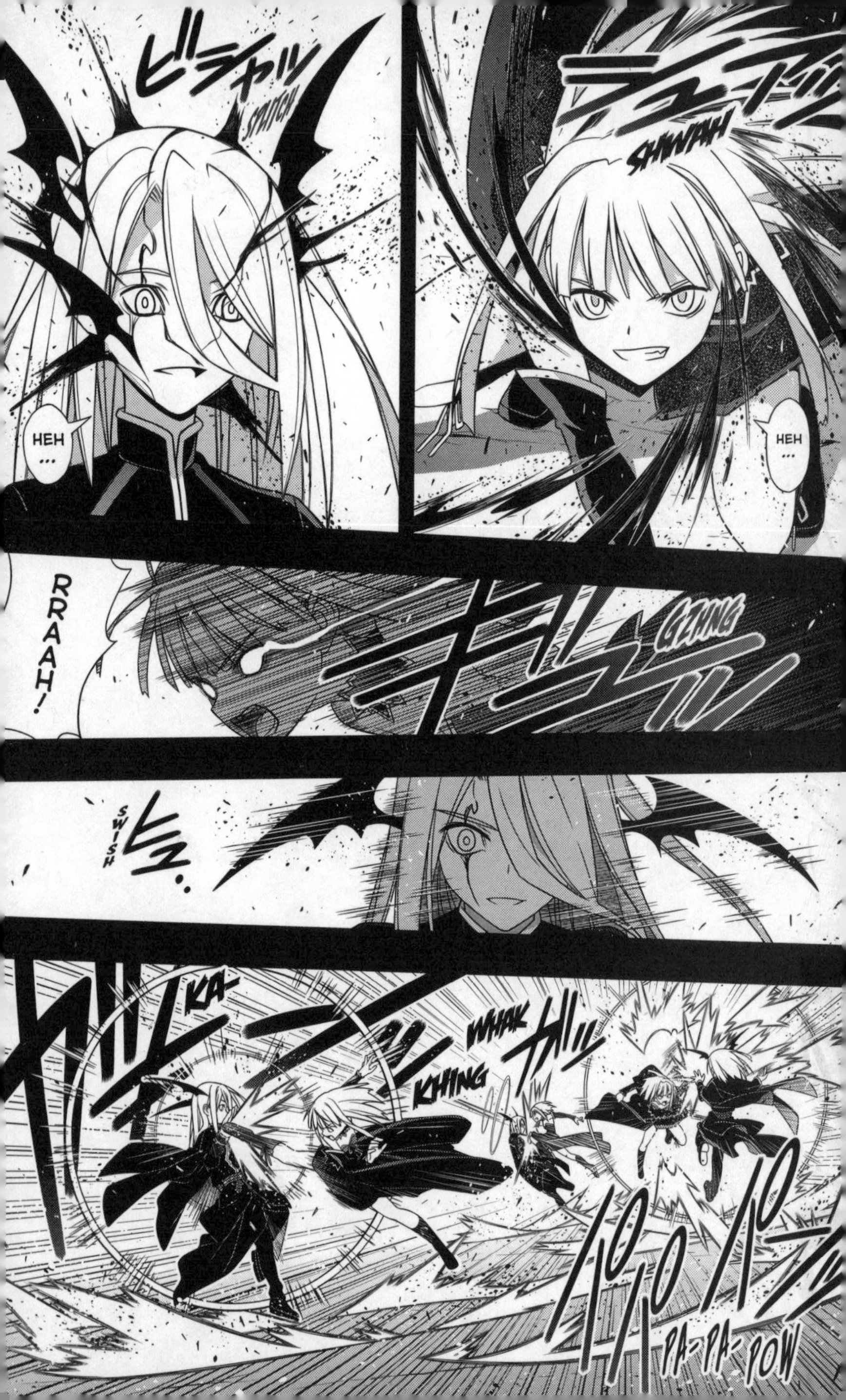
SHWAH
HEH...
SPLITCH
HEH...
GZHNG
RRAAAH!
SWISH
KA-
WHAK
KHING
PA-PA-POW

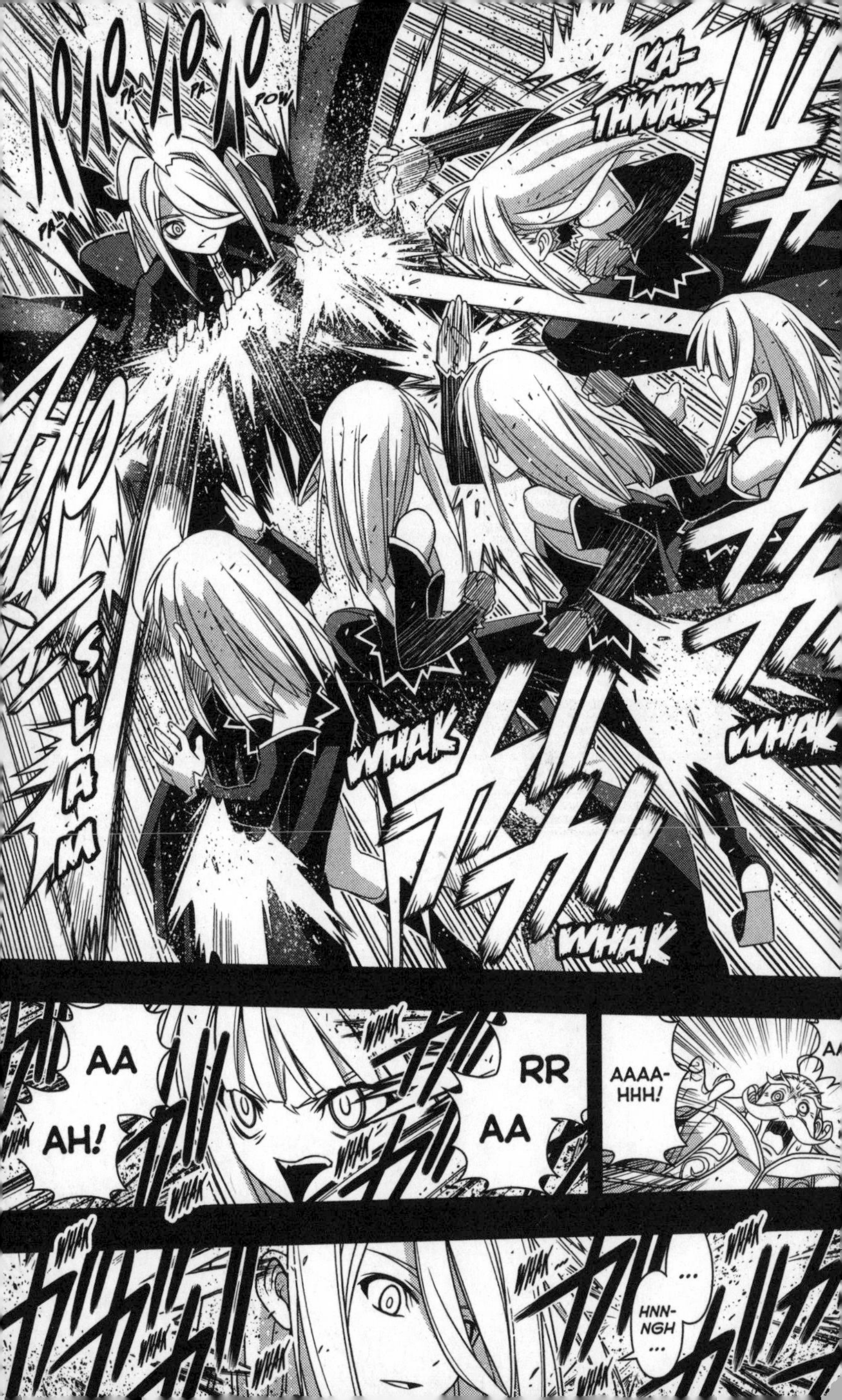

KA-THWAK
POW
PA-
PA-
PA-
WHAK
WHAK
SLAM
PA-
WHAK
AAAA-HHH!
RR AA
AA AH!
... HNN-NGH ...

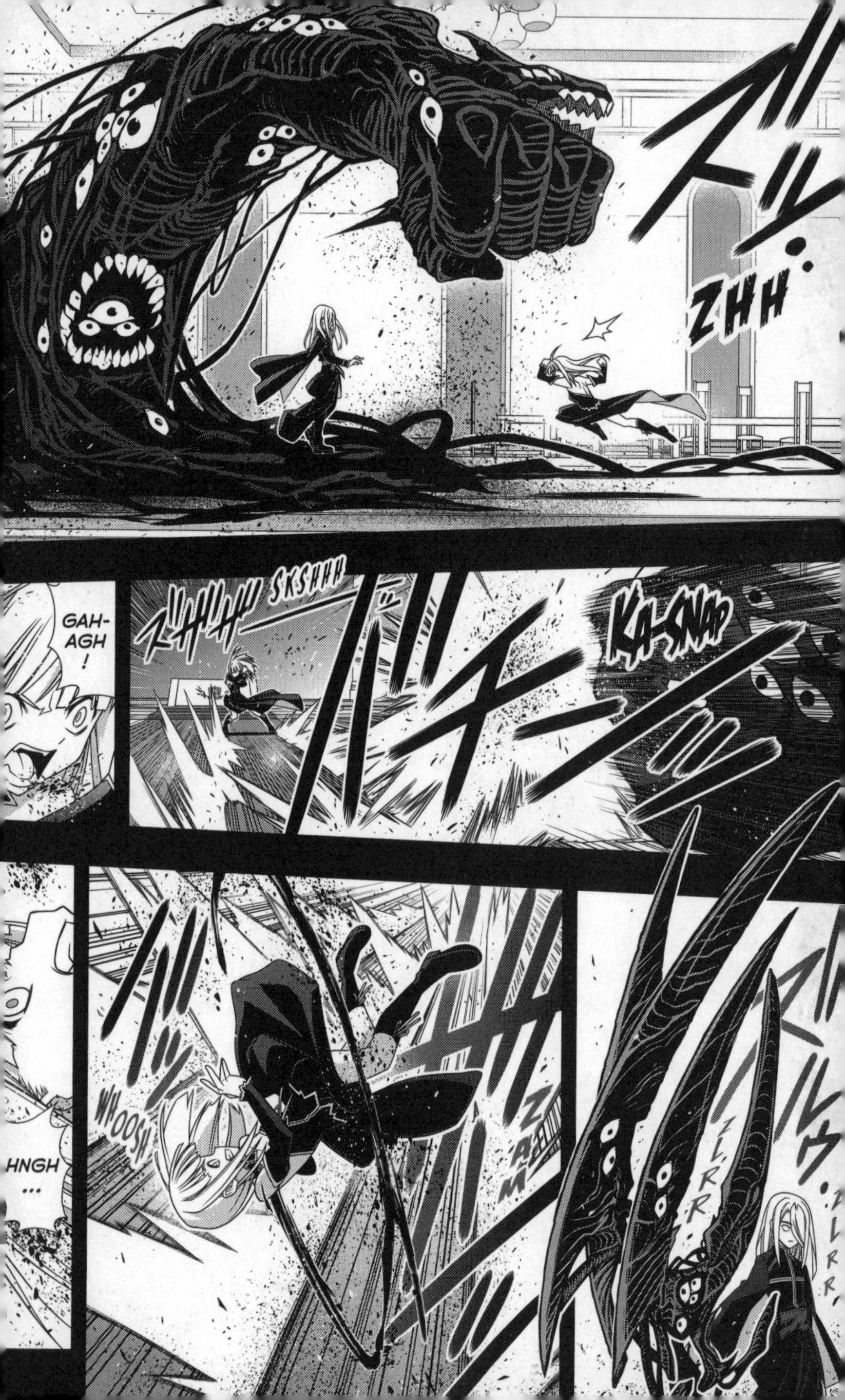
ZHH
KA-SNAP
SKSHHH
GAH-AGH!
ZLRR
ZLRR
ZAM
WHOOSH
HNGH...

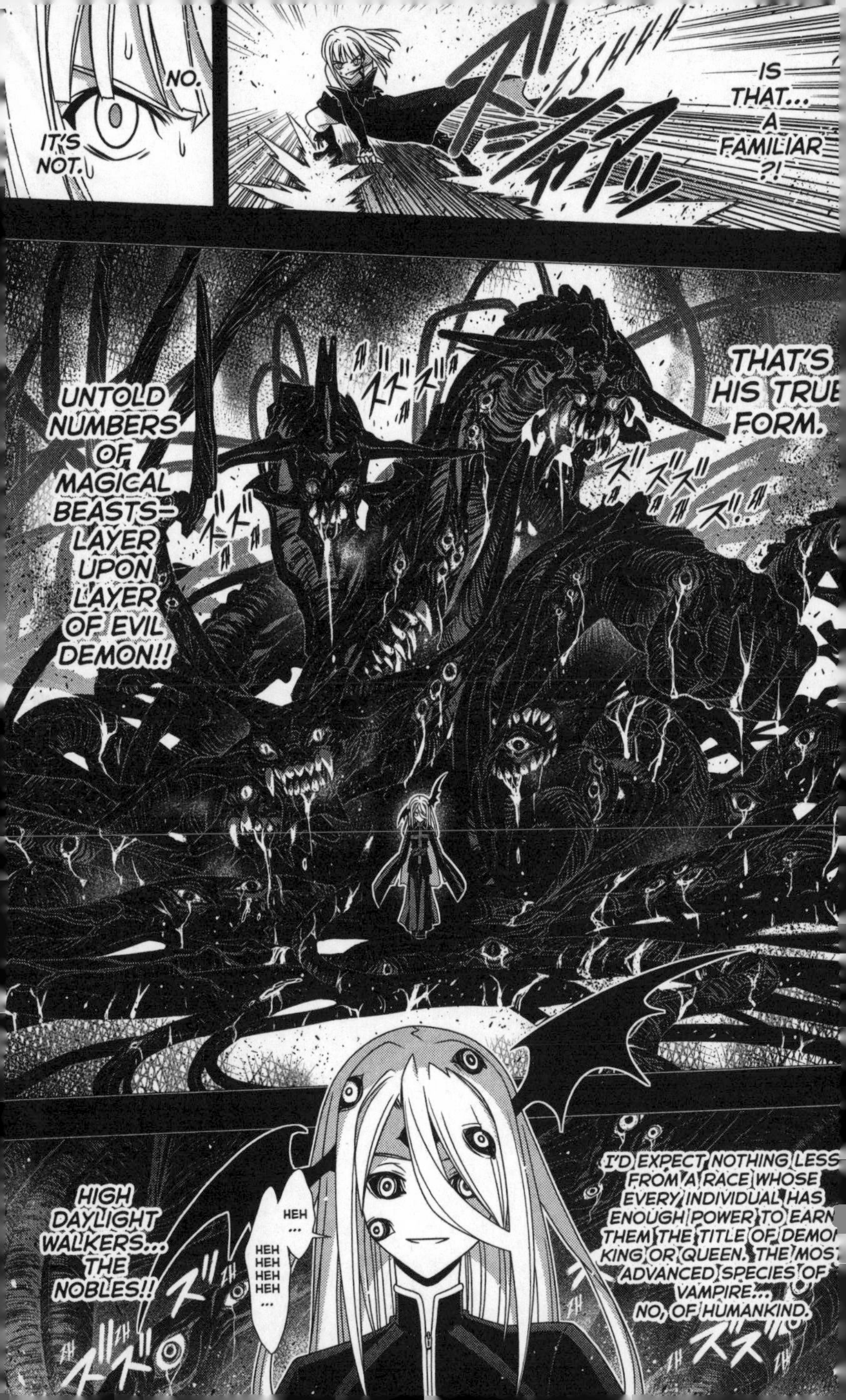
IS THAT... A FAMILIAR?!
NO.
IT'S NOT.
THAT'S HIS TRUE FORM.
UNTOLD NUMBERS OF MAGICAL BEASTS— LAYER UPON LAYER OF EVIL DEMON!!
I'D EXPECT NOTHING LESS FROM A RACE WHOSE EVERY INDIVIDUAL HAS ENOUGH POWER TO EARN THEM THE TITLE OF DEMON KING OR QUEEN. THE MOST ADVANCED SPECIES OF VAMPIRE... NO, OF HUMANKIND.
HEH ...
HEH HEH HEH HEH ...
HIGH DAYLIGHT WALKERS... THE NOBLES!!

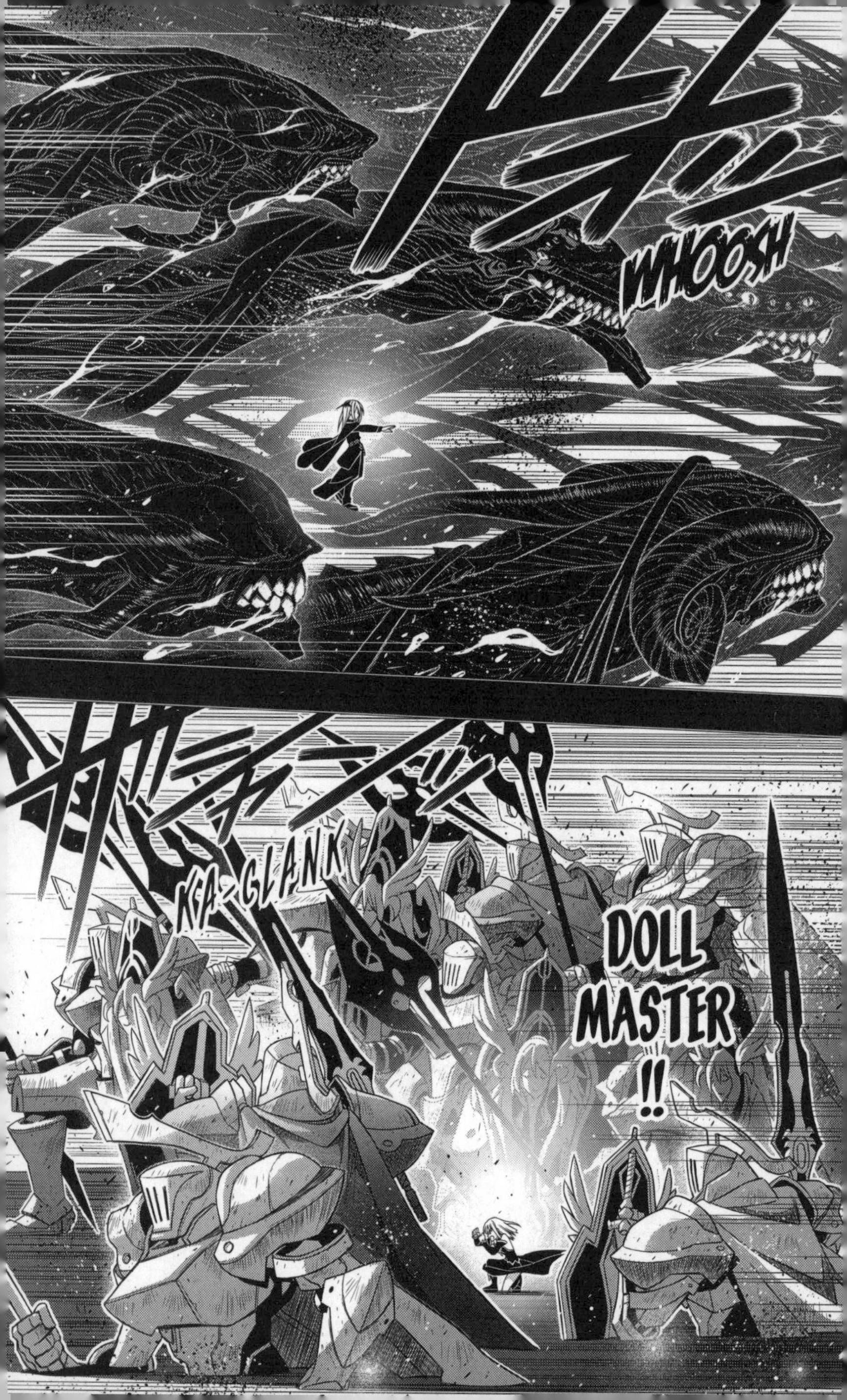
WHOOSH
KA-CLANK
DOLL MASTER!!

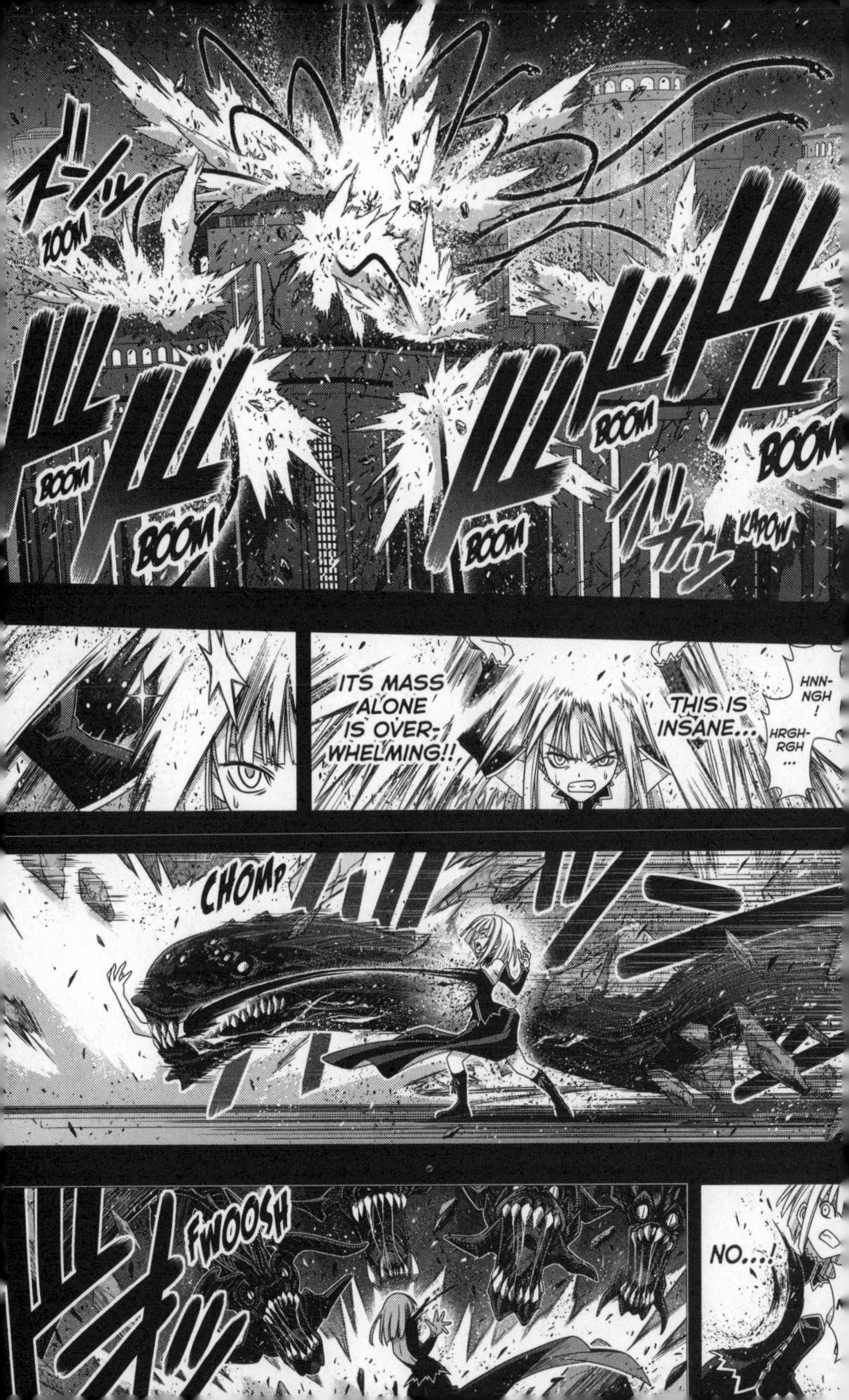
BOOM
BOOM
KAPOW
BOOM
ZOOM
BOOM
BOOM
HNN-NGH!
HRGH-RGH...
THIS IS INSANE...
ITS MASS ALONE IS OVER-WHELMING!!
CHOMP
NO...!
FWOOSH

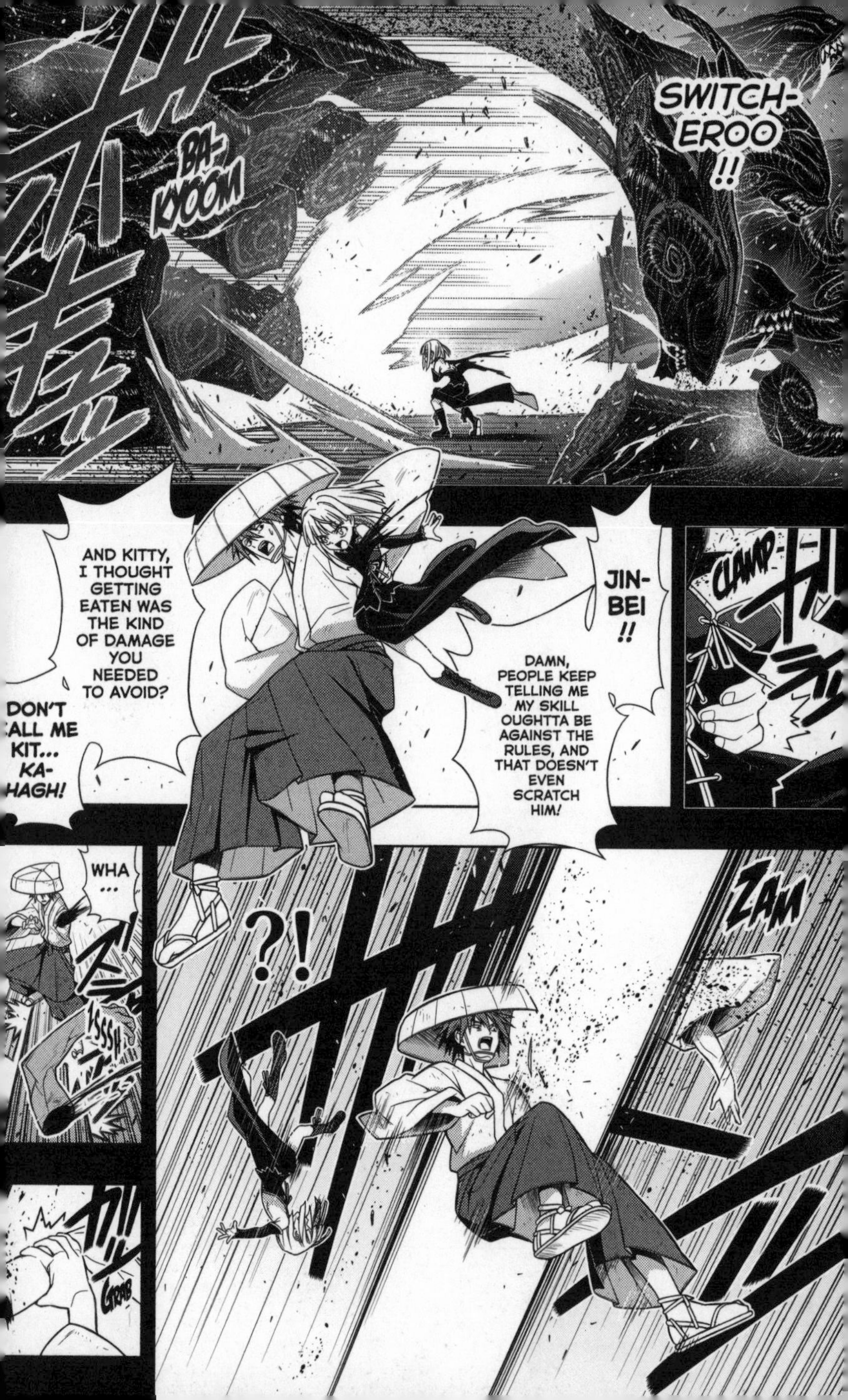
SWITCH-EROO !!
BA-KYOOM
CLAMP
JIN-BEI !!
DAMN, PEOPLE KEEP TELLING ME MY SKILL OUGHTTA BE AGAINST THE RULES, AND THAT DOESN'T EVEN SCRATCH HIM!
AND KITTY, I THOUGHT GETTING EATEN WAS THE KIND OF DAMAGE YOU NEEDED TO AVOID?
DON'T CALL ME KIT... KA-HAGH!
ZAM
?!
WHA ...
VSSSH
GRAB

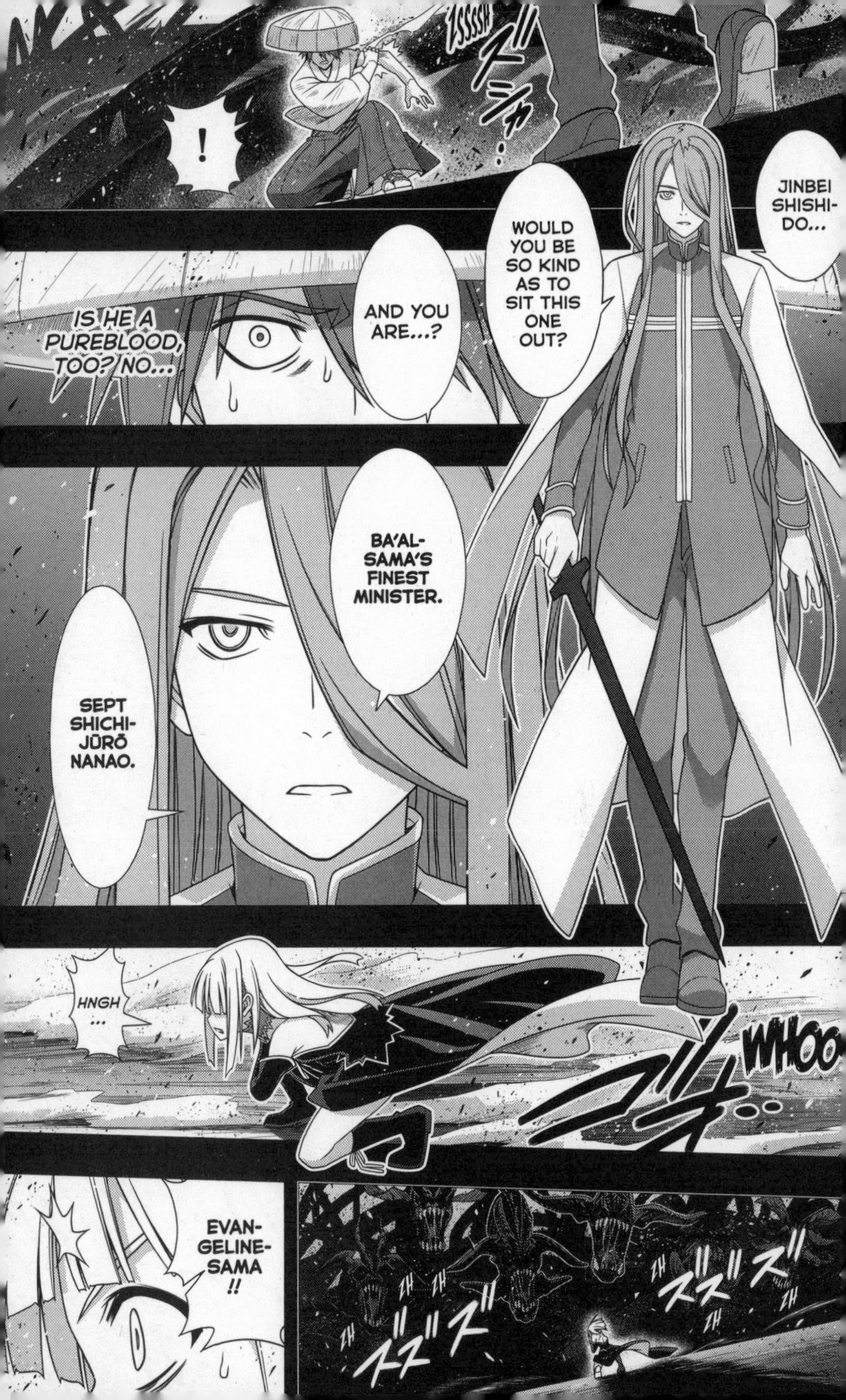
ZSSSSH
!
JINBEI SHISHI-DO...
WOULD YOU BE SO KIND AS TO SIT THIS ONE OUT?
AND YOU ARE...?
IS HE A PUREBLOOD, TOO? NO...
BA'AL-SAMA'S FINEST MINISTER.
SEPT SHICHI-JŪRŌ NANAO.
WHOOO
HNGH ...
ZH
ZH
ZH
ZH
EVAN-GELINE-SAMA !!

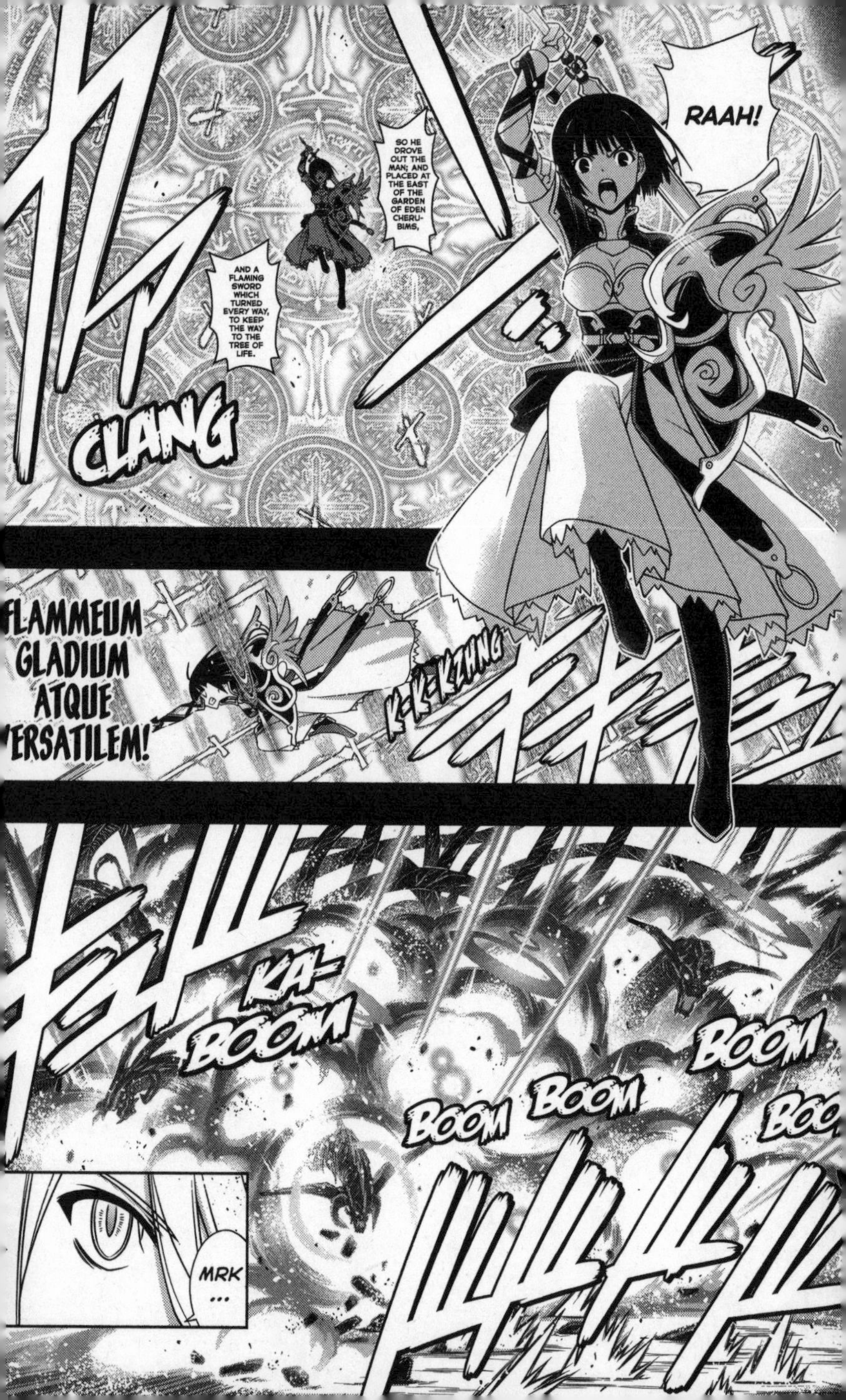
RAAH!
SO HE DROVE OUT THE MAN; AND PLACED AT THE EAST OF THE GARDEN OF EDEN CHERU-BIMS,
AND A FLAMING SWORD WHICH TURNED EVERY WAY, TO KEEP THE WAY TO THE TREE OF LIFE.
CLANG
K-K-KZHNG
FLAMMEUM GLADIUM ATQUE VERSATILEM!
BOOM
BOO
BOOM BOOM
KA-BOOM
MRK ...

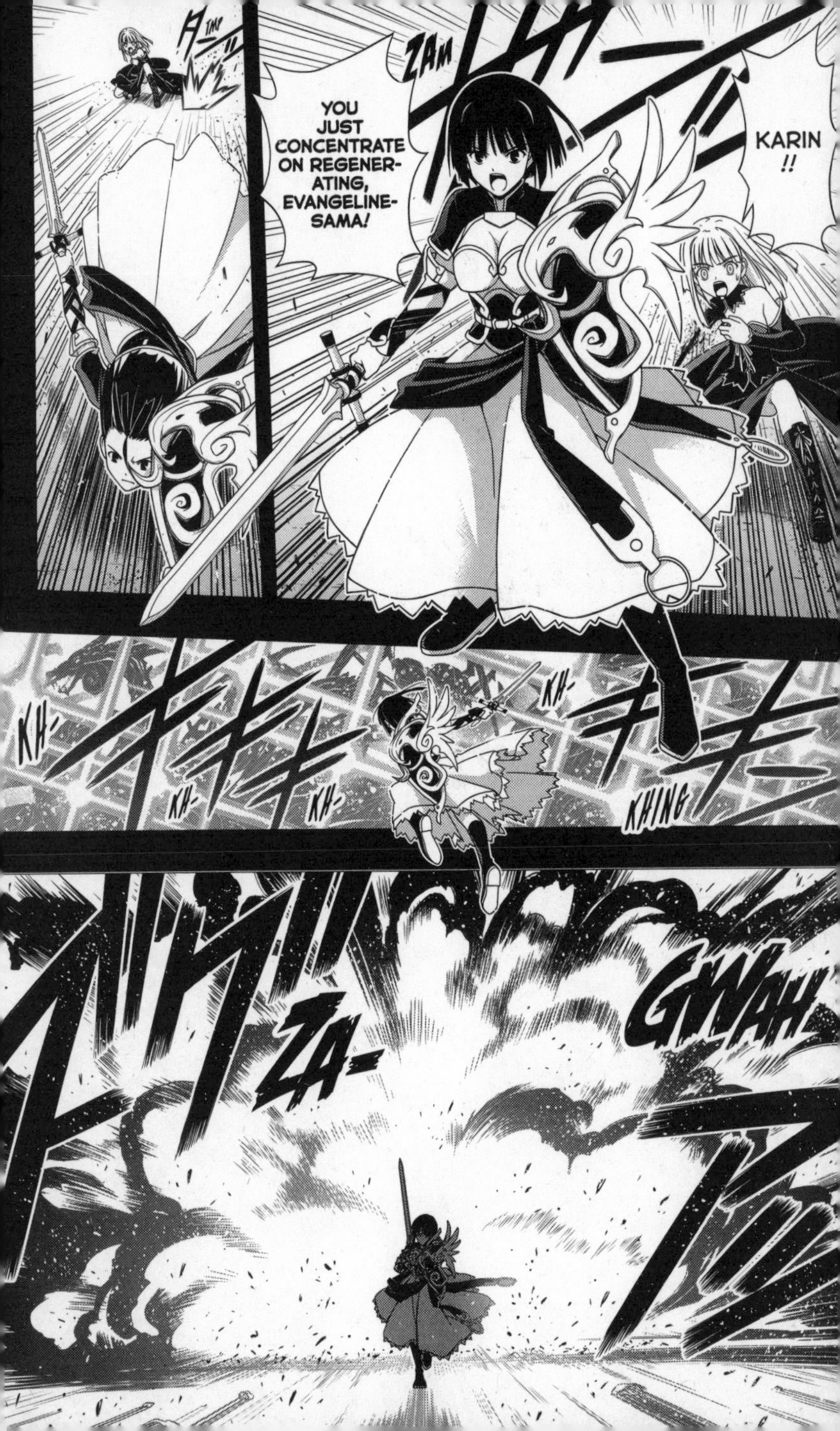

KARIN !!
ZAM
YOU JUST CONCENTRATE ON REGENERATING, EVANGELINE-SAMA!
TMP
KHING
KH-
KH-
KH-
KH-
GWAH
ZA-

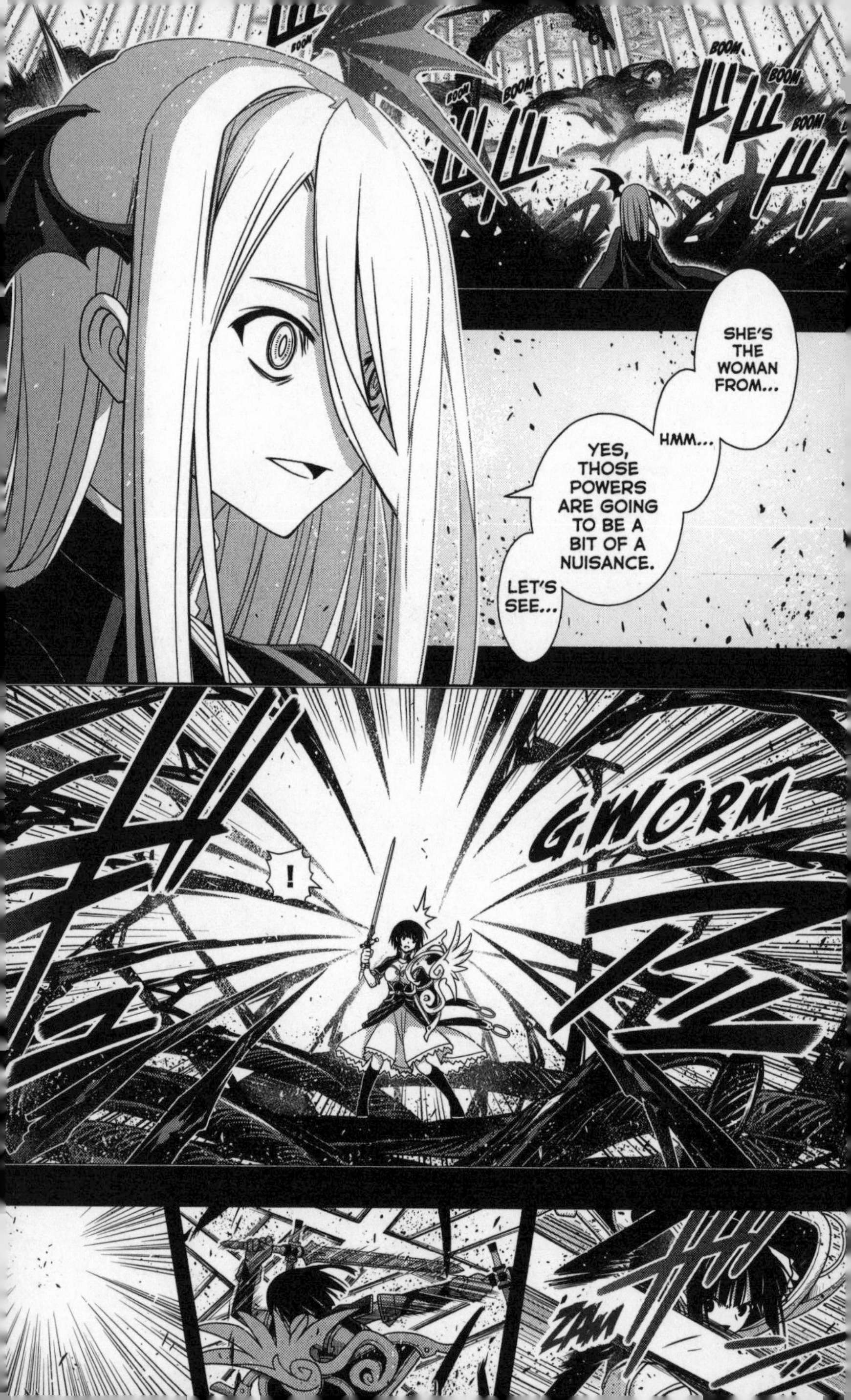
BOOM
BOOM
BOOM
BOOM
BOOM
BOOM
SHE'S THE WOMAN FROM...
HMM...
YES, THOSE POWERS ARE GOING TO BE A BIT OF A NUISANCE.
LET'S SEE...
GWORM
!

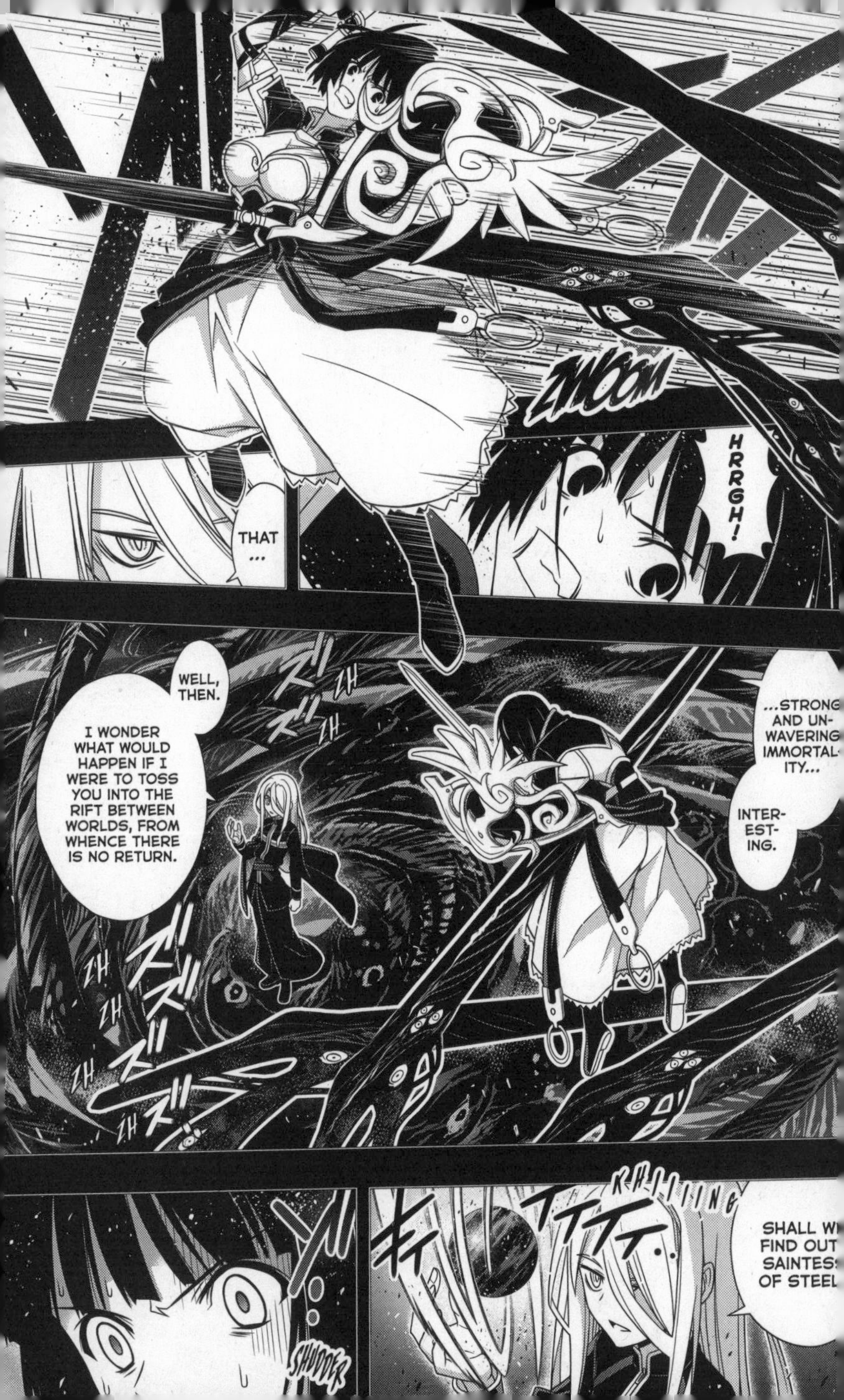
ZWOOM
HRRGH!
THAT ...
...STRONG AND UN-WAVERING IMMORTAL-ITY...
INTER-EST-ING.
WELL, THEN.
I WONDER WHAT WOULD HAPPEN IF I WERE TO TOSS YOU INTO THE RIFT BETWEEN WORLDS, FROM WHENCE THERE IS NO RETURN.
ZH
ZH
ZH
ZH
ZH
ZH
KHIIIING
SHALL W FIND OUT SAINTES OF STEEL
SHUDDER

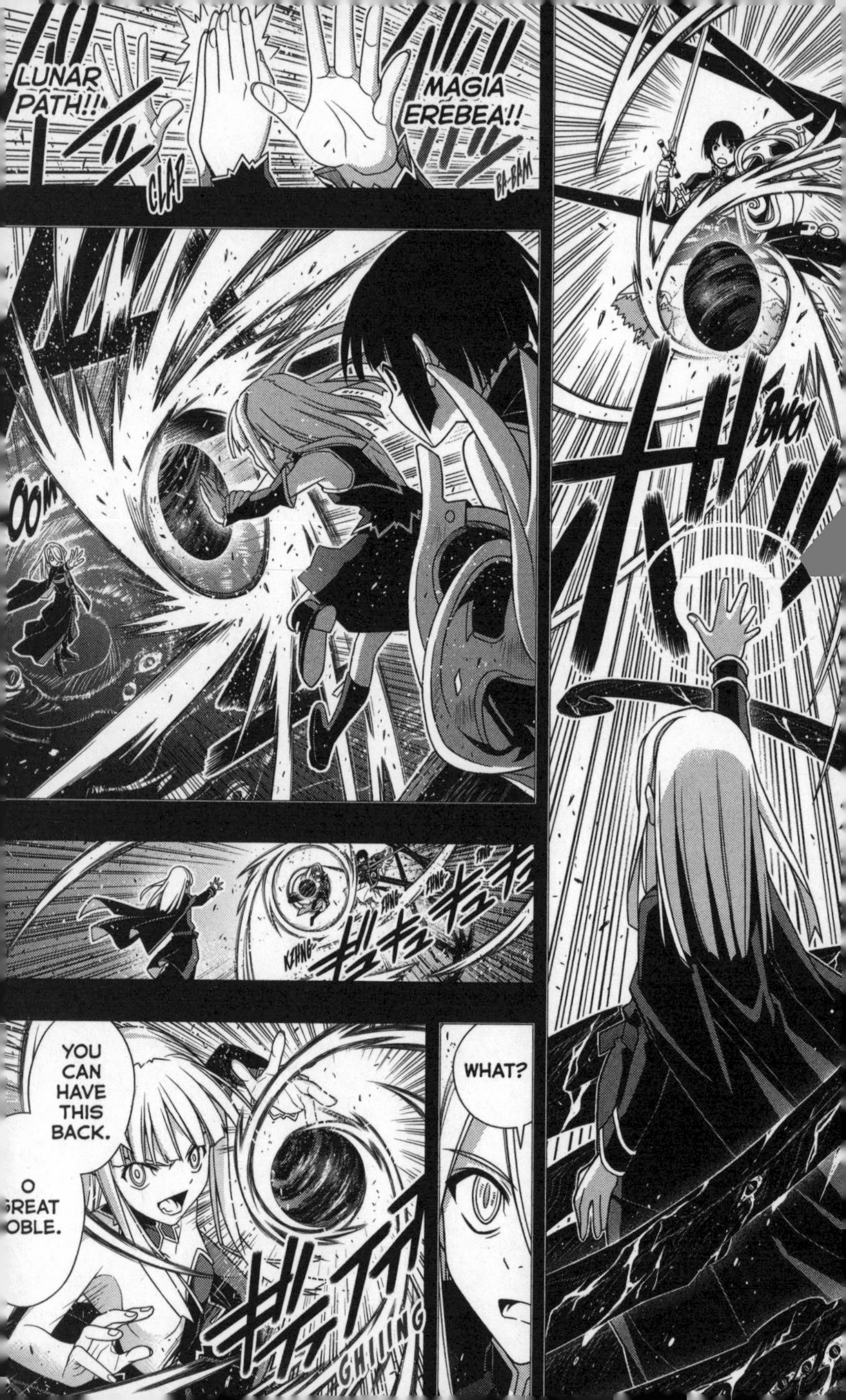
BACH
MAGIA EREBEA!!
LUNAR PATH!!!
CLAP
BA-BAM
OOM
WHAT?
YOU CAN HAVE THIS BACK.
O GREAT
OBLE.
GHIIING

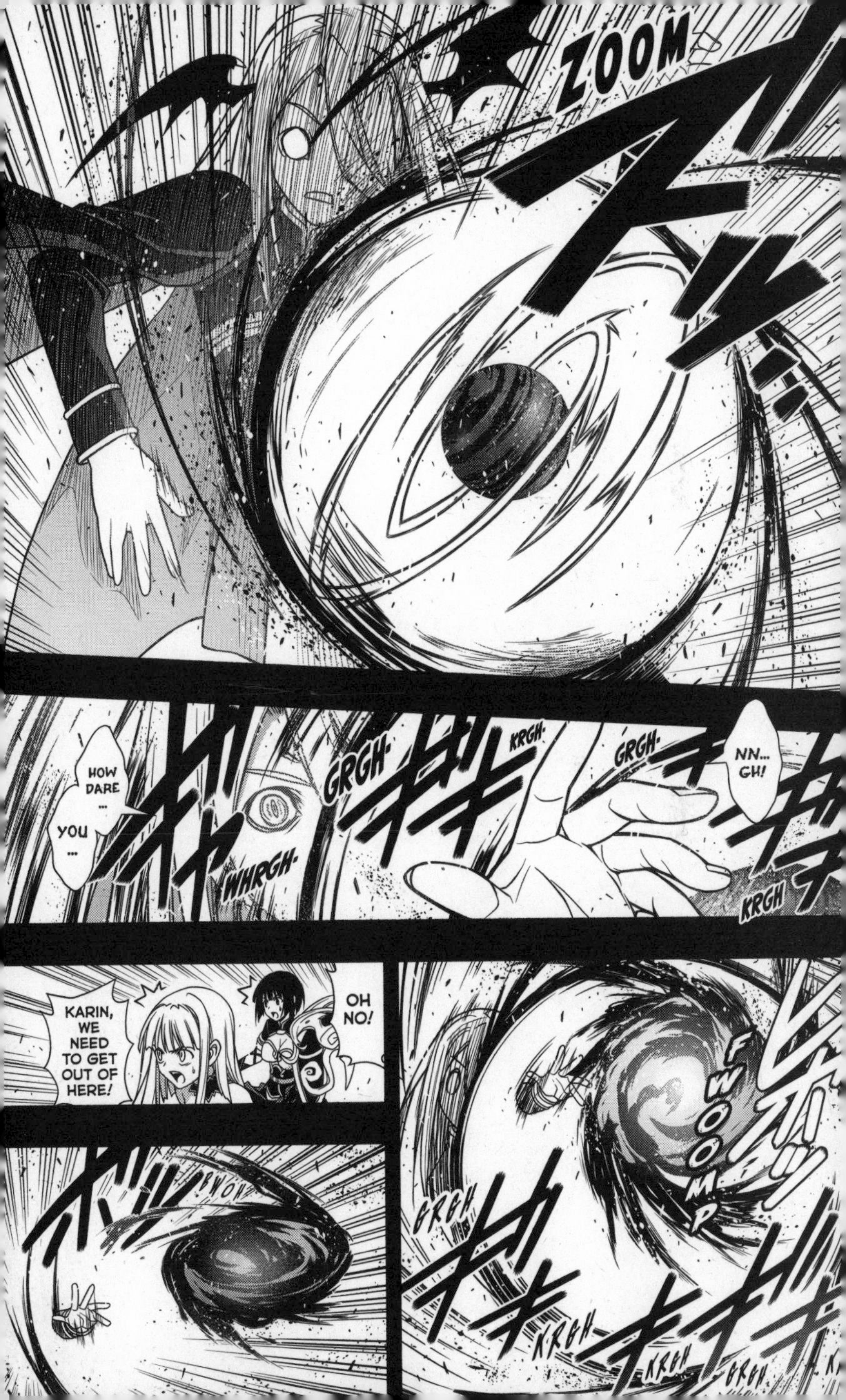
ZOOM
NN... GH!
KRGH
GRGH-
KRGH-
GRGH-
WHRGH-
HOW DARE... YOU...
FWOOOMP
GRGH
KRGH
KRGH
GRGH
OH NO!
KARIN, WE NEED TO GET OUT OF HERE!
BWOH

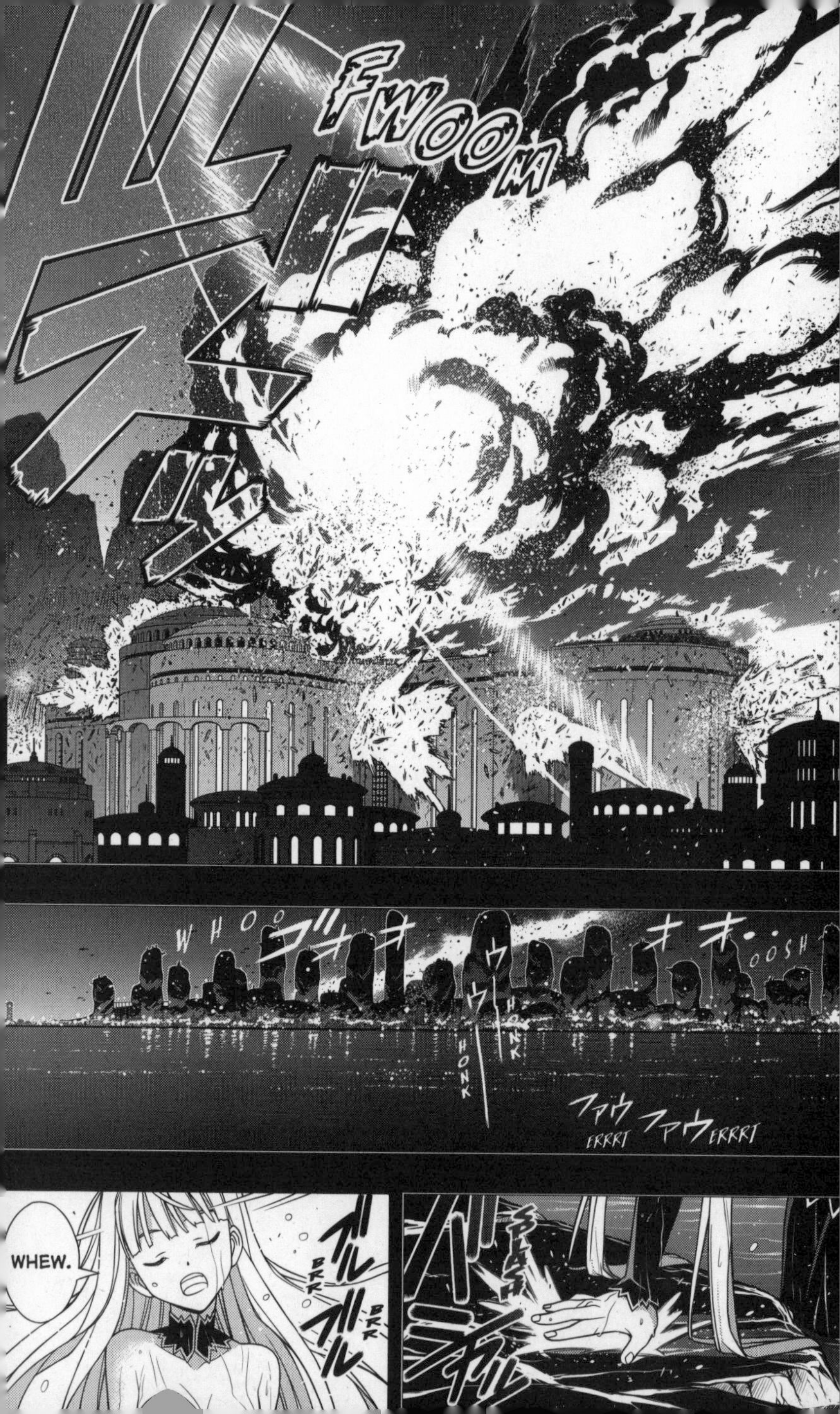
FWOOM
WHOOOSH
HONK
HONK
ファウ
ERRRT
ファウ
ERRRT
SPLASH
WHEW.
BRR
BRR

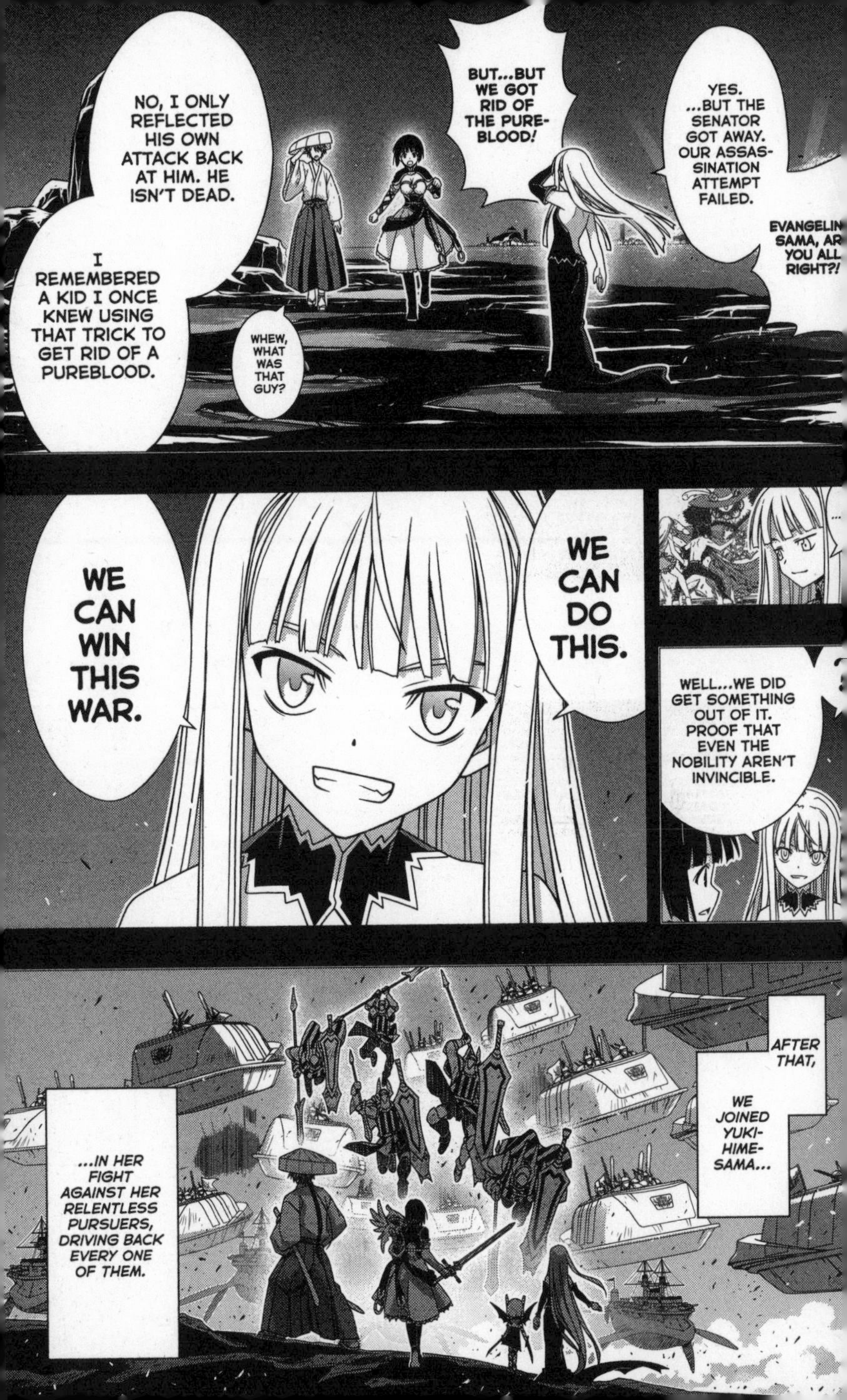
EVANGELIN SAMA, AR YOU ALL RIGHT?!
YES. ...BUT THE SENATOR GOT AWAY. OUR ASSASSINATION ATTEMPT FAILED.
BUT...BUT WE GOT RID OF THE PURE-BLOOD!
WHEW, WHAT WAS THAT GUY?
NO, I ONLY REFLECTED HIS OWN ATTACK BACK AT HIM. HE ISN'T DEAD.
I REMEMBERED A KID I ONCE KNEW USING THAT TRICK TO GET RID OF A PUREBLOOD.
...
WELL...WE DID GET SOMETHING OUT OF IT. PROOF THAT EVEN THE NOBILITY AREN'T INVINCIBLE.
WE CAN DO THIS.
WE CAN WIN THIS WAR.
AFTER THAT,
WE JOINED YUKI-HIME-SAMA...
...IN HER FIGHT AGAINST HER RELENTLESS PURSUERS, DRIVING BACK EVERY ONE OF THEM.

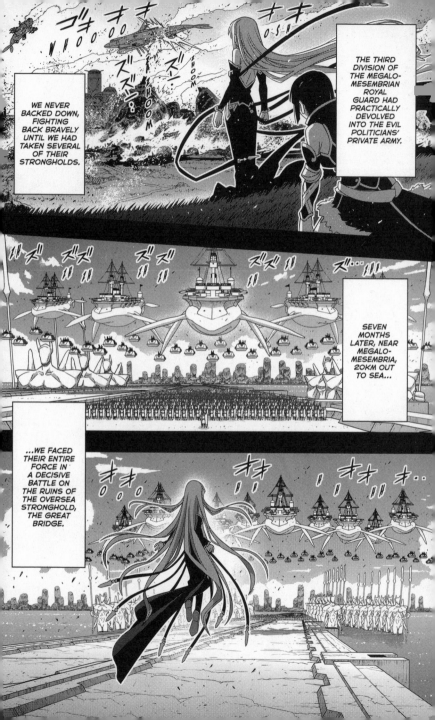

THE THIRD DIVISION OF THE MEGALO-MESEMBRIAN ROYAL GUARD HAD PRACTICALLY DEVOLVED INTO THE EVIL POLITICIANS' PRIVATE ARMY.

WE NEVER BACKED DOWN, FIGHTING BACK BRAVELY UNTIL WE HAD TAKEN SEVERAL OF THEIR STRONGHOLDS.

SEVEN MONTHS LATER, NEAR MEGALO-MESEMBRIA, 20KM OUT TO SEA...

...WE FACED THEIR ENTIRE FORCE IN A DECISIVE BATTLE ON THE RUINS OF THE OVERSEA STRONGHOLD, THE GREAT BRIDGE.

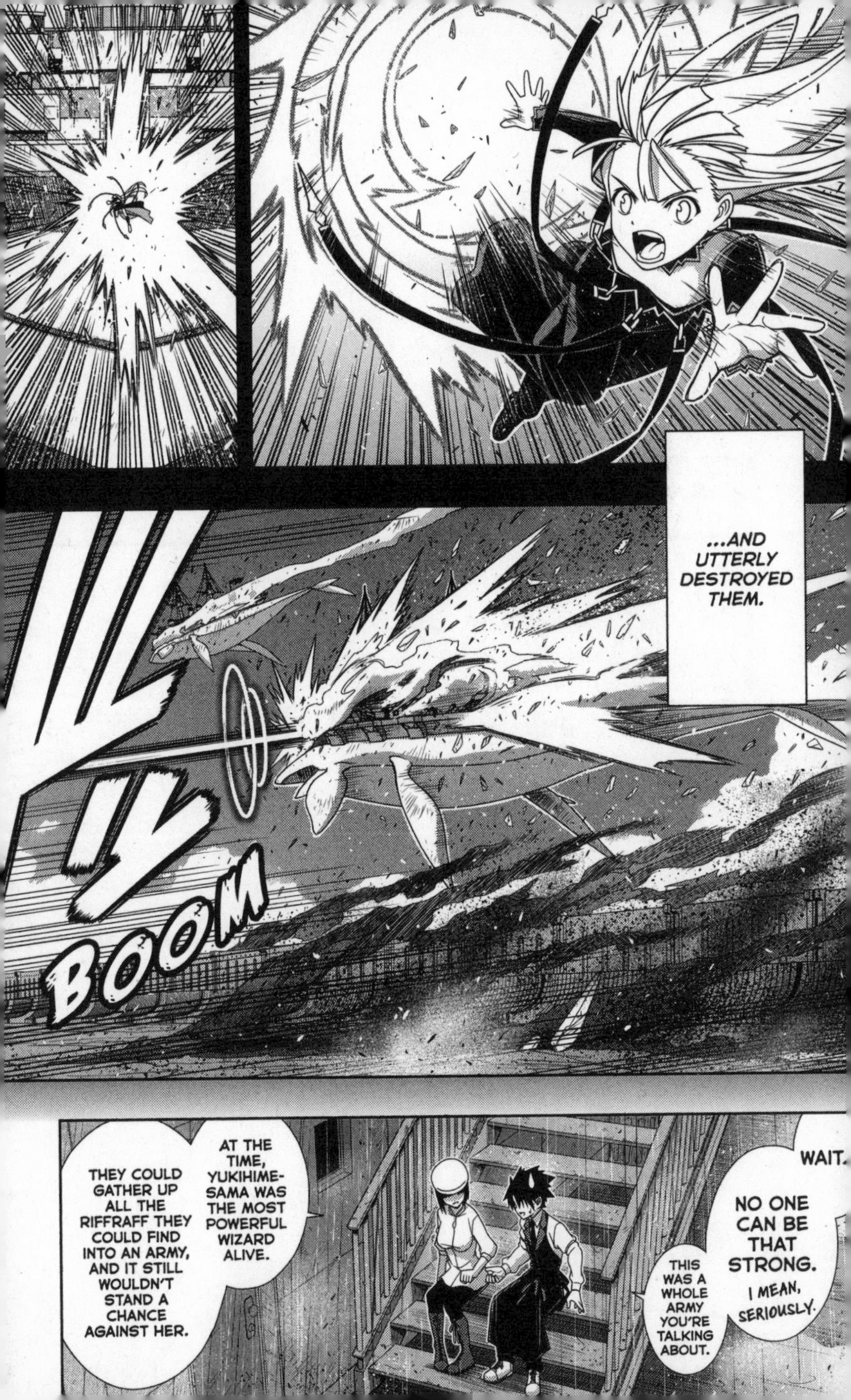
...AND UTTERLY DESTROYED THEM.
BOOM
WAIT.
NO ONE CAN BE THAT STRONG.
I MEAN, SERIOUSLY.
THIS WAS A WHOLE ARMY YOU'RE TALKING ABOUT.
AT THE TIME, YUKIHIME-SAMA WAS THE MOST POWERFUL WIZARD ALIVE.
THEY COULD GATHER UP ALL THE RIFFRAFF THEY COULD FIND INTO AN ARMY, AND IT STILL WOULDN'T STAND A CHANCE AGAINST HER.

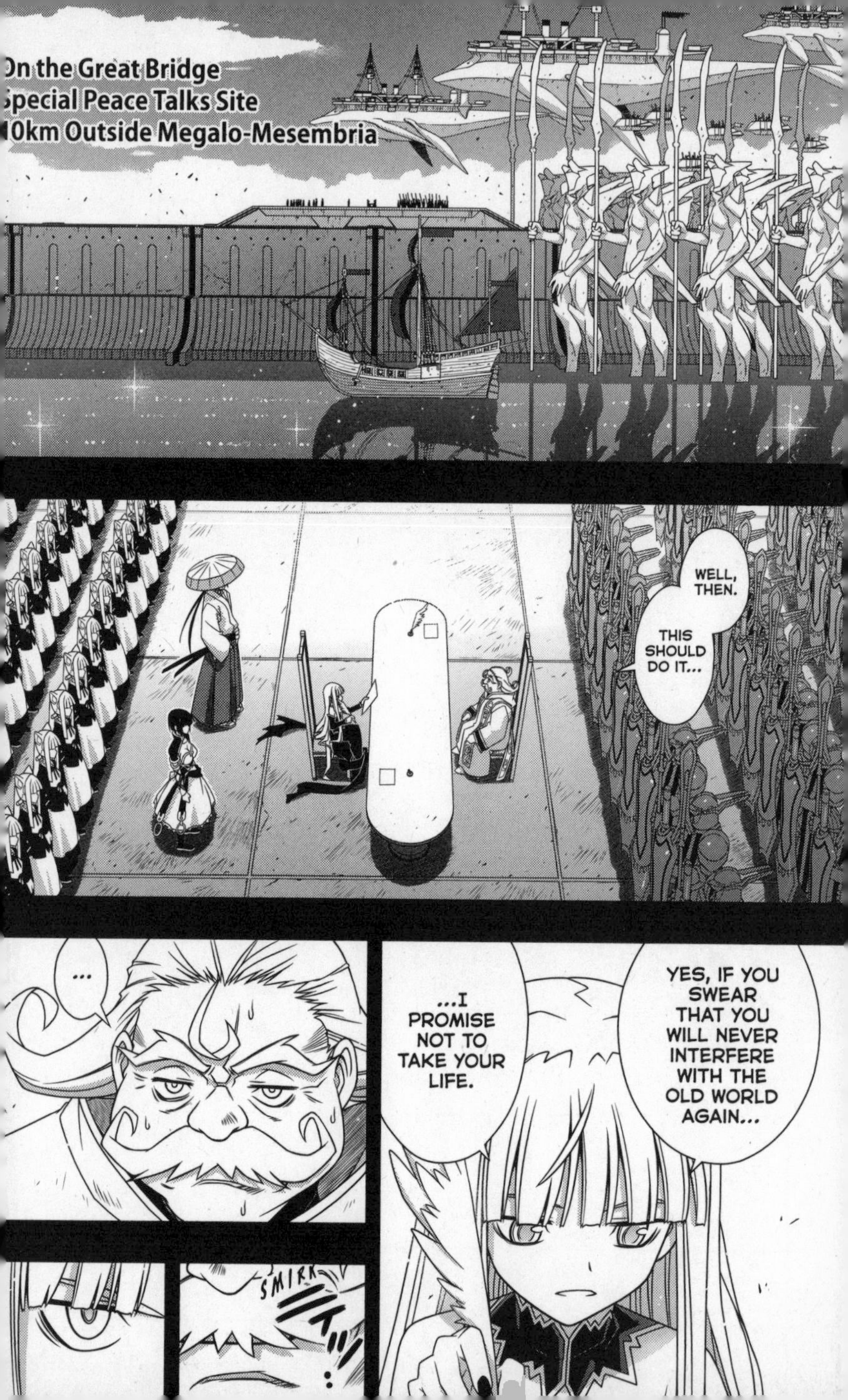
On the Great Bridge
Special Peace Talks Site
10km Outside Megalo-Mesembria
WELL, THEN.
THIS SHOULD DO IT...
YES, IF YOU SWEAR THAT YOU WILL NEVER INTERFERE WITH THE OLD WORLD AGAIN...
...I PROMISE NOT TO TAKE YOUR LIFE.
...
SMIRK

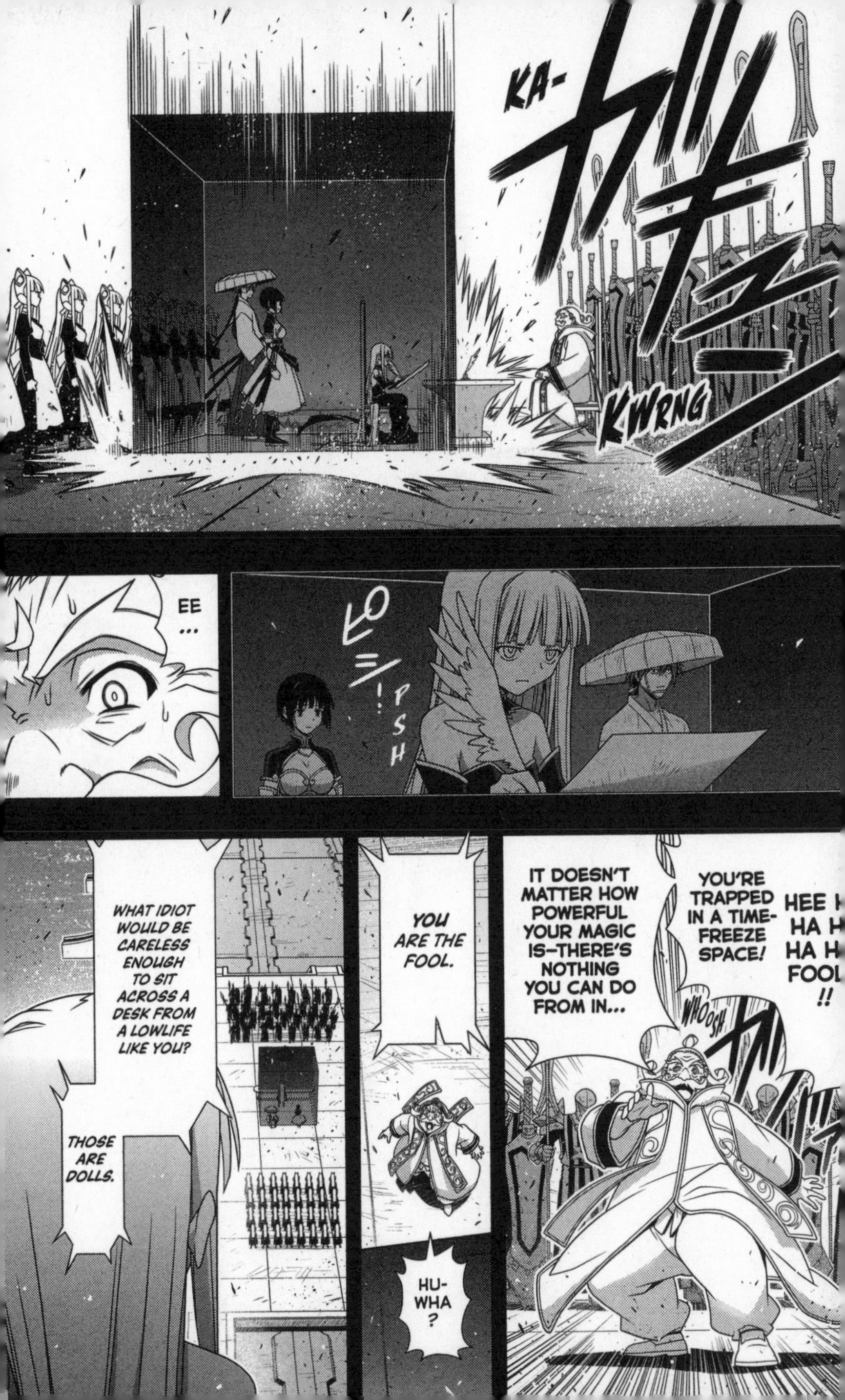
KA-
KWRNG
PSH
EE...
HEE H HA H HA H FOOL!!
YOU'RE TRAPPED IN A TIME-FREEZE SPACE!
IT DOESN'T MATTER HOW POWERFUL YOUR MAGIC IS—THERE'S NOTHING YOU CAN DO FROM IN...
WHOOSH
YOU ARE THE FOOL.
HU-WHA?
WHAT IDIOT WOULD BE CARELESS ENOUGH TO SIT ACROSS A DESK FROM A LOWLIFE LIKE YOU?
THOSE ARE DOLLS.

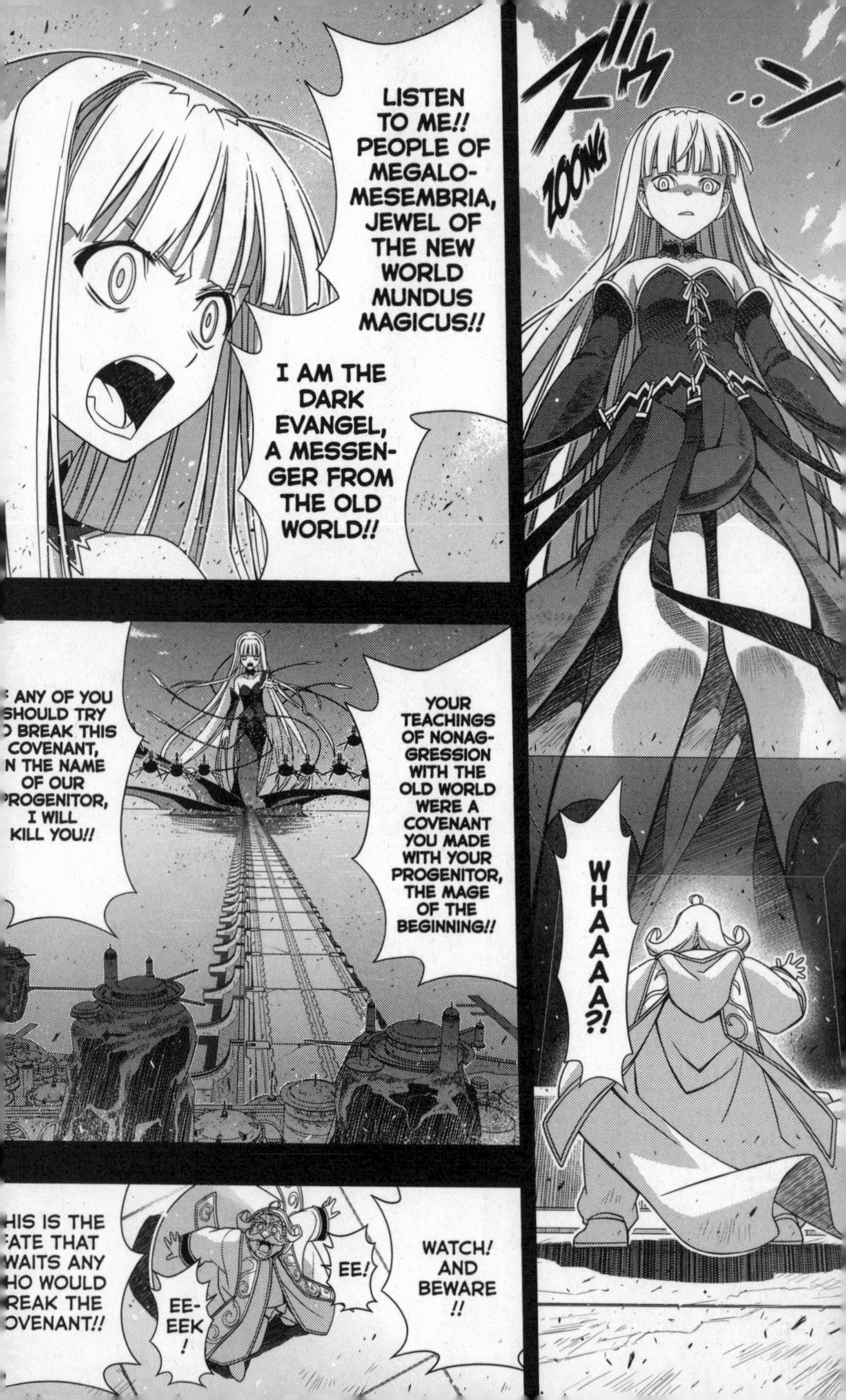
ZOOM
ZOOMG
LISTEN TO ME!! PEOPLE OF MEGALO-MESEMBRIA, JEWEL OF THE NEW WORLD MUNDUS MAGICUS!!
I AM THE DARK EVANGEL, A MESSENGER FROM THE OLD WORLD!!
YOUR TEACHINGS OF NONAGGRESSION WITH THE OLD WORLD WERE A COVENANT YOU MADE WITH YOUR PROGENITOR, THE MAGE OF THE BEGINNING!!
F ANY OF YOU SHOULD TRY O BREAK THIS COVENANT, N THE NAME OF OUR ROGENITOR, I WILL KILL YOU!!
WHAAAA?!
WATCH! AND BEWARE!!
EE!
EE-EEK!
HIS IS THE FATE THAT WAITS ANY HO WOULD REAK THE OVENANT!!

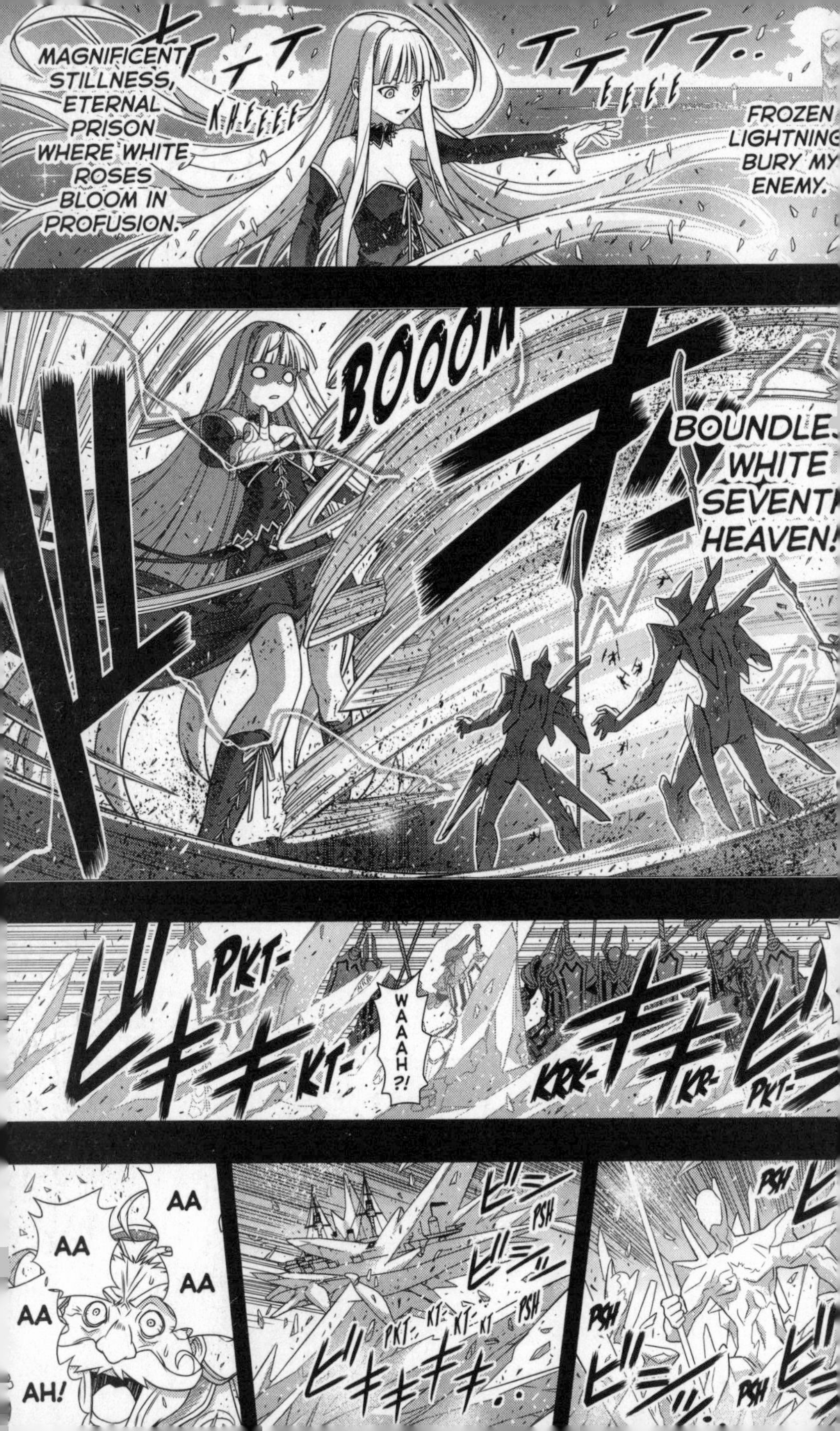
FROZEN LIGHTNING BURY MY ENEMY.
MAGNIFICENT STILLNESS, ETERNAL PRISON WHERE WHITE ROSES BLOOM IN PROFUSION.
BOUNDLE
WHITE
SEVENT
HEAVEN!
BOOOM
PKT-
KRR-
KRK-
WAAAAH?!
KT-
PKT-
PSH
PSH
PSH
PSH
PSH
PSH
KT
KT
KT
PKT
AA
AA
AA
AA
AH!

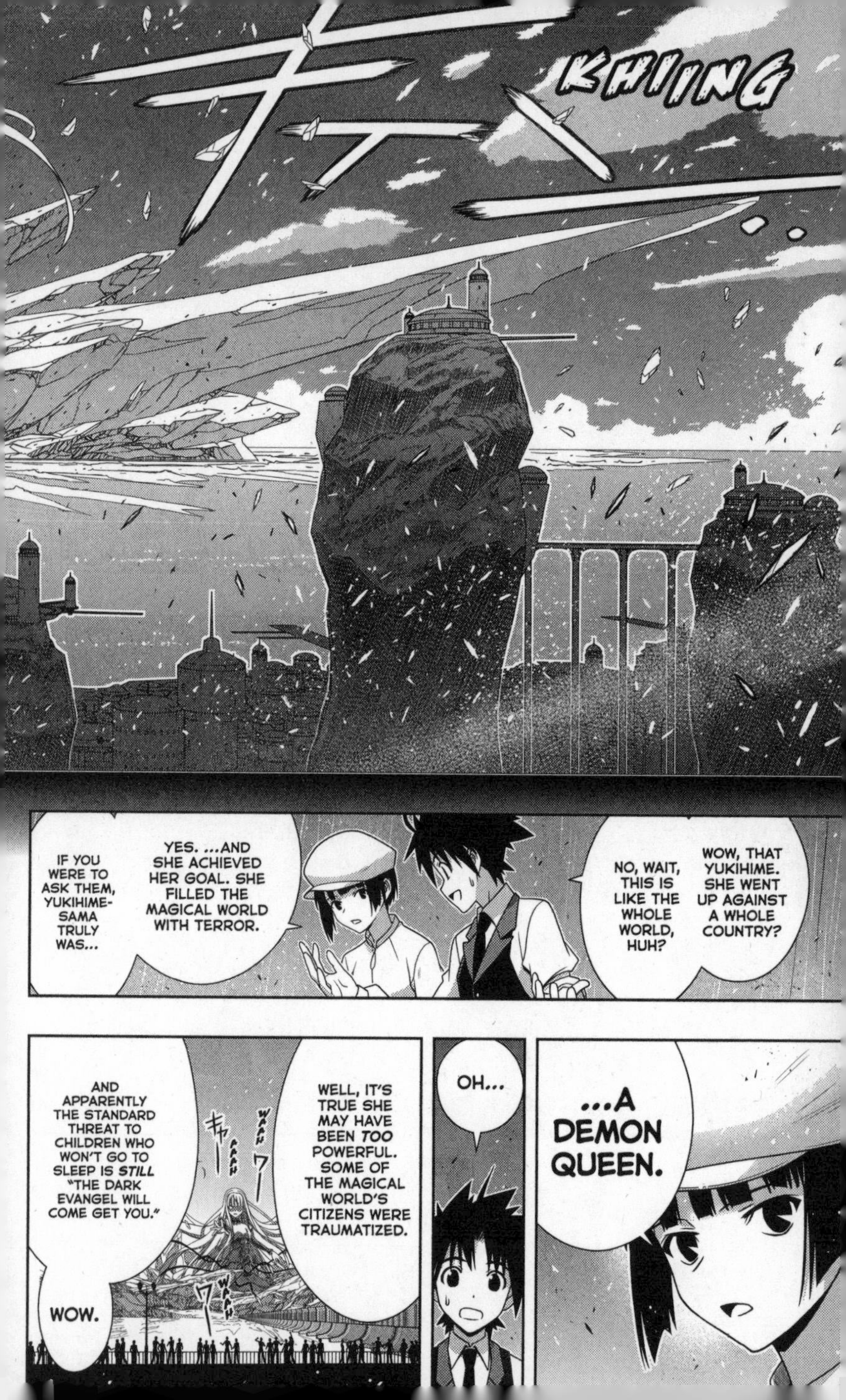
KHIING
WOW, THAT YUKIHIME. SHE WENT UP AGAINST A WHOLE COUNTRY?
NO, WAIT, THIS IS LIKE THE WHOLE WORLD, HUH?
YES. ...AND SHE ACHIEVED HER GOAL. SHE FILLED THE MAGICAL WORLD WITH TERROR.
IF YOU WERE TO ASK THEM, YUKIHIME-SAMA TRULY WAS...
...A DEMON QUEEN.
OH...
WELL, IT'S TRUE SHE MAY HAVE BEEN *TOO* POWERFUL. SOME OF THE MAGICAL WORLD'S CITIZENS WERE TRAUMATIZED.
AND APPARENTLY THE STANDARD THREAT TO CHILDREN WHO WON'T GO TO SLEEP IS *STILL* "THE DARK EVANGEL WILL COME GET YOU."
WAAH
AAAH
WAAH
WOW.

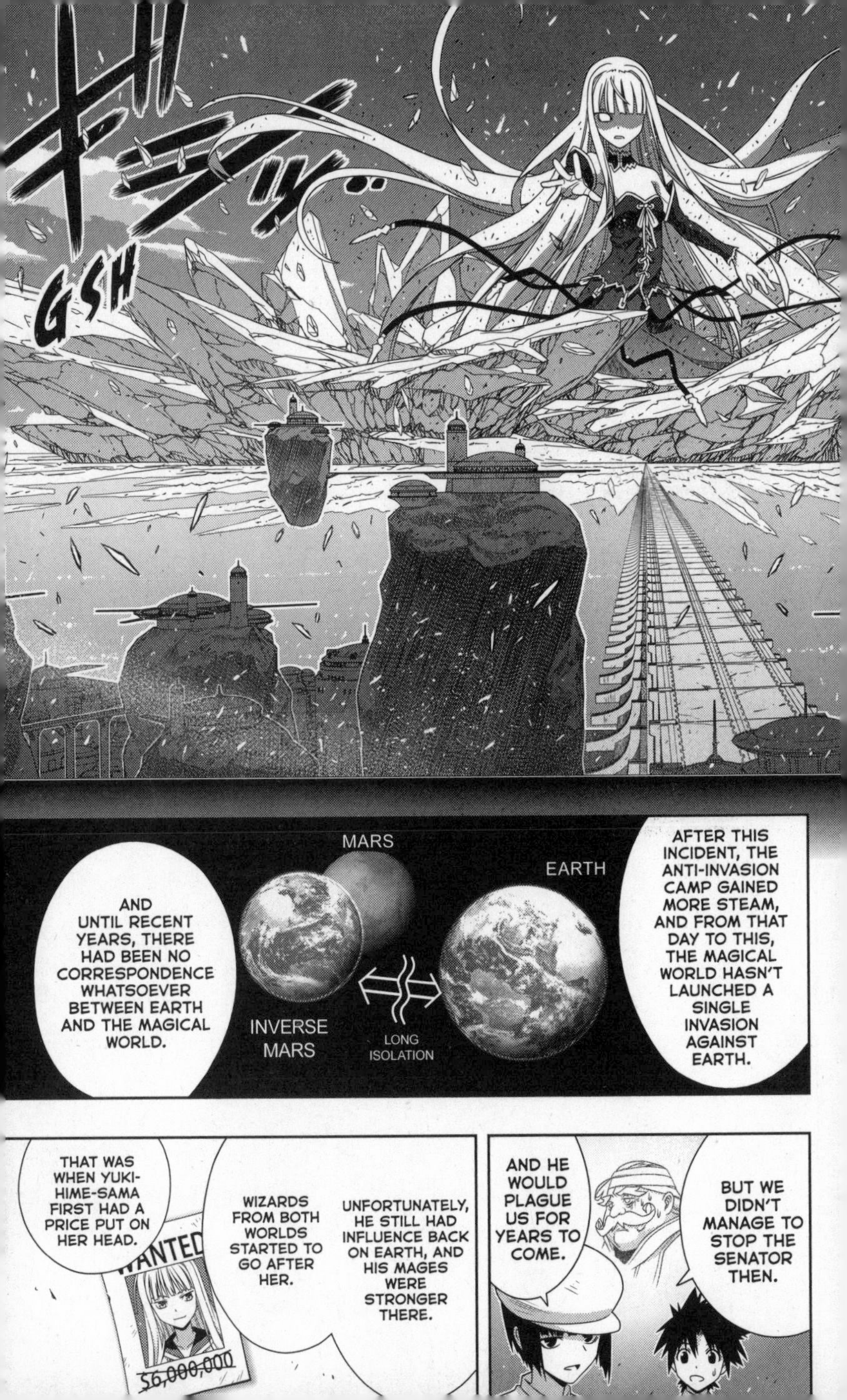
GSH
AFTER THIS INCIDENT, THE ANTI-INVASION CAMP GAINED MORE STEAM, AND FROM THAT DAY TO THIS, THE MAGICAL WORLD HASN'T LAUNCHED A SINGLE INVASION AGAINST EARTH.
EARTH
MARS
LONG ISOLATION
INVERSE MARS
AND UNTIL RECENT YEARS, THERE HAD BEEN NO CORRESPONDENCE WHATSOEVER BETWEEN EARTH AND THE MAGICAL WORLD.
BUT WE DIDN'T MANAGE TO STOP THE SENATOR THEN.
AND HE WOULD PLAGUE US FOR YEARS TO COME.
UNFORTUNATELY, HE STILL HAD INFLUENCE BACK ON EARTH, AND HIS MAGES WERE STRONGER THERE.
WIZARDS FROM BOTH WORLDS STARTED TO GO AFTER HER.
THAT WAS WHEN YUKI-HIME-SAMA FIRST HAD A PRICE PUT ON HER HEAD.
WANTED
$6,000,000

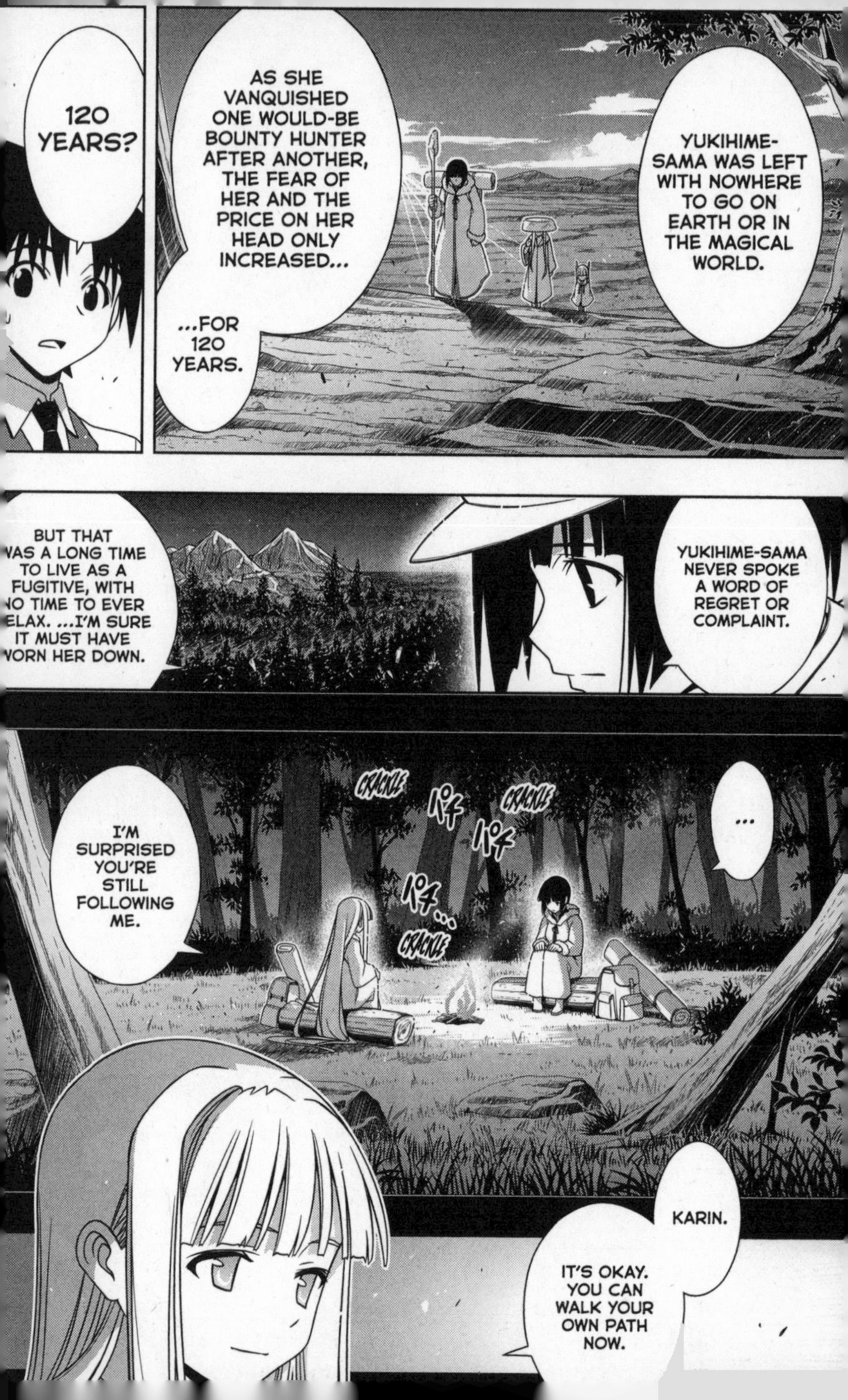
YUKIHIME-SAMA WAS LEFT WITH NOWHERE TO GO ON EARTH OR IN THE MAGICAL WORLD.
AS SHE VANQUISHED ONE WOULD-BE BOUNTY HUNTER AFTER ANOTHER, THE FEAR OF HER AND THE PRICE ON HER HEAD ONLY INCREASED...
...FOR 120 YEARS.
120 YEARS?
YUKIHIME-SAMA NEVER SPOKE A WORD OF REGRET OR COMPLAINT.
BUT THAT VAS A LONG TIME TO LIVE AS A FUGITIVE, WITH IO TIME TO EVER ELAX. ...I'M SURE IT MUST HAVE VORN HER DOWN.
...
CRACKLE
パチ
CRACKLE
パチ
パチ...
CRACKLE
I'M SURPRISED YOU'RE STILL FOLLOWING ME.
KARIN.
IT'S OKAY. YOU CAN WALK YOUR OWN PATH NOW.

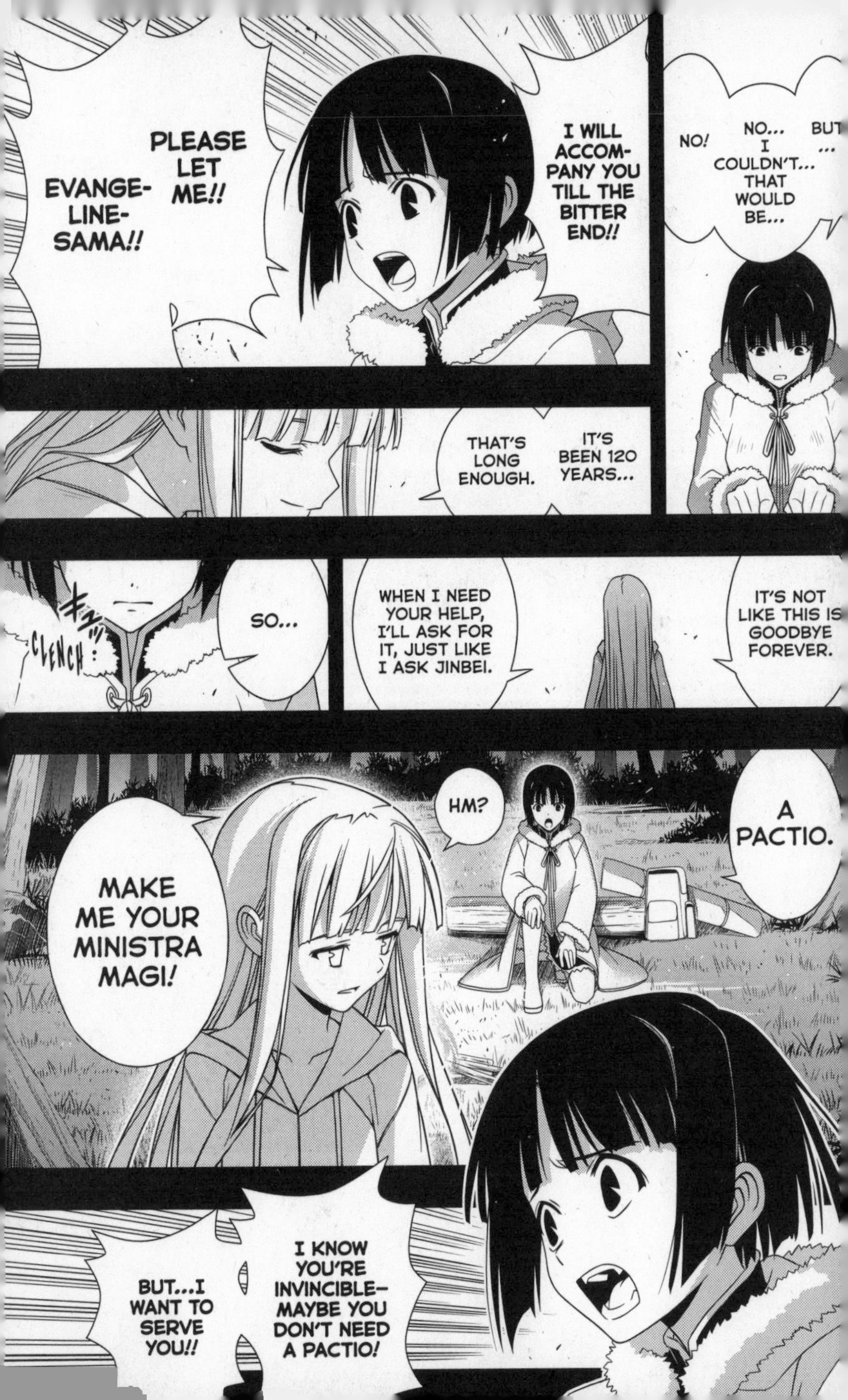

BUT...
NO... I COULDN'T... THAT WOULD BE...
NO!
I WILL ACCOMPANY YOU TILL THE BITTER END!!
PLEASE LET ME!!
EVANGELINE-SAMA!!
IT'S BEEN 120 YEARS...
THAT'S LONG ENOUGH.
IT'S NOT LIKE THIS IS GOODBYE FOREVER.
WHEN I NEED YOUR HELP, I'LL ASK FOR IT, JUST LIKE I ASK JINBEI.
SO...
CLENCH
A PACTIO.
HM?
MAKE ME YOUR MINISTRA MAGI!
I KNOW YOU'RE INVINCIBLE—MAYBE YOU DON'T NEED A PACTIO!
BUT...I WANT TO SERVE YOU!!

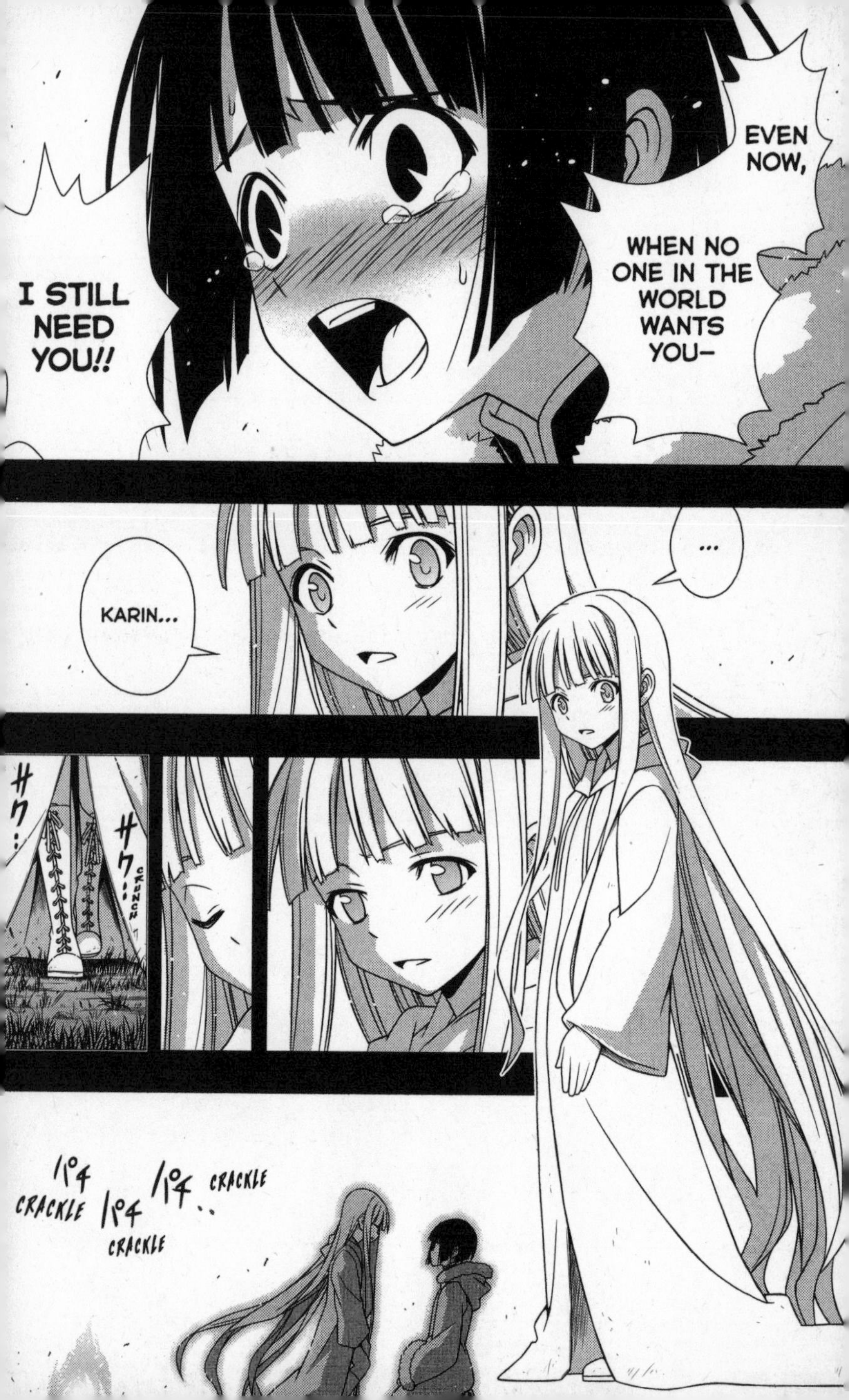
EVEN NOW,
WHEN NO ONE IN THE WORLD WANTS YOU–
I STILL NEED YOU!!
...
KARIN...
サク‥
サク‥
CRUNCH
パチ‥
CRACKLE
パチ
CRACKLE
パチ
CRACKLE

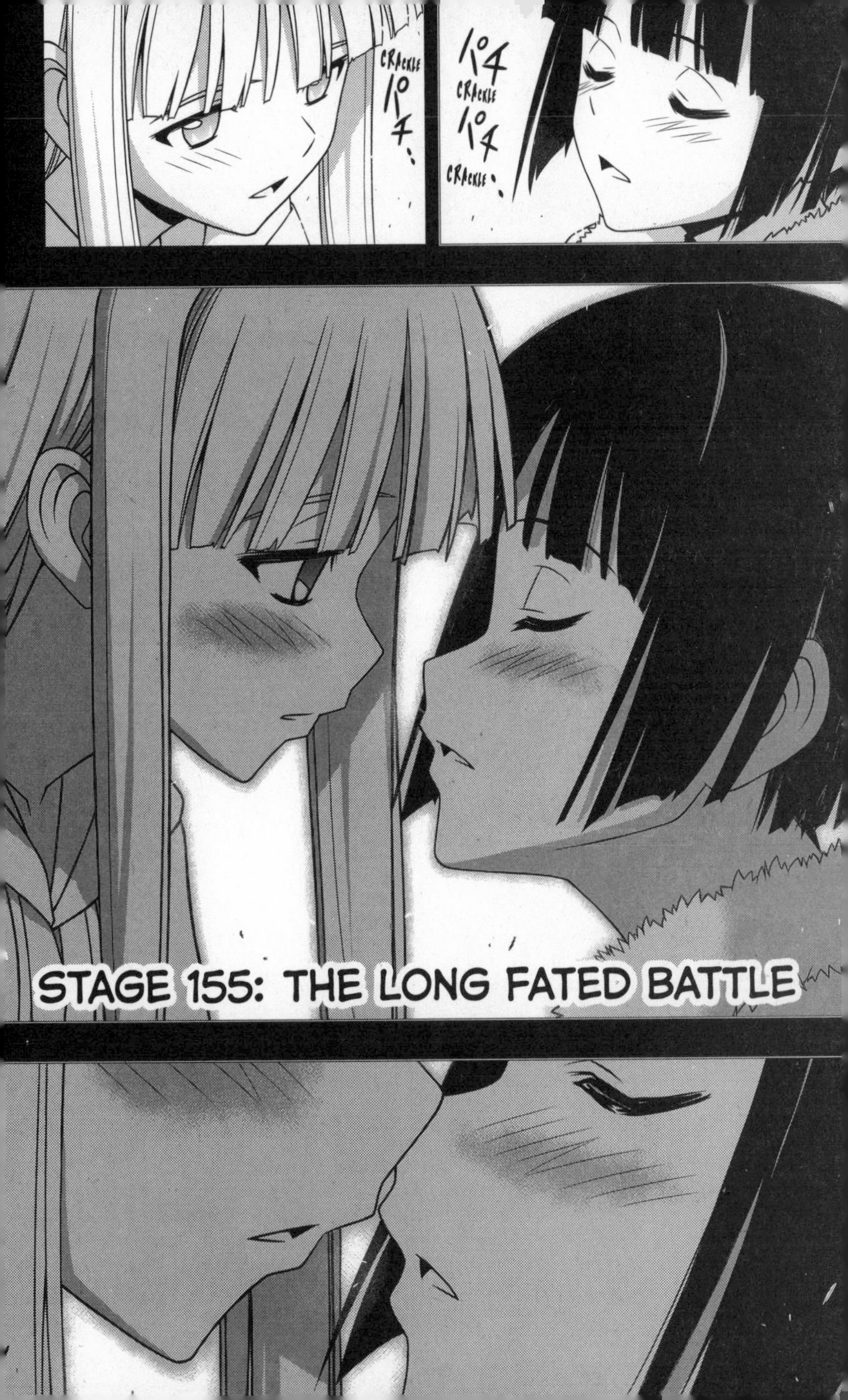
パチ
CRACKLE
パチ
CRACKLE
CRACKLE
パチ…
STAGE 155: THE LONG FATED BATTLE

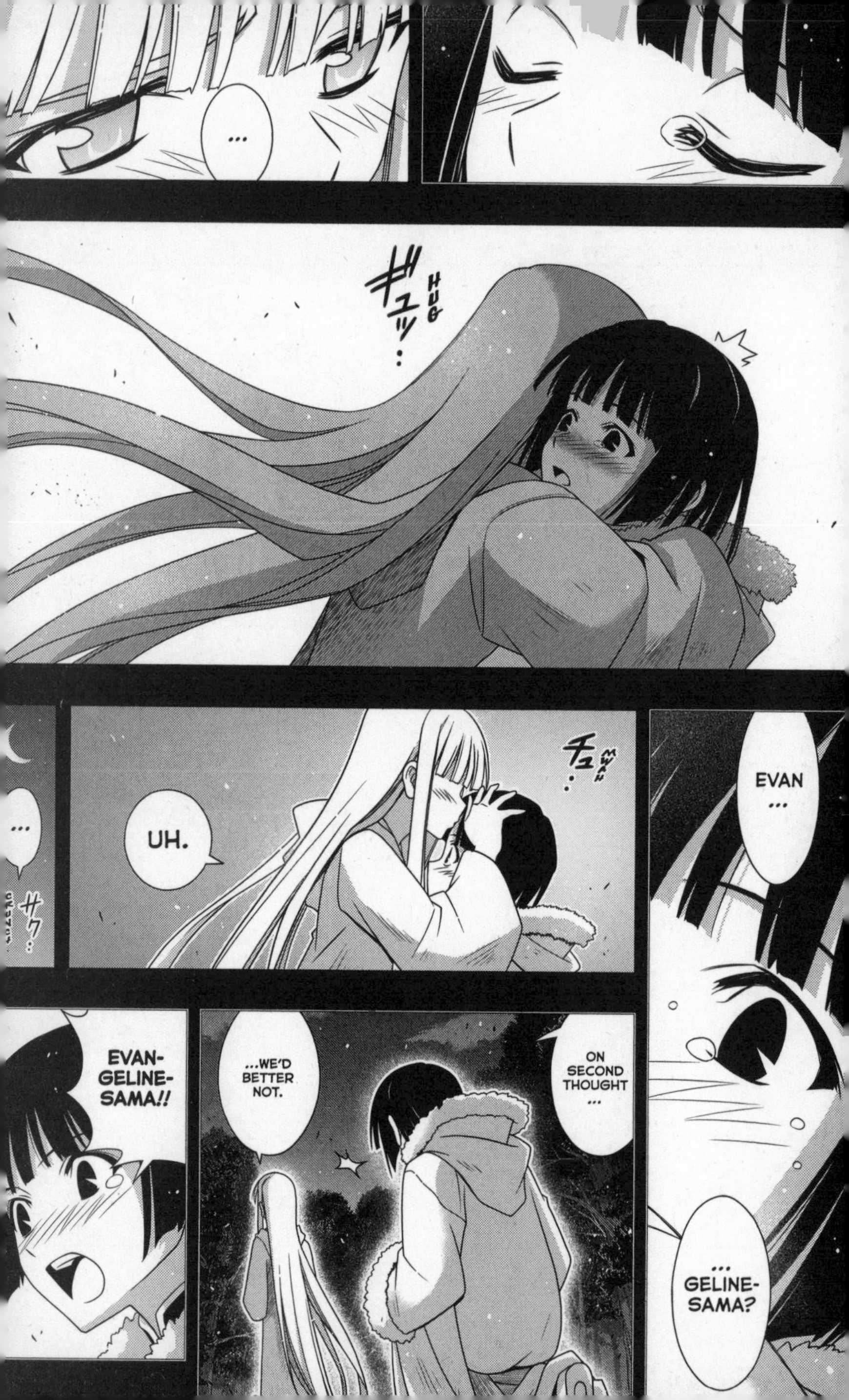

...
ギュッ
HUG
EVAN ...
... GELINE-SAMA?
チュ
MWAH
UH.
...
サク
ON SECOND THOUGHT ...
...WE'D BETTER NOT.
EVAN-GELINE-SAMA!!

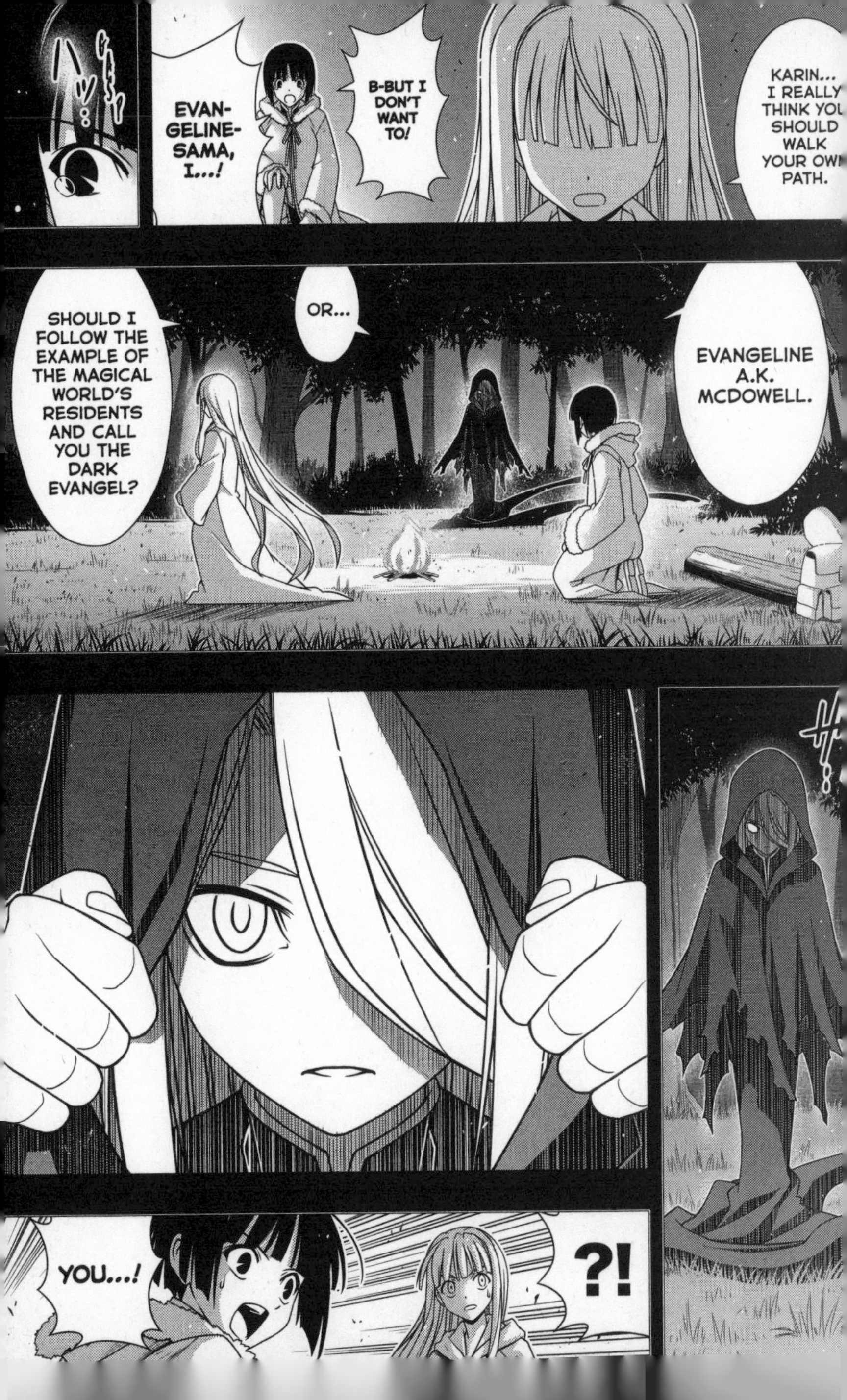
KARIN... I REALLY THINK YOU SHOULD WALK YOUR OWN PATH.
B-BUT I DON'T WANT TO!
EVAN-GELINE-SAMA, I...!
EVANGELINE A.K. MCDOWELL.
OR...
SHOULD I FOLLOW THE EXAMPLE OF THE MAGICAL WORLD'S RESIDENTS AND CALL YOU THE DARK EVANGEL?
?!
YOU...!

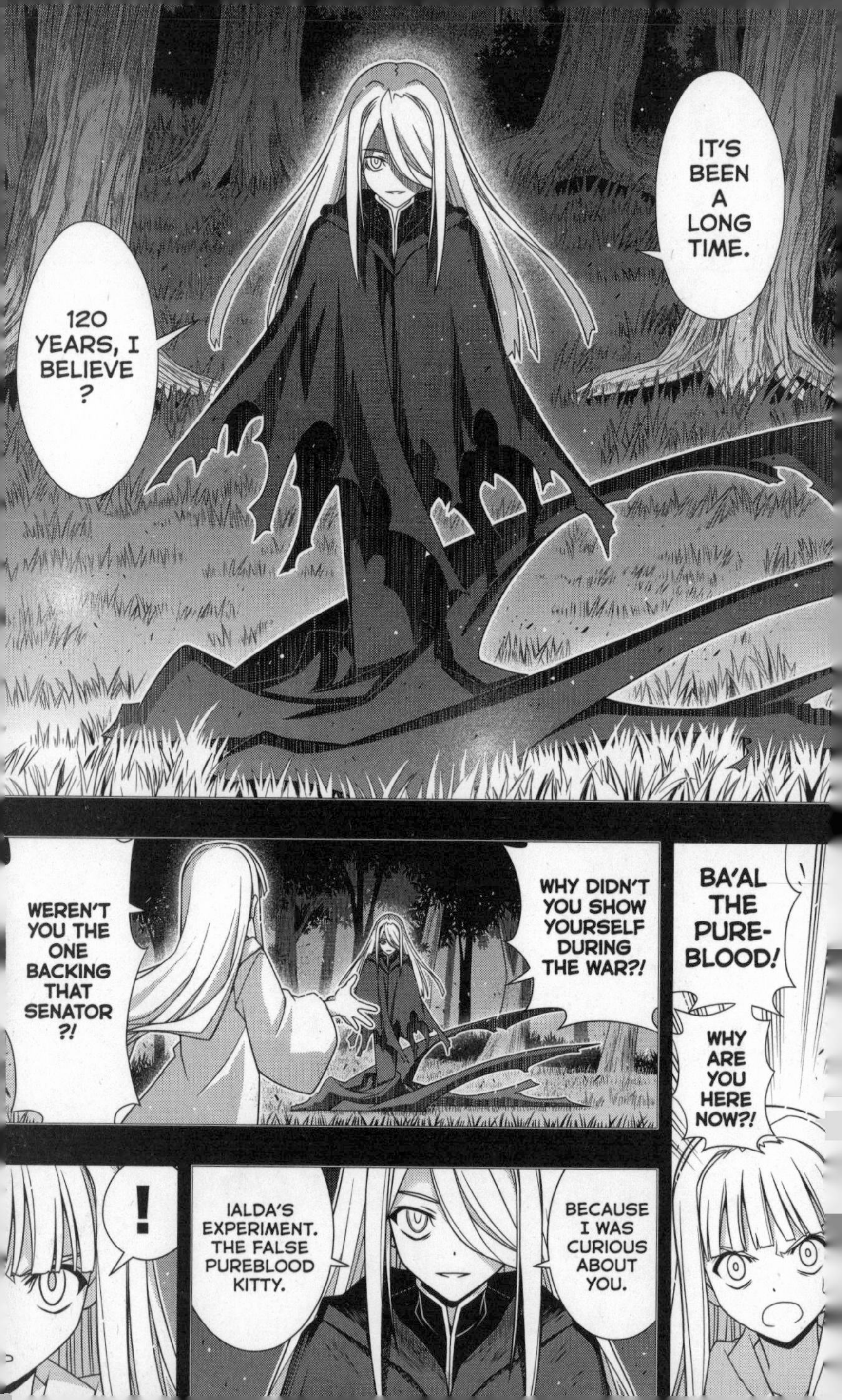
IT'S BEEN A LONG TIME.
120 YEARS, I BELIEVE?
BA'AL THE PURE-BLOOD!
WHY ARE YOU HERE NOW?!
WHY DIDN'T YOU SHOW YOURSELF DURING THE WAR?!
WEREN'T YOU THE ONE BACKING THAT SENATOR?!
BECAUSE I WAS CURIOUS ABOUT YOU.
IALDA'S EXPERIMENT. THE FALSE PUREBLOOD KITTY.
!

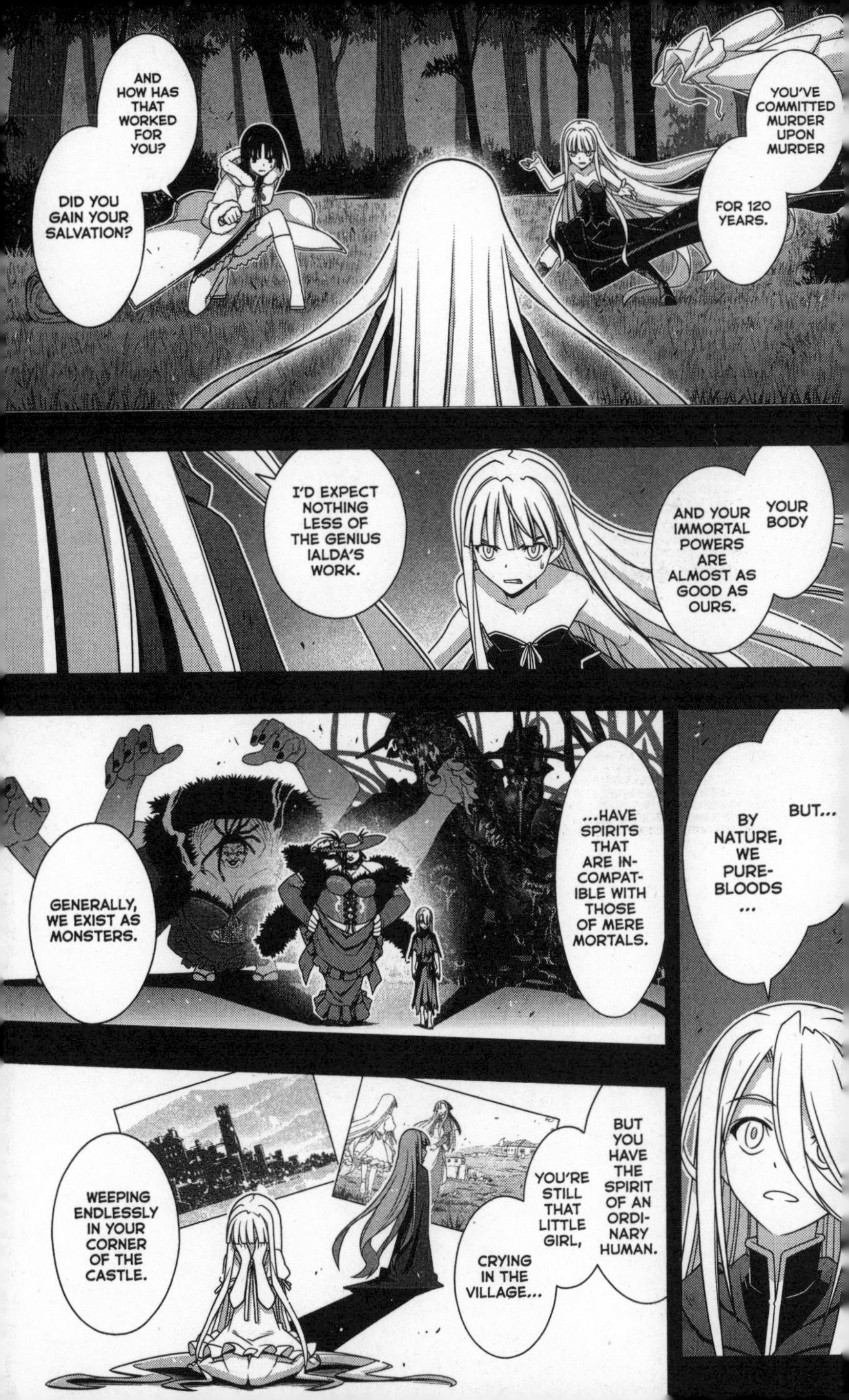
YOU'VE COMMITTED MURDER UPON MURDER
FOR 120 YEARS.
AND HOW HAS THAT WORKED FOR YOU?
DID YOU GAIN YOUR SALVATION?
YOUR BODY
AND YOUR IMMORTAL POWERS ARE ALMOST AS GOOD AS OURS.
I'D EXPECT NOTHING LESS OF THE GENIUS IALDA'S WORK.
BUT...
BY NATURE, WE PURE-BLOODS...
...HAVE SPIRITS THAT ARE INCOMPATIBLE WITH THOSE OF MERE MORTALS.
GENERALLY, WE EXIST AS MONSTERS.
BUT YOU HAVE THE SPIRIT OF AN ORDINARY HUMAN.
YOU'RE STILL THAT LITTLE GIRL,
CRYING IN THE VILLAGE...
WEEPING ENDLESSLY IN YOUR CORNER OF THE CASTLE.

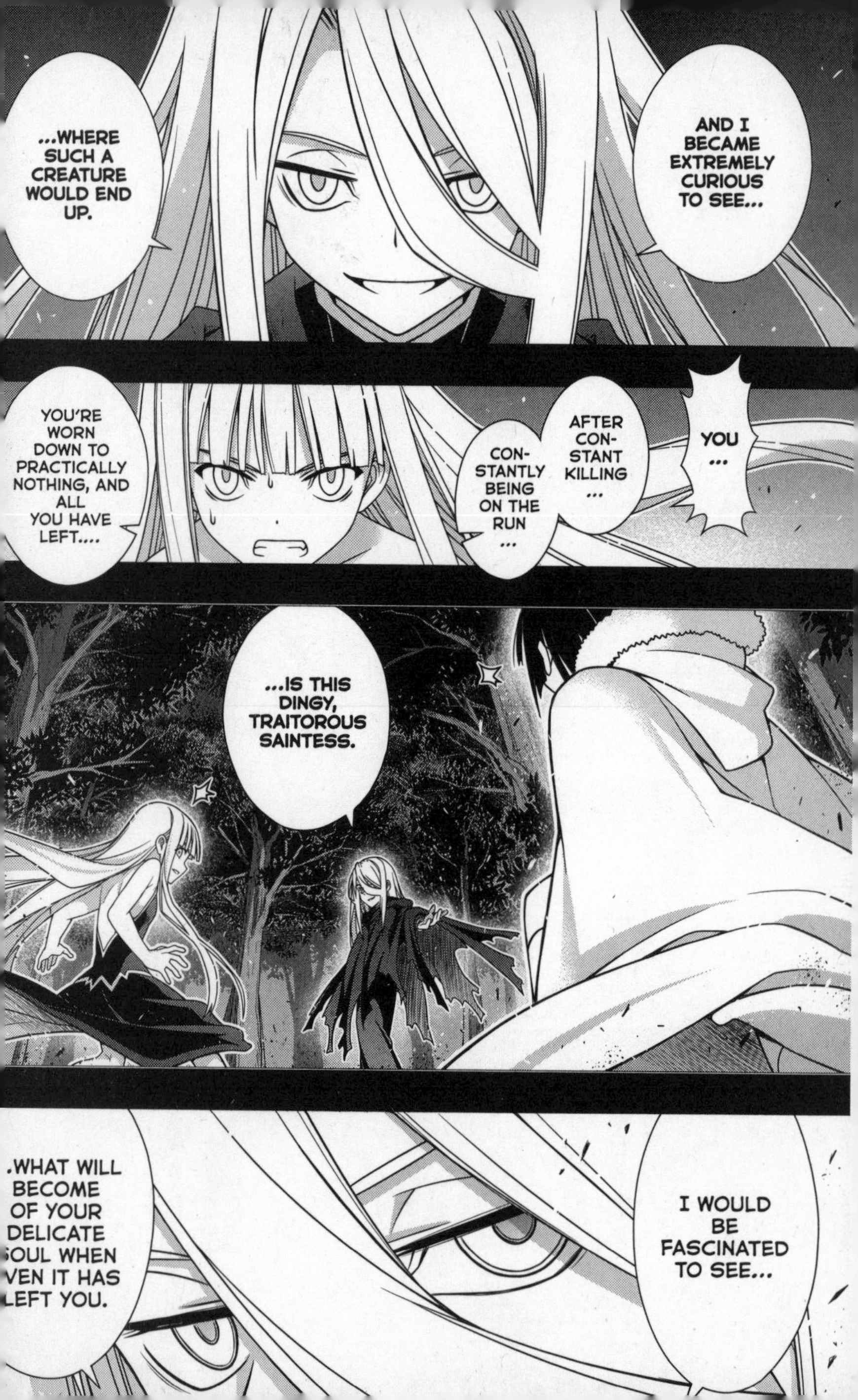
AND I BECAME EXTREMELY CURIOUS TO SEE...
...WHERE SUCH A CREATURE WOULD END UP.
YOU ...
AFTER CON-STANT KILLING ...
CON-STANTLY BEING ON THE RUN ...
YOU'RE WORN DOWN TO PRACTICALLY NOTHING, AND ALL YOU HAVE LEFT....
...IS THIS DINGY, TRAITOROUS SAINTESS.
I WOULD BE FASCINATED TO SEE...
.WHAT WILL BECOME OF YOUR DELICATE SOUL WHEN VEN IT HAS LEFT YOU.

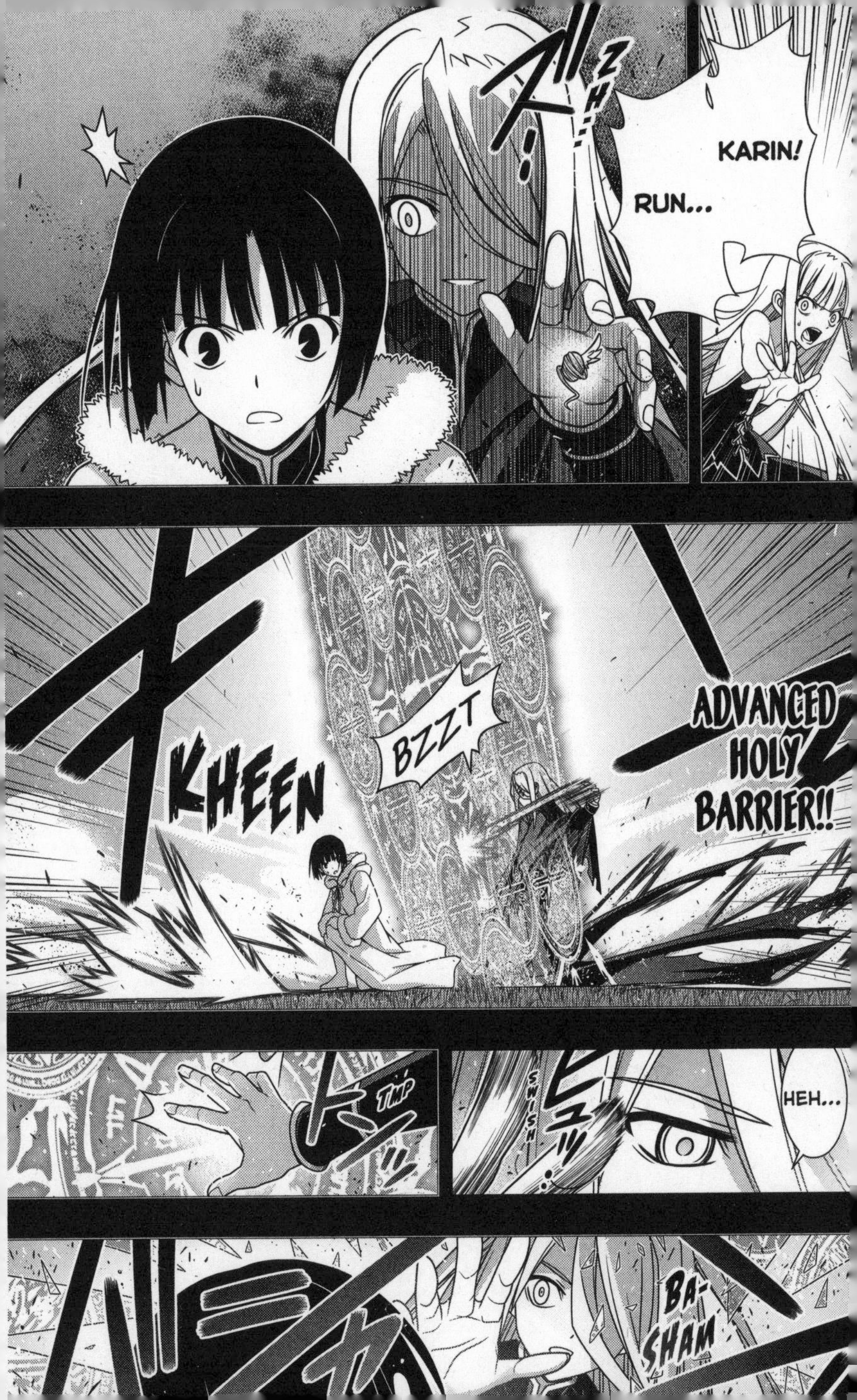

KARIN!
RUN...
ZHI!!
ADVANCED HOLY BARRIER!!
BZZT
KHEEN
HEH...
SWISH
TMP
BA-SHAM

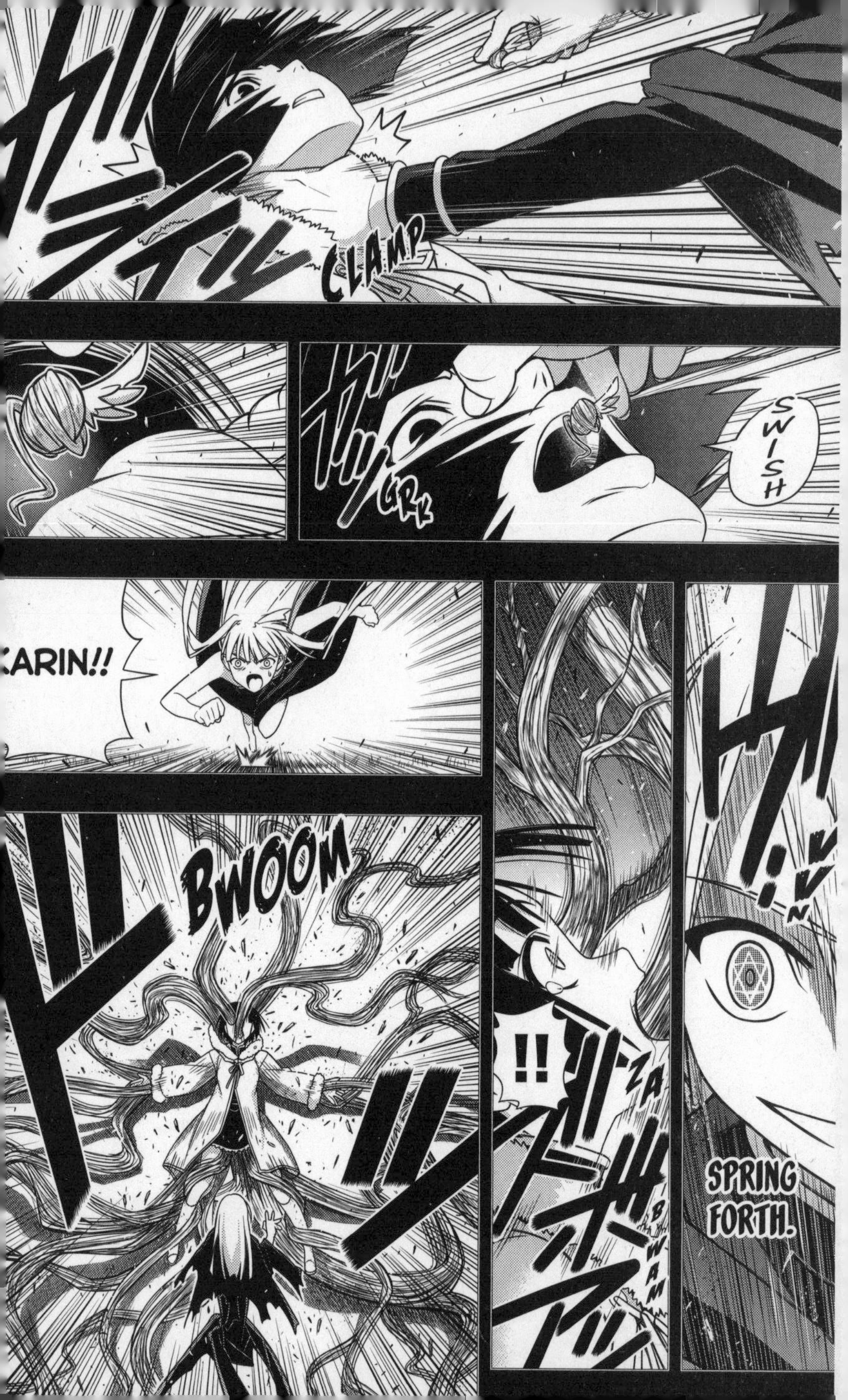
CLAMP
SWISH
GRK
VVVN
SPRING FORTH.
!!
ZA
BWAM
KARIN!!
BWOOM

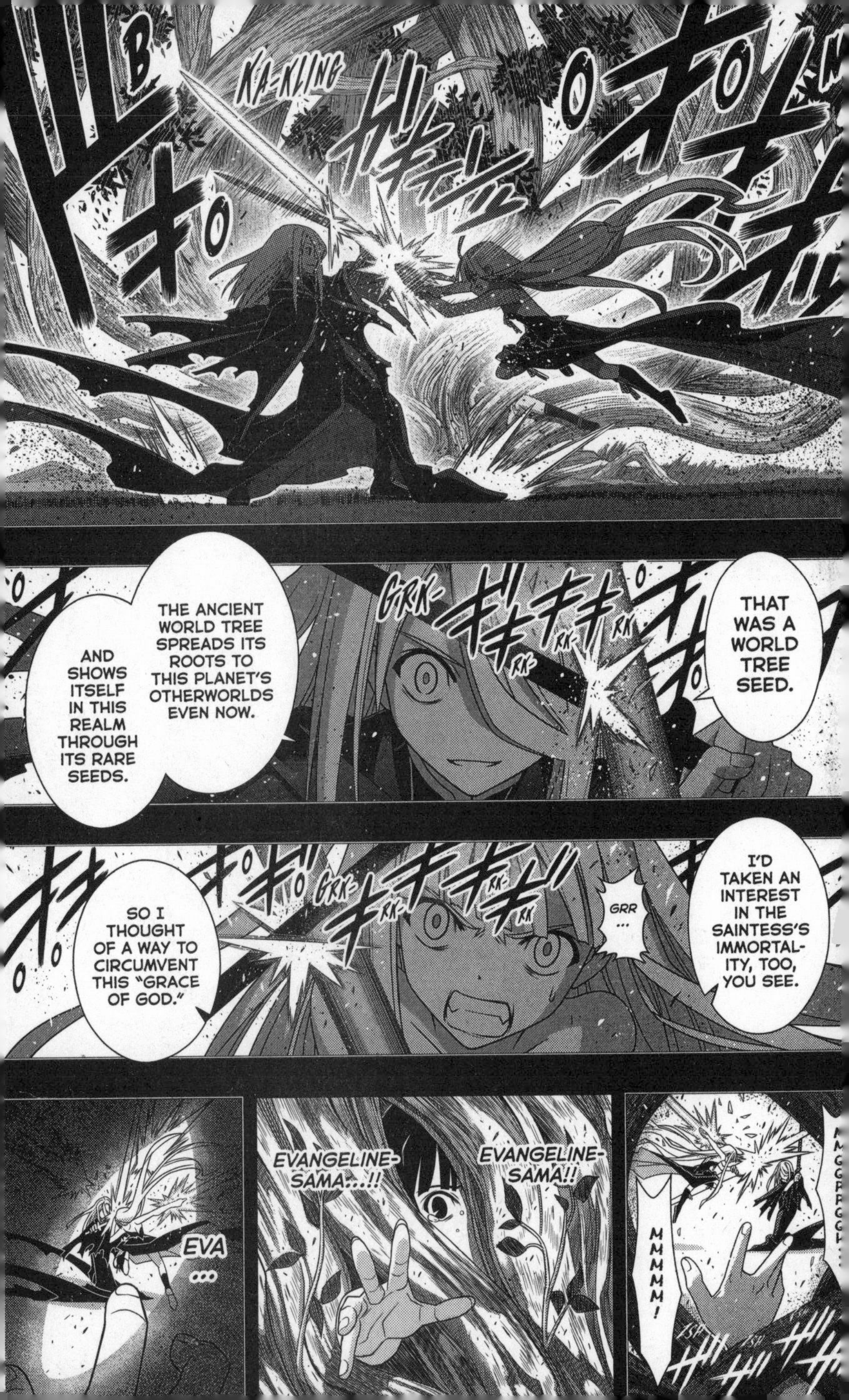
KA-KLING
THAT WAS A WORLD TREE SEED.
GRK-
RK-
RK
RK
THE ANCIENT WORLD TREE SPREADS ITS ROOTS TO THIS PLANET'S OTHERWORLDS EVEN NOW.
AND SHOWS ITSELF IN THIS REALM THROUGH ITS RARE SEEDS.
I'D TAKEN AN INTEREST IN THE SAINTESS'S IMMORTAL-ITY, TOO, YOU SEE.
GRR ...
GRK-
RK-
RK-
RK
SO I THOUGHT OF A WAY TO CIRCUMVENT THIS "GRACE OF GOD."
AGGRRGGH...
MMMMM!
TSH
TSH
EVANGELINE-SAMA!!
EVANGELINE-SAMA...!!
EVA ...

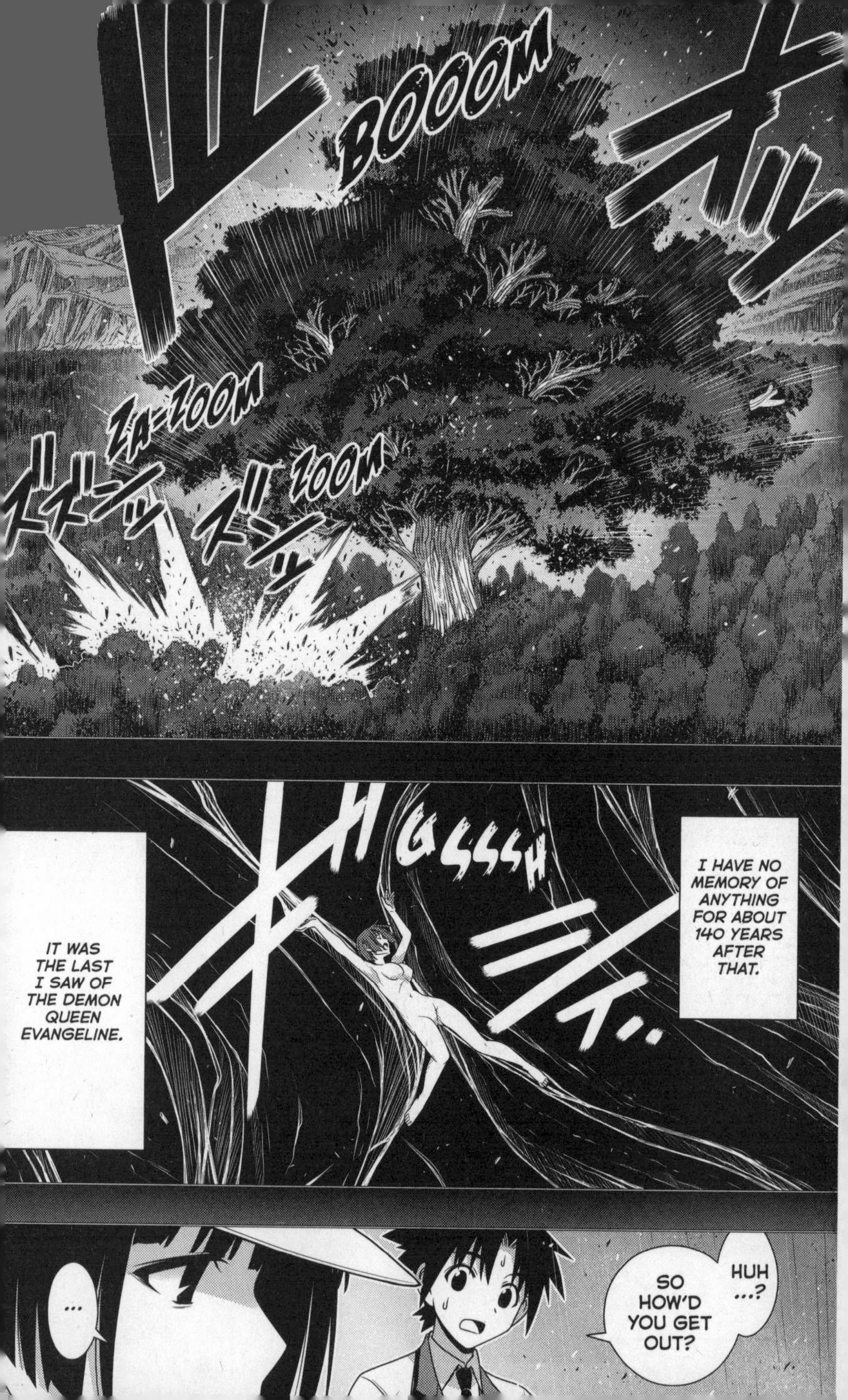
BOOOM
ZA-ZOOM
ZOOM
HGSSSH
IT WAS THE LAST I SAW OF THE DEMON QUEEN EVANGELINE.
I HAVE NO MEMORY OF ANYTHING FOR ABOUT 140 YEARS AFTER THAT.
HUH ...?
SO HOW'D YOU GET OUT?
...

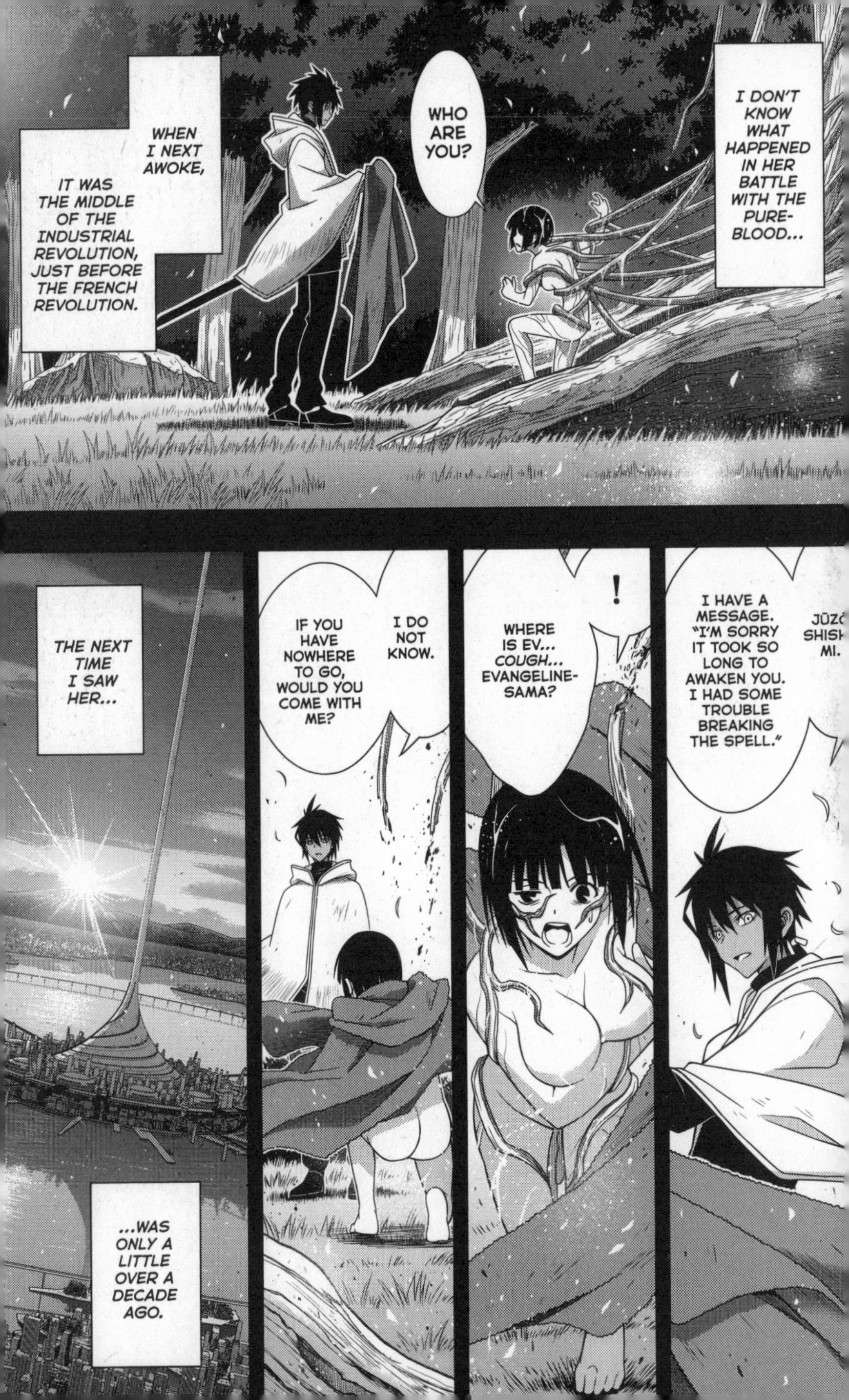
I DON'T KNOW WHAT HAPPENED IN HER BATTLE WITH THE PURE-BLOOD...
WHO ARE YOU?
WHEN I NEXT AWOKE,
IT WAS THE MIDDLE OF THE INDUSTRIAL REVOLUTION, JUST BEFORE THE FRENCH REVOLUTION.
JŪZŌ SHISH MI.
I HAVE A MESSAGE. “I'M SORRY IT TOOK SO LONG TO AWAKEN YOU. I HAD SOME TROUBLE BREAKING THE SPELL.”
!
WHERE IS EV... *COUGH*... EVANGELINE-SAMA?
I DO NOT KNOW.
IF YOU HAVE NOWHERE TO GO, WOULD YOU COME WITH ME?
THE NEXT TIME I SAW HER...
...WAS ONLY A LITTLE OVER A DECADE AGO.

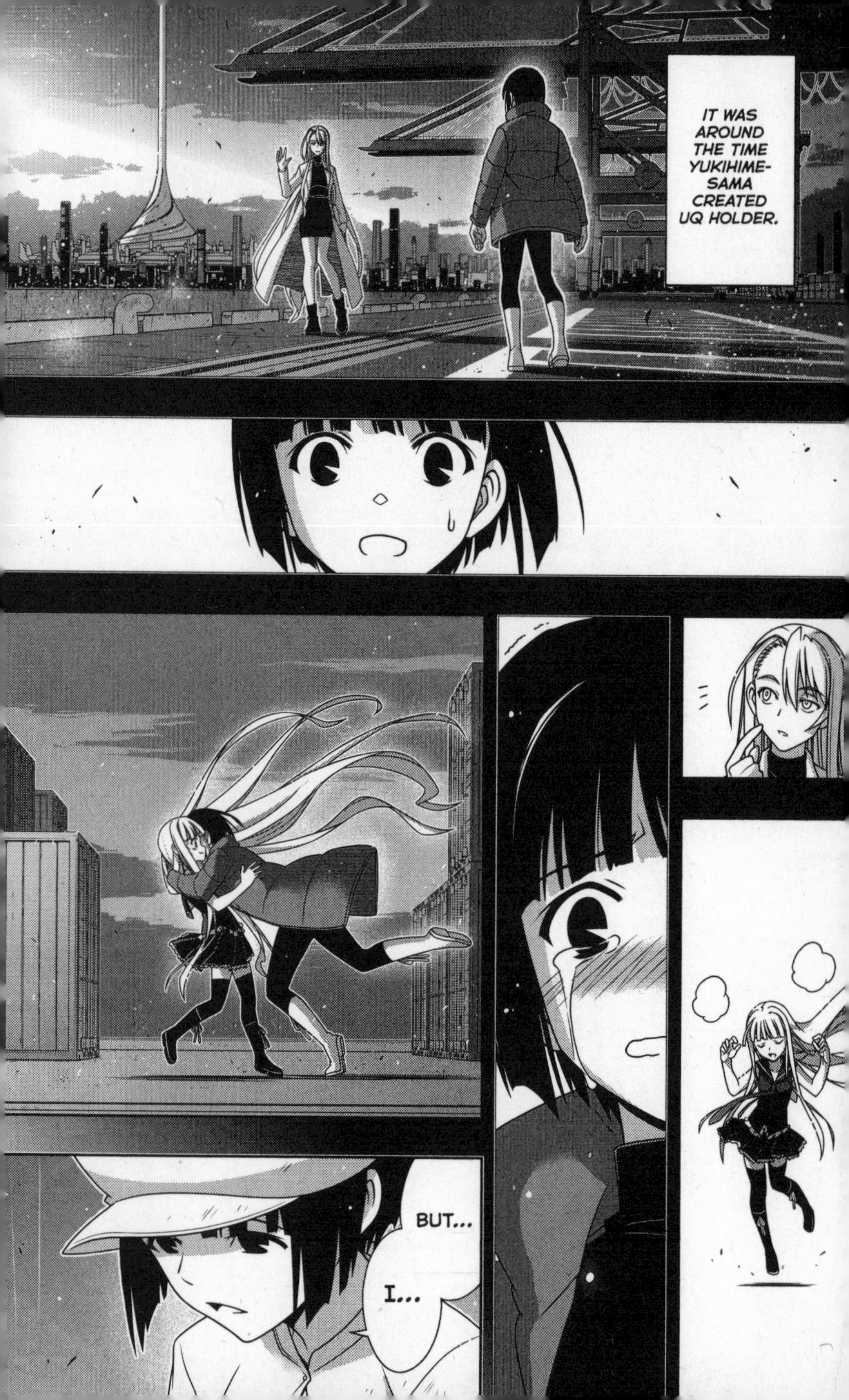
IT WAS AROUND THE TIME YUKIHIME-SAMA CREATED UQ HOLDER.
BUT...
I...

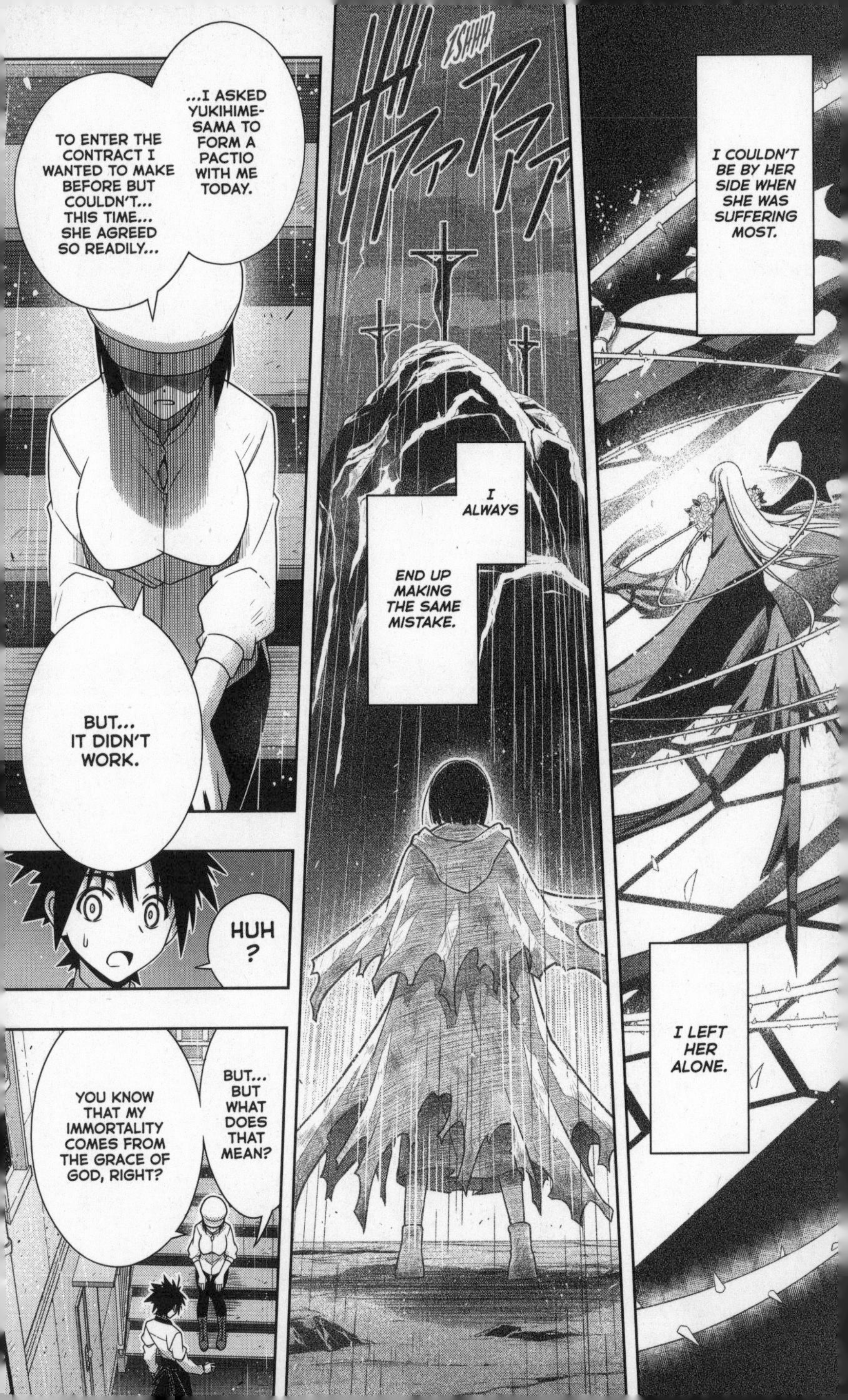
I COULDN'T BE BY HER SIDE WHEN SHE WAS SUFFERING MOST.
I LEFT HER ALONE.
ZSHHH
I ALWAYS
END UP MAKING THE SAME MISTAKE.
...I ASKED YUKIHIME-SAMA TO FORM A PACTIO WITH ME TODAY.
TO ENTER THE CONTRACT I WANTED TO MAKE BEFORE BUT COULDN'T... THIS TIME... SHE AGREED SO READILY...
BUT... IT DIDN'T WORK.
HUH?
BUT... BUT WHAT DOES THAT MEAN?
YOU KNOW THAT MY IMMORTALITY COMES FROM THE GRACE OF GOD, RIGHT?

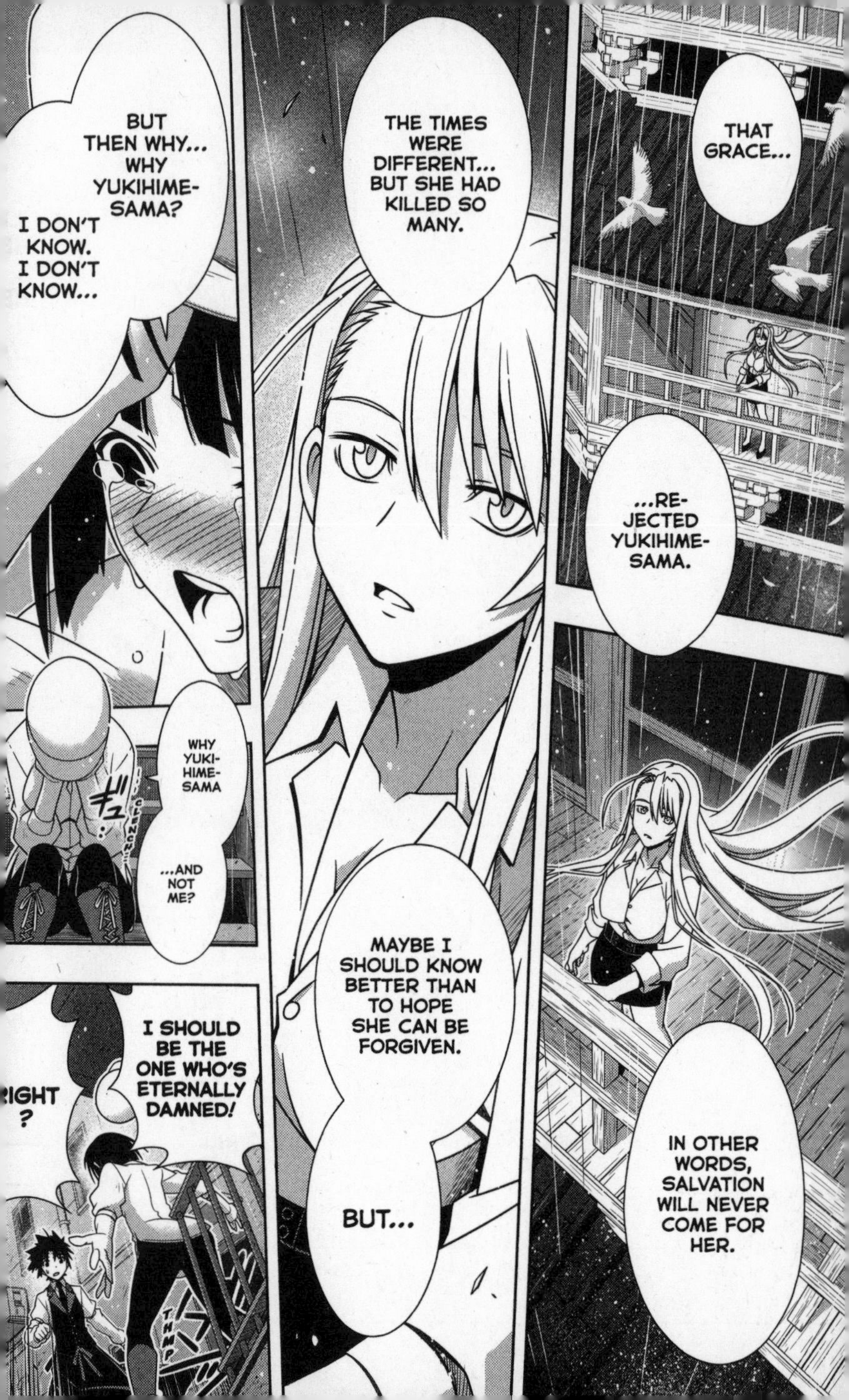

THAT GRACE...
...REJECTED YUKIHIME-SAMA.
IN OTHER WORDS, SALVATION WILL NEVER COME FOR HER.
THE TIMES WERE DIFFERENT... BUT SHE HAD KILLED SO MANY.
MAYBE I SHOULD KNOW BETTER THAN TO HOPE SHE CAN BE FORGIVEN.
BUT...
BUT THEN WHY... WHY YUKIHIME-SAMA?
I DON'T KNOW. I DON'T KNOW...
WHY YUKIHIME-SAMA
...AND NOT ME?
CLENCH
I SHOULD BE THE ONE WHO'S ETERNALLY DAMNED!
IGHT ?
THMP

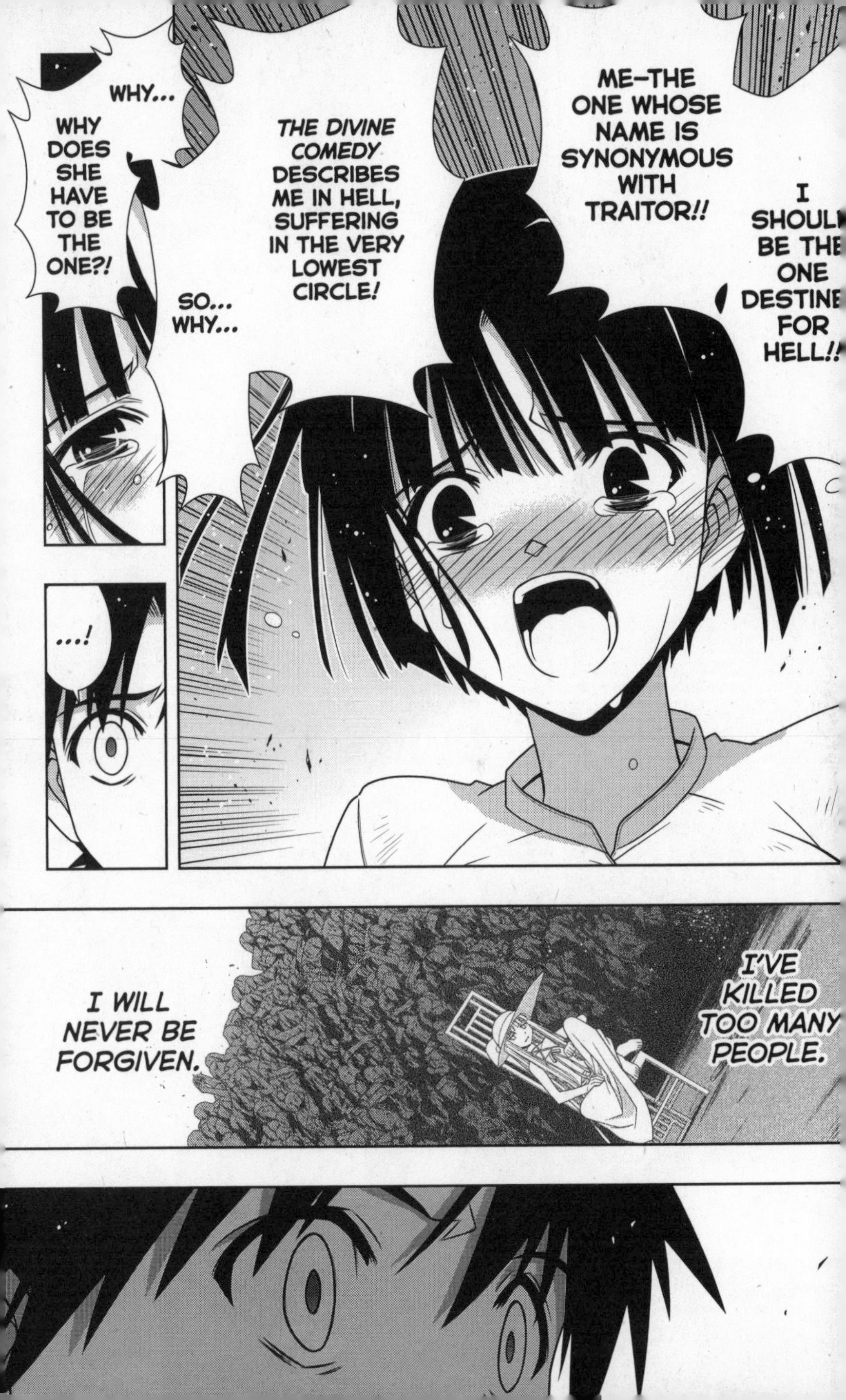
I SHOUL BE THE ONE DESTINE FOR HELL!!
ME—THE ONE WHOSE NAME IS SYNONYMOUS WITH TRAITOR!!
THE DIVINE COMEDY DESCRIBES ME IN HELL, SUFFERING IN THE VERY LOWEST CIRCLE!
SO... WHY...
WHY...
WHY DOES SHE HAVE TO BE THE ONE?!
...!
I'VE KILLED TOO MANY PEOPLE.
I WILL NEVER BE FORGIVEN.

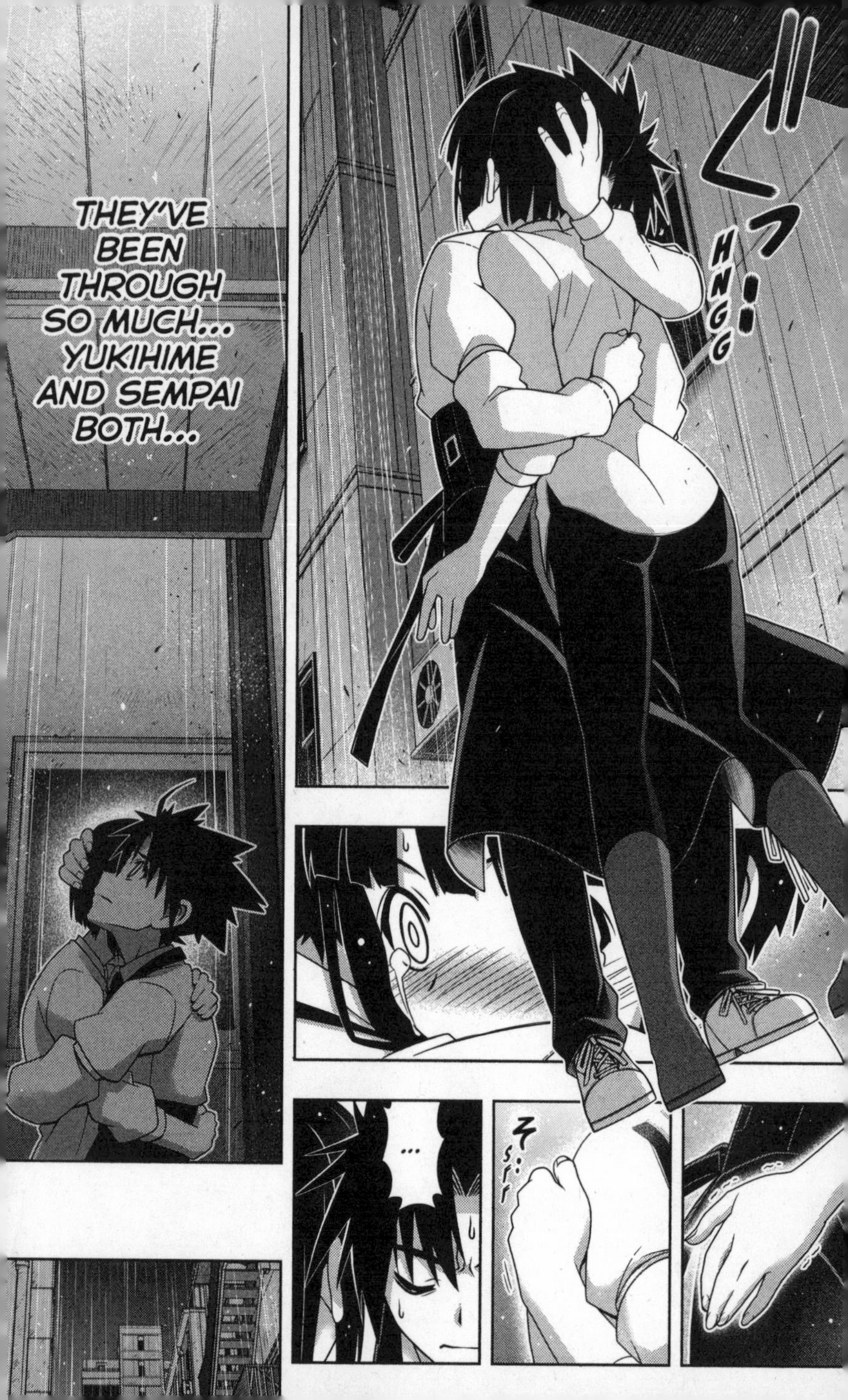
HNGG
SFFF
...
THEY'VE BEEN THROUGH SO MUCH... YUKIHIME AND SEMPAI BOTH...

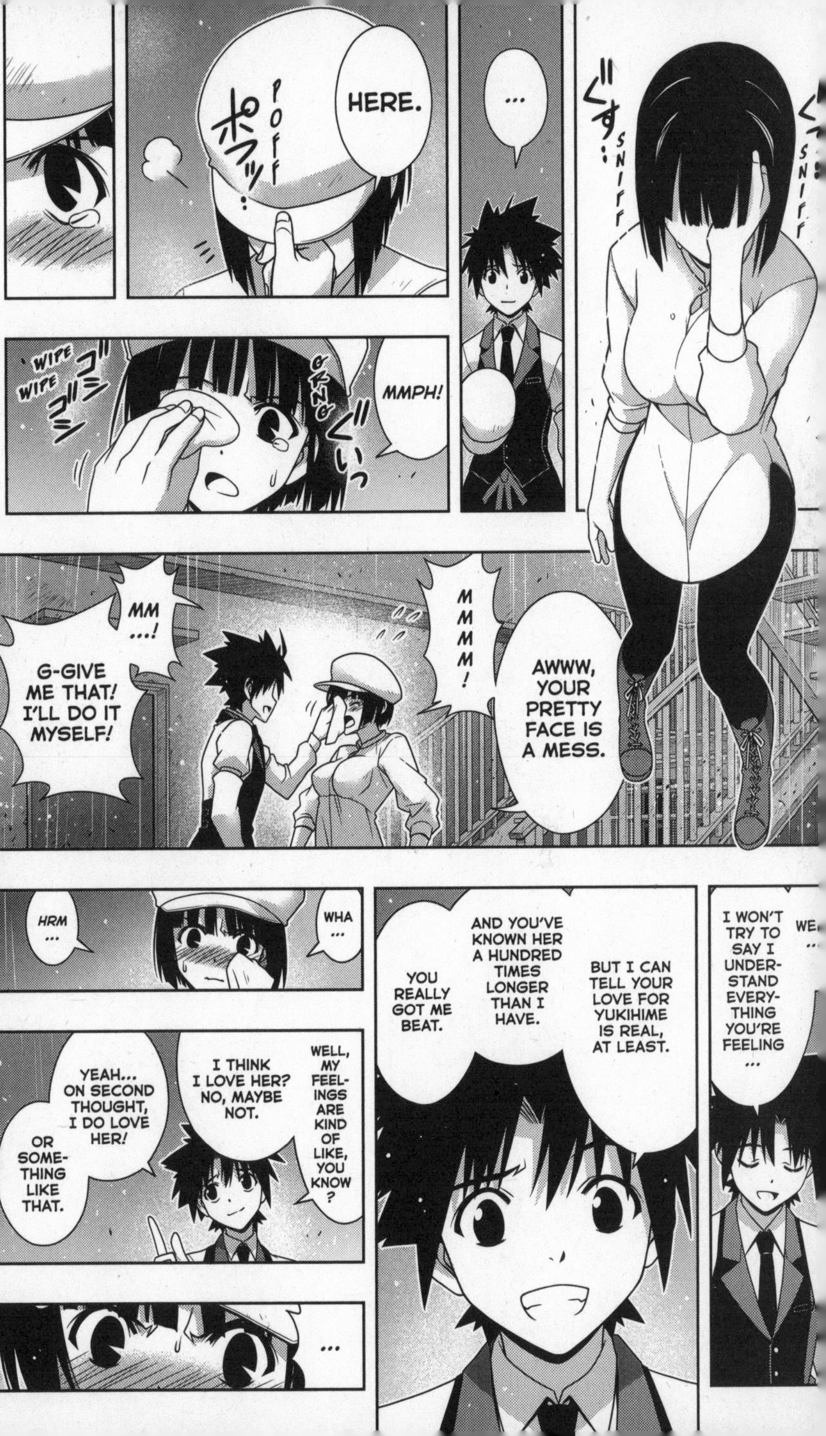

ぐす SNIFF
ぐす SNIFF
...
HERE.
ポフッ POFF
MMPH!
ぐいっ GRNG
ゴシゴシ WIPE WIPE
AWWW, YOUR PRETTY FACE IS A MESS.
MMMMM!
MM...!
G-GIVE ME THAT! I'LL DO IT MYSELF!
WE...
I WON'T TRY TO SAY I UNDERSTAND EVERYTHING YOU'RE FEELING...
BUT I CAN TELL YOUR LOVE FOR YUKIHIME IS REAL, AT LEAST.
AND YOU'VE KNOWN HER A HUNDRED TIMES LONGER THAN I HAVE.
YOU REALLY GOT ME BEAT.
WHA...
HRM...
WELL, MY FEELINGS ARE KIND OF LIKE, YOU KNOW?
I THINK I LOVE HER? NO, MAYBE NOT.
YEAH... ON SECOND THOUGHT, I DO LOVE HER!
OR SOMETHING LIKE THAT.
...

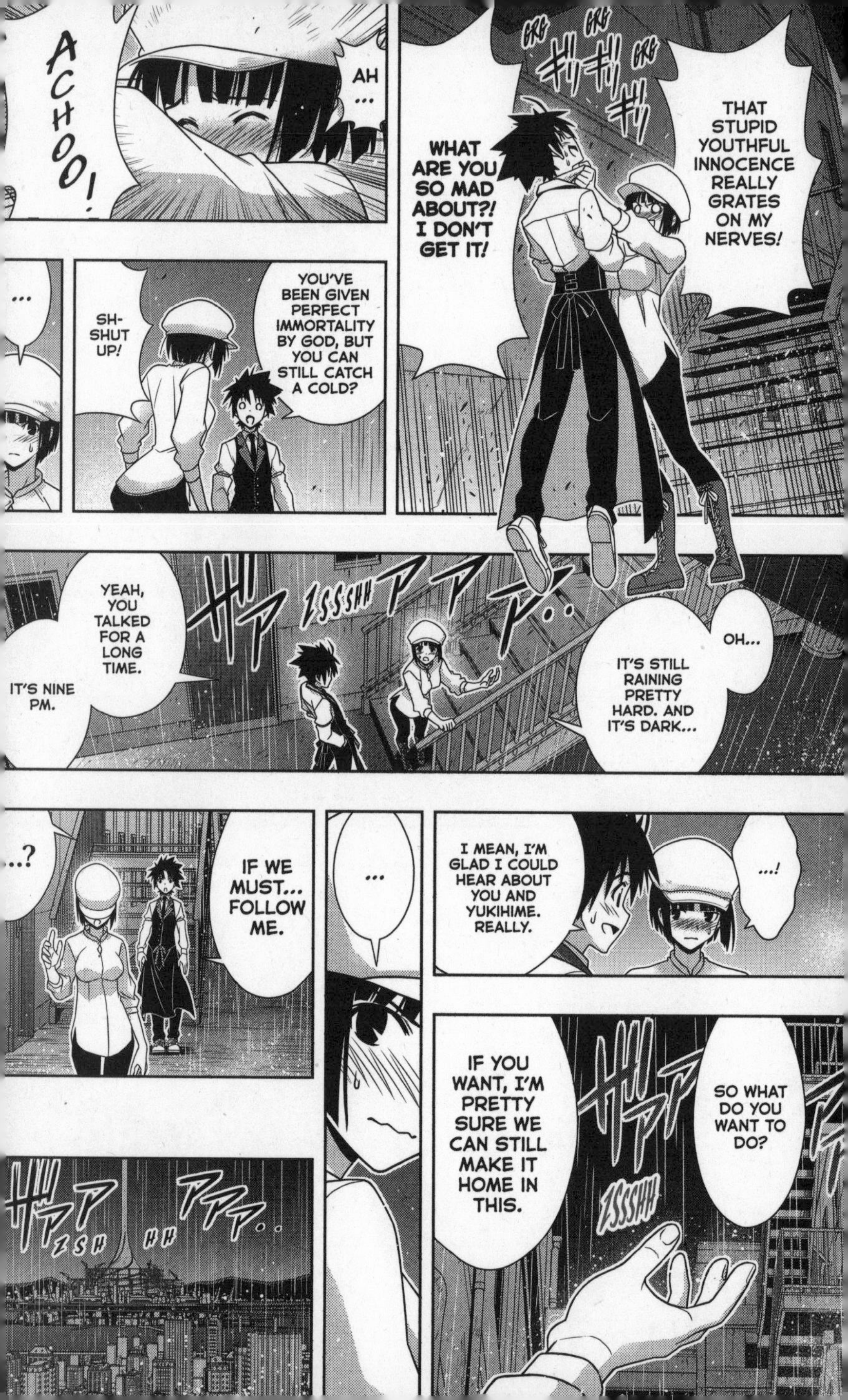
GRG GRG GRG
THAT STUPID YOUTHFUL INNOCENCE REALLY GRATES ON MY NERVES!
WHAT ARE YOU SO MAD ABOUT?! I DON'T GET IT!
AH ...
ACHOO!
YOU'VE BEEN GIVEN PERFECT IMMORTALITY BY GOD, BUT YOU CAN STILL CATCH A COLD?
SH- SHUT UP!
...
OH...
IT'S STILL RAINING PRETTY HARD. AND IT'S DARK...
ZSSSHH
YEAH, YOU TALKED FOR A LONG TIME.
IT'S NINE PM.
...!
I MEAN, I'M GLAD I COULD HEAR ABOUT YOU AND YUKIHIME. REALLY.
SO WHAT DO YOU WANT TO DO?
ZSSSHH
IF YOU WANT, I'M PRETTY SURE WE CAN STILL MAKE IT HOME IN THIS.
...
IF WE MUST... FOLLOW ME.
...?
ZSH HH

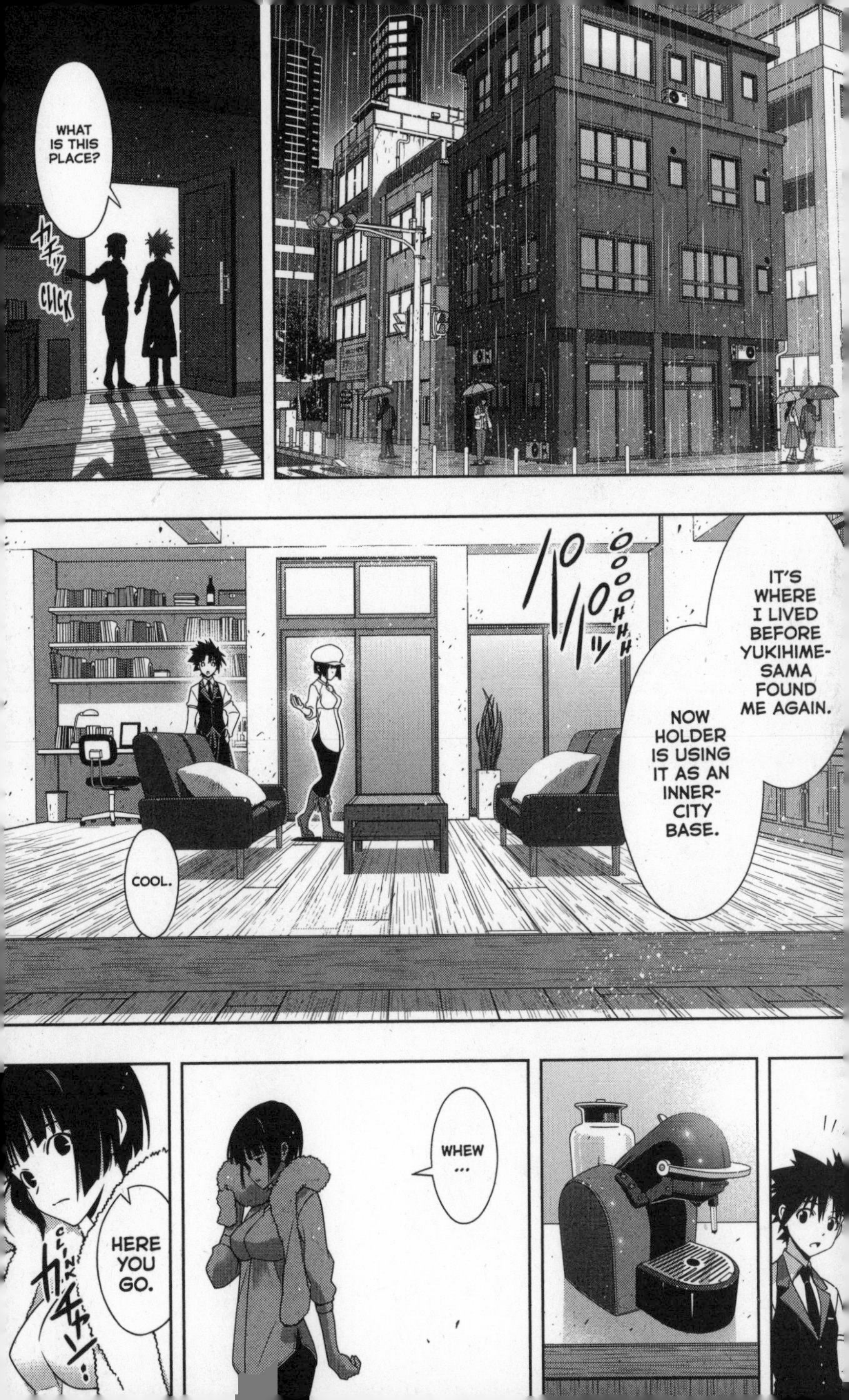
WHAT IS THIS PLACE?
CLICK
IT'S WHERE I LIVED BEFORE YUKIHIME-SAMA FOUND ME AGAIN.
NOW HOLDER IS USING IT AS AN INNER-CITY BASE.
COOL.
WHEW ...
HERE YOU GO.
CLINK

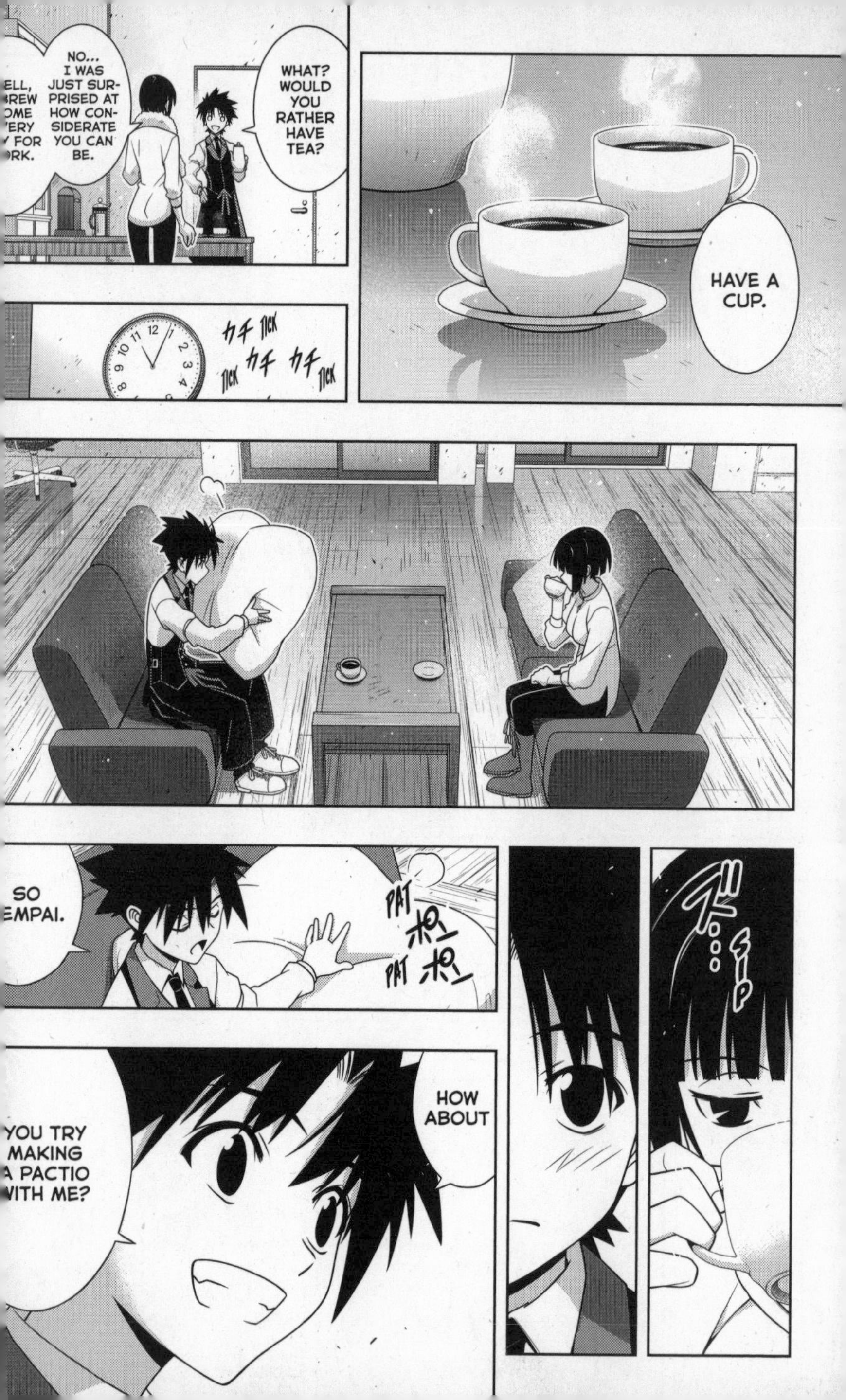
HAVE A CUP.
WHAT? WOULD YOU RATHER HAVE TEA?
NO... I WAS JUST SURPRISED AT HOW CONSIDERATE YOU CAN BE.
ELL, BREW OME ERY FOR ORK.
カチ TICK カチ TICK カチ TICK
ズ... SIP
SO EMPAI.
PAT ポン PAT ポン
HOW ABOUT
YOU TRY MAKING A PACTIO WITH ME?

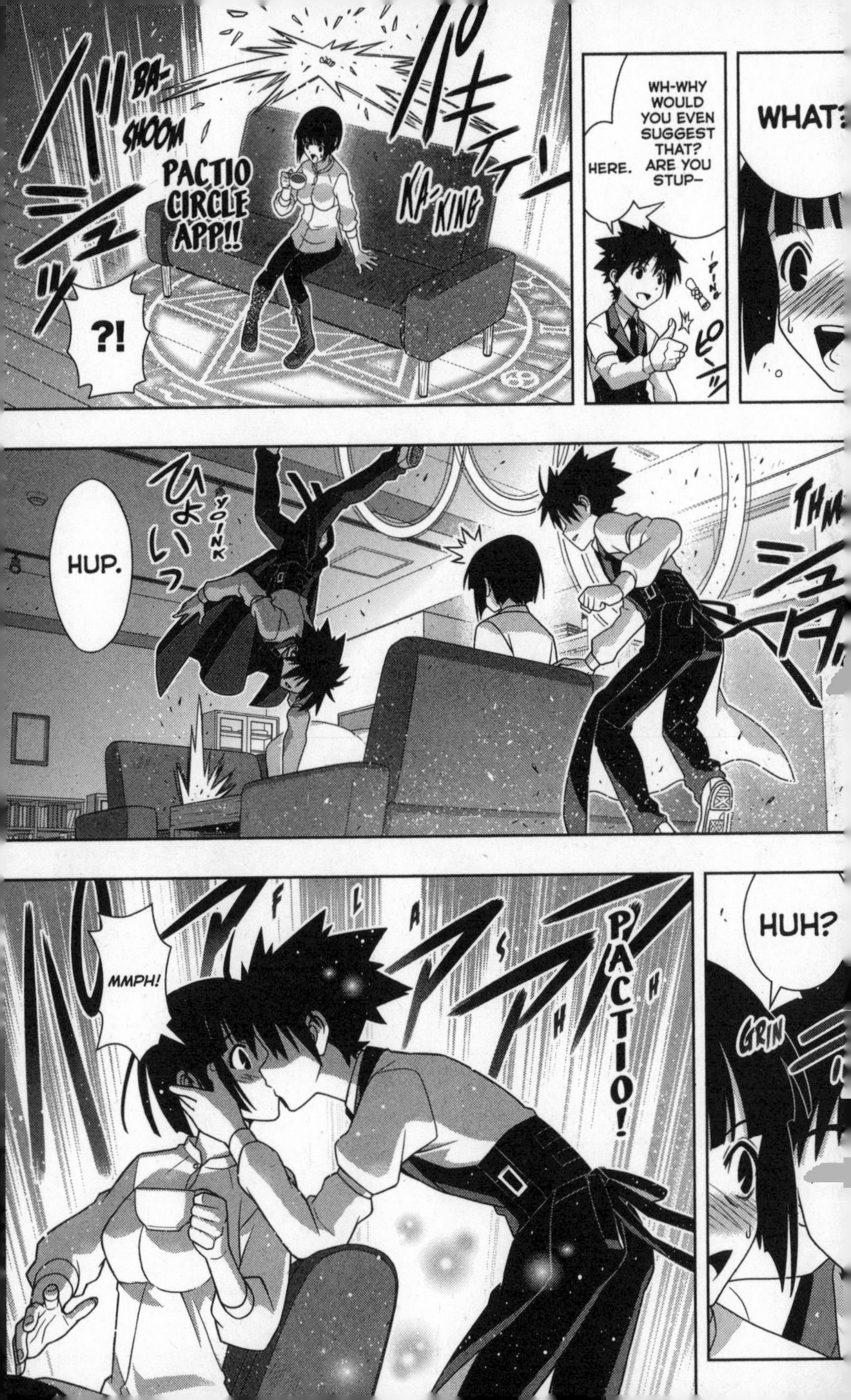
WHAT?
WH-WHY WOULD YOU EVEN SUGGEST THAT? ARE YOU STUP–
HERE.
PING
BA-SHOOM
PACTIO CIRCLE APP!!
KA-KING
?!
THM
YOINK
HUP.
HUH?
GRIN
FLASH
PACTIO!
MMPH!

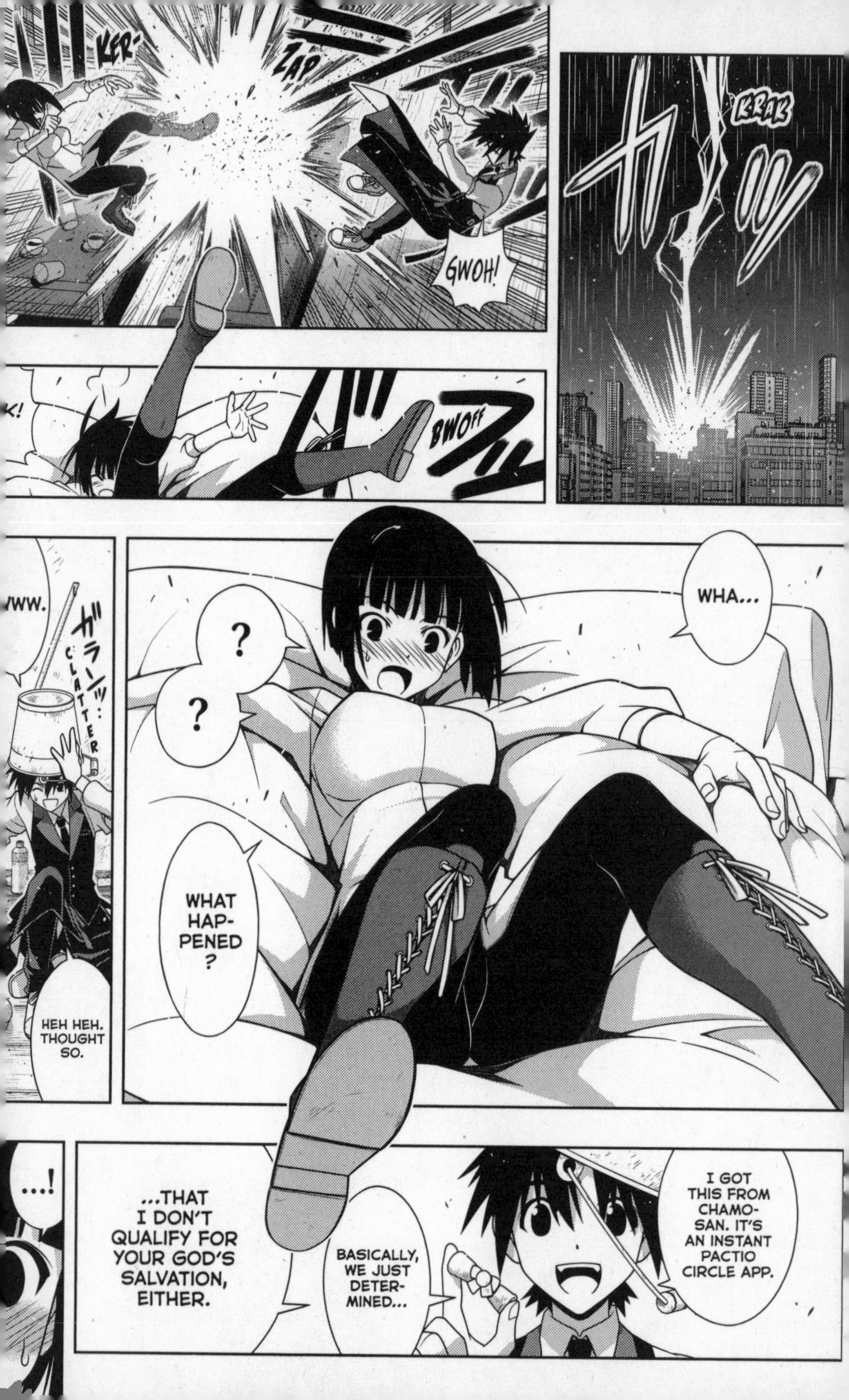
KRAK
KER-
ZAP
GWOH!
K!
BWOFF
WHA...
?
?
WHAT HAP-PENED?
WWW.
ガラーンッ
CLATTER
HEH HEH. THOUGHT SO.
I GOT THIS FROM CHAMO-SAN. IT'S AN INSTANT PACTIO CIRCLE APP.
BASICALLY, WE JUST DETER-MINED...
...THAT I DON'T QUALIFY FOR YOUR GOD'S SALVATION, EITHER.
...!

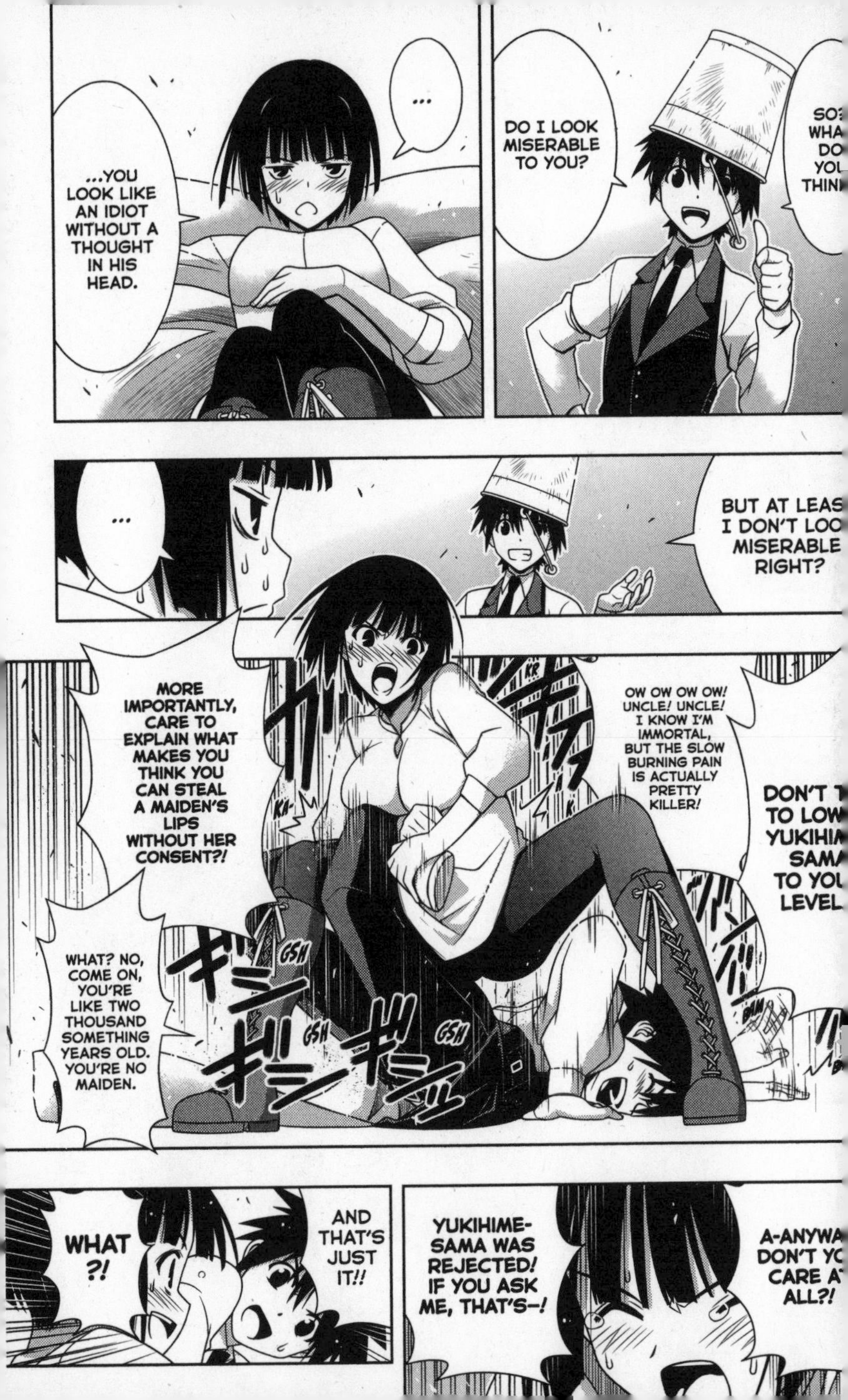
SO? WHA DO YOU THINK
DO I LOOK MISERABLE TO YOU?
...
...YOU LOOK LIKE AN IDIOT WITHOUT A THOUGHT IN HIS HEAD.
BUT AT LEAS I DON'T LOO MISERABLE RIGHT?
...
DON'T T TO LOW YUKIHIM SAMA TO YOU LEVEL.
OW OW OW OW! UNCLE! UNCLE! I KNOW I'M IMMORTAL, BUT THE SLOW BURNING PAIN IS ACTUALLY PRETTY KILLER!
KR
K
MORE IMPORTANTLY, CARE TO EXPLAIN WHAT MAKES YOU THINK YOU CAN STEAL A MAIDEN'S LIPS WITHOUT HER CONSENT?!
KA-
GSH
GSH
GSH
WHAT? NO, COME ON, YOU'RE LIKE TWO THOUSAND SOMETHING YEARS OLD. YOU'RE NO MAIDEN.
A-ANYWA DON'T YO CARE A ALL?!
YUKIHIME-SAMA WAS REJECTED! IF YOU ASK ME, THAT'S–!
AND THAT'S JUST IT!!
WHAT ?!

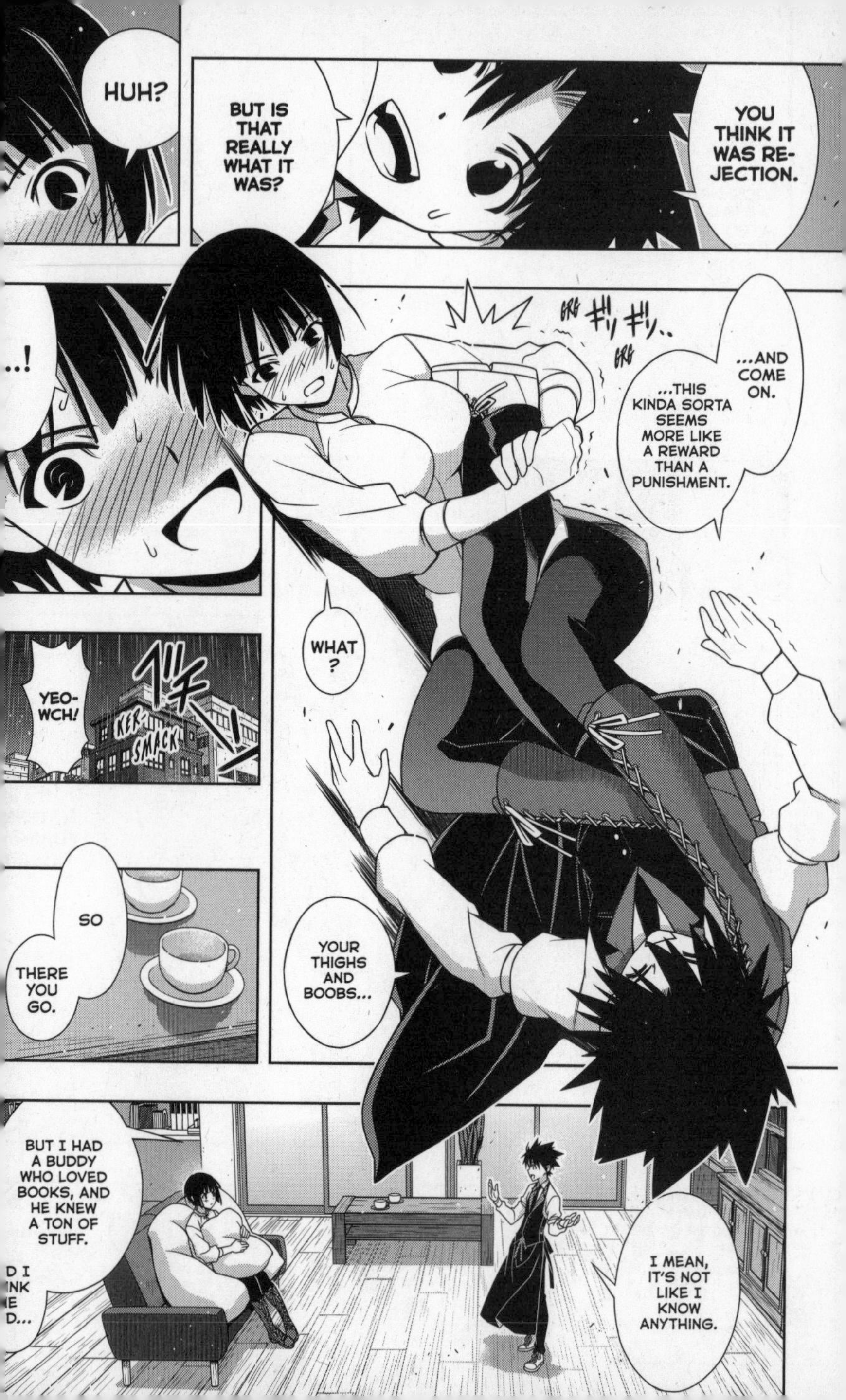
YOU THINK IT WAS RE-JECTION.
BUT IS THAT REALLY WHAT IT WAS?
HUH?
...AND COME ON.
...THIS KINDA SORTA SEEMS MORE LIKE A REWARD THAN A PUNISHMENT.
GRG
GRG
WHAT?
YOUR THIGHS AND BOOBS...
...!
YEO-WCH!
KER-SMACK
SO
THERE YOU GO.
I MEAN, IT'S NOT LIKE I KNOW ANYTHING.
BUT I HAD A BUDDY WHO LOVED BOOKS, AND HE KNEW A TON OF STUFF.

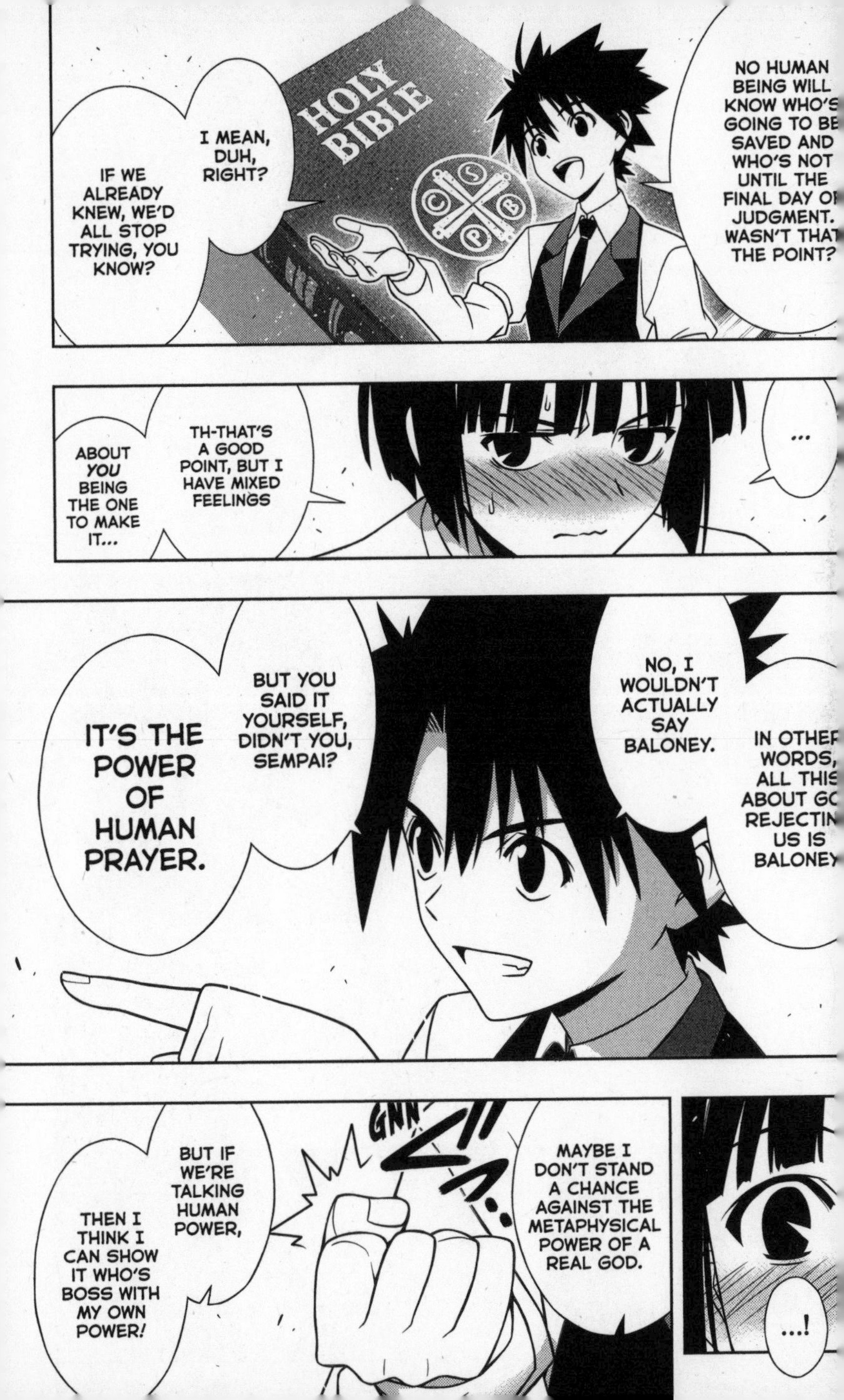
NO HUMAN BEING WILL KNOW WHO'S GOING TO BE SAVED AND WHO'S NOT UNTIL THE FINAL DAY OF JUDGMENT. WASN'T THAT THE POINT?
HOLY BIBLE
I MEAN, DUH, RIGHT?
IF WE ALREADY KNEW, WE'D ALL STOP TRYING, YOU KNOW?
...
TH-THAT'S A GOOD POINT, BUT I HAVE MIXED FEELINGS
ABOUT *YOU* BEING THE ONE TO MAKE IT...
IN OTHER WORDS, ALL THIS ABOUT GOD REJECTING US IS BALONEY
NO, I WOULDN'T ACTUALLY SAY BALONEY.
BUT YOU SAID IT YOURSELF, DIDN'T YOU, SEMPAI?
IT'S THE POWER OF HUMAN PRAYER.
...!
MAYBE I DON'T STAND A CHANCE AGAINST THE METAPHYSICAL POWER OF A REAL GOD.
GNN
BUT IF WE'RE TALKING HUMAN POWER,
THEN I THINK I CAN SHOW IT WHO'S BOSS WITH MY OWN POWER!

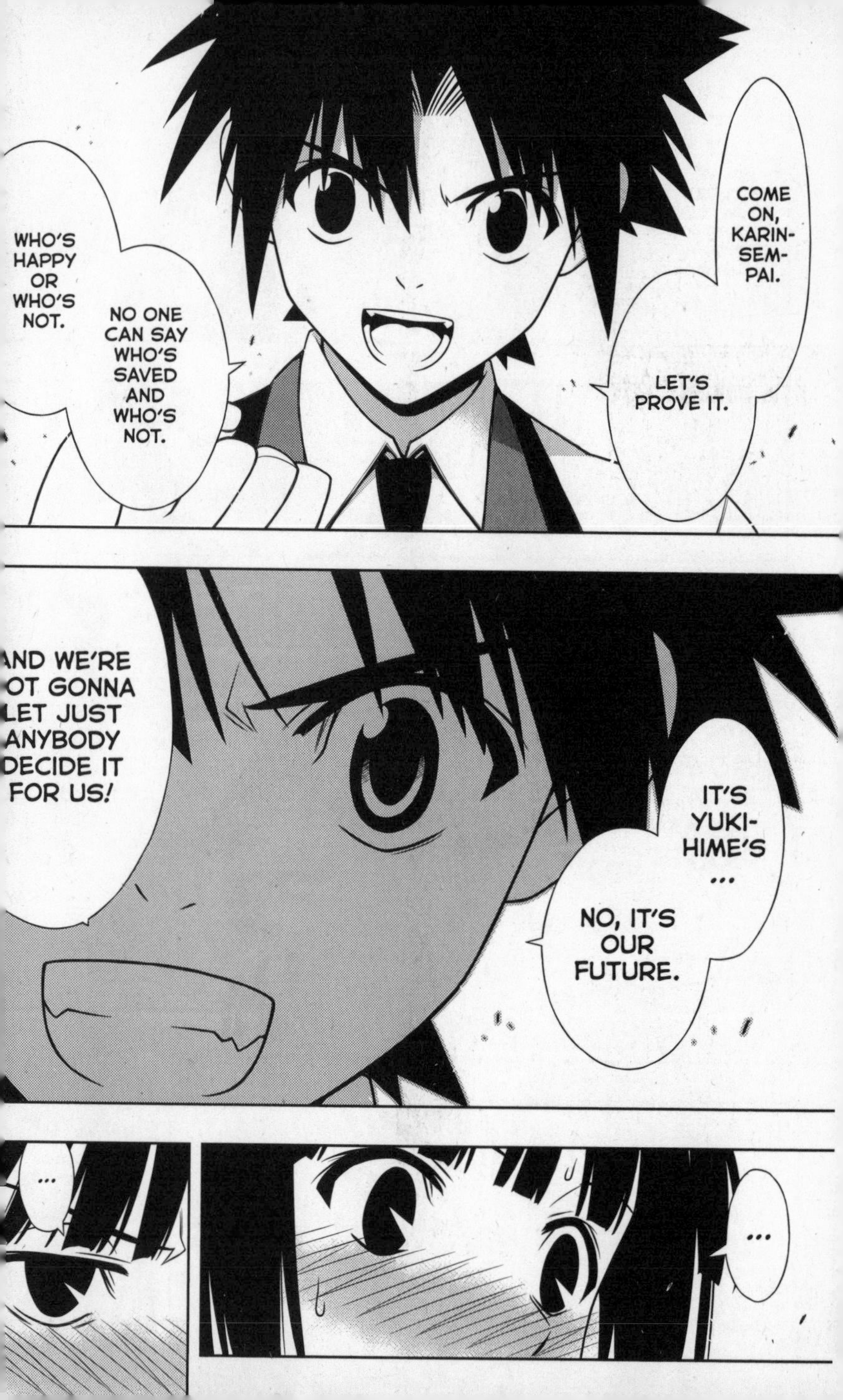
COME ON, KARIN-SEMPAI.
LET'S PROVE IT.
NO ONE CAN SAY WHO'S SAVED AND WHO'S NOT.
WHO'S HAPPY OR WHO'S NOT.
IT'S YUKI-HIME'S ...
NO, IT'S OUR FUTURE.
AND WE'RE OT GONNA LET JUST ANYBODY DECIDE IT FOR US!
...
...

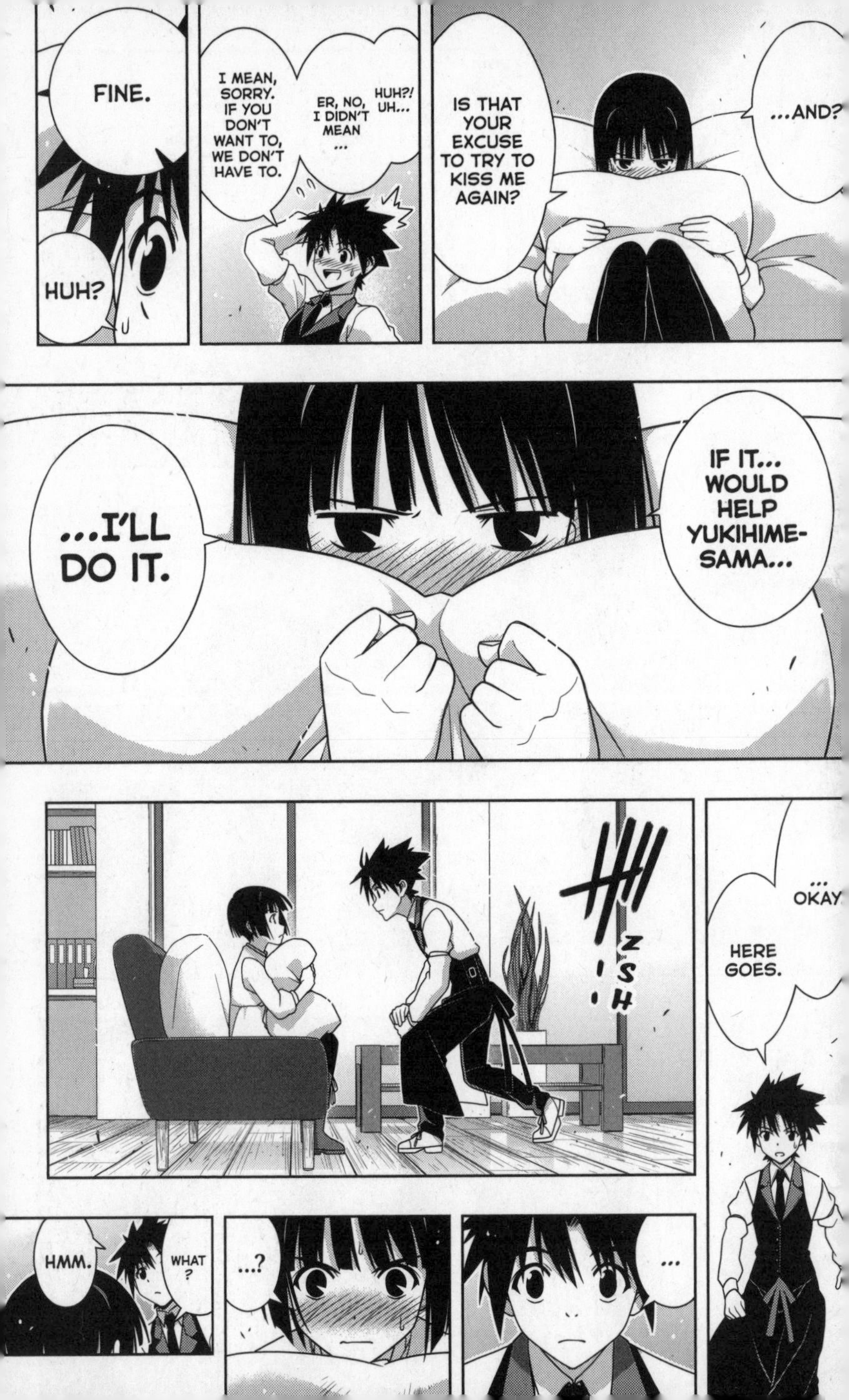
...AND?
IS THAT YOUR EXCUSE TO TRY TO KISS ME AGAIN?
HUH?! UH...
ER, NO, I DIDN'T MEAN ...
I MEAN, SORRY. IF YOU DON'T WANT TO, WE DON'T HAVE TO.
FINE.
HUH?
IF IT... WOULD HELP YUKIHIME-SAMA...
...I'LL DO IT.
... OKAY.
HERE GOES.
ZSH
...
...?
WHAT?
HMM.

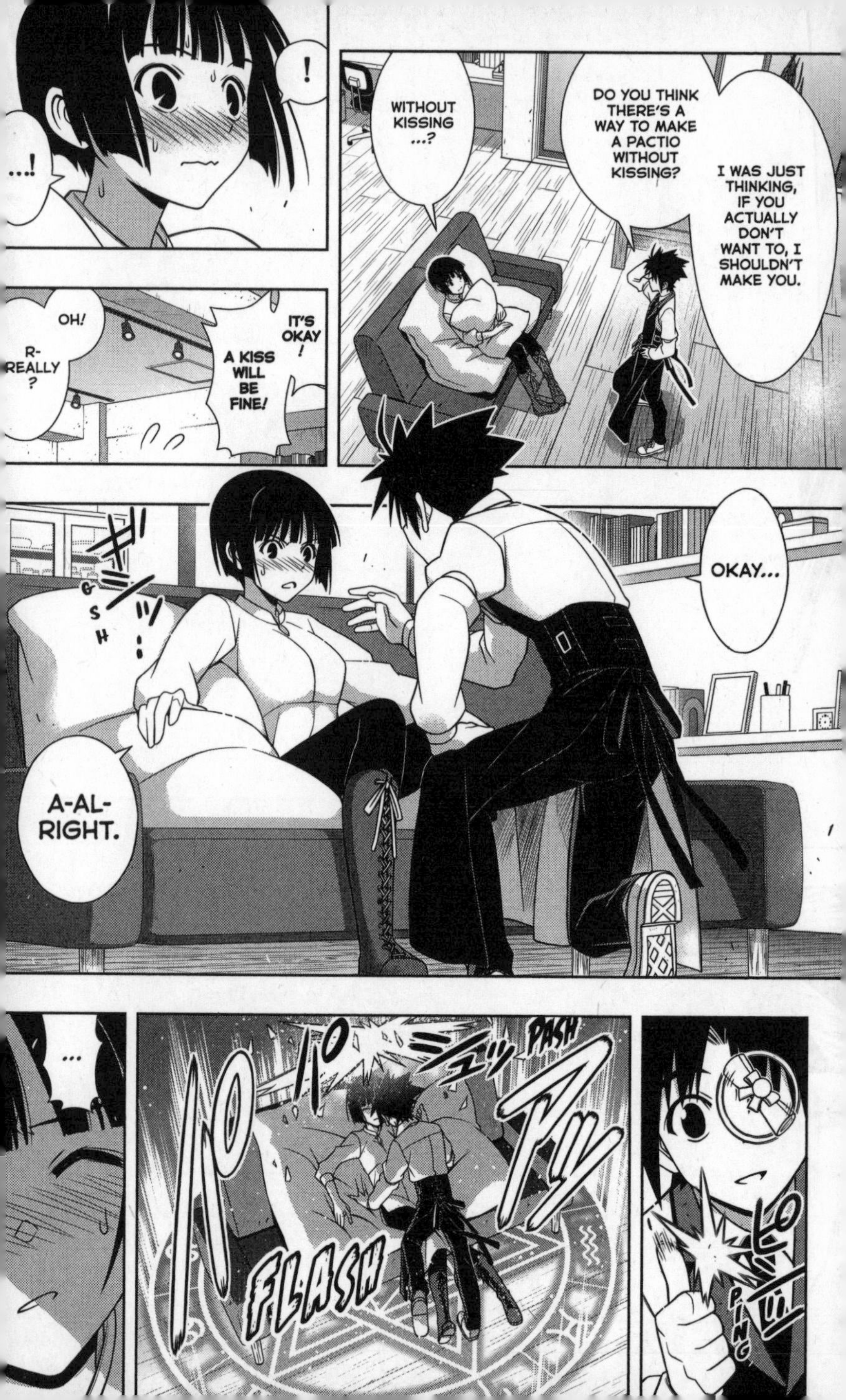
I WAS JUST THINKING, IF YOU ACTUALLY DON'T WANT TO, I SHOULDN'T MAKE YOU.
DO YOU THINK THERE'S A WAY TO MAKE A PACTIO WITHOUT KISSING?
WITHOUT KISSING ...?
!
...!
IT'S OKAY!
A KISS WILL BE FINE!
OH!
R-REALLY?
OKAY...
GSH
A-AL-RIGHT.
PING
DASH
FLASH
...

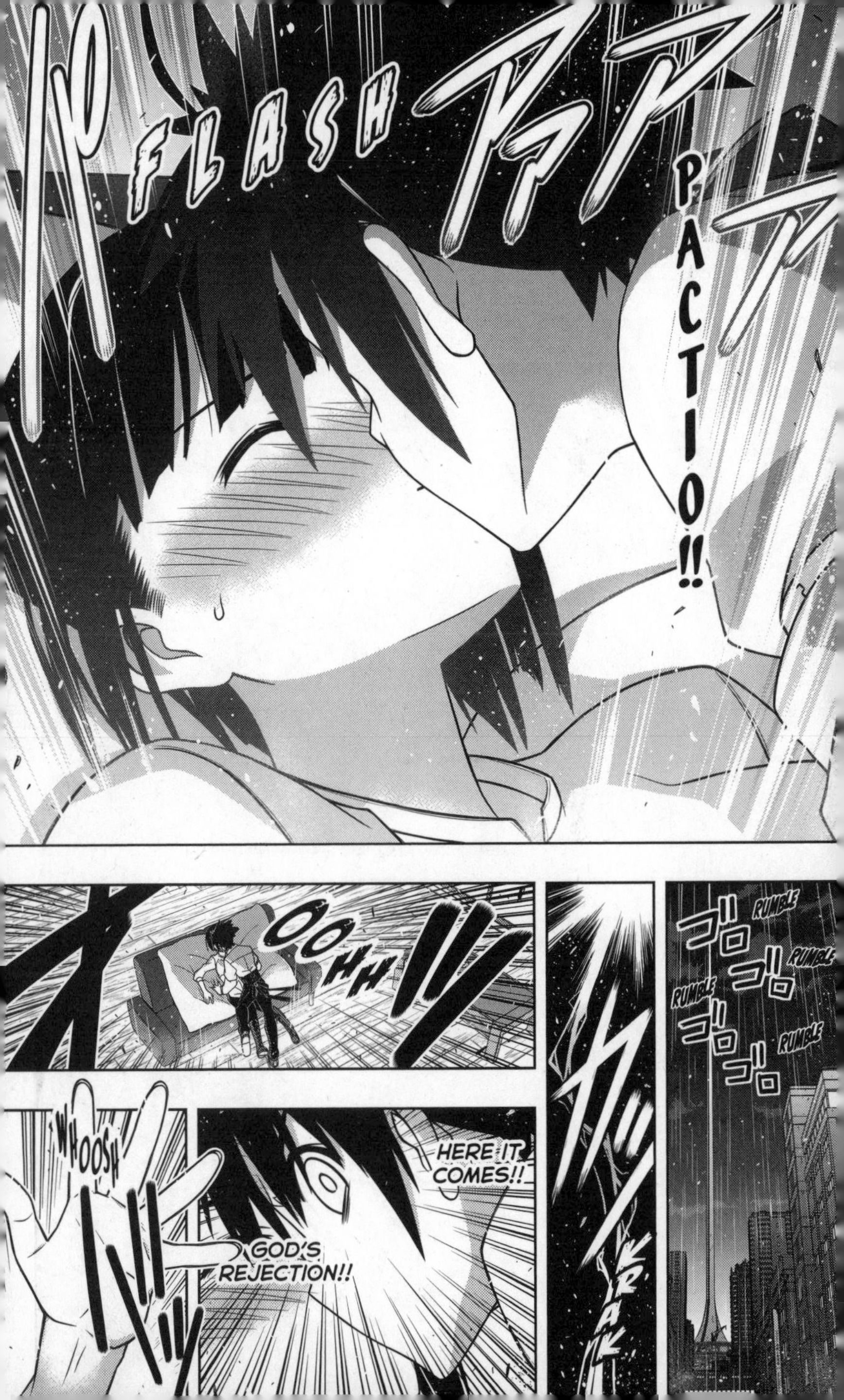
FLASH
PACTIO!!
RUMBLE
RUMBLE
RUMBLE
RUMBLE
KRAK
OOHH
HERE IT COMES!!
GOD'S REJECTION!!
WHOOSH

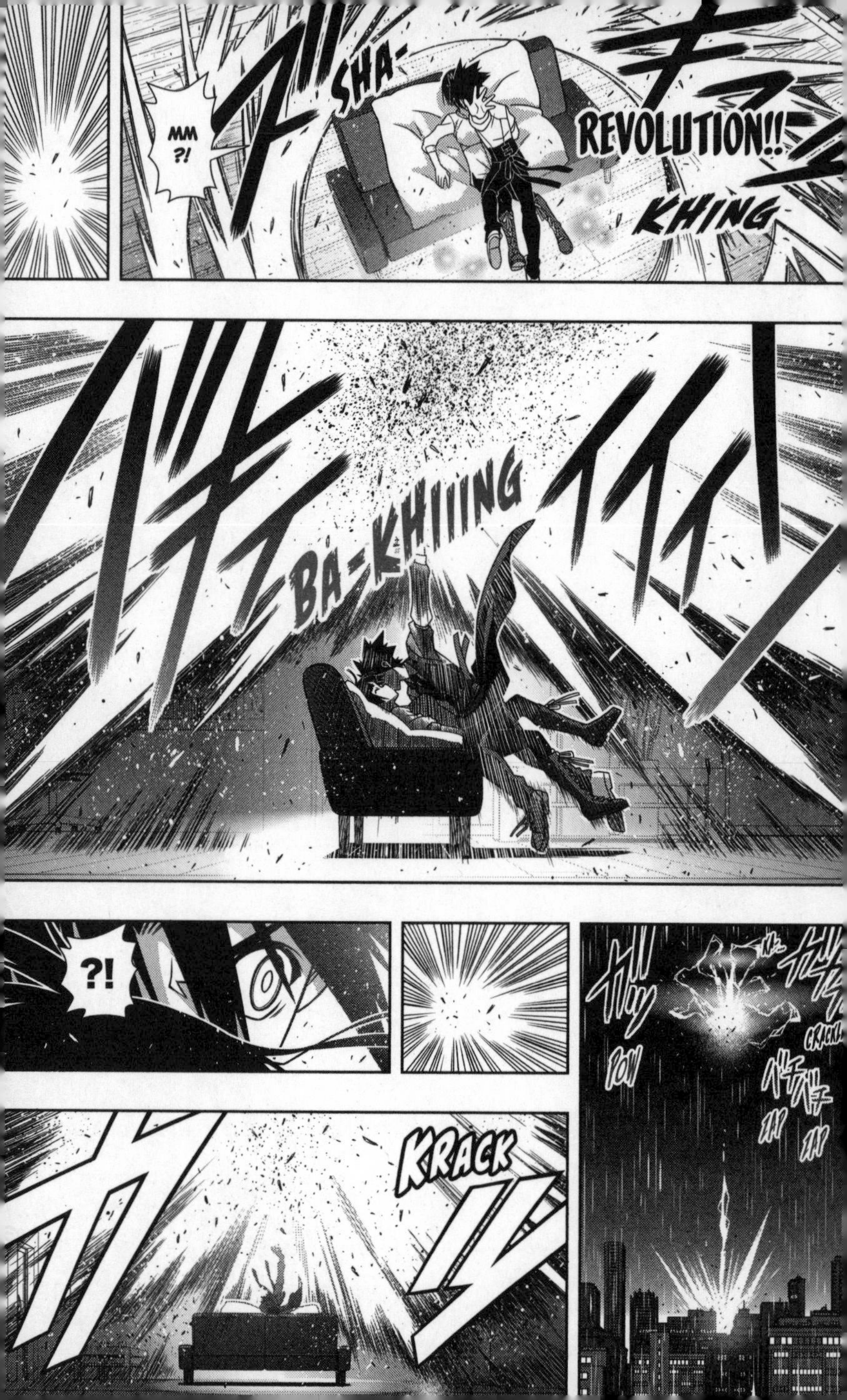
REVOLUTION!!
KHING
SHA-
MM ?!
BA-KHIIING
CRACKL
POW
ZAP
ZAP
?!
KRACK

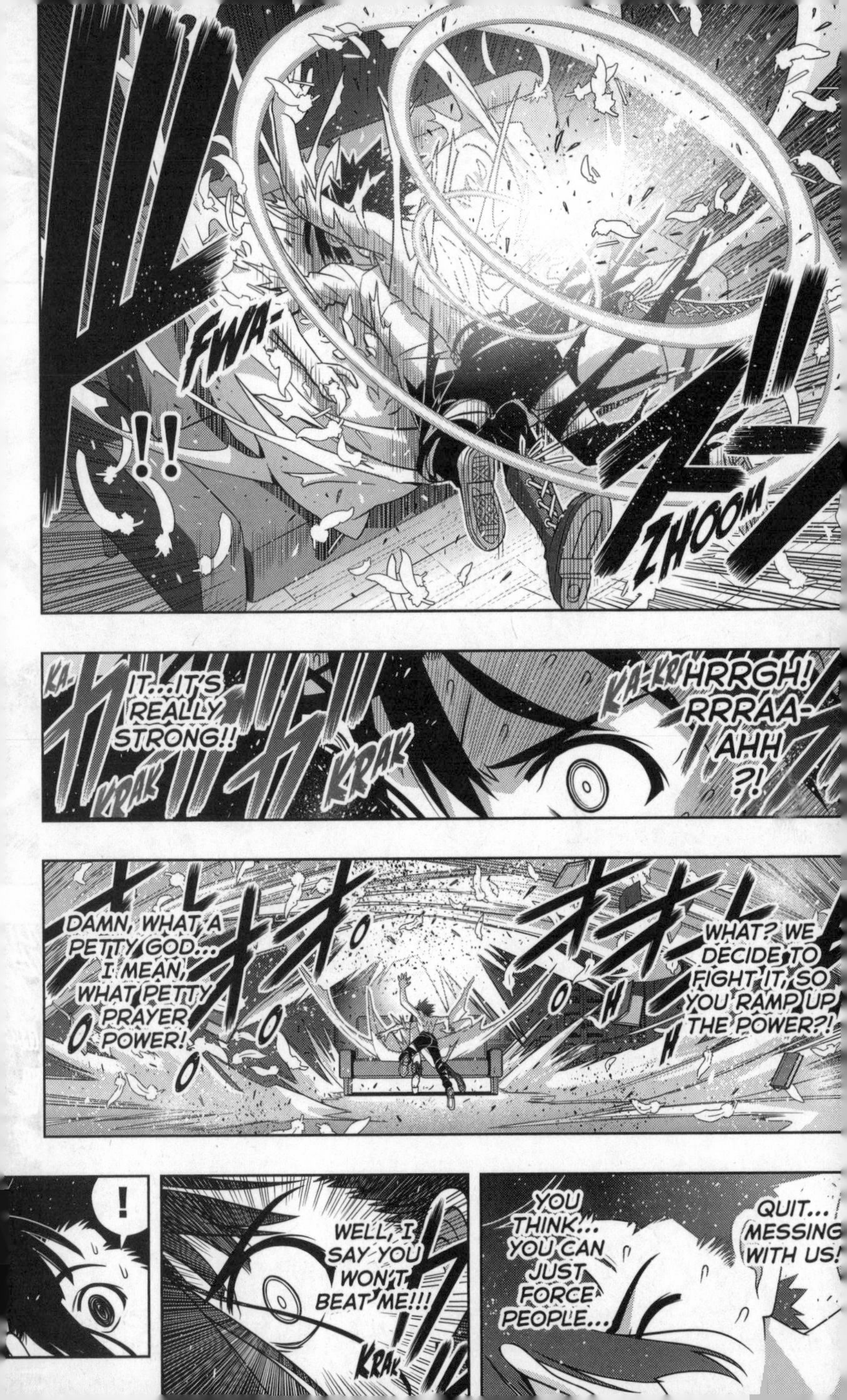
ZHOOM
FWA-
!!
KA-KRI
HRRGH! RRRAA-AHH?!
KRAK
IT...IT'S REALLY STRONG!!
KA-
KRAK
WHAT? WE DECIDE TO FIGHT IT, SO YOU RAMP UP THE POWER?!
DAMN, WHAT A PETTY GOD... I MEAN, WHAT PETTY PRAYER POWER!
QUIT... MESSING WITH US!
YOU THINK... YOU CAN JUST FORCE PEOPLE...
WELL, I SAY YOU WON'T BEAT ME!!!
KRAK
!

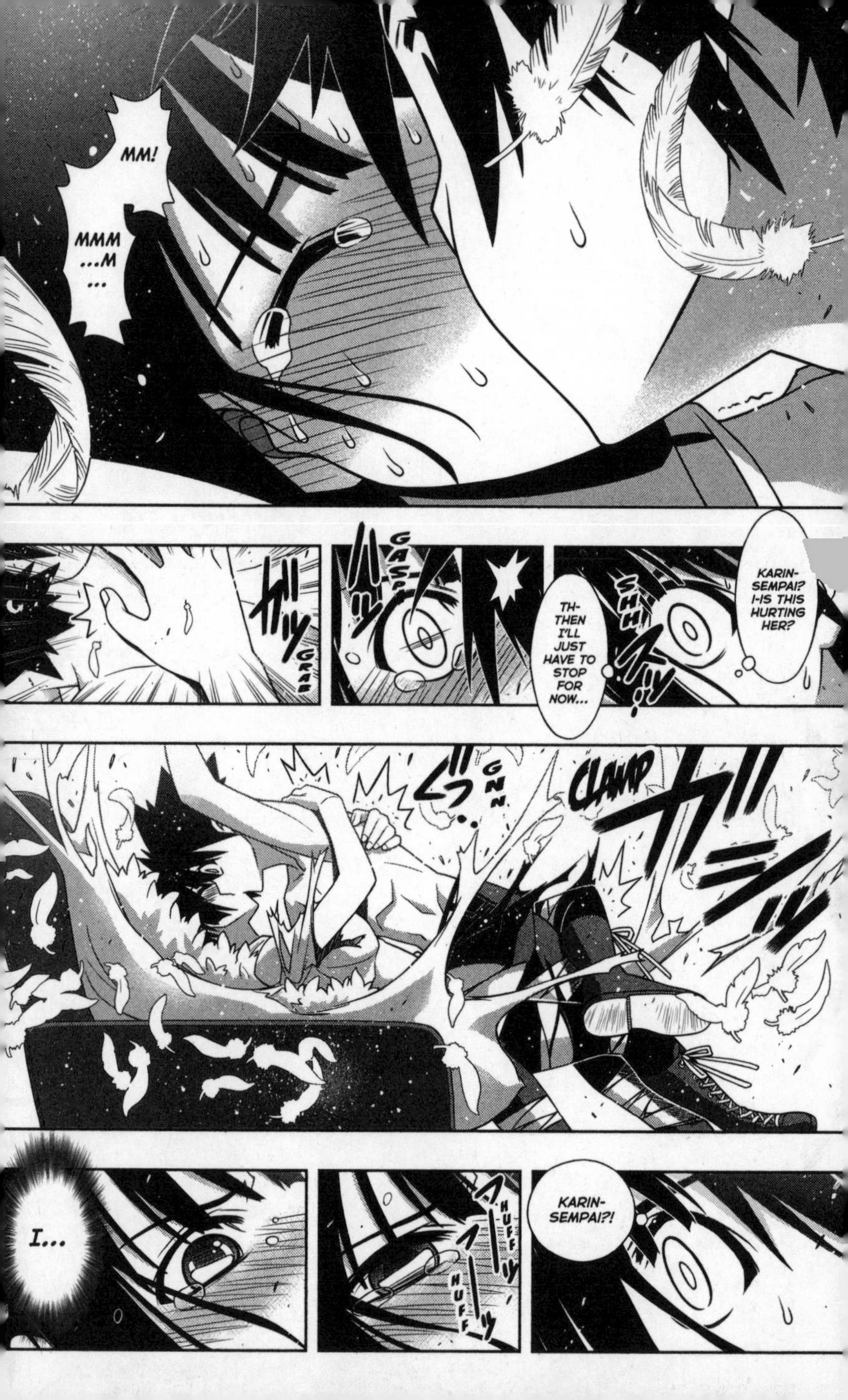
MM!
MMM ...M ...
KARIN-SEMPAI? I-IS THIS HURTING HER?
SHH
TH-THEN I'LL JUST HAVE TO STOP FOR NOW...
GASP
GRAB
CLAMP
GNN
KARIN-SEMPAI?!
HUFF
HUFF
I...

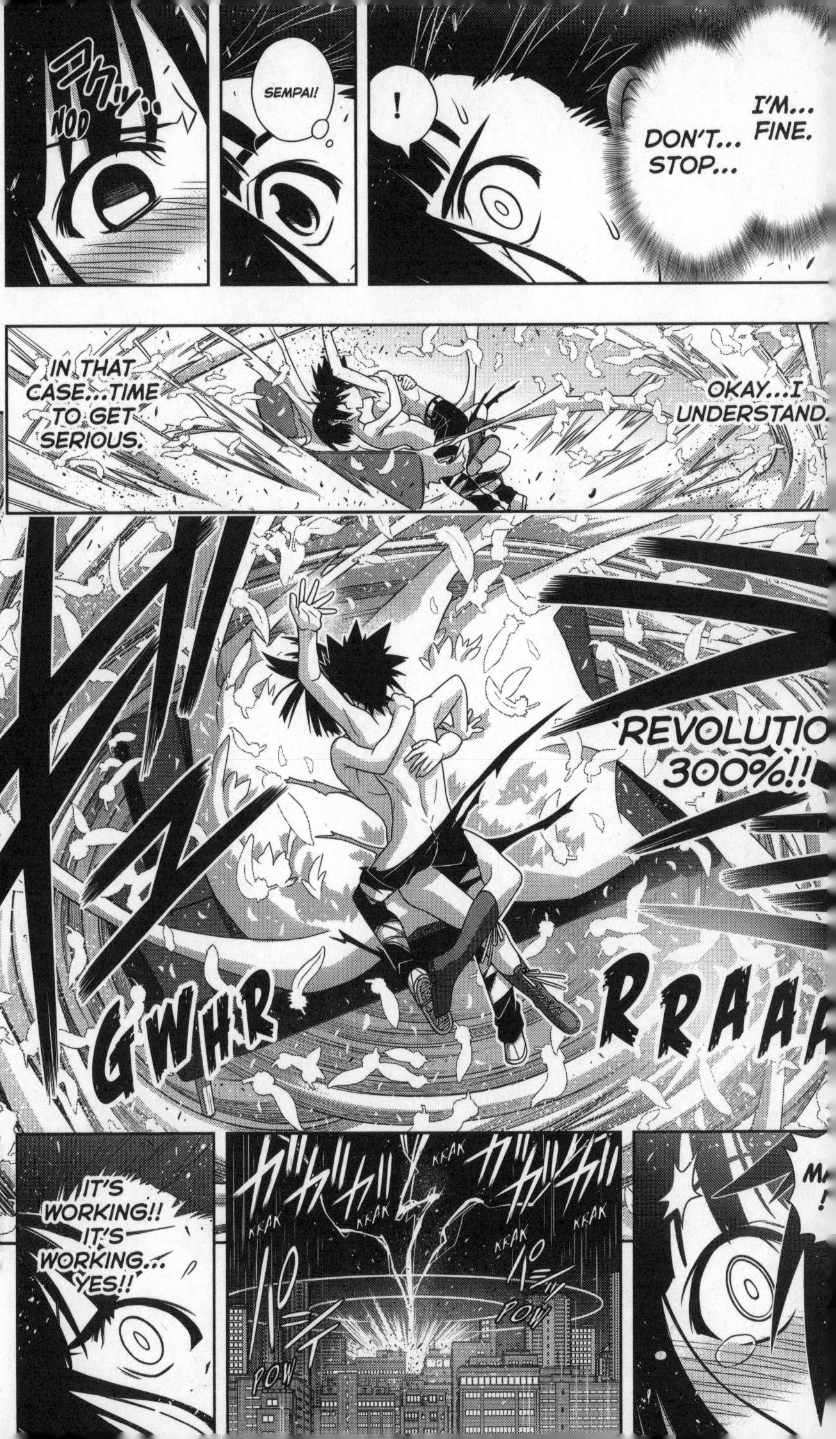
I'M... FINE.
DON'T... STOP...
!
SEMPAI!
NOD
OKAY...I UNDERSTAND.
IN THAT CASE...TIME TO GET SERIOUS.
REVOLUTIO
300%!!
RRAA
GWHR
M...
!
KRAK
KRAK
KRAK
KRAK
KRAK
POW
POW
IT'S WORKING!! IT'S WORKING... YES!!

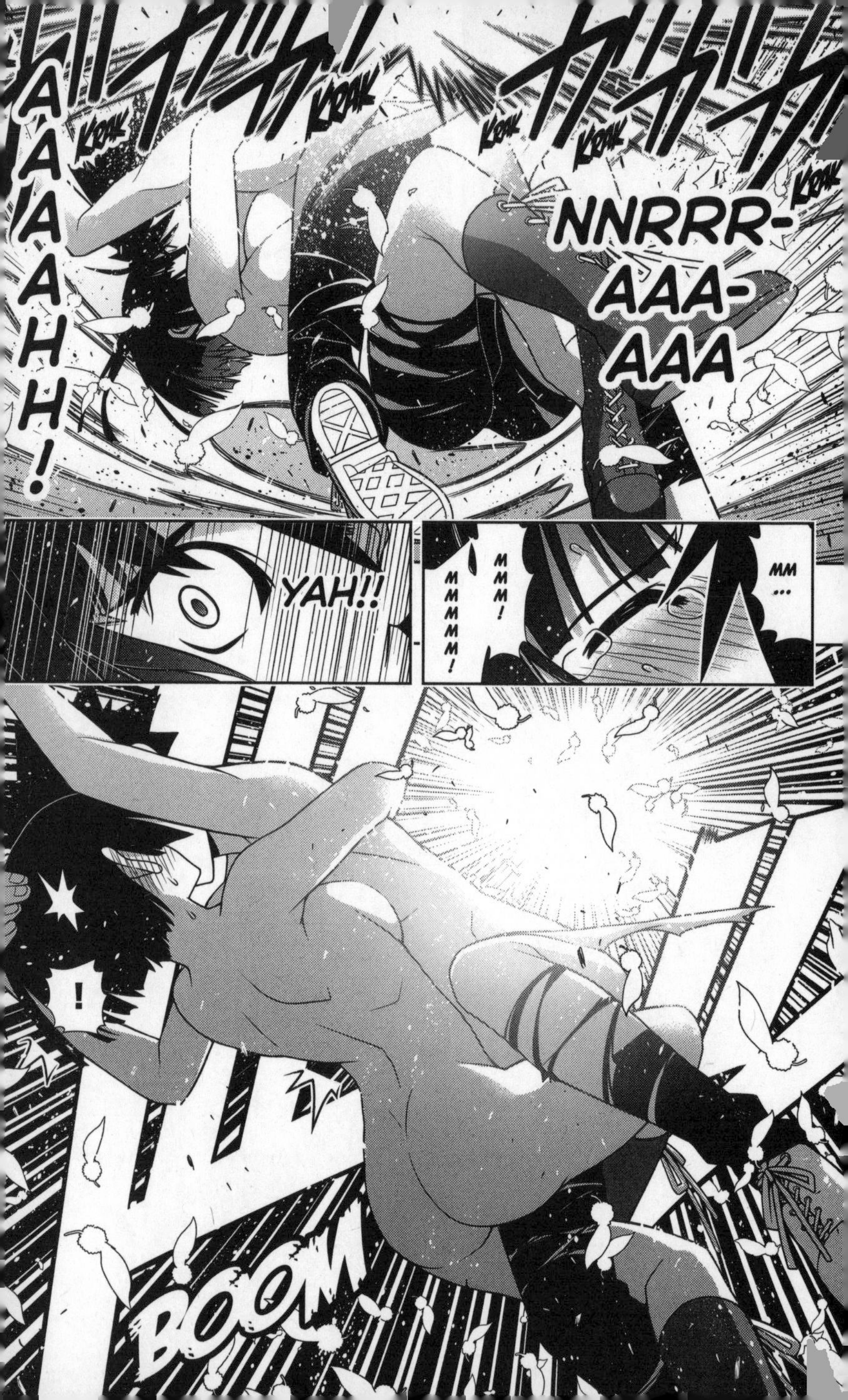
KRAK
NNRRRR-AAA-AAA
KRAK
KRAK
KRAK
KRAK
AAAAAHH!
MM...
MMM! MMMMM!
YAH!!
!
BOO

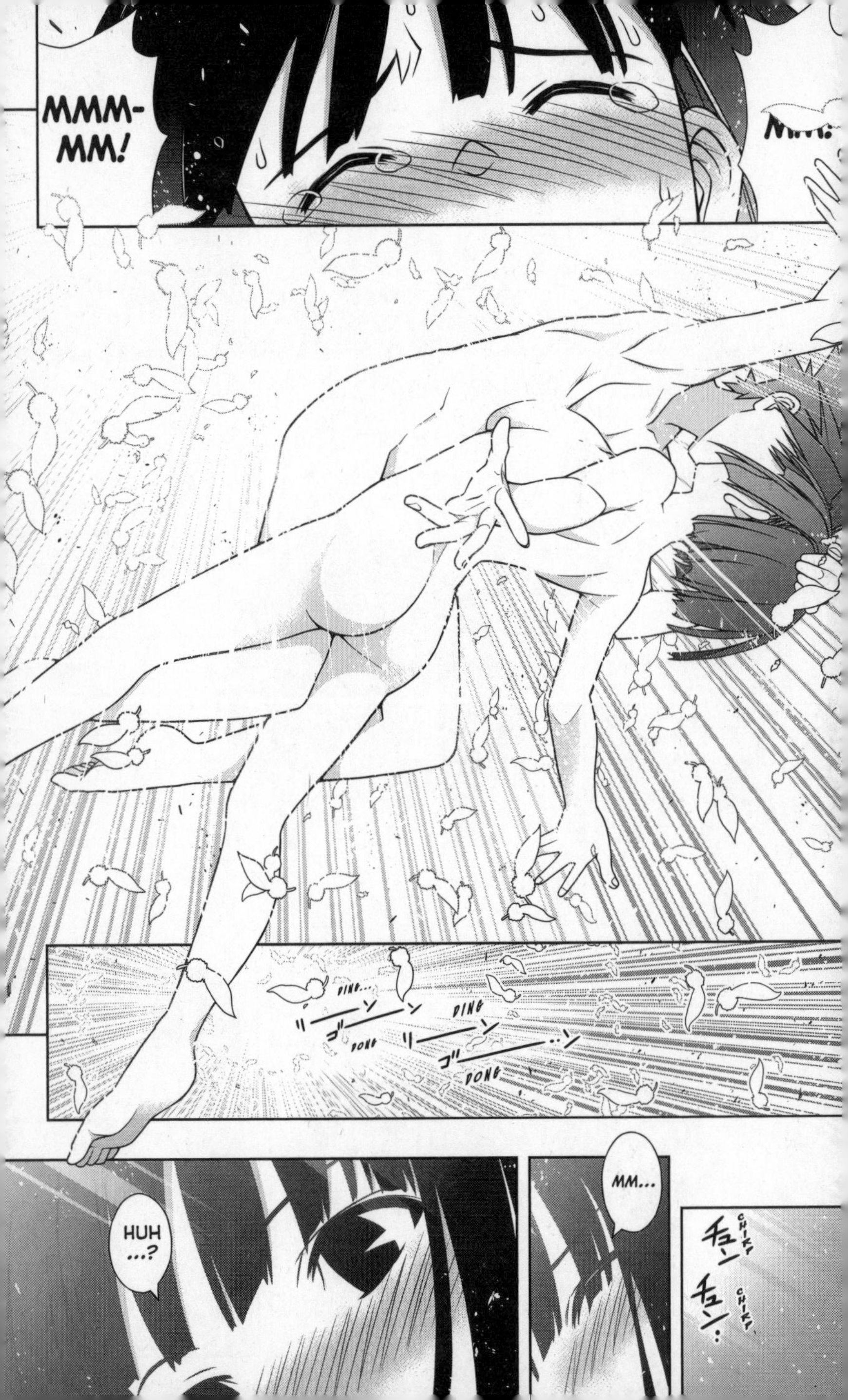
MMM-
MM!
DING...
リーーン
ゴーーン
DONG
DING
リーーン
ゴーーー…ン
DONG
チュン
CHIRP
チュン。
CHIRP
MM...
HUH
...?

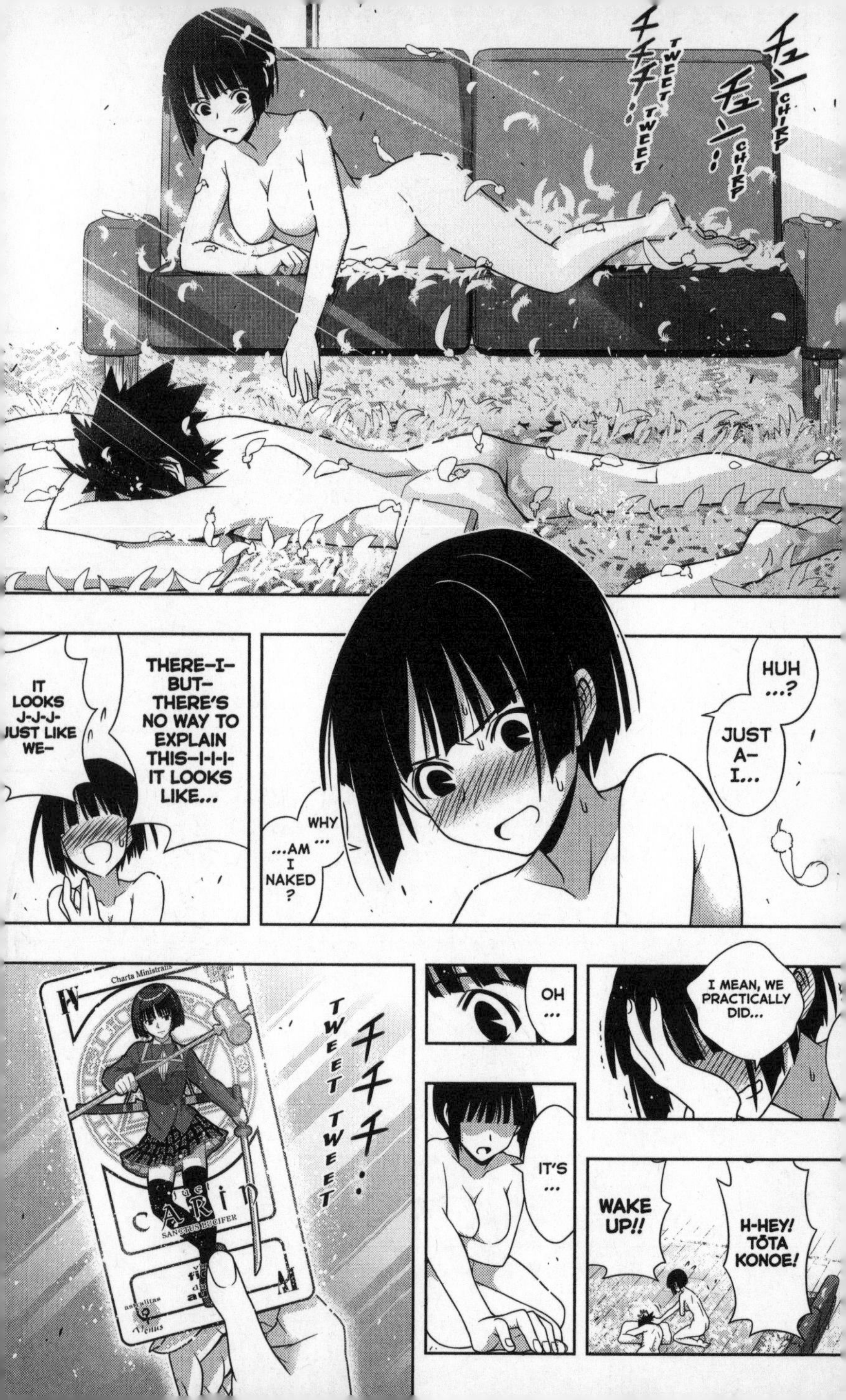
チュ
CHIRP
チュン…
CHIRP
チチチ…
TWEET TWEET TWEET
HUH ...?
JUST A– I...
WHY ...
...AM I NAKED?
THERE–I– BUT– THERE'S NO WAY TO EXPLAIN THIS–I–I–I– IT LOOKS LIKE...
IT LOOKS J-J-J- JUST LIKE WE–
I MEAN, WE PRACTICALLY DID...
OH ...
H-HEY! TŌTA KONOE!
WAKE UP!!
IT'S ...
チチチ…
TWEET TWEET
Charta Ministralis
IV
CARIN
SANCTUS LUCIFER
Venus

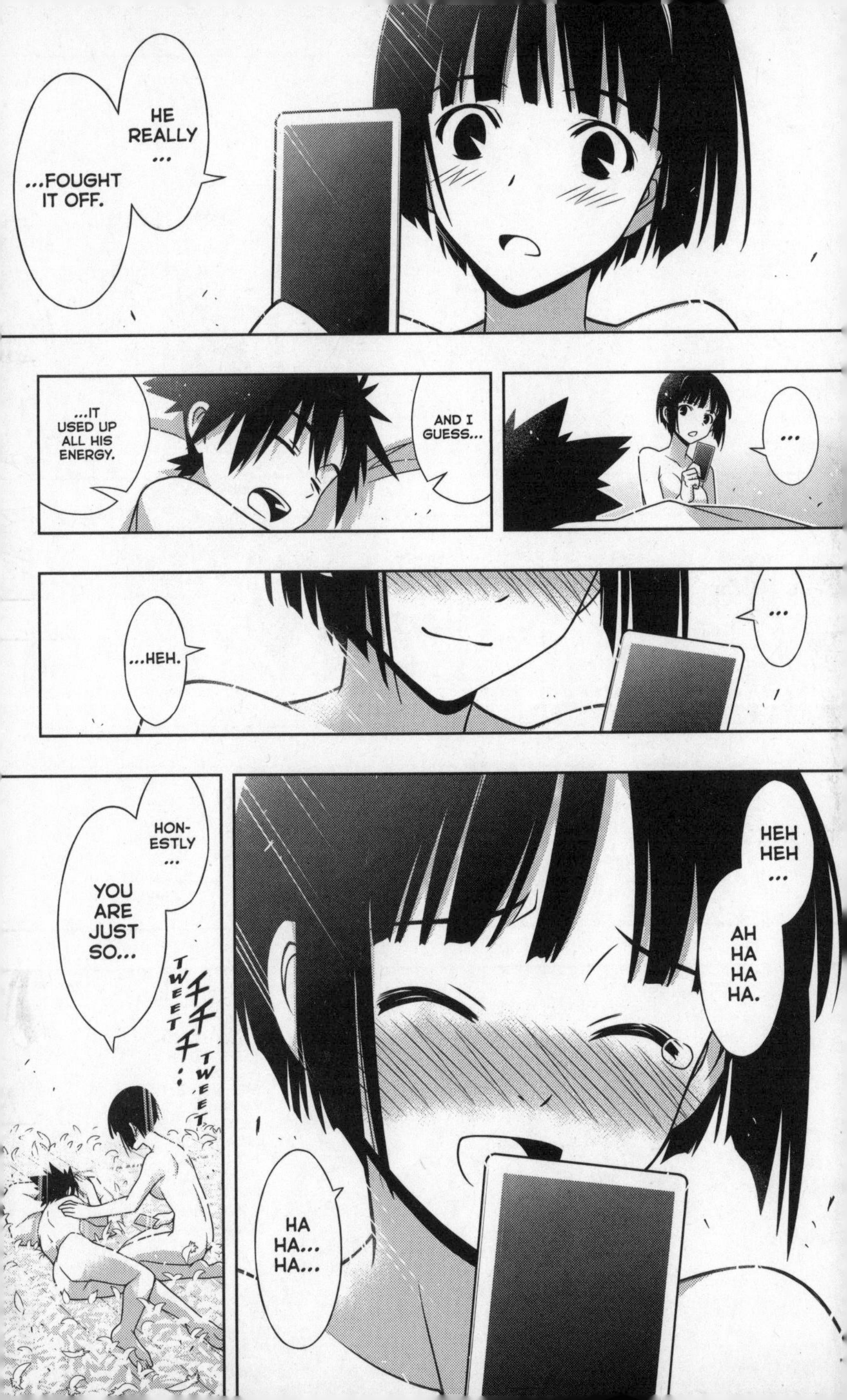
HE REALLY ...
...FOUGHT IT OFF.
...
AND I GUESS...
...IT USED UP ALL HIS ENERGY.
...
...HEH.
HEH HEH ...
AH HA HA HA.
HA HA... HA...
HON-ESTLY ...
YOU ARE JUST SO...
TWEET TWEET

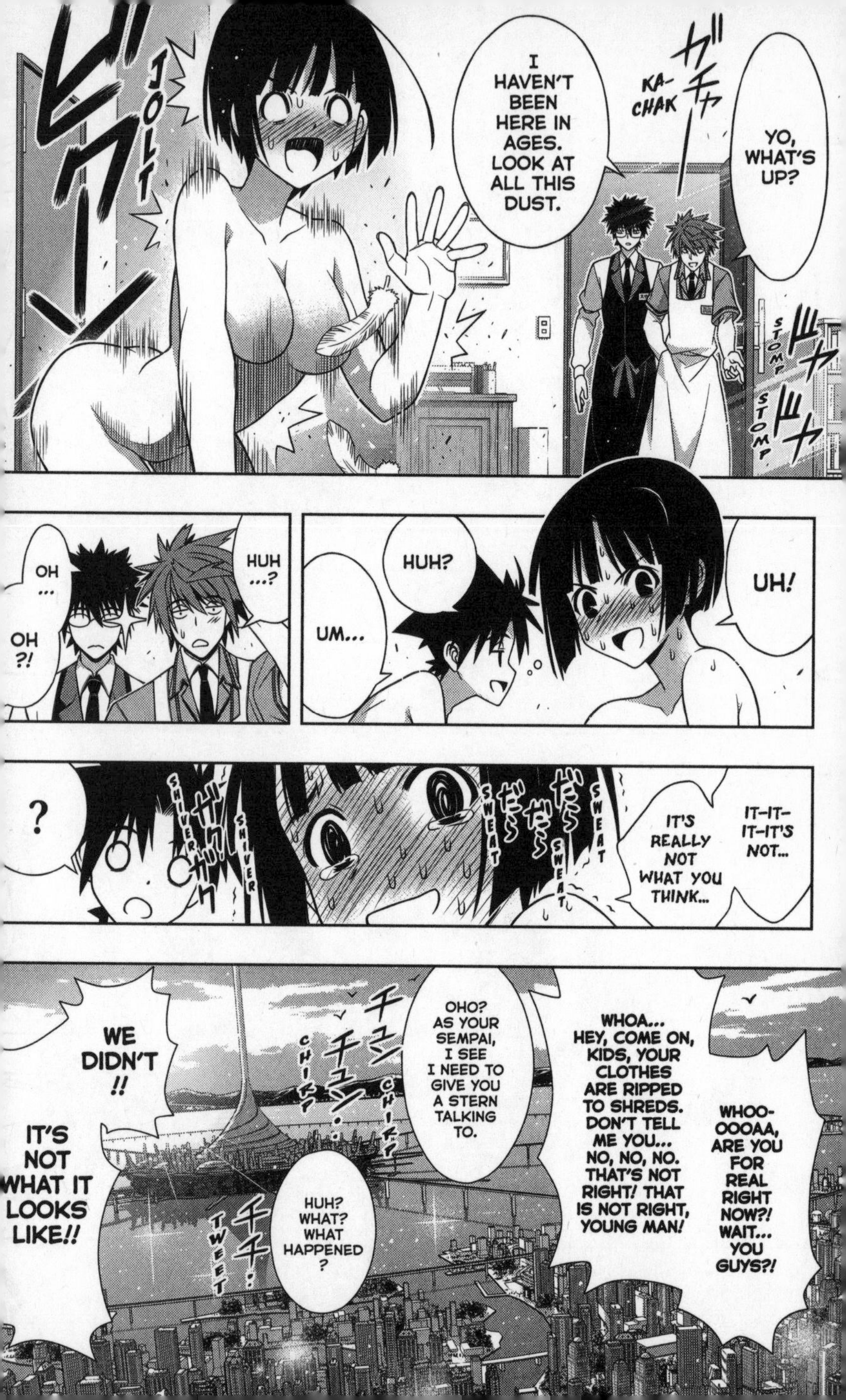
YO, WHAT'S UP?
KA-CHAK
I HAVEN'T BEEN HERE IN AGES. LOOK AT ALL THIS DUST.
STOMP STOMP
JOLT
UH!
HUH?
UM...
HUH ...?
OH ... OH ?!
IT-IT-IT-IT'S NOT...
IT'S REALLY NOT WHAT YOU THINK...
SWEAT SWEAT SWEAT
SHIVER SHIVER
?
WHOO-OOOAA, ARE YOU FOR REAL RIGHT NOW?! WAIT... YOU GUYS?!
WHOA... HEY, COME ON, KIDS, YOUR CLOTHES ARE RIPPED TO SHREDS. DON'T TELL ME YOU... NO, NO, NO. THAT'S NOT RIGHT! THAT IS NOT RIGHT, YOUNG MAN!
OHO? AS YOUR SEMPAI, I SEE I NEED TO GIVE YOU A STERN TALKING TO.
CHIRP CHIRP
HUH? WHAT? WHAT HAPPENED ?
TWEET
WE DIDN'T !!
IT'S NOT WHAT IT LOOKS LIKE!!

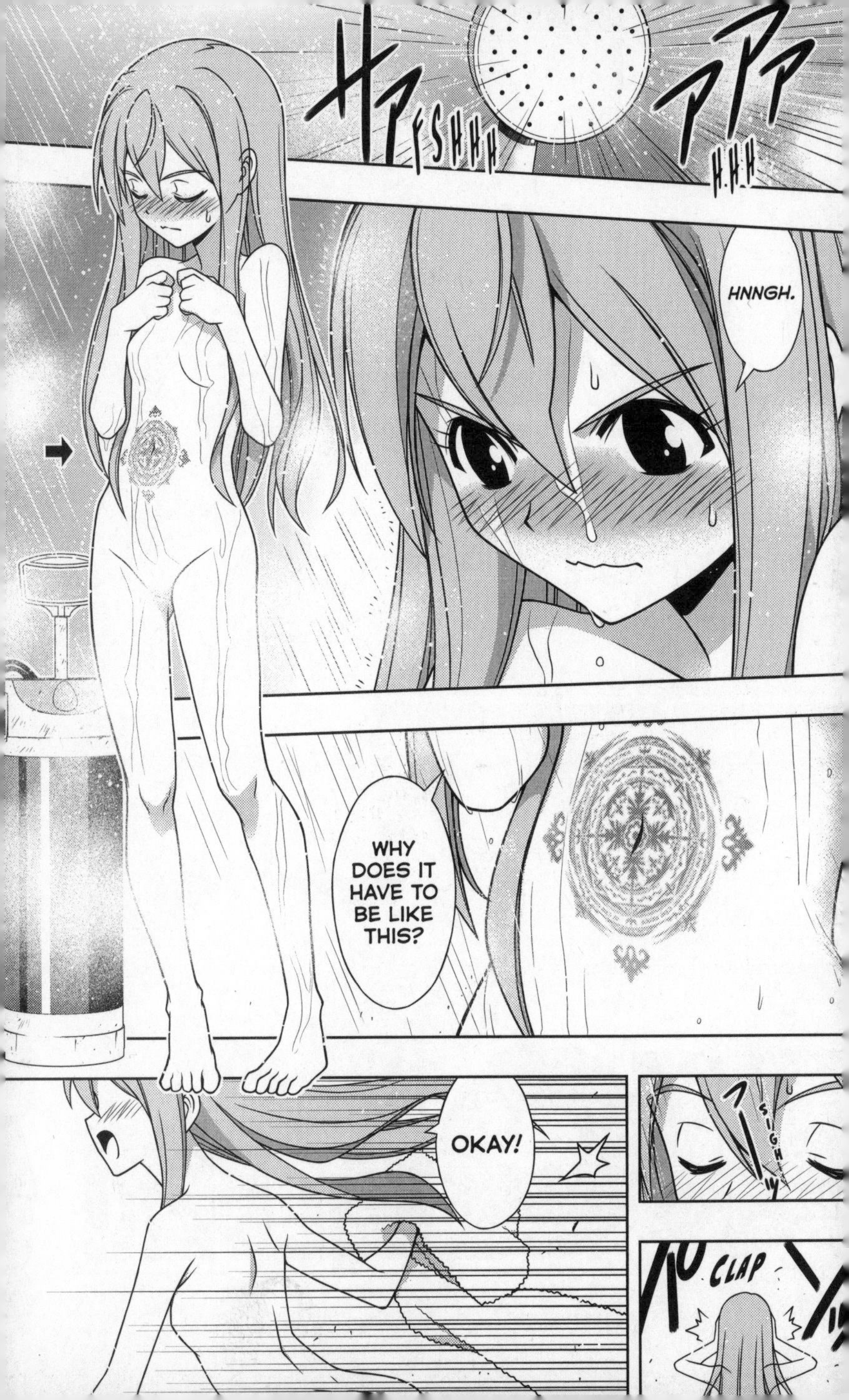
FSHHHH
HHH
HNNGH.
WHY DOES IT HAVE TO BE LIKE THIS?
SIGH
CLAP
OKAY!

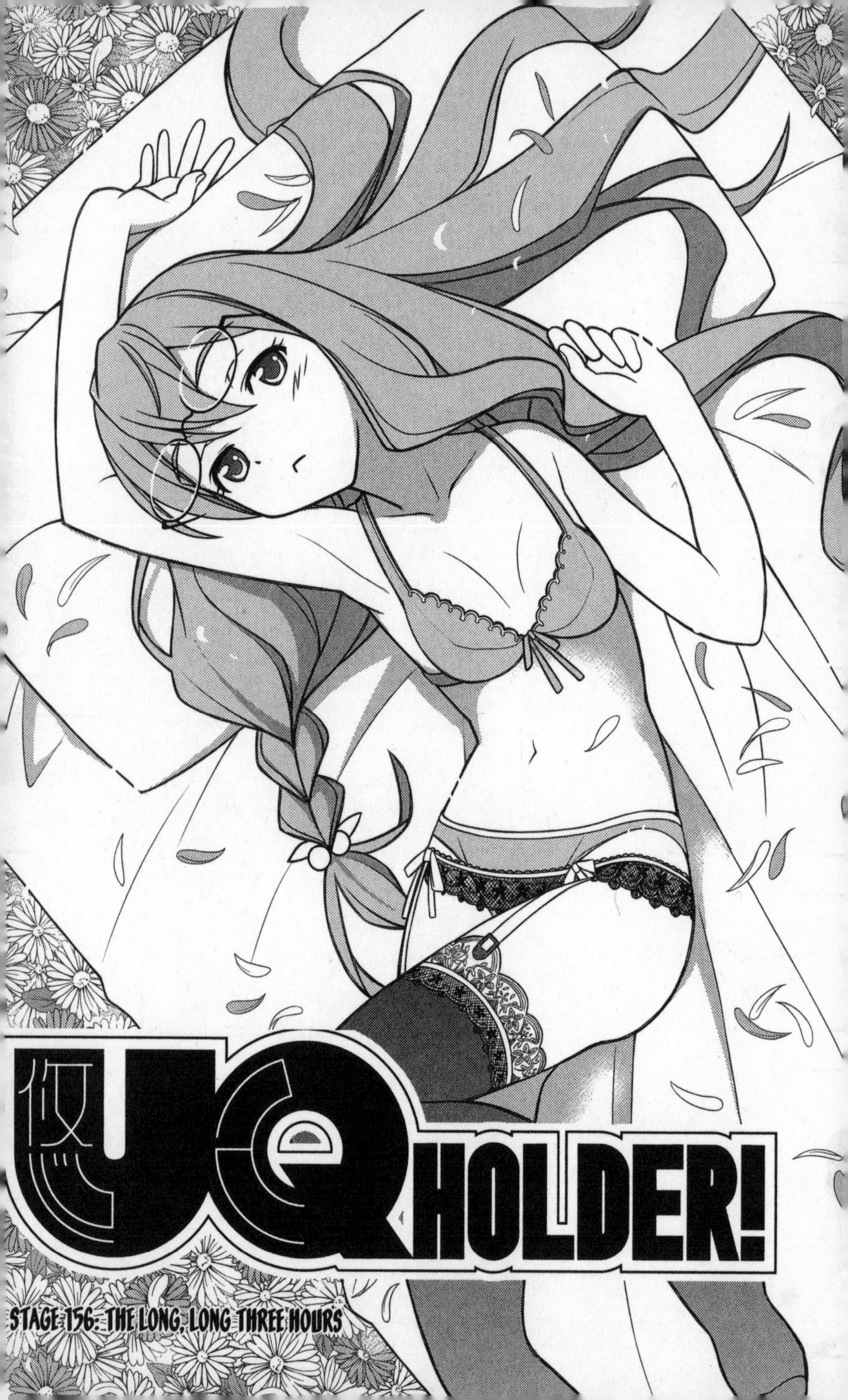

UQ HOLDER!
STAGE 156: THE LONG, LONG THREE HOURS

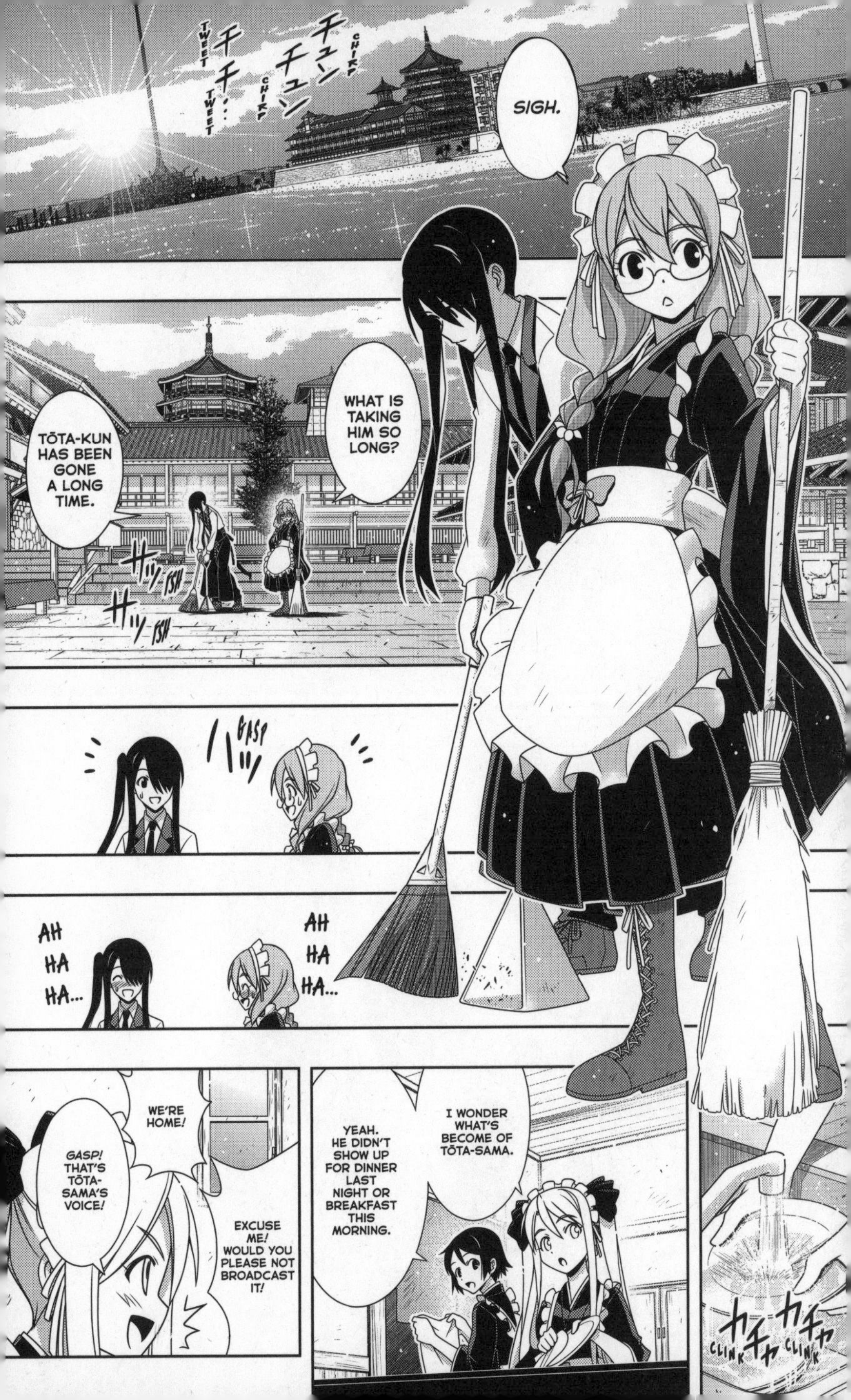
チュンチュン
CHIRP CHIRP
チチ…
TWEET TWEET
SIGH.
WHAT IS TAKING HIM SO LONG?
TŌTA-KUN HAS BEEN GONE A LONG TIME.
ザッ FSH
ザッ FSH
GASP
AH HA HA...
AH HA HA...
カチャ CLINK
カチャ CLINK
I WONDER WHAT'S BECOME OF TŌTA-SAMA.
YEAH. HE DIDN'T SHOW UP FOR DINNER LAST NIGHT OR BREAKFAST THIS MORNING.
WE'RE HOME!
GASP! THAT'S TŌTA-SAMA'S VOICE!
EXCUSE ME! WOULD YOU PLEASE NOT BROADCAST IT!

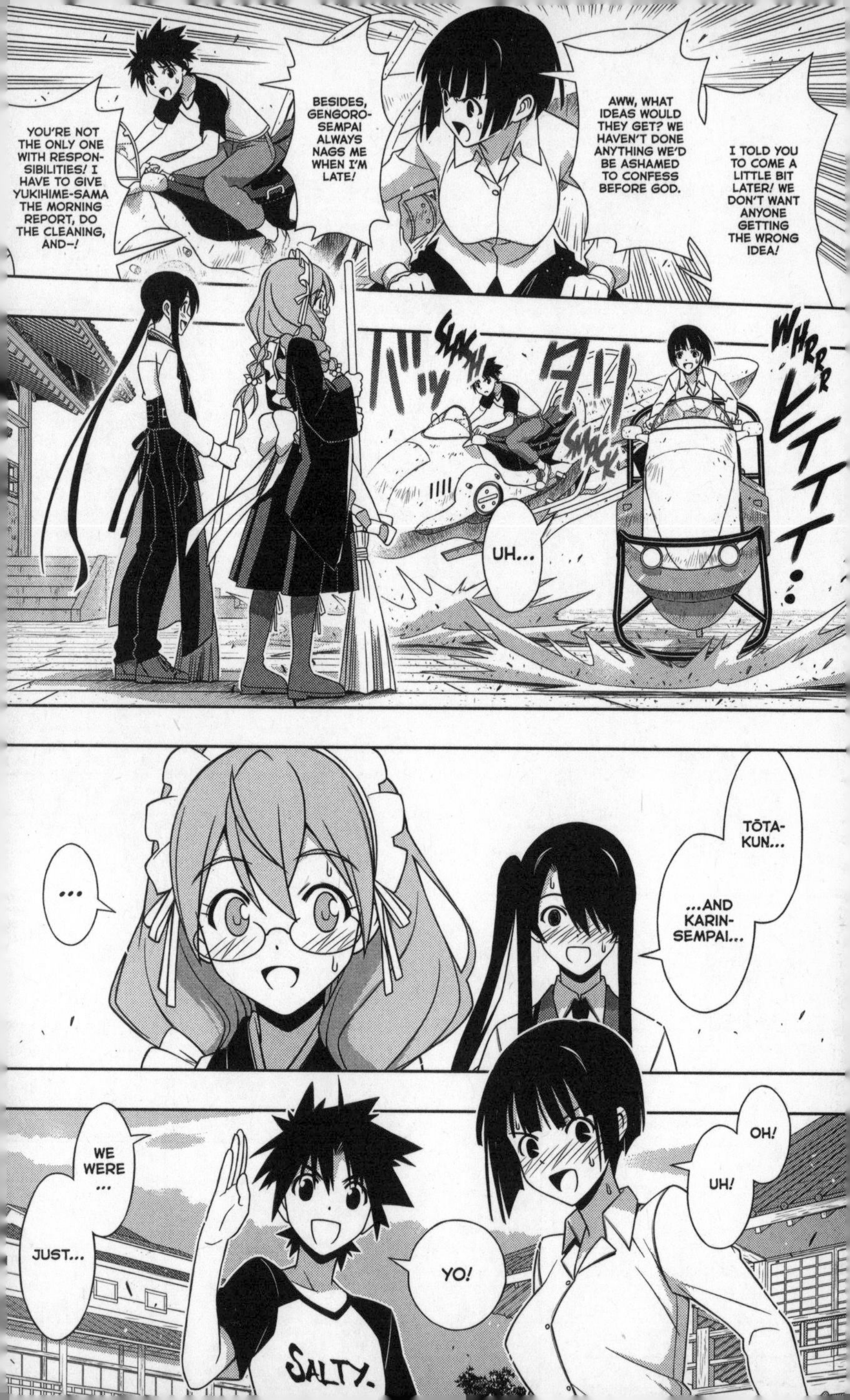
I TOLD YOU TO COME A LITTLE BIT LATER! WE DON'T WANT ANYONE GETTING THE WRONG IDEA!
AWW, WHAT IDEAS WOULD THEY GET? WE HAVEN'T DONE ANYTHING WE'D BE ASHAMED TO CONFESS BEFORE GOD.
BESIDES, GENGORO-SEMPAI ALWAYS NAGS ME WHEN I'M LATE!
YOU'RE NOT THE ONLY ONE WITH RESPON-SIBILITIES! I HAVE TO GIVE YUKIHIME-SAMA THE MORNING REPORT, DO THE CLEANING, AND-!
WHRRR
SMACK
SLASH
UH...
TŌTA-KUN...
...AND KARIN-SEMPAI...
...
OH!
UH!
YO!
WE WERE...
JUST...
SALTY.

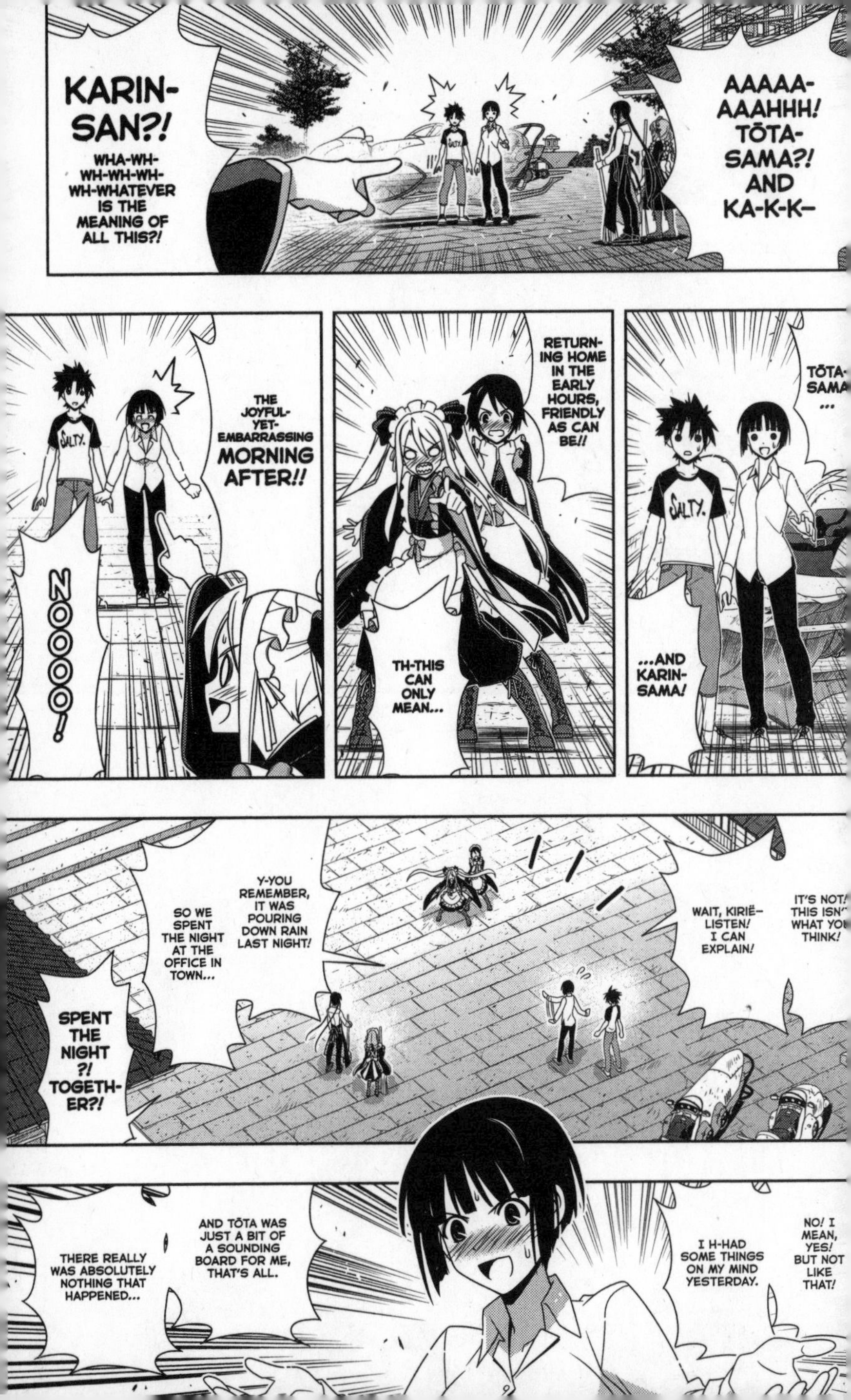
AAAAA-AAAHHH! TŌTA-SAMA?! AND KA-K-K–
KARIN-SAN?!
WHA-WH-WH-WH-WH-WH-WHATEVER IS THE MEANING OF ALL THIS?!
TŌTA-SAMA...
...AND KARIN-SAMA!
RETURNING HOME IN THE EARLY HOURS, FRIENDLY AS CAN BE!!
TH-THIS CAN ONLY MEAN...
THE JOYFUL-YET-EMBARRASSING MORNING AFTER!!
NOOOOO!
IT'S NOT! THIS ISN' WHAT YO THINK!
WAIT, KIRIË– LISTEN! I CAN EXPLAIN!
Y-YOU REMEMBER, IT WAS POURING DOWN RAIN LAST NIGHT!
SO WE SPENT THE NIGHT AT THE OFFICE IN TOWN...
SPENT THE NIGHT?! TOGETHER?!
NO! I MEAN, YES! BUT NOT LIKE THAT!
I H-HAD SOME THINGS ON MY MIND YESTERDAY.
AND TŌTA WAS JUST A BIT OF A SOUNDING BOARD FOR ME, THAT'S ALL.
THERE REALLY WAS ABSOLUTELY NOTHING THAT HAPPENED...

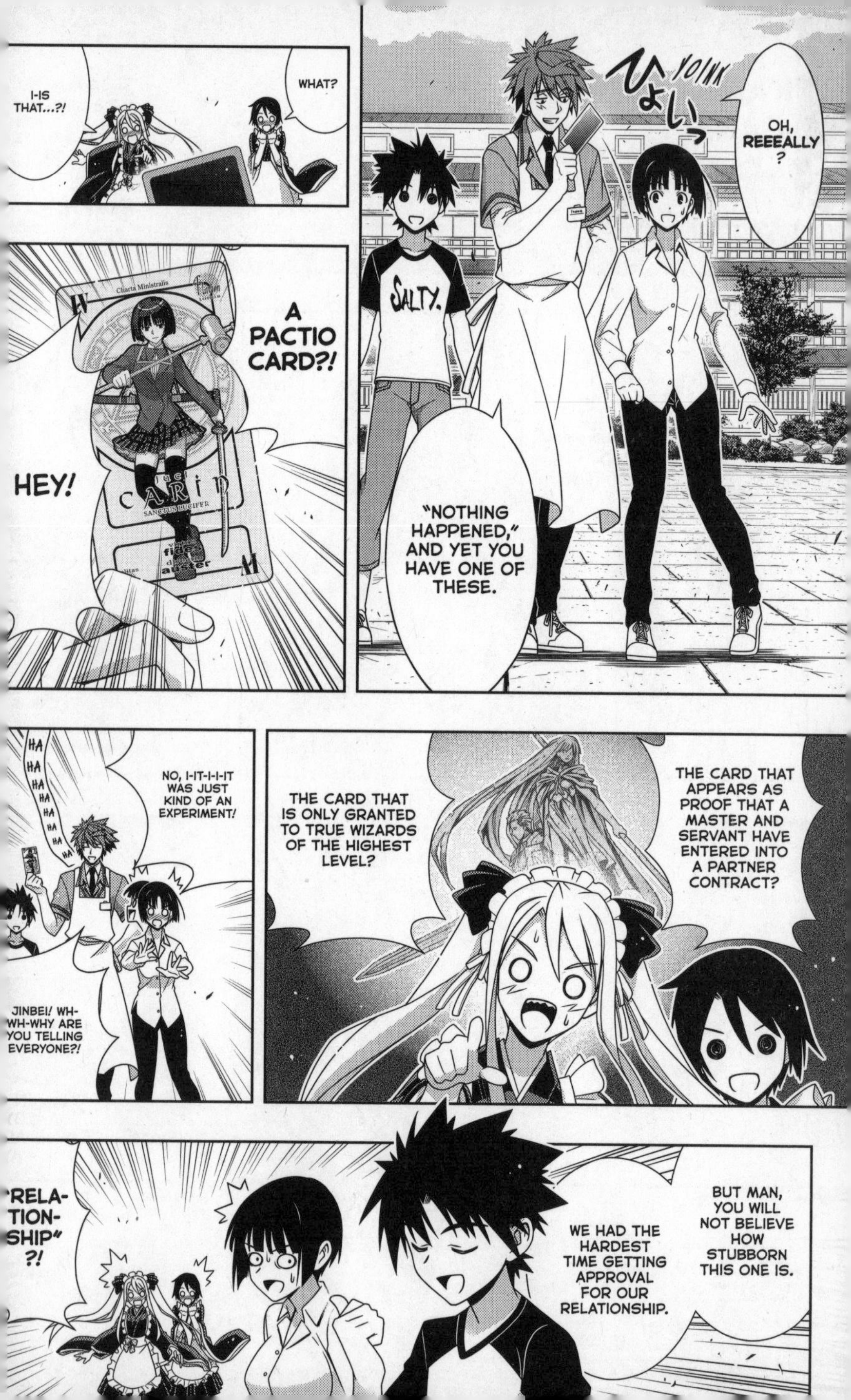
ひょいっ YOINK
OH, REEEALLY?
"NOTHING HAPPENED," AND YET YOU HAVE ONE OF THESE.
WHAT?
I-IS THAT...?!
A PACTIO CARD?!
HEY!
THE CARD THAT APPEARS AS PROOF THAT A MASTER AND SERVANT HAVE ENTERED INTO A PARTNER CONTRACT?
THE CARD THAT IS ONLY GRANTED TO TRUE WIZARDS OF THE HIGHEST LEVEL?
NO, I-IT-I-I-IT WAS JUST KIND OF AN EXPERIMENT!
HA HA HA HA HA HA HA HA
JINBEI! WH-WH-WHY ARE YOU TELLING EVERYONE?!
BUT MAN, YOU WILL NOT BELIEVE HOW STUBBORN THIS ONE IS.
WE HAD THE HARDEST TIME GETTING APPROVAL FOR OUR RELATIONSHIP.
"RELATIONSHIP"?!

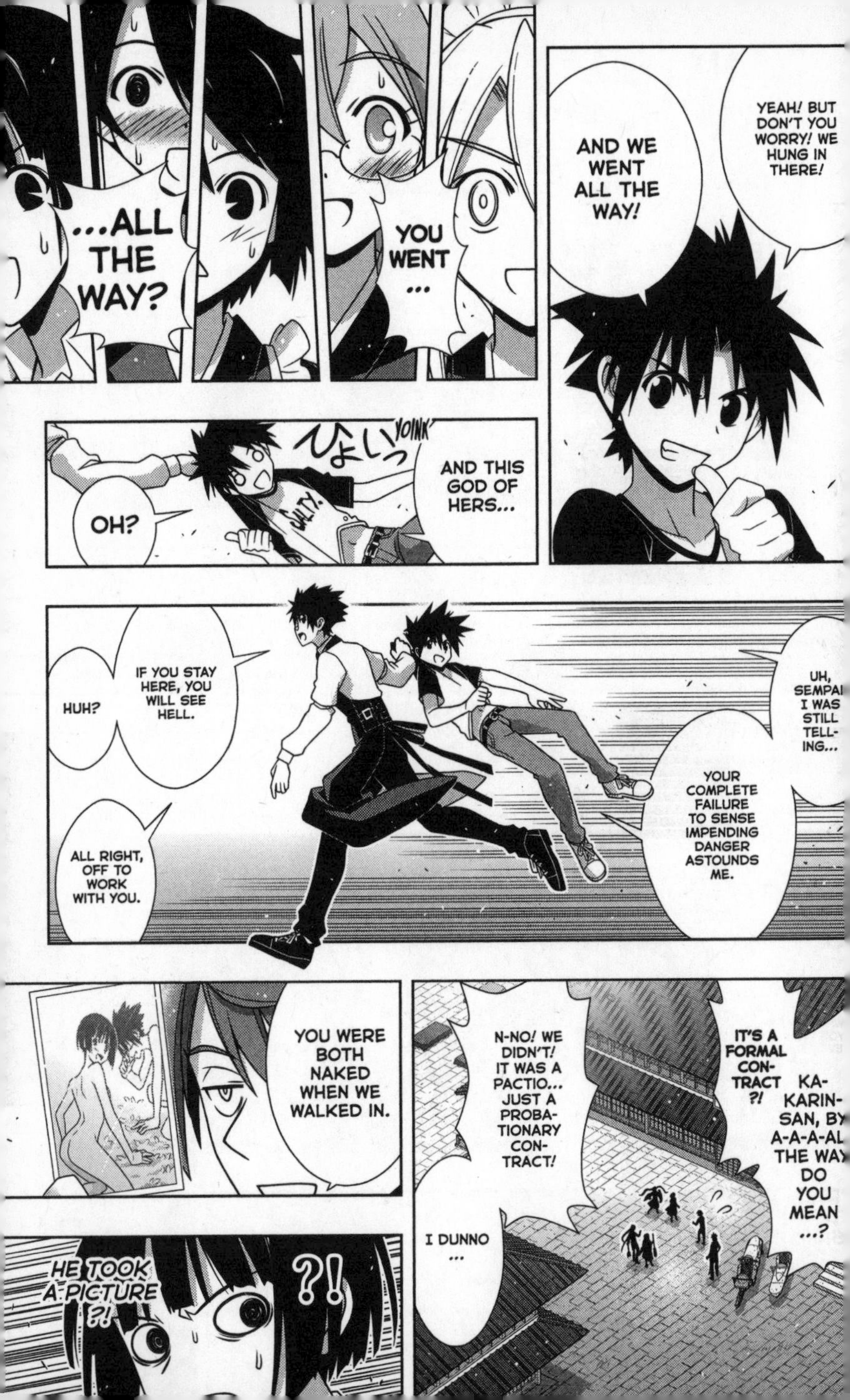
YEAH! BUT DON'T YOU WORRY! WE HUNG IN THERE!
AND WE WENT ALL THE WAY!
YOU WENT ...
...ALL THE WAY?
AND THIS GOD OF HERS...
ひょいっ YOINK
OH?
UH, SEMPAI I WAS STILL TELLING...
YOUR COMPLETE FAILURE TO SENSE IMPENDING DANGER ASTOUNDS ME.
IF YOU STAY HERE, YOU WILL SEE HELL.
HUH?
ALL RIGHT, OFF TO WORK WITH YOU.
KA-KARIN-SAN, BY A-A-A-AL THE WAY DO YOU MEAN ...?
IT'S A FORMAL CONTRACT ?!
N-NO! WE DIDN'T! IT WAS A PACTIO... JUST A PROBATIONARY CONTRACT!
I DUNNO ...
YOU WERE BOTH NAKED WHEN WE WALKED IN.
?!
HE TOOK A PICTURE ?!

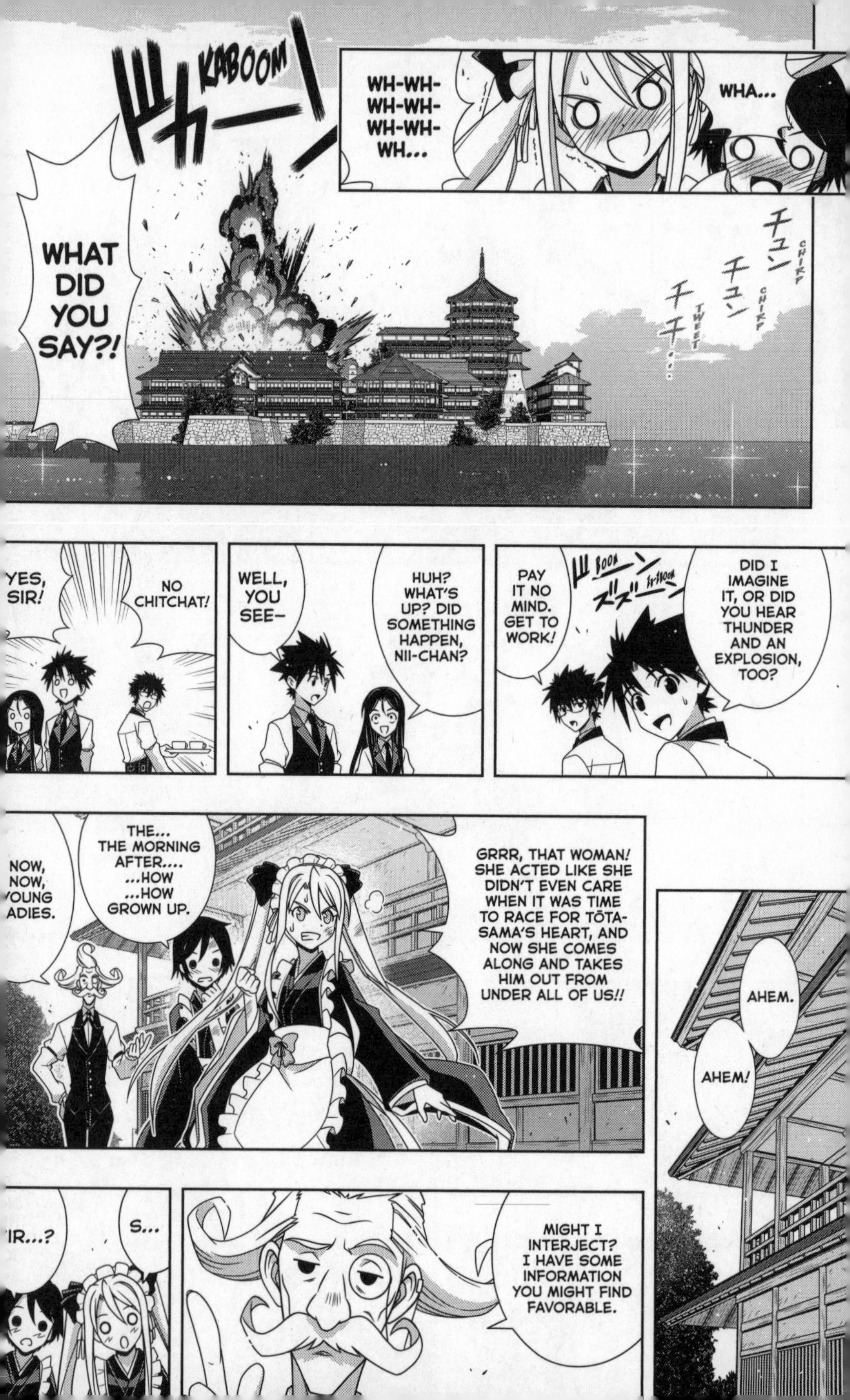
WHA...
WH-WH-
WH-WH-
WH-WH-
WH...
KABOOM
WHAT DID YOU SAY?!
CHIRP
CHIRP
TWEET
DID I IMAGINE IT, OR DID YOU HEAR THUNDER AND AN EXPLOSION, TOO?
BOOM
FWOOM
PAY IT NO MIND. GET TO WORK!
HUH? WHAT'S UP? DID SOMETHING HAPPEN, NII-CHAN?
WELL, YOU SEE—
NO CHITCHAT!
YES, SIR!
AHEM.
AHEM!
GRRR, THAT WOMAN! SHE ACTED LIKE SHE DIDN'T EVEN CARE WHEN IT WAS TIME TO RACE FOR TŌTA-SAMA'S HEART, AND NOW SHE COMES ALONG AND TAKES HIM OUT FROM UNDER ALL OF US!!
THE... THE MORNING AFTER.... ...HOW ...HOW GROWN UP.
NOW, NOW, YOUNG LADIES.
MIGHT I INTERJECT? I HAVE SOME INFORMATION YOU MIGHT FIND FAVORABLE.
S...
IR...?

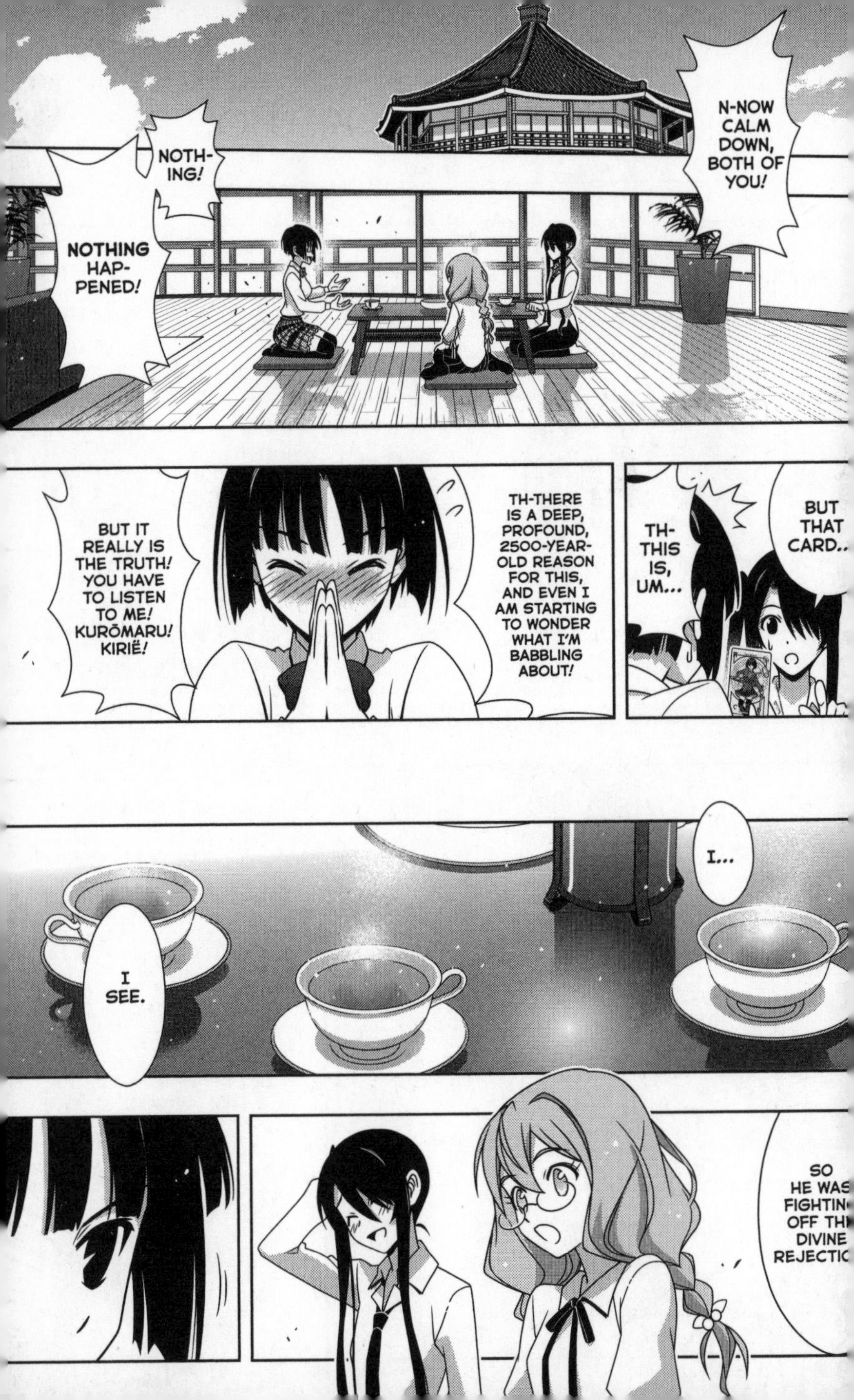
N-NOW CALM DOWN, BOTH OF YOU!
NOTH-ING!
NOTHING HAP-PENED!
BUT THAT CARD..
TH-THIS IS, UM...
TH-THERE IS A DEEP, PROFOUND, 2500-YEAR-OLD REASON FOR THIS, AND EVEN I AM STARTING TO WONDER WHAT I'M BABBLING ABOUT!
BUT IT REALLY IS THE TRUTH! YOU HAVE TO LISTEN TO ME! KURŌMARU! KIRIË!
I...
I SEE.
SO HE WAS FIGHTIN OFF TH DIVINE REJECTIO

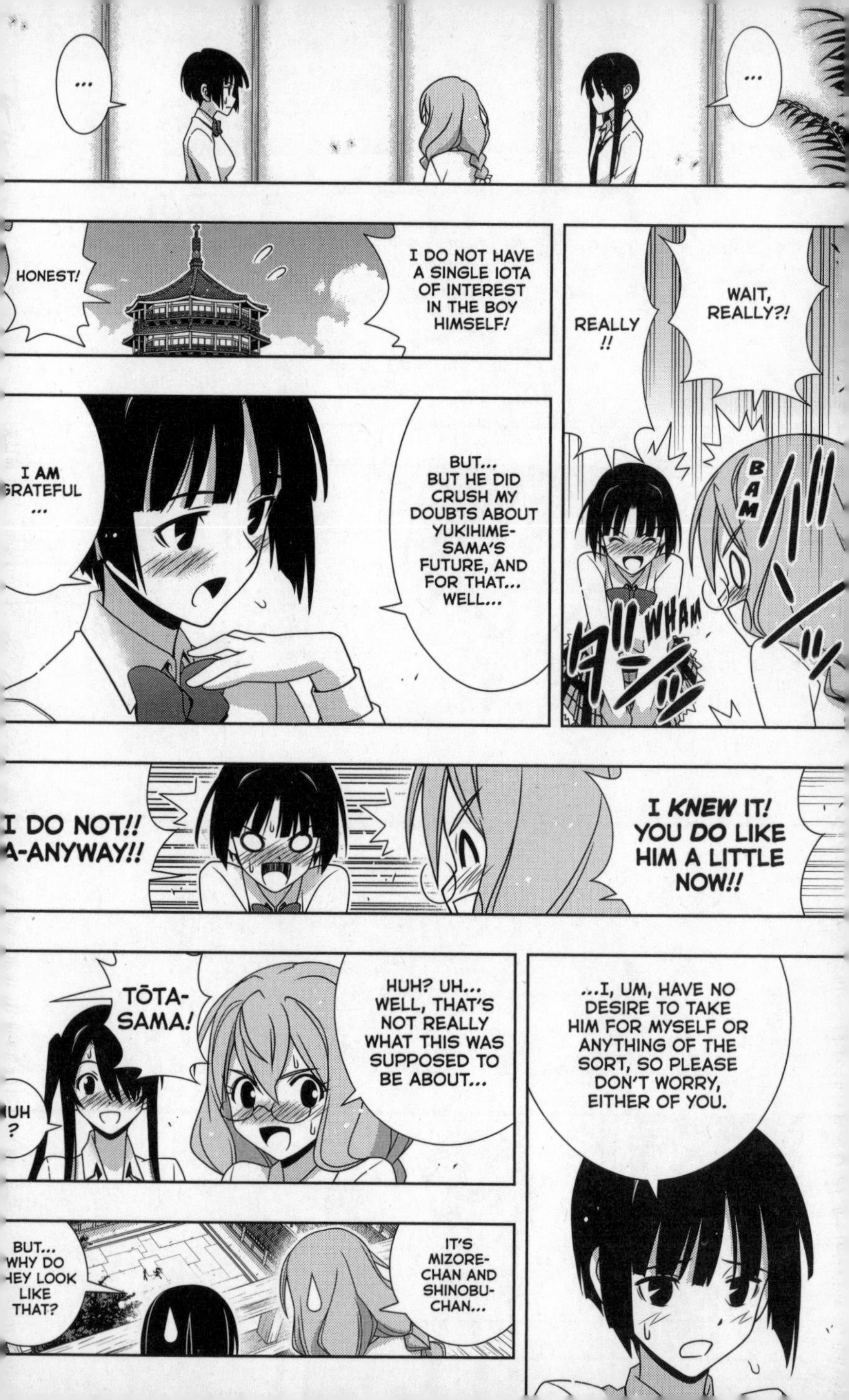
...
...
WAIT, REALLY?!
REALLY!!
BAM
WHAM
I DO NOT HAVE A SINGLE IOTA OF INTEREST IN THE BOY HIMSELF!
HONEST!
BUT... BUT HE DID CRUSH MY DOUBTS ABOUT YUKIHIME-SAMA'S FUTURE, AND FOR THAT... WELL...
I AM GRATEFUL ...
I *KNEW* IT! YOU *DO* LIKE HIM A LITTLE NOW!!
I DO NOT!! A-ANYWAY!!
...I, UM, HAVE NO DESIRE TO TAKE HIM FOR MYSELF OR ANYTHING OF THE SORT, SO PLEASE DON'T WORRY, EITHER OF YOU.
HUH? UH... WELL, THAT'S NOT REALLY WHAT THIS WAS SUPPOSED TO BE ABOUT...
TŌTA-SAMA!
HUH?
IT'S MIZORE-CHAN AND SHINOBU-CHAN...
BUT... WHY DO THEY LOOK LIKE THAT?

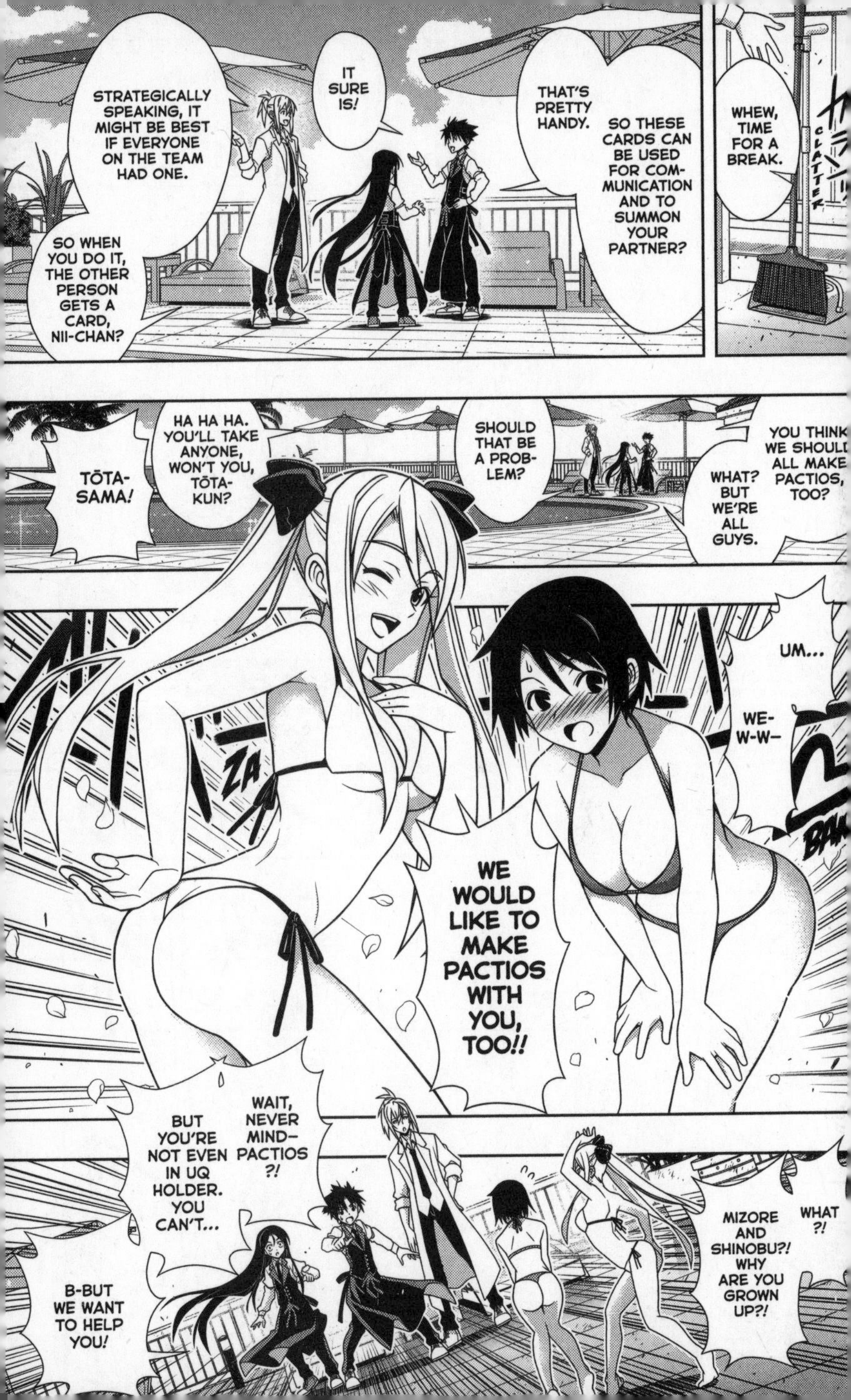
WHEW, TIME FOR A BREAK.
CLATTER
THAT'S PRETTY HANDY.
SO THESE CARDS CAN BE USED FOR COM-MUNICATION AND TO SUMMON YOUR PARTNER?
IT SURE IS!
STRATEGICALLY SPEAKING, IT MIGHT BE BEST IF EVERYONE ON THE TEAM HAD ONE.
SO WHEN YOU DO IT, THE OTHER PERSON GETS A CARD, NII-CHAN?
YOU THINK WE SHOULD ALL MAKE PACTIOS, TOO?
WHAT? BUT WE'RE ALL GUYS.
SHOULD THAT BE A PROB-LEM?
HA HA HA. YOU'LL TAKE ANYONE, WON'T YOU, TŌTA-KUN?
TŌTA-SAMA!
UM...
WE-W-W–
ZA
WE WOULD LIKE TO MAKE PACTIOS WITH YOU, TOO!!
WHAT?!
MIZORE AND SHINOBU?! WHY ARE YOU GROWN UP?!
WAIT, NEVER MIND– PACTIOS?!
BUT YOU'RE NOT EVEN IN UQ HOLDER. YOU CAN'T...
B-BUT WE WANT TO HELP YOU!

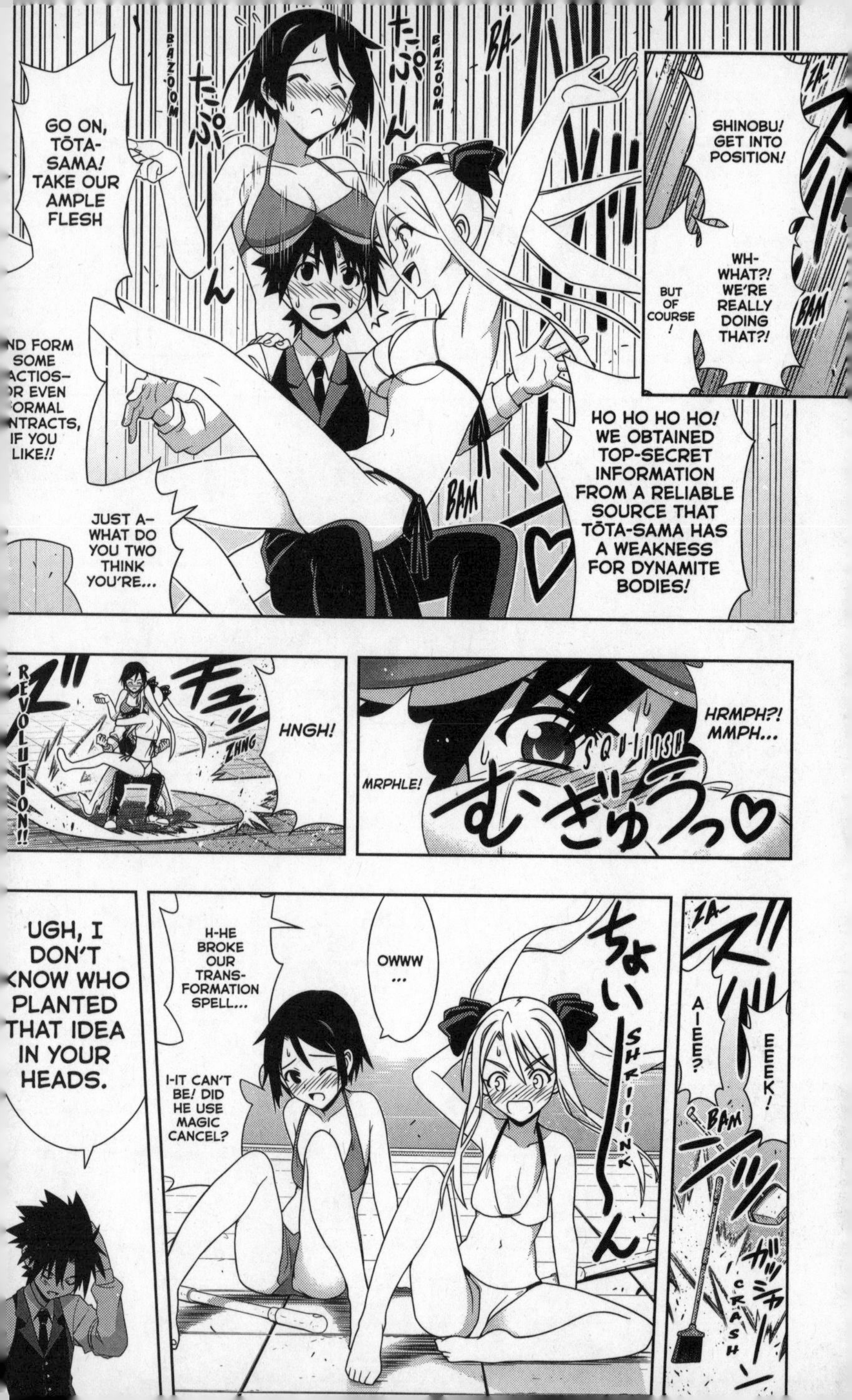
ZA-
SHINOBU! GET INTO POSITION!
WH-WHAT?! WE'RE REALLY DOING THAT?!
BUT OF COURSE!
BAM
BA-
BAZOOM
たぷーん
BAZOOM
たぷーん
GO ON, TŌTA-SAMA! TAKE OUR AMPLE FLESH
ND FORM SOME ACTIOS— OR EVEN ORMAL NTRACTS, IF YOU LIKE!!
HO HO HO HO! WE OBTAINED TOP-SECRET INFORMATION FROM A RELIABLE SOURCE THAT TŌTA-SAMA HAS A WEAKNESS FOR DYNAMITE BODIES!
BAM
JUST A— WHAT DO YOU TWO THINK YOU'RE...
HRMPH?! MMPH...
SQU-IIISH
むぎゅうっ♡
MRPHLE!
HNGH!
ZHNG
REVOLUTION!!
ZA-
EEEK!
AIEE?
BAM
CRASH
ちょいーん
SHRIIIINK
OWWW...
H-HE BROKE OUR TRANS-FORMATION SPELL...
I-IT CAN'T BE! DID HE USE MAGIC CANCEL?
UGH, I DON'T KNOW WHO PLANTED THAT IDEA IN YOUR HEADS.

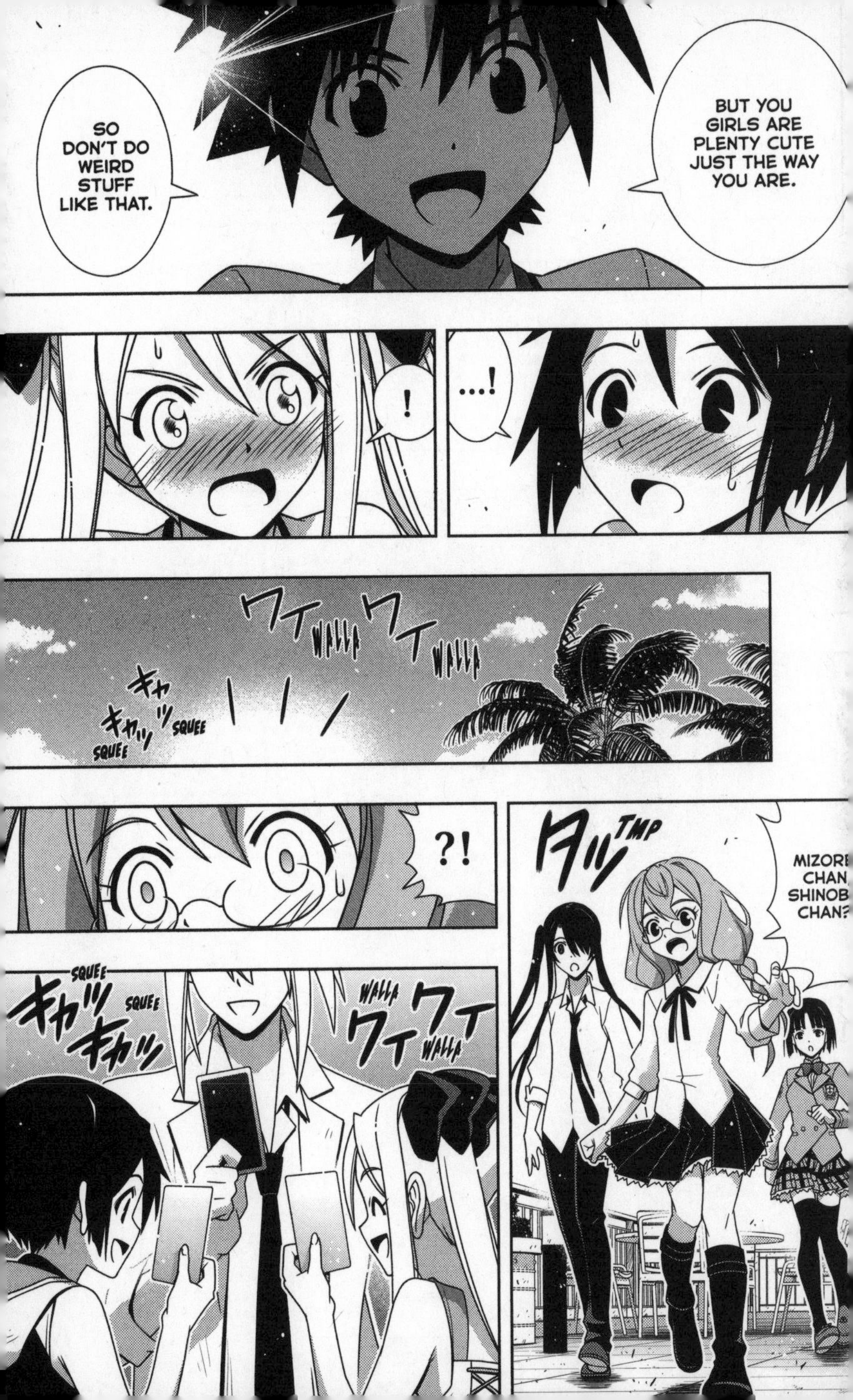
BUT YOU GIRLS ARE PLENTY CUTE JUST THE WAY YOU ARE.
SO DON'T DO WEIRD STUFF LIKE THAT.
...!
!
ワイ WALLA
ワイ WALLA
キャ キャッ SQUEE
SQUEE
タッ TMP
MIZORE CHAN, SHINOB CHAN?
?!
SQUEE
キャッ キャッ
SQUEE
WALLA
ワイワイ
WALLA

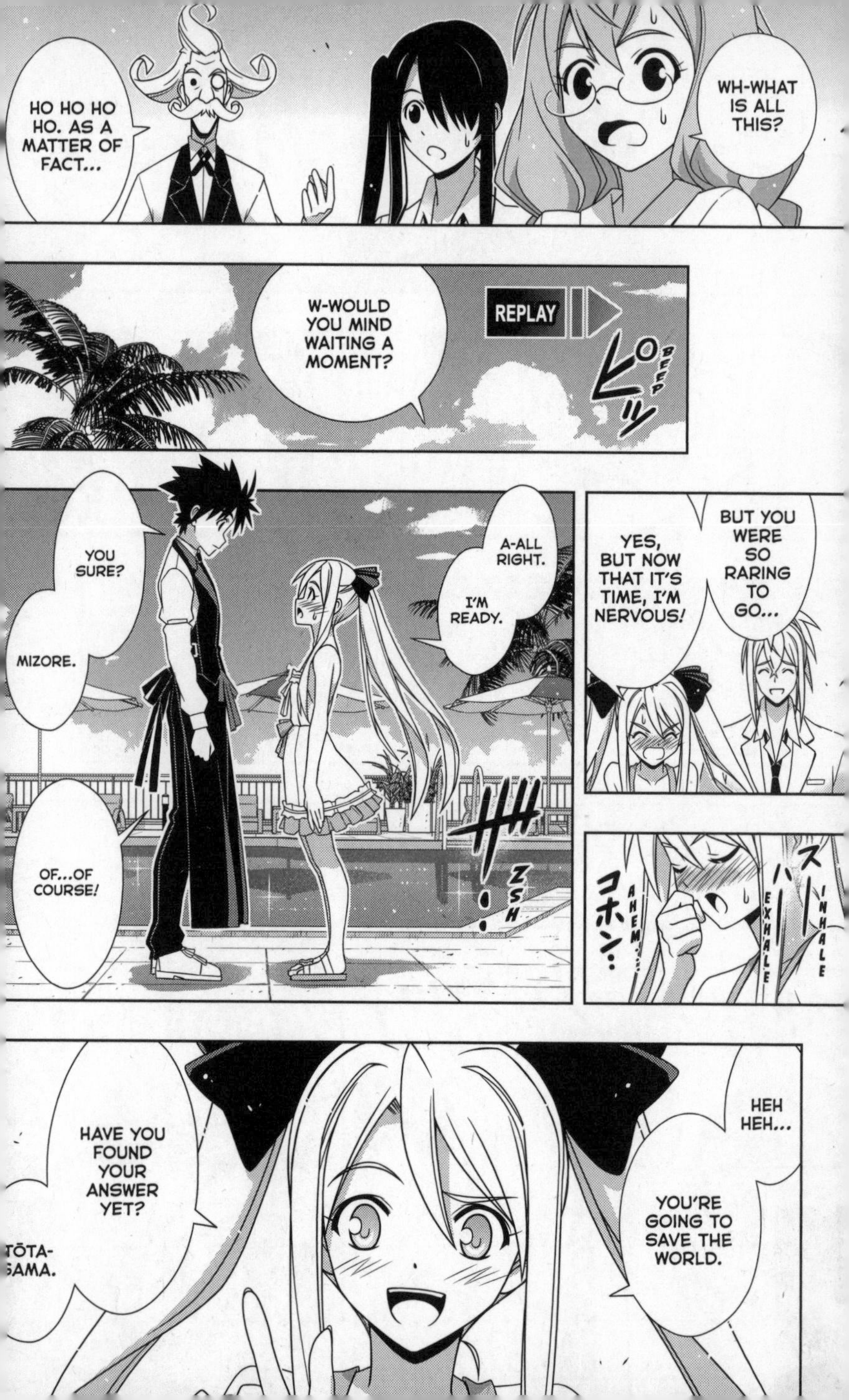
WH-WHAT IS ALL THIS?
HO HO HO. AS A MATTER OF FACT...
ピッ BEEP
REPLAY
W-WOULD YOU MIND WAITING A MOMENT?
BUT YOU WERE SO RARING TO GO...
YES, BUT NOW THAT IT'S TIME, I'M NERVOUS!
スーハー INHALE EXHALE
コホン AHEM...
A-ALL RIGHT.
I'M READY.
ZSH
YOU SURE?
MIZORE.
OF...OF COURSE!
HEH HEH...
YOU'RE GOING TO SAVE THE WORLD.
HAVE YOU FOUND YOUR ANSWER YET?
TŌTA-SAMA.

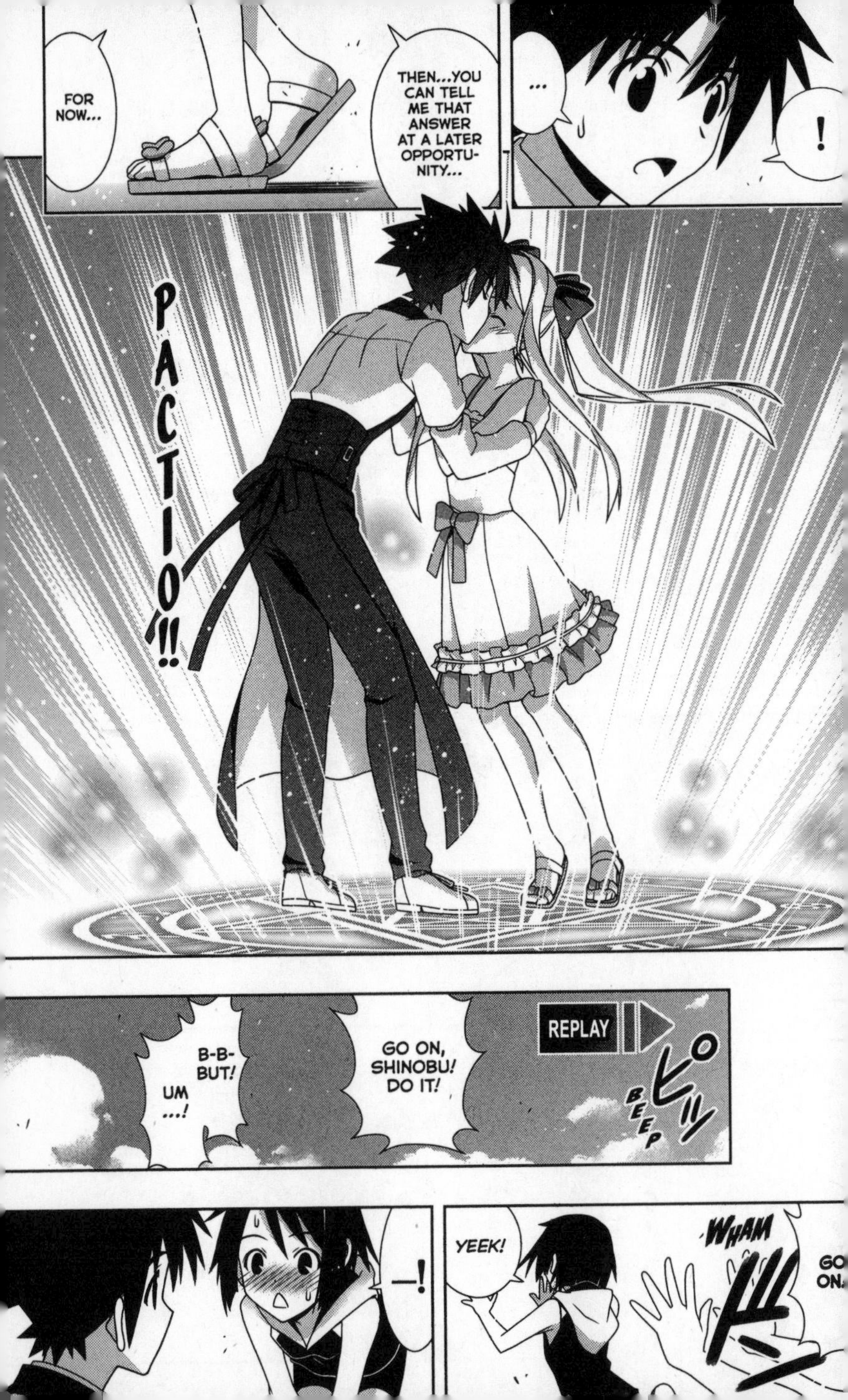
...
!
THEN...YOU CAN TELL ME THAT ANSWER AT A LATER OPPORTUNITY...
FOR NOW...
PACTIO!!
REPLAY
BEEP
GO ON, SHINOBU! DO IT!
B-B-BUT!
UM ...!
GO ON.
WHAM
YEEK!
—!

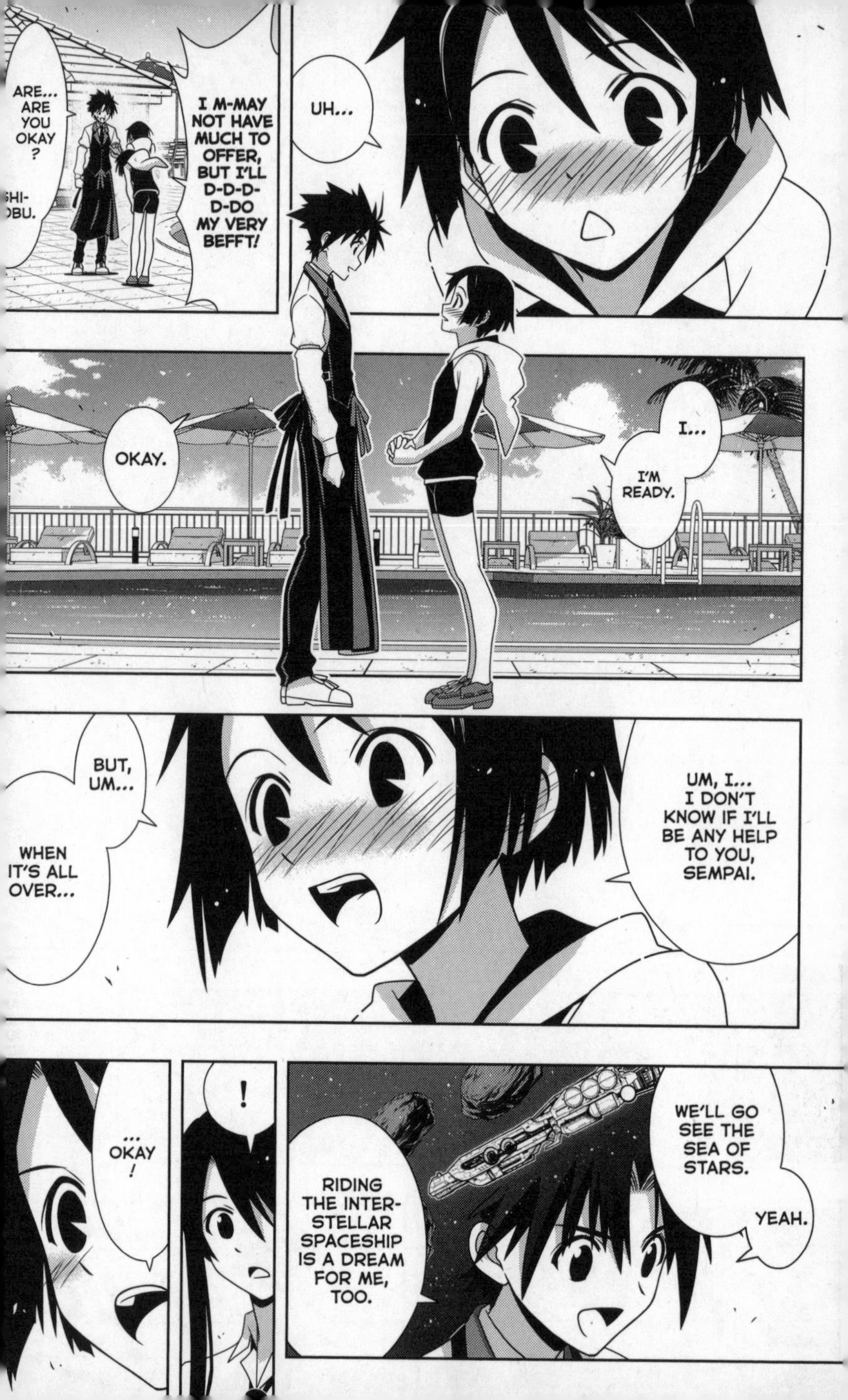
UH...
I M-MAY NOT HAVE MUCH TO OFFER, BUT I'LL D-D-D-D-DO MY VERY BEFFT!
ARE... ARE YOU OKAY?
SHI-OBU.
I...
I'M READY.
OKAY.
UM, I... I DON'T KNOW IF I'LL BE ANY HELP TO YOU, SEMPAI.
BUT, UM...
WHEN IT'S ALL OVER...
WE'LL GO SEE THE SEA OF STARS.
YEAH.
RIDING THE INTER-STELLAR SPACESHIP IS A DREAM FOR ME, TOO.
!
...OKAY!

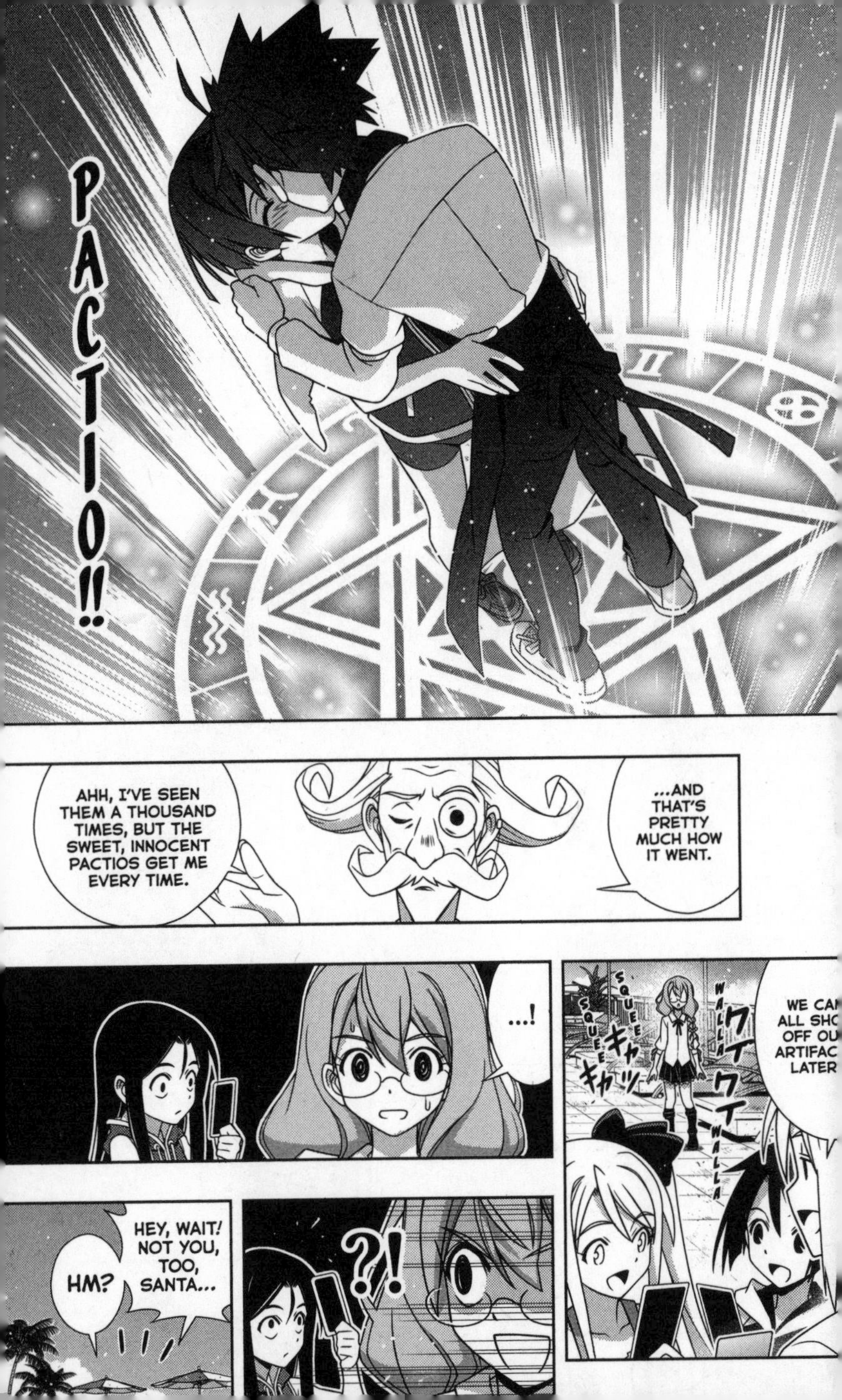
PACTIO!!
...AND THAT'S PRETTY MUCH HOW IT WENT.
AHH, I'VE SEEN THEM A THOUSAND TIMES, BUT THE SWEET, INNOCENT PACTIOS GET ME EVERY TIME.
WE CA
ALL SHO
OFF OU
ARTIFAC
LATER
WALLA ワイ
WALLA ワイ
SQUEE キャッ
SQUEE キャ
...!
?!
HEY, WAIT! NOT YOU, TOO, SANTA...
HM?

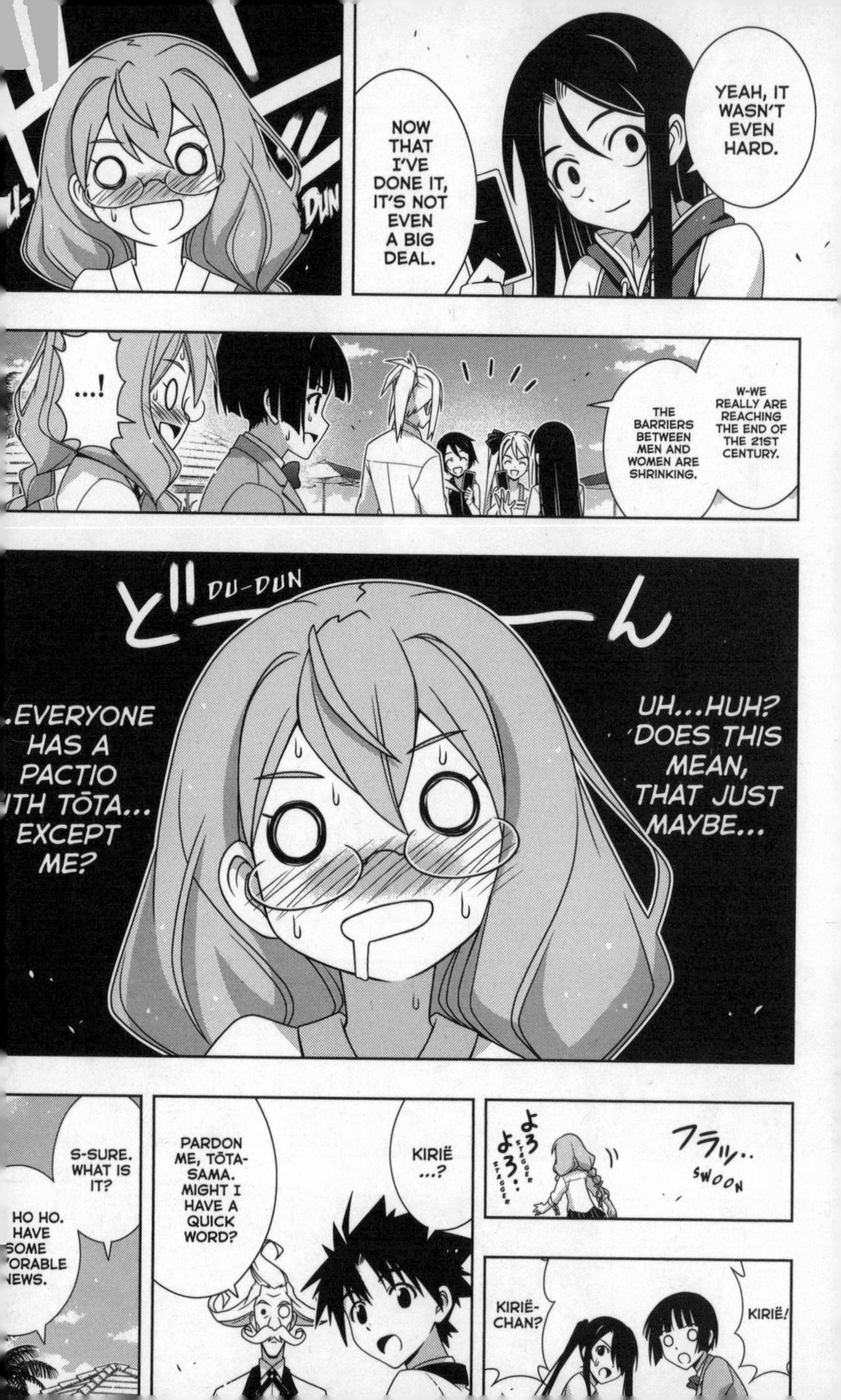
YEAH, IT WASN'T EVEN HARD.
NOW THAT I'VE DONE IT, IT'S NOT EVEN A BIG DEAL.
DUN
W-WE REALLY ARE REACHING THE END OF THE 21ST CENTURY.
THE BARRIERS BETWEEN MEN AND WOMEN ARE SHRINKING.
...!
とーーーん DU-DUN
UH...HUH? DOES THIS MEAN, THAT JUST MAYBE...
.EVERYONE HAS A PACTIO ITH TŌTA... EXCEPT ME?
フラッ.. SWOON
よろよろ.. STAGGER STAGGER
KIRIË!
KIRIË-CHAN?
KIRIË ...?
PARDON ME, TŌTA-SAMA. MIGHT I HAVE A QUICK WORD?
S-SURE. WHAT IS IT?
HO HO. HAVE SOME ORABLE NEWS.

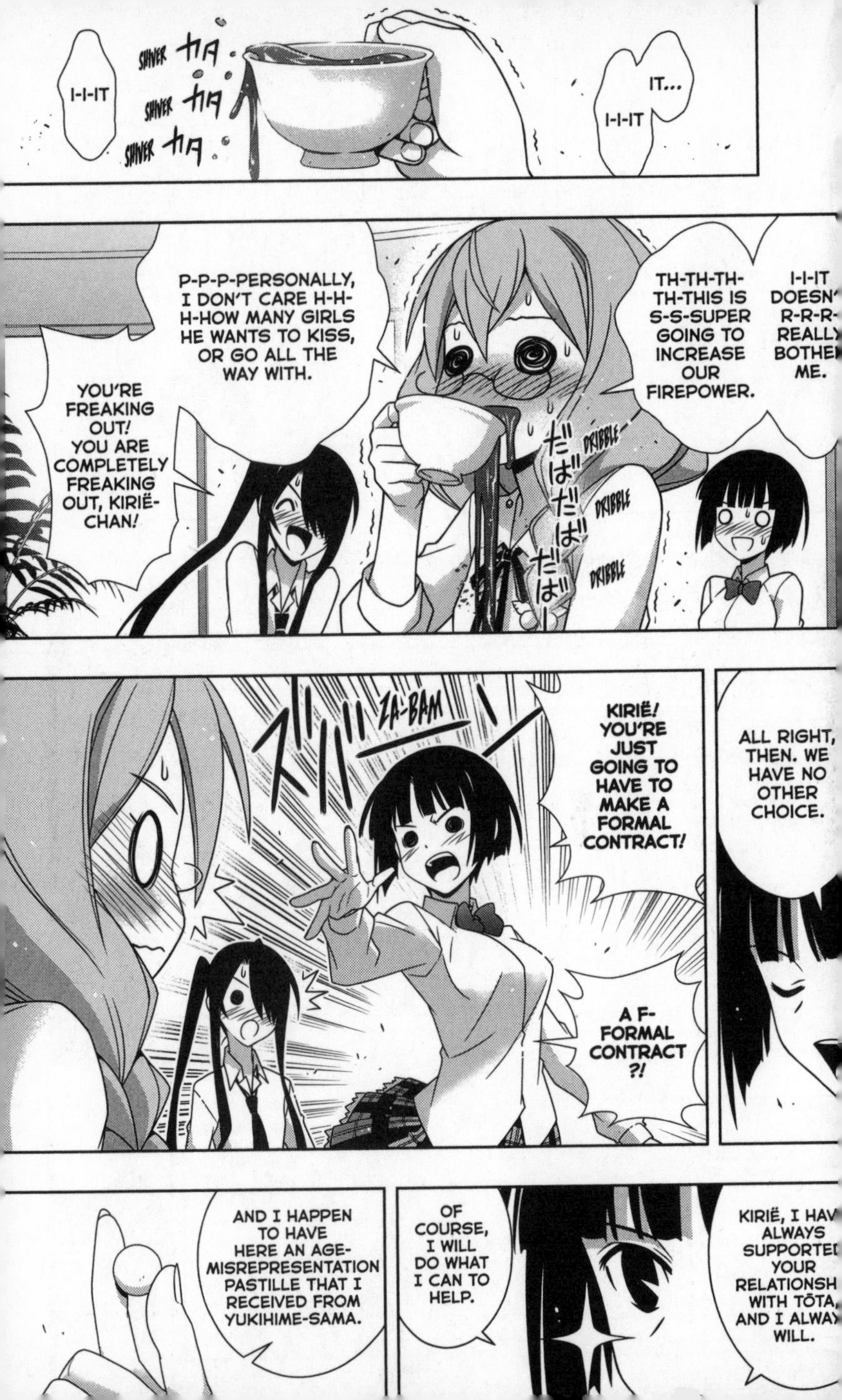

I-I-IT IT...
SHIVER
SHIVER
SHIVER
I-I-IT
I-I-IT DOESN' R-R-R-REALLY BOTHEI ME.
TH-TH-TH-TH-THIS IS S-S-SUPER GOING TO INCREASE OUR FIREPOWER.
DRIBBLE
DRIBBLE
DRIBBLE
P-P-P-PERSONALLY, I DON'T CARE H-H-H-HOW MANY GIRLS HE WANTS TO KISS, OR GO ALL THE WAY WITH.
YOU'RE FREAKING OUT! YOU ARE COMPLETELY FREAKING OUT, KIRIË-CHAN!
ALL RIGHT, THEN. WE HAVE NO OTHER CHOICE.
KIRIË! YOU'RE JUST GOING TO HAVE TO MAKE A FORMAL CONTRACT!
ZA-BAM
A F-FORMAL CONTRACT ?!
KIRIË, I HAV ALWAYS SUPPORTEI YOUR RELATIONSH WITH TŌTA, AND I ALWAY WILL.
OF COURSE, I WILL DO WHAT I CAN TO HELP.
AND I HAPPEN TO HAVE HERE AN AGE-MISREPRESENTATION PASTILLE THAT I RECEIVED FROM YUKIHIME-SAMA.

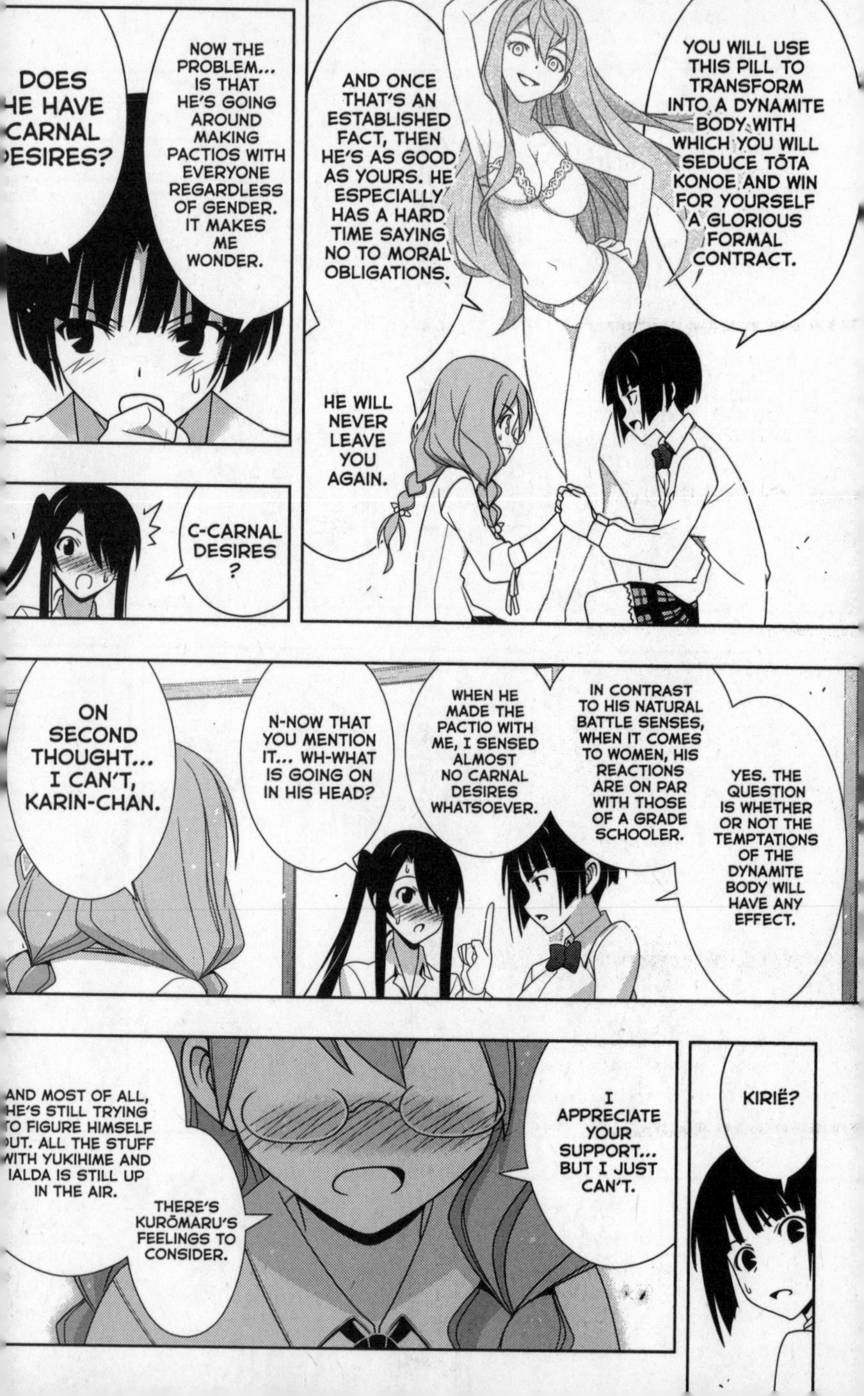
YOU WILL USE THIS PILL TO TRANSFORM INTO A DYNAMITE BODY WITH WHICH YOU WILL SEDUCE TŌTA KONOE AND WIN FOR YOURSELF A GLORIOUS FORMAL CONTRACT.
AND ONCE THAT'S AN ESTABLISHED FACT, THEN HE'S AS GOOD AS YOURS. HE ESPECIALLY HAS A HARD TIME SAYING NO TO MORAL OBLIGATIONS.
HE WILL NEVER LEAVE YOU AGAIN.
NOW THE PROBLEM... IS THAT HE'S GOING AROUND MAKING PACTIOS WITH EVERYONE REGARDLESS OF GENDER. IT MAKES ME WONDER.
DOES HE HAVE CARNAL DESIRES?
C-CARNAL DESIRES ?
YES. THE QUESTION IS WHETHER OR NOT THE TEMPTATIONS OF THE DYNAMITE BODY WILL HAVE ANY EFFECT.
IN CONTRAST TO HIS NATURAL BATTLE SENSES, WHEN IT COMES TO WOMEN, HIS REACTIONS ARE ON PAR WITH THOSE OF A GRADE SCHOOLER.
WHEN HE MADE THE PACTIO WITH ME, I SENSED ALMOST NO CARNAL DESIRES WHATSOEVER.
N-NOW THAT YOU MENTION IT... WH-WHAT IS GOING ON IN HIS HEAD?
ON SECOND THOUGHT... I CAN'T, KARIN-CHAN.
KIRIË?
I APPRECIATE YOUR SUPPORT... BUT I JUST CAN'T.
THERE'S KURŌMARU'S FEELINGS TO CONSIDER.
AND MOST OF ALL, HE'S STILL TRYING TO FIGURE HIMSELF OUT. ALL THE STUFF WITH YUKIHIME AND IALDA IS STILL UP IN THE AIR.

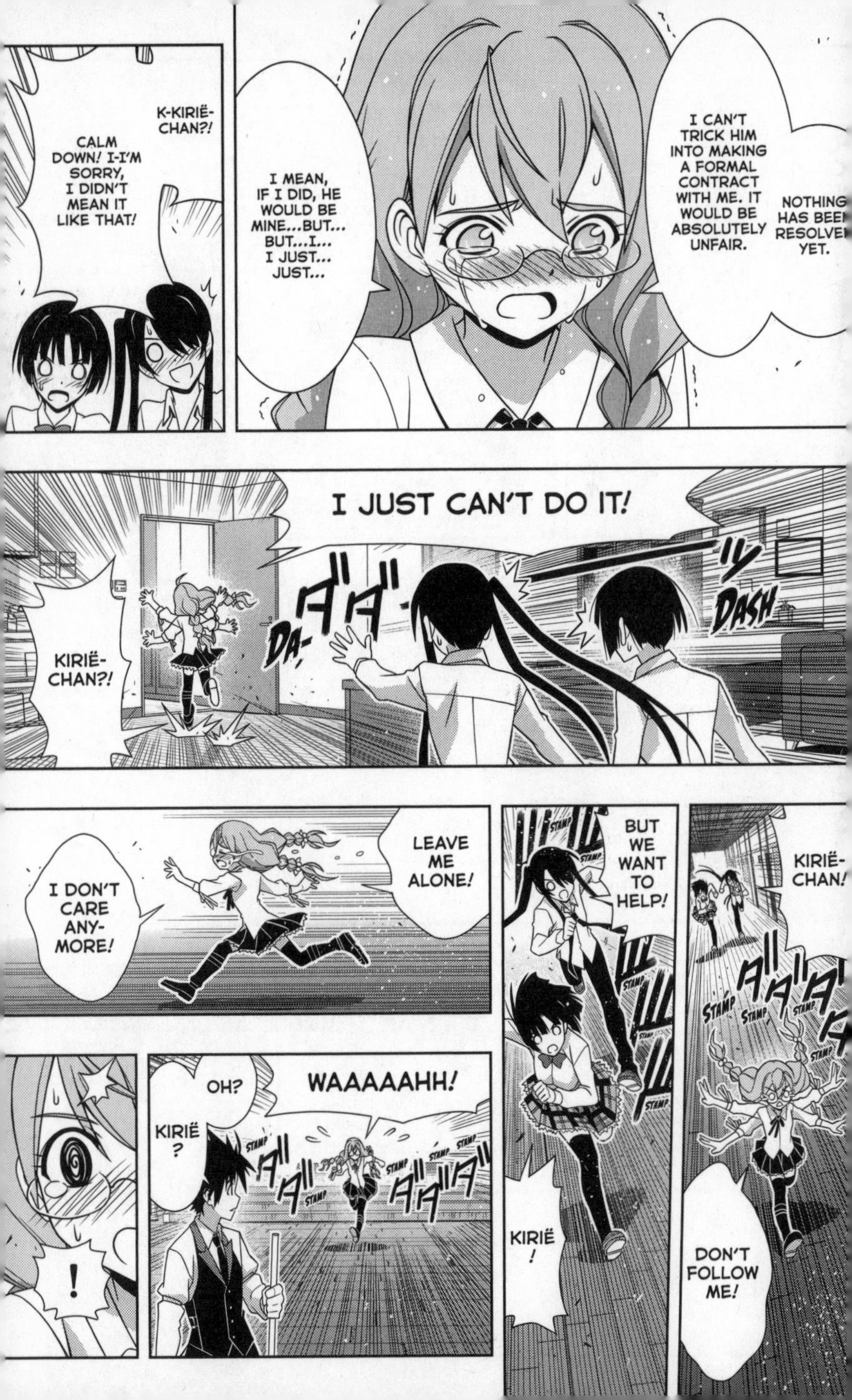
I CAN'T TRICK HIM INTO MAKING A FORMAL CONTRACT WITH ME. IT WOULD BE ABSOLUTELY UNFAIR.
NOTHING HAS BEE RESOLVE YET.
I MEAN, IF I DID, HE WOULD BE MINE...BUT... BUT...I... I JUST... JUST...
K-KIRIË-CHAN?!
CALM DOWN! I-I'M SORRY, I DIDN'T MEAN IT LIKE THAT!
I JUST CAN'T DO IT!
DASH
DA-
KIRIË-CHAN?!
KIRIË-CHAN!
STAMP STAMP STAMP STAMP
DON'T FOLLOW ME!
BUT WE WANT TO HELP!
STAMP STAMP STAMP STAMP STAMP
KIRIË!
LEAVE ME ALONE!
I DON'T CARE ANYMORE!
WAAAAAHH!
STAMP STAMP STAMP STAMP STAMP
OH?
KIRIË?
!

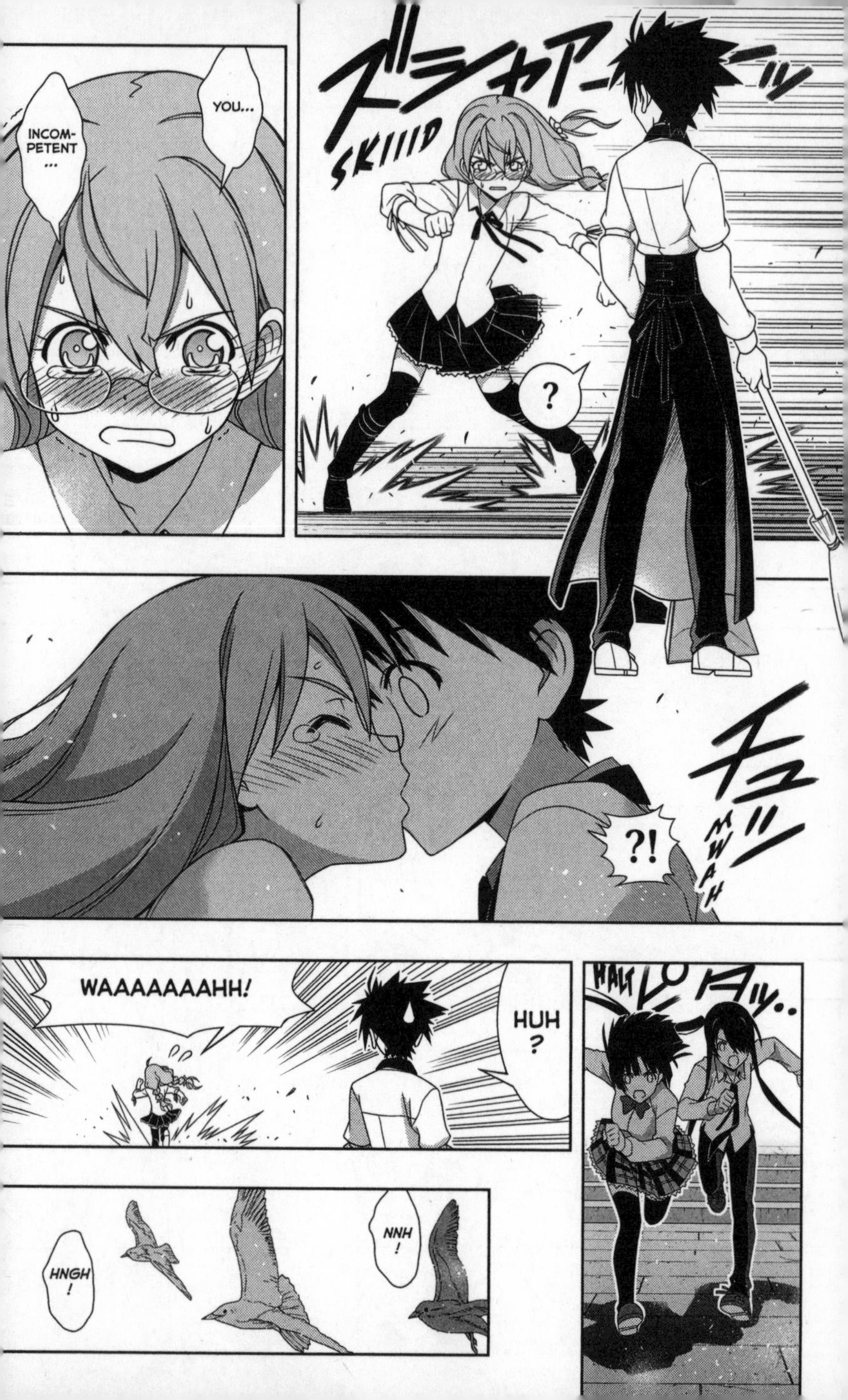
SKIIID
?
YOU...
INCOM-PETENT ...
?!
MWAH
HALT
HUH ?
WAAAAAAAHH!
NNH !
HNGH !

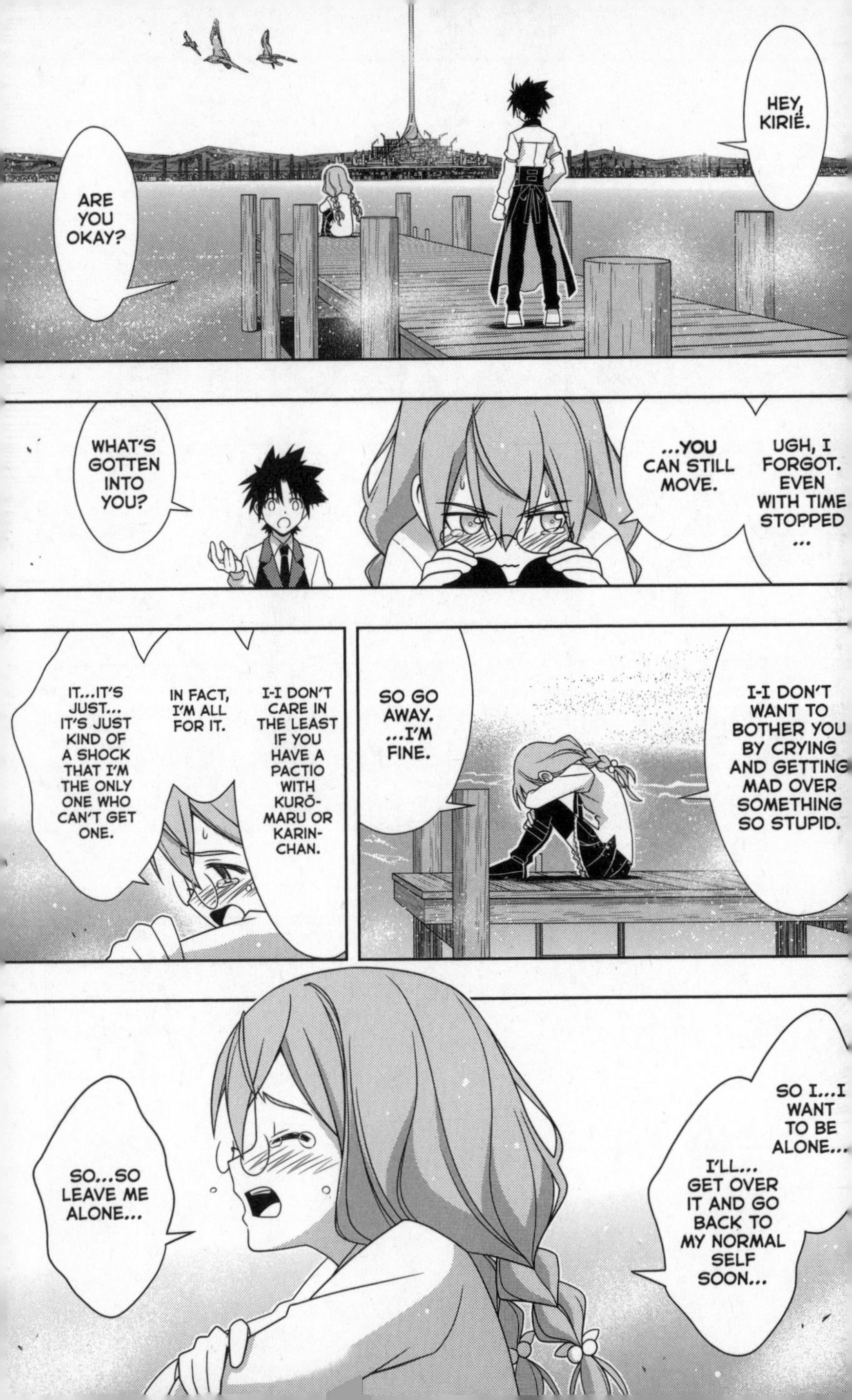
HEY, KIRIË.
ARE YOU OKAY?
UGH, I FORGOT. EVEN WITH TIME STOPPED...
...YOU CAN STILL MOVE.
WHAT'S GOTTEN INTO YOU?
I-I DON'T WANT TO BOTHER YOU BY CRYING AND GETTING MAD OVER SOMETHING SO STUPID.
SO GO AWAY. ...I'M FINE.
I-I DON'T CARE IN THE LEAST IF YOU HAVE A PACTIO WITH KURŌ-MARU OR KARIN-CHAN.
IN FACT, I'M ALL FOR IT.
IT...IT'S JUST... IT'S JUST KIND OF A SHOCK THAT I'M THE ONLY ONE WHO CAN'T GET ONE.
SO I...I WANT TO BE ALONE...
I'LL... GET OVER IT AND GO BACK TO MY NORMAL SELF SOON...
SO...SO LEAVE ME ALONE...

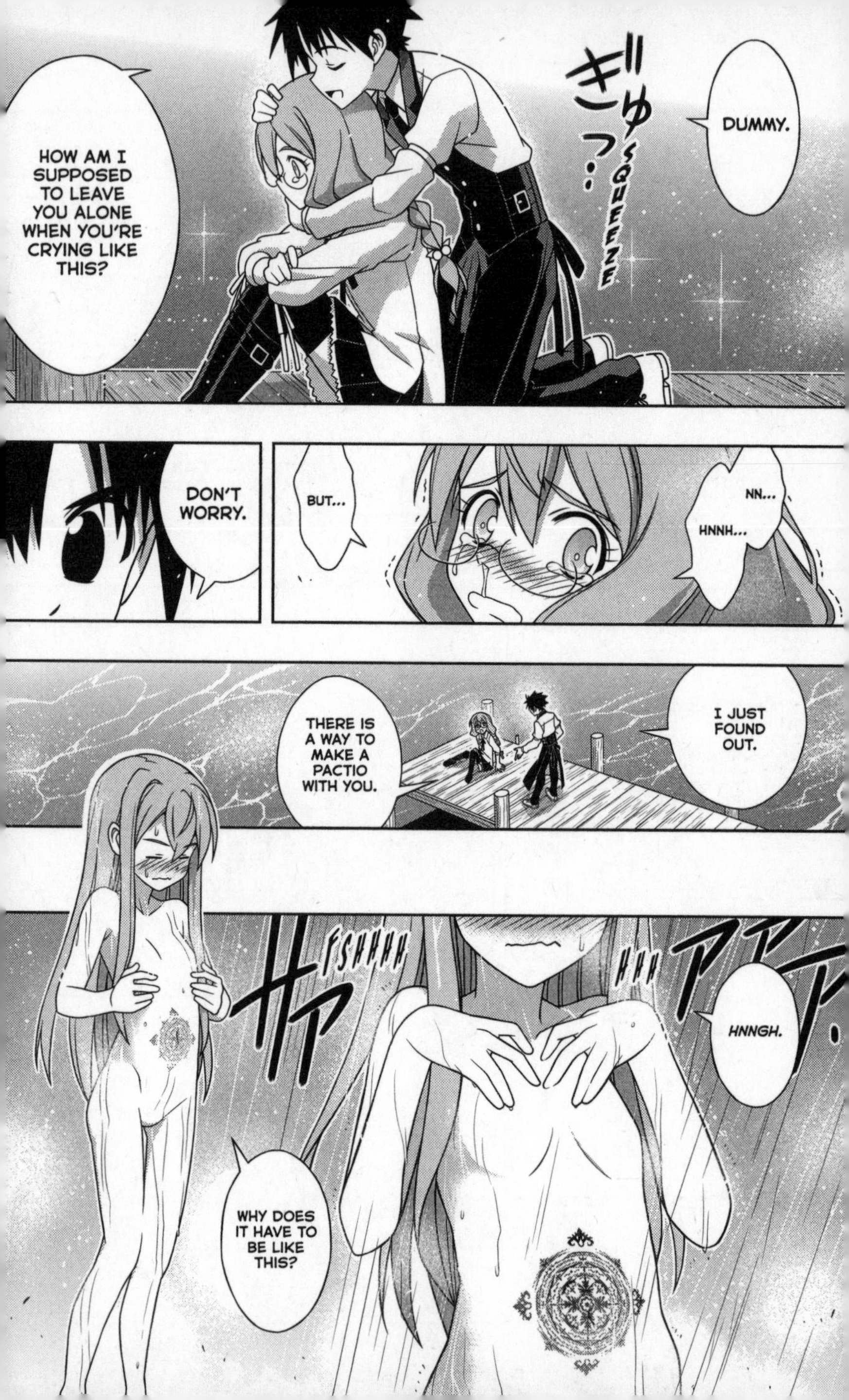
DUMMY.
ぎゅっ
SQUEEZE
HOW AM I SUPPOSED TO LEAVE YOU ALONE WHEN YOU'RE CRYING LIKE THIS?
NN... HNNH...
BUT...
DON'T WORRY.
I JUST FOUND OUT.
THERE IS A WAY TO MAKE A PACTIO WITH YOU.
HHH
HNNGH.
FSHHHH
WHY DOES IT HAVE TO BE LIKE THIS?

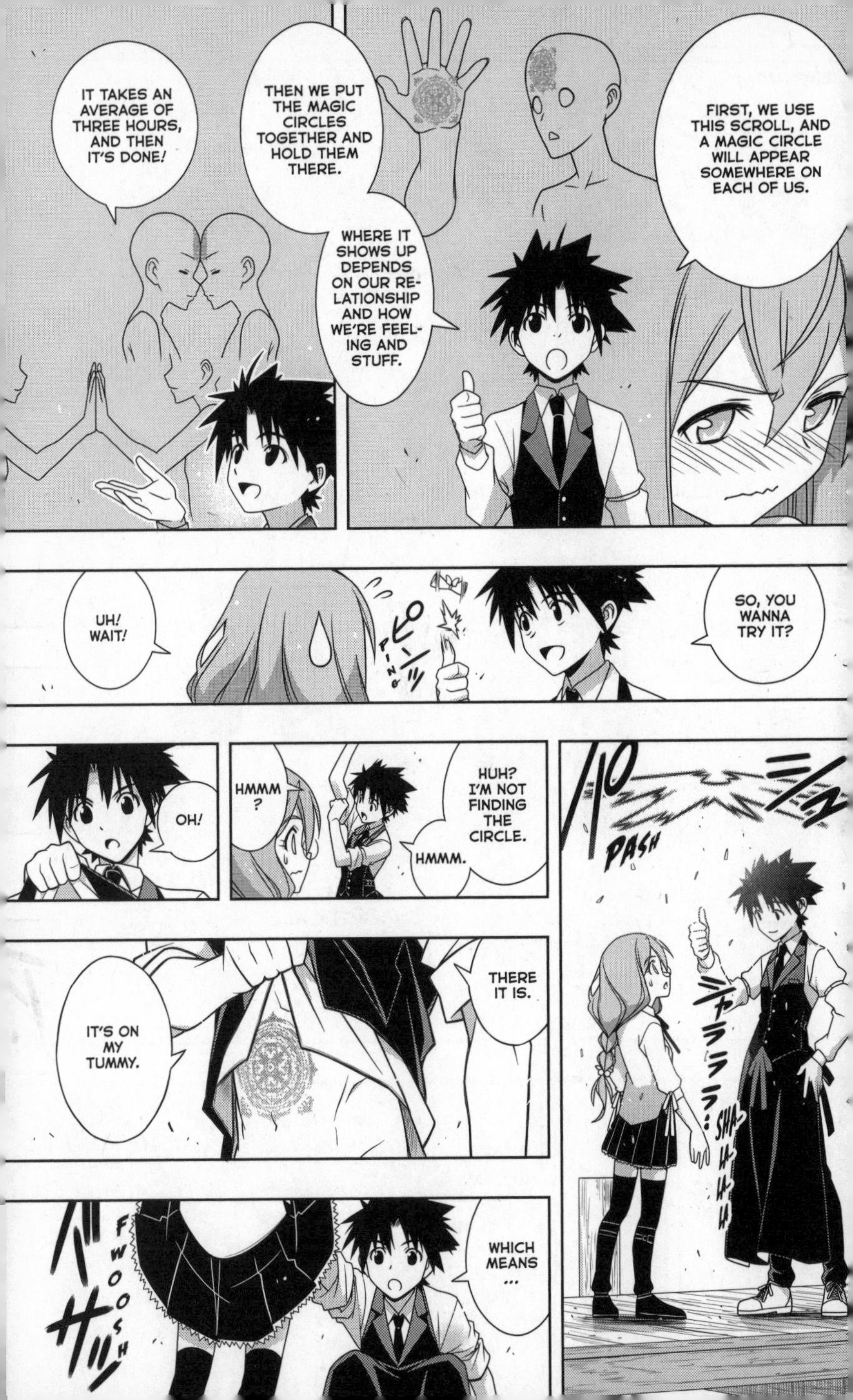
FIRST, WE USE THIS SCROLL, AND A MAGIC CIRCLE WILL APPEAR SOMEWHERE ON EACH OF US.
WHERE IT SHOWS UP DEPENDS ON OUR RE-LATIONSHIP AND HOW WE'RE FEEL-ING AND STUFF.
THEN WE PUT THE MAGIC CIRCLES TOGETHER AND HOLD THEM THERE.
IT TAKES AN AVERAGE OF THREE HOURS, AND THEN IT'S DONE!
SO, YOU WANNA TRY IT?
PING
UH! WAIT!
PASH
SHA LA LA LA LA
HUH? I'M NOT FINDING THE CIRCLE.
HMMM.
HMMM ?
OH!
THERE IT IS.
IT'S ON MY TUMMY.
WHICH MEANS ...
FWOOSH

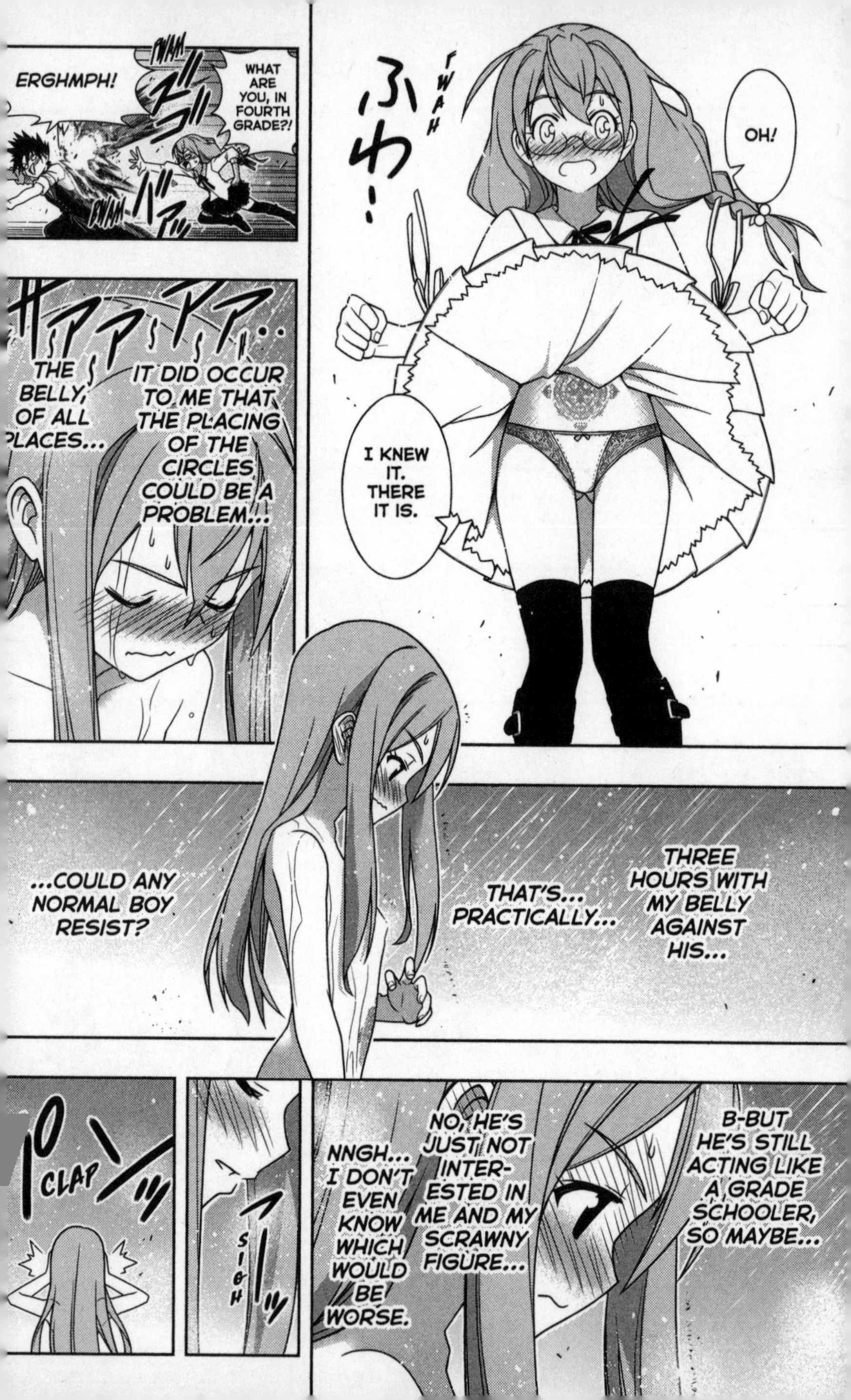
ふわ…
FWAH
OH!
I KNEW IT. THERE IT IS.
WHAT ARE YOU, IN FOURTH GRADE?!
PWAM
ERGHMPH!
BWAM
IT DID OCCUR TO ME THAT THE PLACING OF THE CIRCLES COULD BE A PROBLEM...
THE BELLY, OF ALL PLACES...
THREE HOURS WITH MY BELLY AGAINST HIS...
THAT'S... PRACTICALLY...
...COULD ANY NORMAL BOY RESIST?
B-BUT HE'S STILL ACTING LIKE A GRADE SCHOOLER, SO MAYBE...
NO, HE'S JUST NOT INTER-ESTED IN ME AND MY SCRAWNY FIGURE...
NNGH... I DON'T EVEN KNOW WHICH WOULD BE WORSE.
SIGH
CLAP

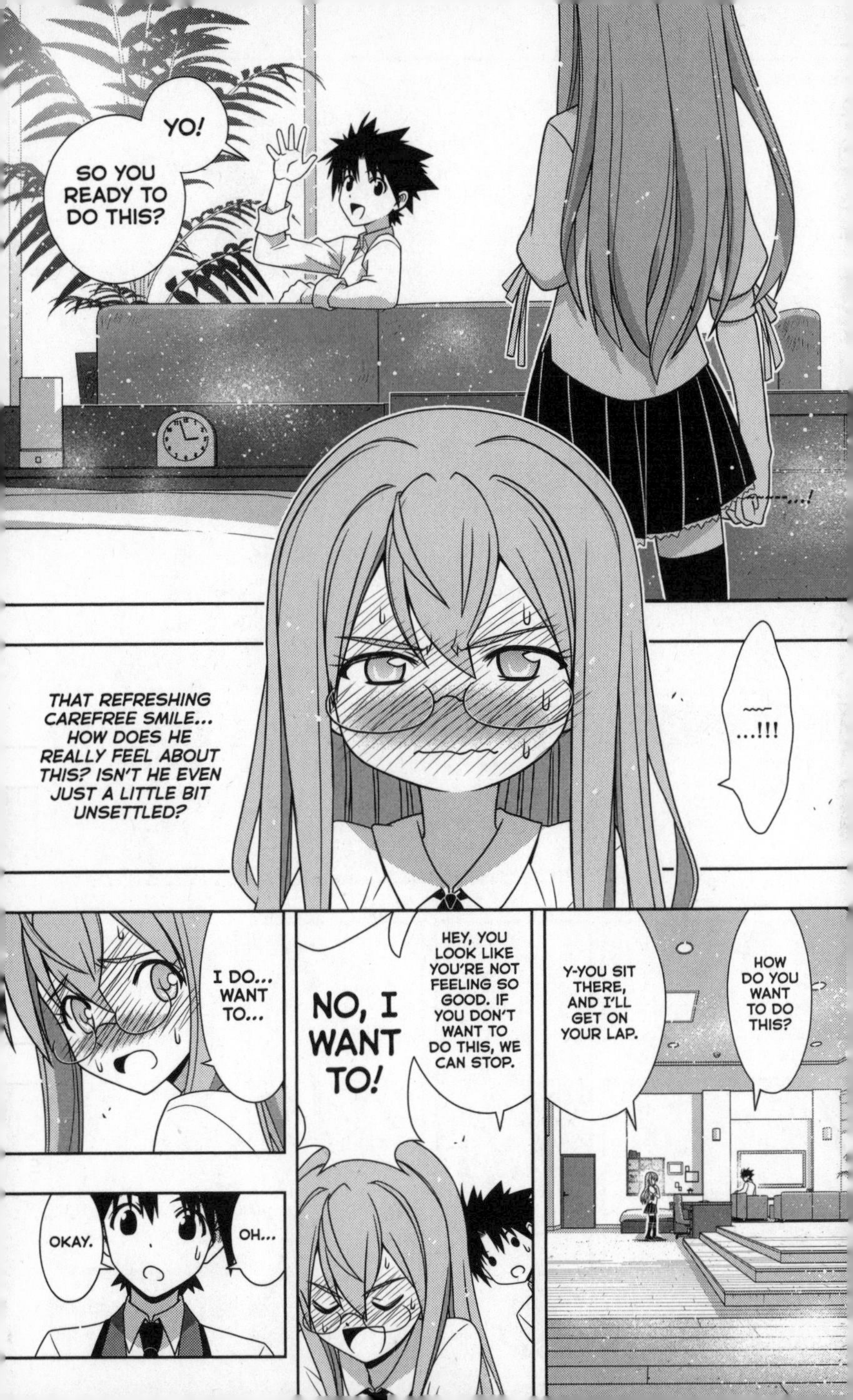
YO!
SO YOU READY TO DO THIS?
~~ ...!!!
THAT REFRESHING CAREFREE SMILE... HOW DOES HE REALLY FEEL ABOUT THIS? ISN'T HE EVEN JUST A LITTLE BIT UNSETTLED?
HOW DO YOU WANT TO DO THIS?
Y-YOU SIT THERE, AND I'LL GET ON YOUR LAP.
HEY, YOU LOOK LIKE YOU'RE NOT FEELING SO GOOD. IF YOU DON'T WANT TO DO THIS, WE CAN STOP.
NO, I WANT TO!
I DO... WANT TO...
OH...
OKAY.

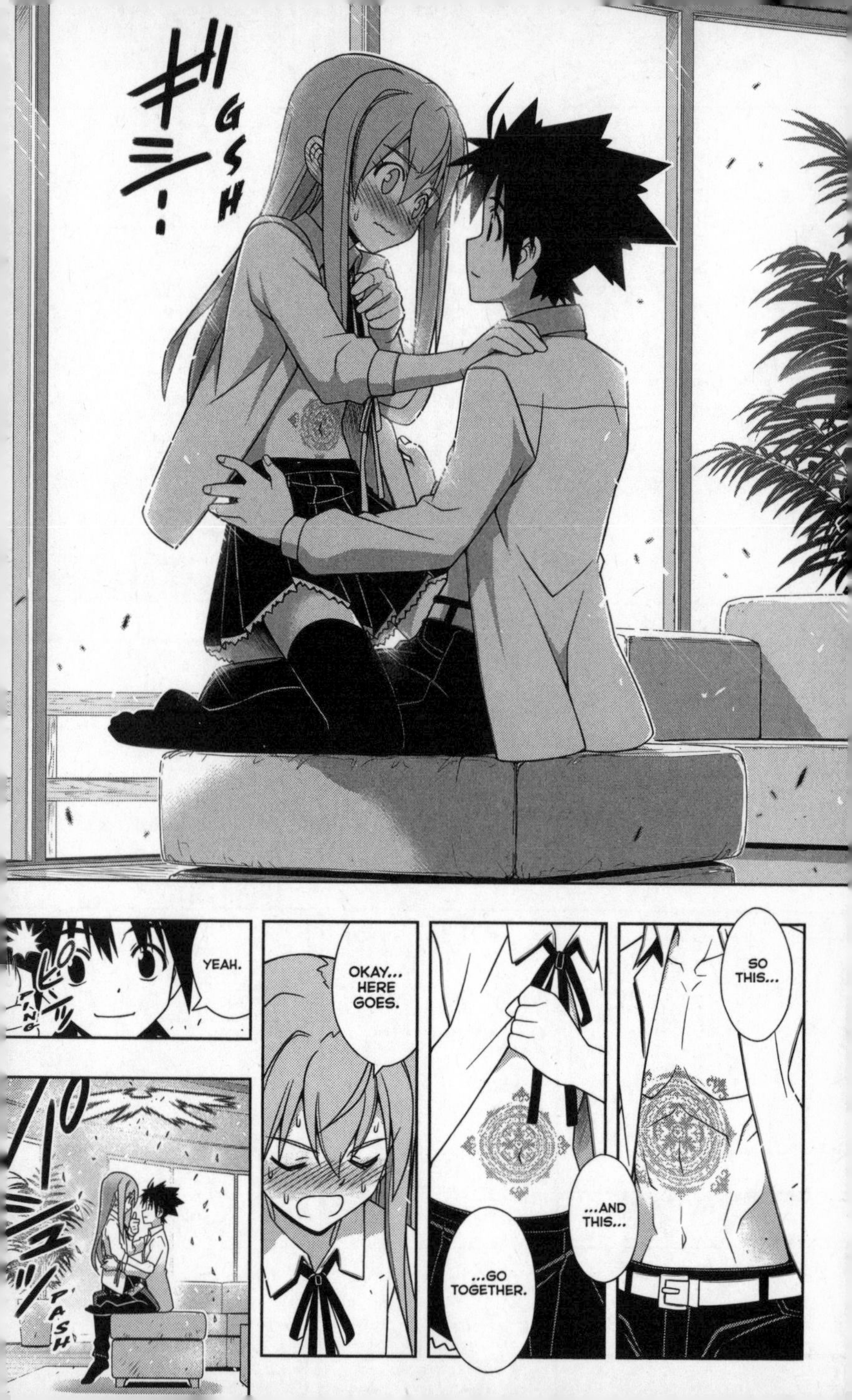
GSH
SO THIS...
...AND THIS...
...GO TOGETHER.
OKAY... HERE GOES.
YEAH.
TING
PASH

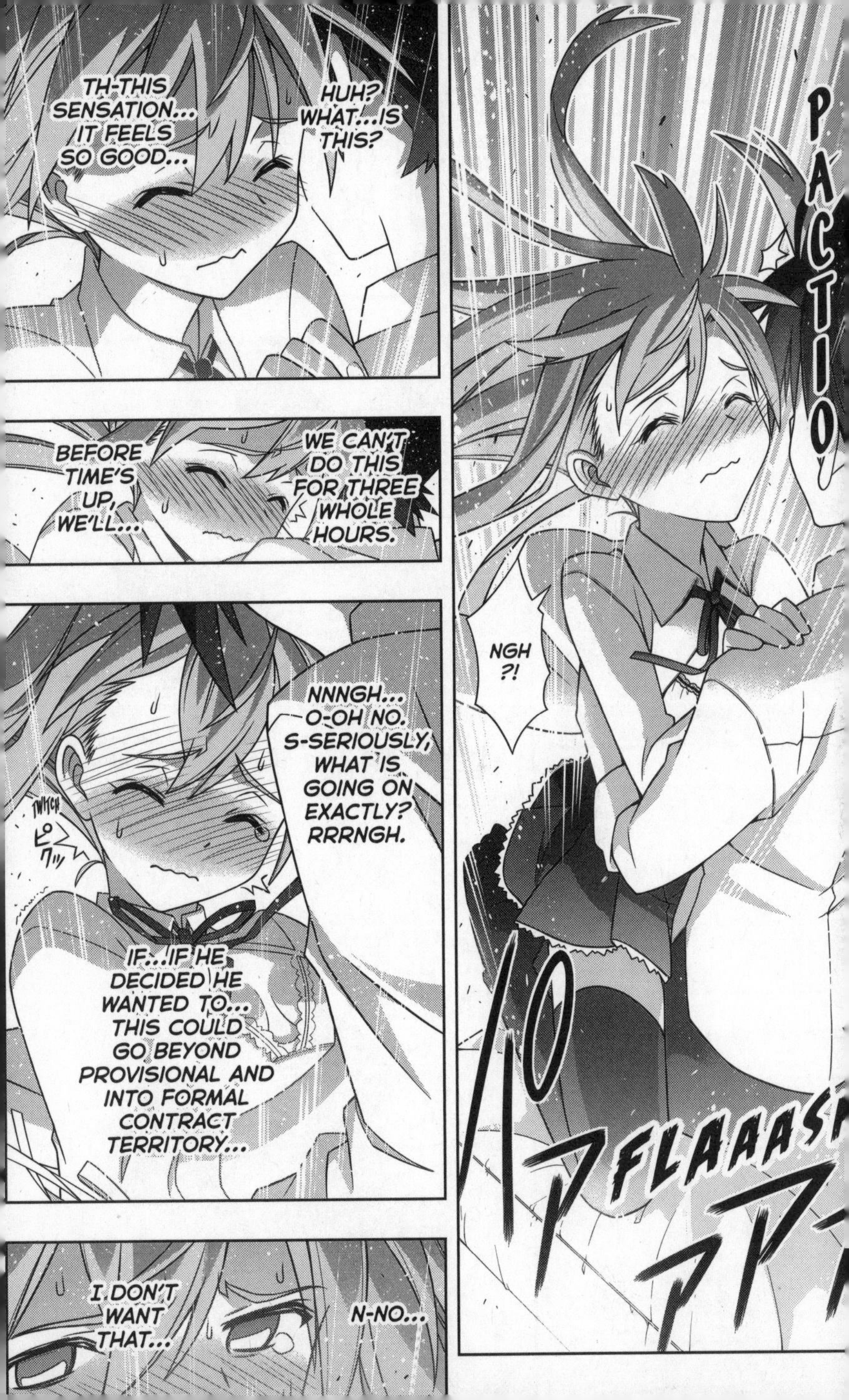
PACTIO
NGH ?!
FLAAASH
HUH? WHAT...IS THIS?
TH-THIS SENSATION... IT FEELS SO GOOD...
WE CAN'T DO THIS FOR THREE WHOLE HOURS.
BEFORE TIME'S UP, WE'LL...
NNNGH... O-OH NO. S-SERIOUSLY, WHAT IS GOING ON EXACTLY? RRRNGH.
TWITCH
IF...IF HE DECIDED HE WANTED TO... THIS COULD GO BEYOND PROVISIONAL AND INTO FORMAL CONTRACT TERRITORY...
N-NO...
I DON'T WANT THAT...

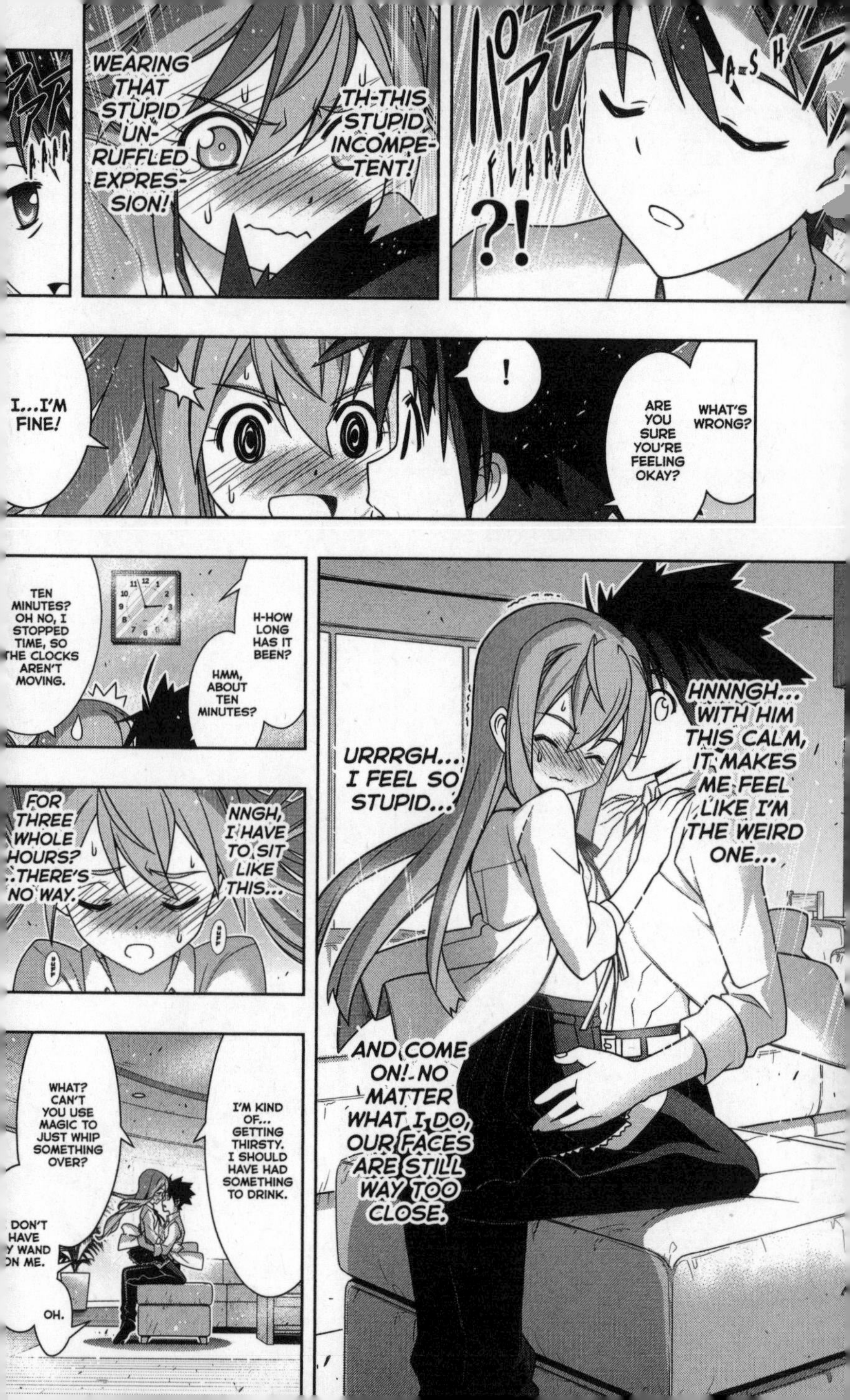

A-S-H
FLAAAA
?!
TH-THIS STUPID INCOMPE-TENT!
WEARING THAT STUPID UN-RUFFLED EXPRES-SION!
WHAT'S WRONG?
ARE YOU SURE YOU'RE FEELING OKAY?
!
I...I'M FINE!
HNNNGH... WITH HIM THIS CALM, IT MAKES ME FEEL LIKE I'M THE WEIRD ONE...
URRRGH... I FEEL SO STUPID...
AND COME ON! NO MATTER WHAT I DO, OUR FACES ARE STILL WAY TOO CLOSE.
H-HOW LONG HAS IT BEEN?
HMM, ABOUT TEN MINUTES?
TEN MINUTES? OH NO, I STOPPED TIME, SO THE CLOCKS AREN'T MOVING.
NNGH, I HAVE TO SIT LIKE THIS...
FOR THREE WHOLE HOURS? .THERE'S NO WAY.
I'M KIND OF... GETTING THIRSTY. I SHOULD HAVE HAD SOMETHING TO DRINK.
WHAT? CAN'T YOU USE MAGIC TO JUST WHIP SOMETHING OVER?
DON'T HAVE Y WAND ON ME.
OH.

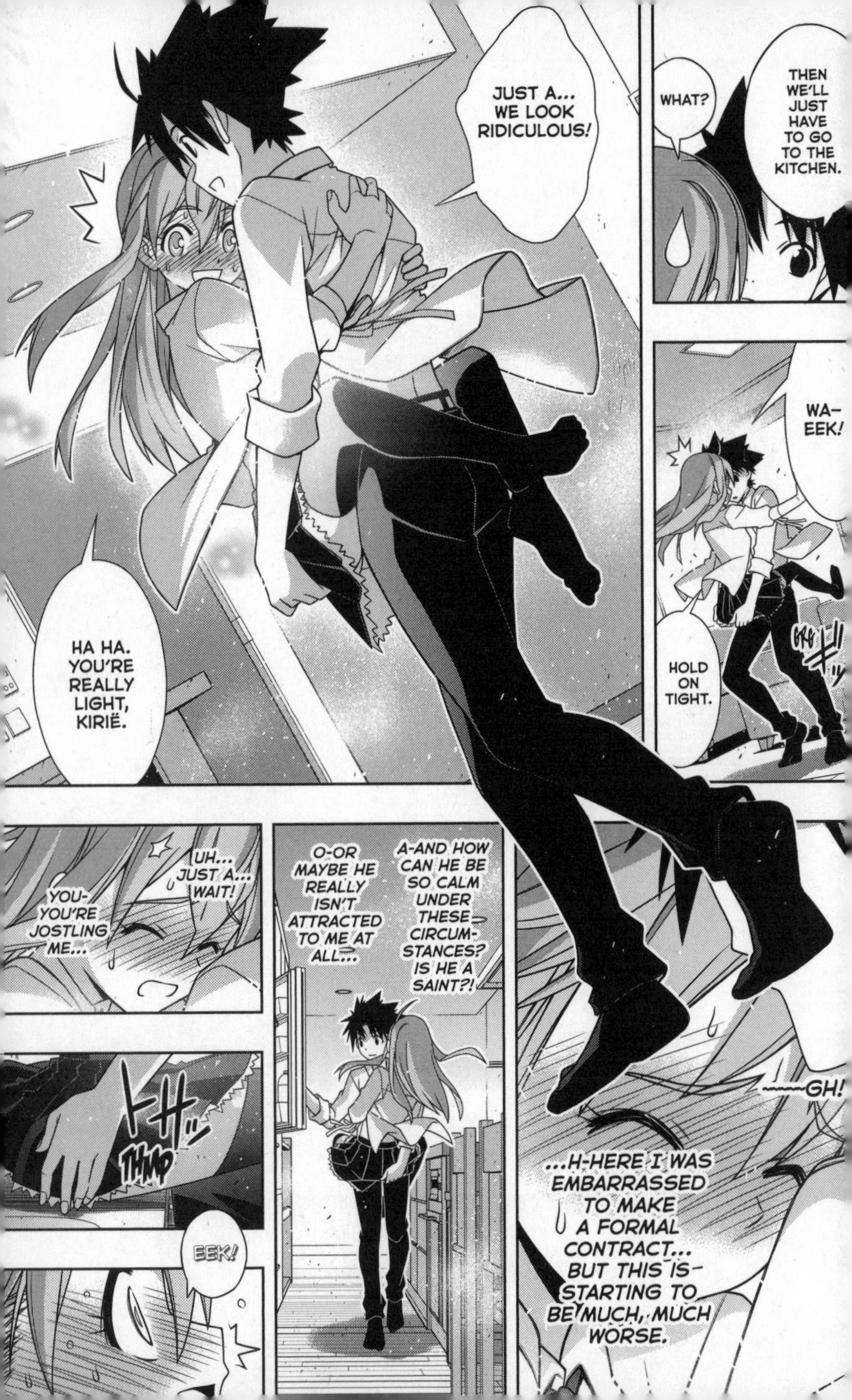
THEN WE'LL JUST HAVE TO GO TO THE KITCHEN.
WHAT?
WA—EEK!
HOLD ON TIGHT.
JUST A... WE LOOK RIDICULOUS!
HA HA. YOU'RE REALLY LIGHT, KIRIË.
——GH!
...H-HERE I WAS EMBARRASSED TO MAKE A FORMAL CONTRACT... BUT THIS IS— STARTING TO BE MUCH, MUCH WORSE.
A-AND HOW CAN HE BE SO CALM UNDER THESE CIRCUM-STANCES? IS HE A SAINT?!
O-OR MAYBE HE REALLY ISN'T ATTRACTED TO ME AT ALL...
UH... JUST A... WAIT!
YOU-YOU'RE JOSTLING ME...
THMP
EEK!

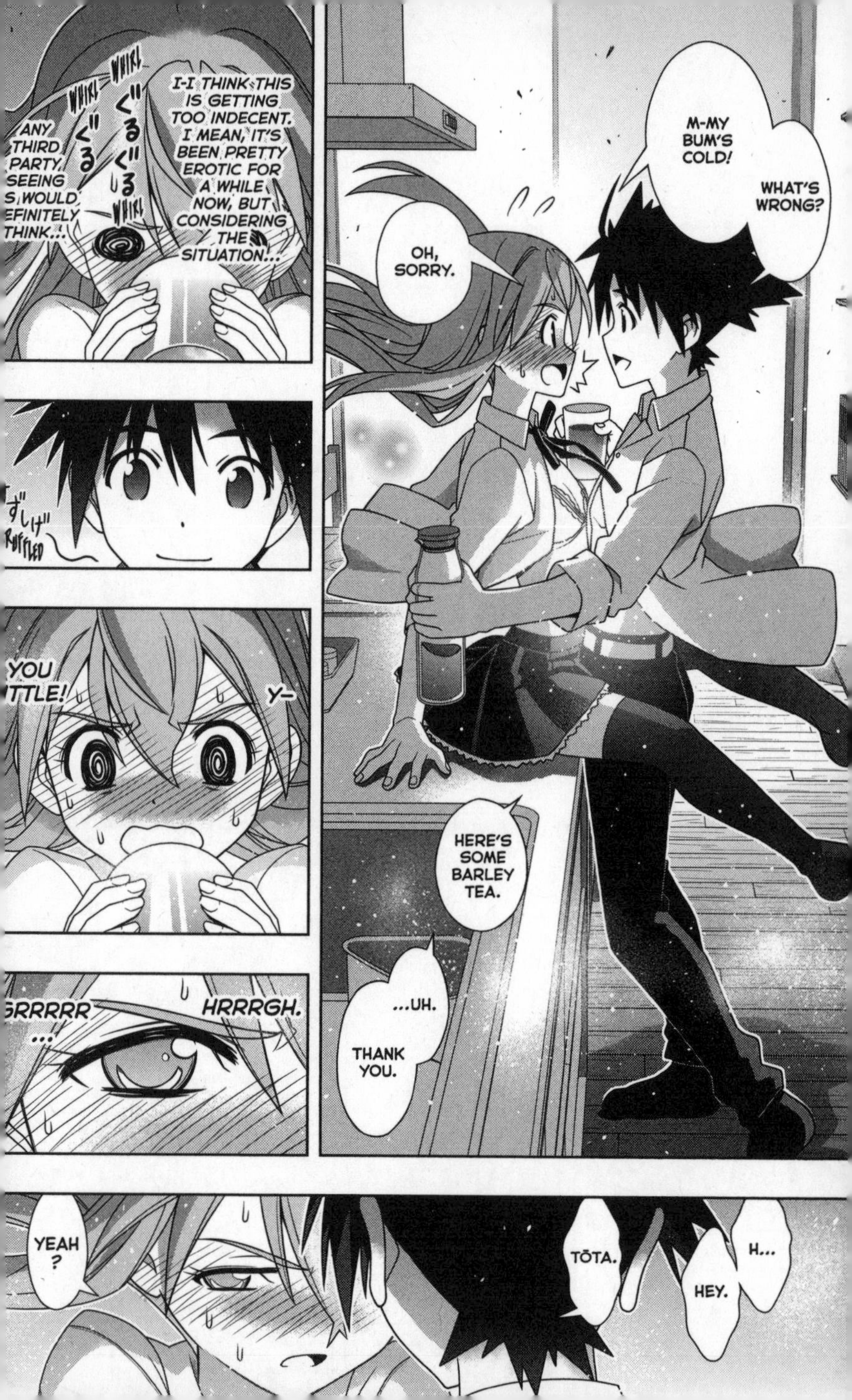
WHAT'S WRONG?
M-MY BUM'S COLD!
OH, SORRY.
HERE'S SOME BARLEY TEA.
...UH.
THANK YOU.
I-I THINK THIS IS GETTING TOO INDECENT. I MEAN, IT'S BEEN PRETTY EROTIC FOR A WHILE NOW, BUT CONSIDERING THE SITUATION...
WHIRL WHIRL WHIRL
ぐるぐるぐるぐる
ANY THIRD PARTY SEEING S WOULD EFINITELY THINK...
RUFFLED
Y–
YOU TTLE!
HRRRGH.
GRRRRR ...
H...
HEY.
TŌTA.
YEAH?

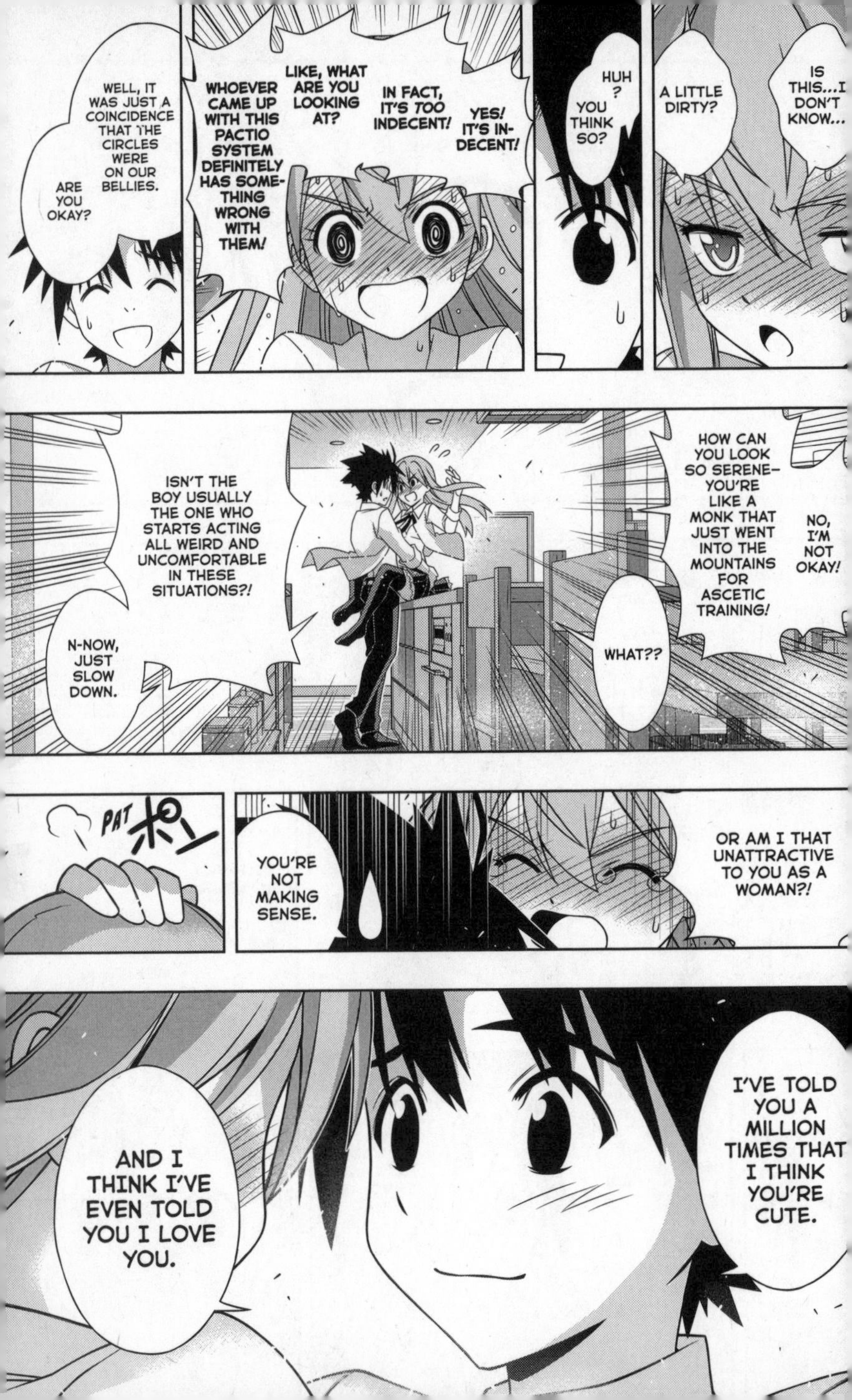
IS THIS...I DON'T KNOW...
A LITTLE DIRTY?
HUH? YOU THINK SO?
YES! IT'S IN-DECENT!
IN FACT, IT'S *TOO* INDECENT!
LIKE, WHAT ARE YOU LOOKING AT?
WHOEVER CAME UP WITH THIS PACTIO SYSTEM DEFINITELY HAS SOME-THING WRONG WITH THEM!
WELL, IT WAS JUST A COINCIDENCE THAT THE CIRCLES WERE ON OUR BELLIES.
ARE YOU OKAY?
NO, I'M NOT OKAY!
HOW CAN YOU LOOK SO SERENE—YOU'RE LIKE A MONK THAT JUST WENT INTO THE MOUNTAINS FOR ASCETIC TRAINING!
WHAT??
ISN'T THE BOY USUALLY THE ONE WHO STARTS ACTING ALL WEIRD AND UNCOMFORTABLE IN THESE SITUATIONS?!
N-NOW, JUST SLOW DOWN.
OR AM I THAT UNATTRACTIVE TO YOU AS A WOMAN?!
YOU'RE NOT MAKING SENSE.
PAT
I'VE TOLD YOU A MILLION TIMES THAT I THINK YOU'RE CUTE.
AND I THINK I'VE EVEN TOLD YOU I LOVE YOU.

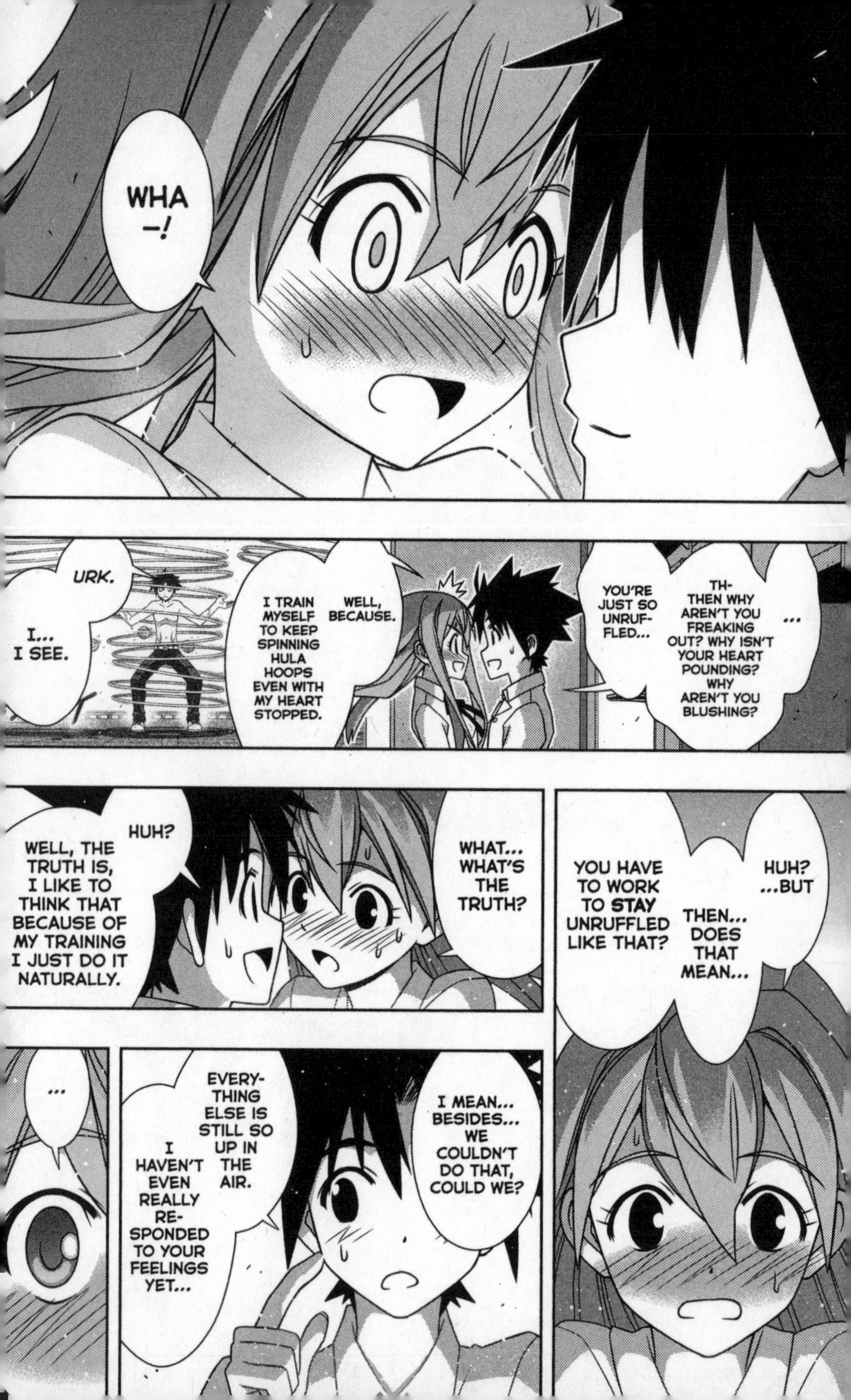
WHA —!
...
TH- THEN WHY AREN'T YOU FREAKING OUT? WHY ISN'T YOUR HEART POUNDING? WHY AREN'T YOU BLUSHING?
YOU'RE JUST SO UNRUF- FLED...
WELL, BECAUSE.
I TRAIN MYSELF TO KEEP SPINNING HULA HOOPS EVEN WITH MY HEART STOPPED.
URK.
I... I SEE.
HUH? ...BUT
YOU HAVE TO WORK TO STAY UNRUFFLED LIKE THAT?
THEN... DOES THAT MEAN...
WHAT... WHAT'S THE TRUTH?
HUH?
WELL, THE TRUTH IS, I LIKE TO THINK THAT BECAUSE OF MY TRAINING I JUST DO IT NATURALLY.
I MEAN... BESIDES... WE COULDN'T DO THAT, COULD WE?
EVERY- THING ELSE IS STILL SO UP IN THE AIR.
I HAVEN'T EVEN REALLY RE- SPONDED TO YOUR FEELINGS YET...
...

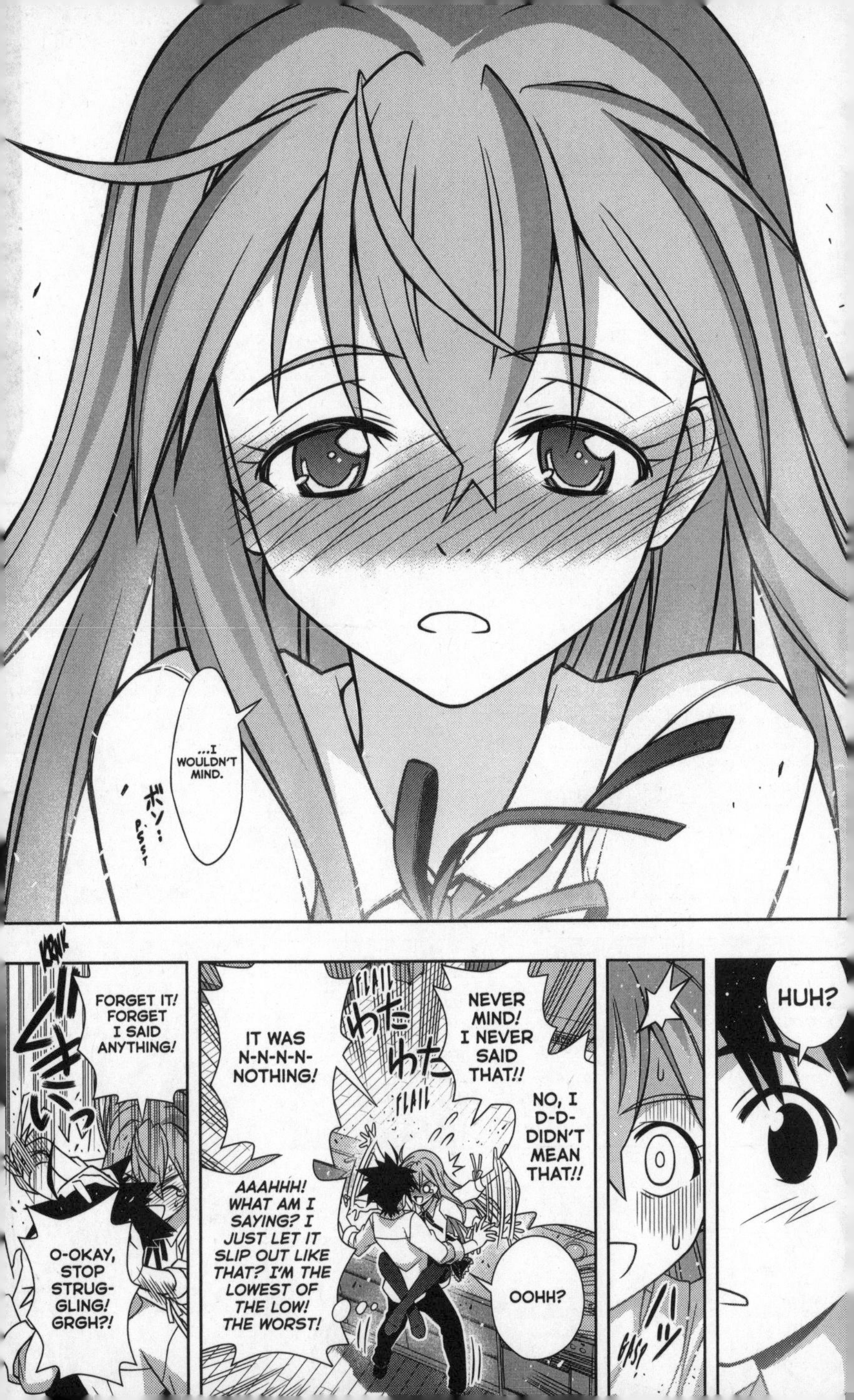
...I WOULDN'T MIND.
PSST
HUH?
GASP
NEVER MIND! I NEVER SAID THAT!!
NO, I D-D-DIDN'T MEAN THAT!!
FLAIL
わたわた
FLAIL
IT WAS N-N-N-N-NOTHING!
AAAHHH! WHAT AM I SAYING? I JUST LET IT SLIP OUT LIKE THAT? I'M THE LOWEST OF THE LOW! THE WORST!
OOHH?
FORGET IT! FORGET I SAID ANYTHING!
O-OKAY, STOP STRUG-GLING! GRGH?!

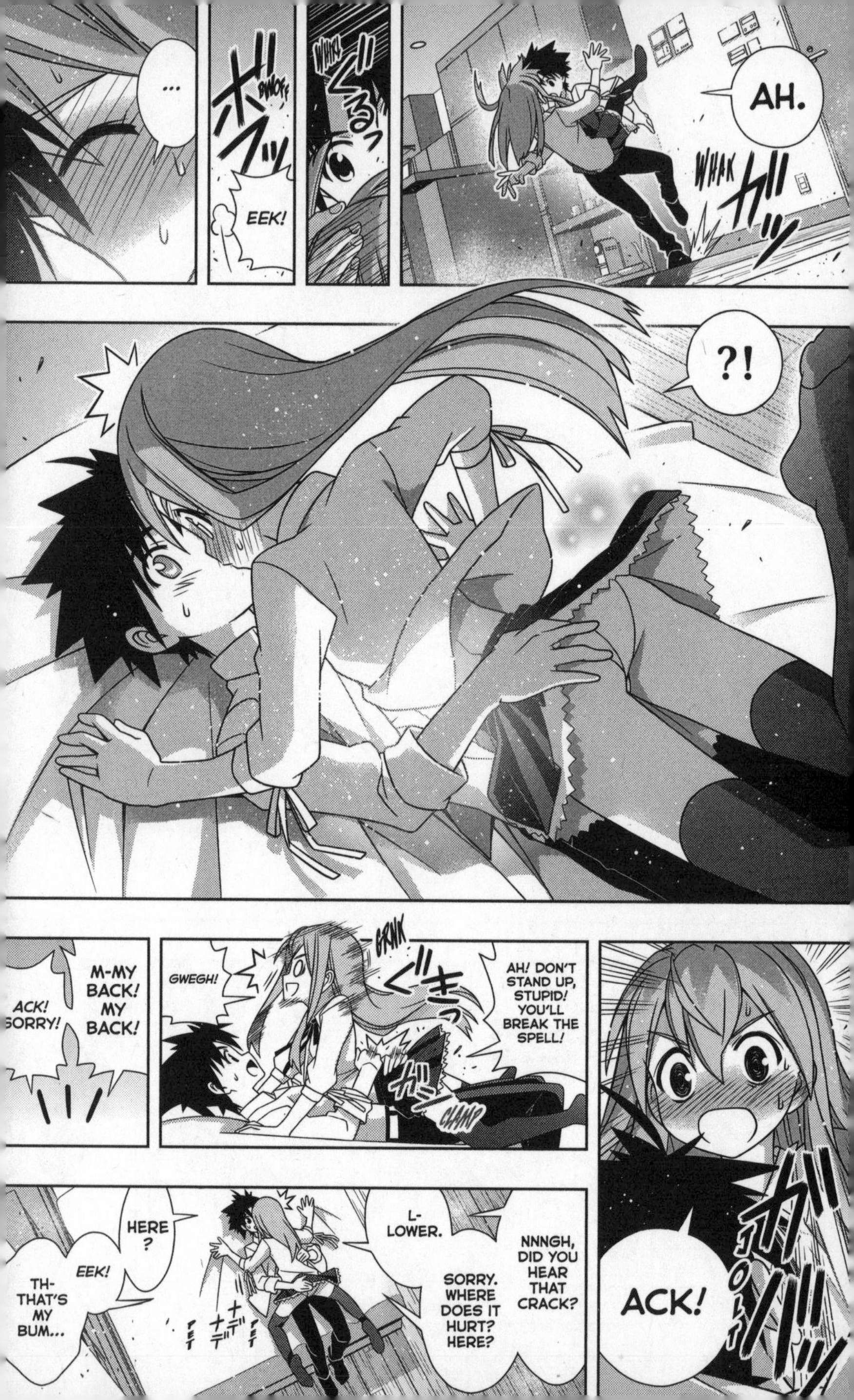
AH.
WHAK
WHIRL
BWOFF
EEK!
...
?!
ACK!
AH! DON'T STAND UP, STUPID! YOU'LL BREAK THE SPELL!
GRNK
GWEGH!
CLAMP
M-MY BACK! MY BACK!
ACK! SORRY!
NNNGH, DID YOU HEAR THAT CRACK?
SORRY. WHERE DOES IT HURT? HERE?
L-LOWER.
HERE?
PET
PET
EEK!
TH-THAT'S MY BUM...

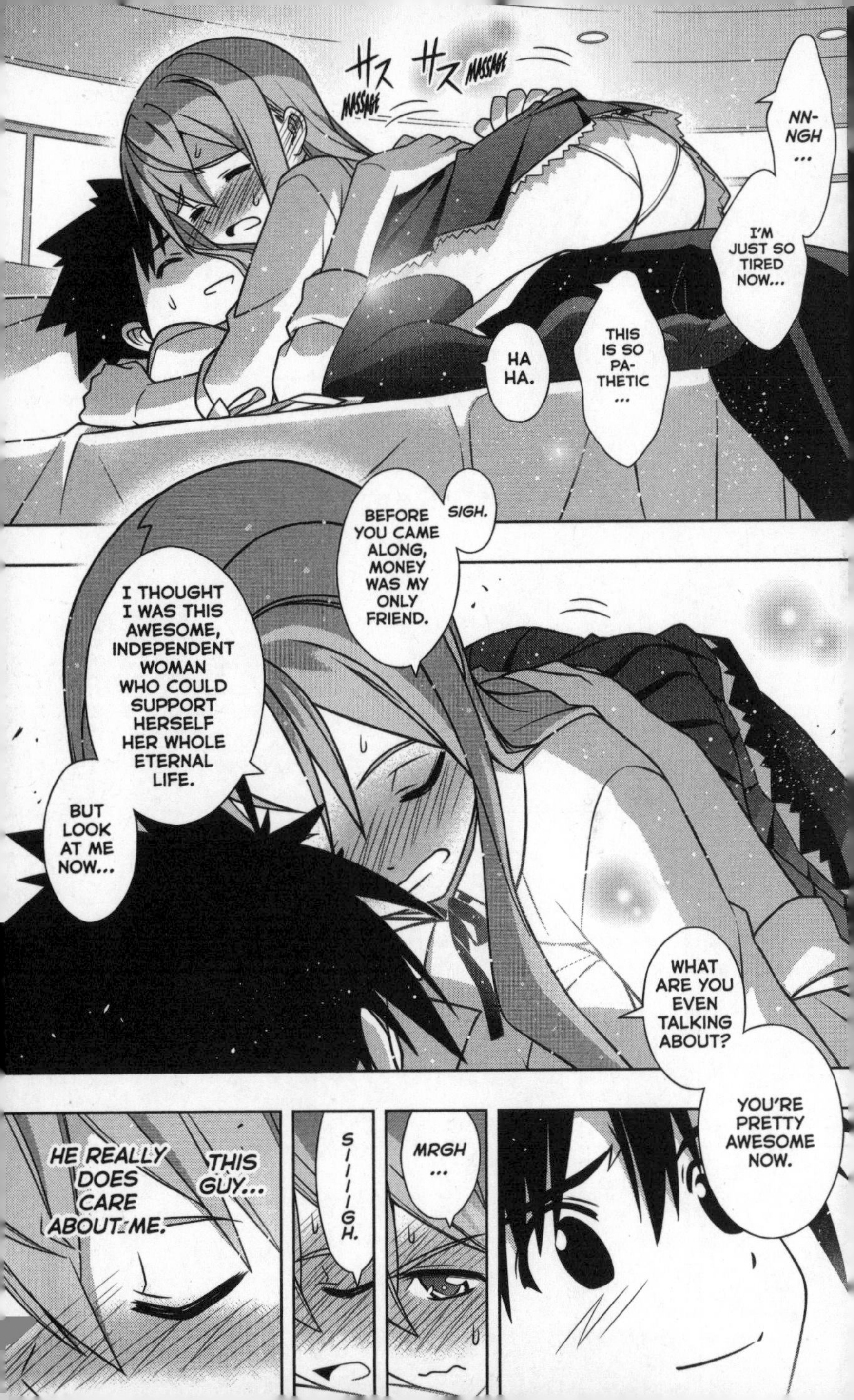
サス MASSAGE
サス MASSAGE
NN-NGH...
I'M JUST SO TIRED NOW...
THIS IS SO PATHETIC...
HA HA.
SIGH.
BEFORE YOU CAME ALONG, MONEY WAS MY ONLY FRIEND.
I THOUGHT I WAS THIS AWESOME, INDEPENDENT WOMAN WHO COULD SUPPORT HERSELF HER WHOLE ETERNAL LIFE.
BUT LOOK AT ME NOW...
WHAT ARE YOU EVEN TALKING ABOUT?
YOU'RE PRETTY AWESOME NOW.
MRGH...
SIIIIGH.
THIS GUY...
HE REALLY DOES CARE ABOUT ME.

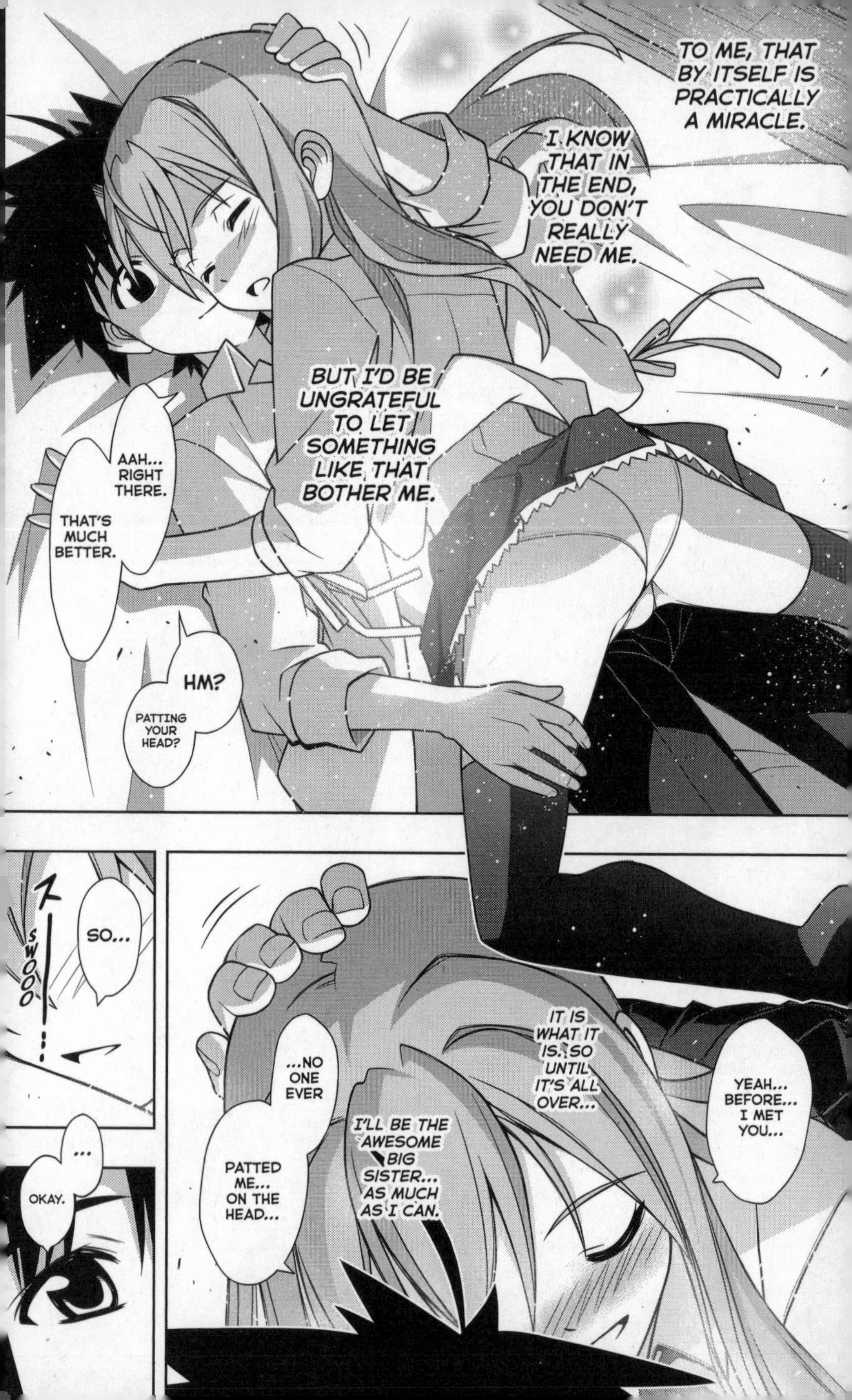
TO ME, THAT BY ITSELF IS PRACTICALLY A MIRACLE.
I KNOW THAT IN THE END, YOU DON'T REALLY NEED ME.
BUT I'D BE UNGRATEFUL TO LET SOMETHING LIKE THAT BOTHER ME.
AAH... RIGHT THERE.
THAT'S MUCH BETTER.
HM?
PATTING YOUR HEAD?
YEAH... BEFORE... I MET YOU...
IT IS WHAT IT IS. SO UNTIL IT'S ALL OVER...
...NO ONE EVER
PATTED ME... ON THE HEAD...
I'LL BE THE AWESOME BIG SISTER... AS MUCH AS I CAN.
SWOOOO...!
SO...
...
OKAY.

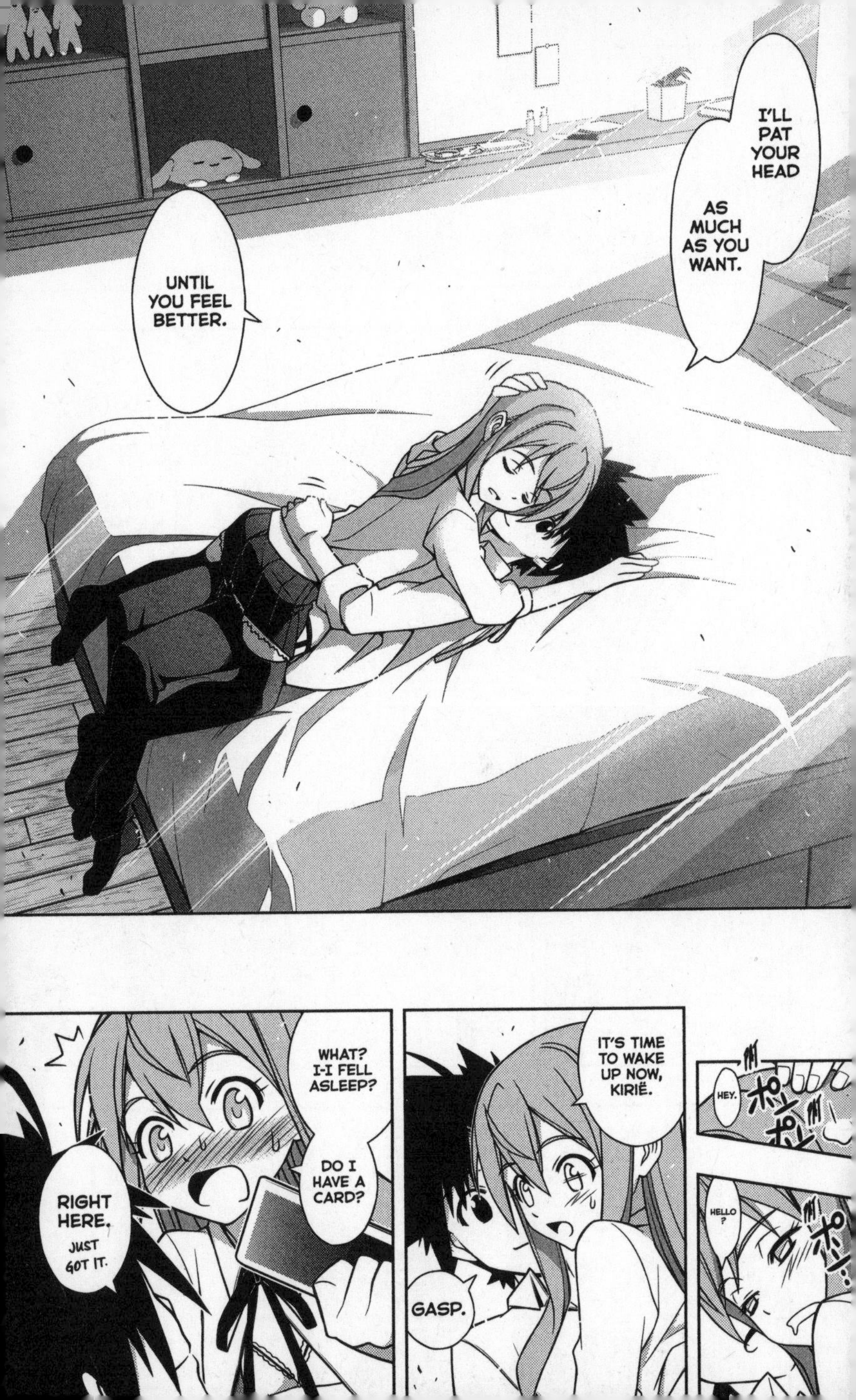
I'LL PAT YOUR HEAD
AS MUCH AS YOU WANT.
UNTIL YOU FEEL BETTER.
HEY.
HELLO?
IT'S TIME TO WAKE UP NOW, KIRIË.
GASP.
WHAT? I-I FELL ASLEEP?
DO I HAVE A CARD?
RIGHT HERE.
JUST GOT IT.

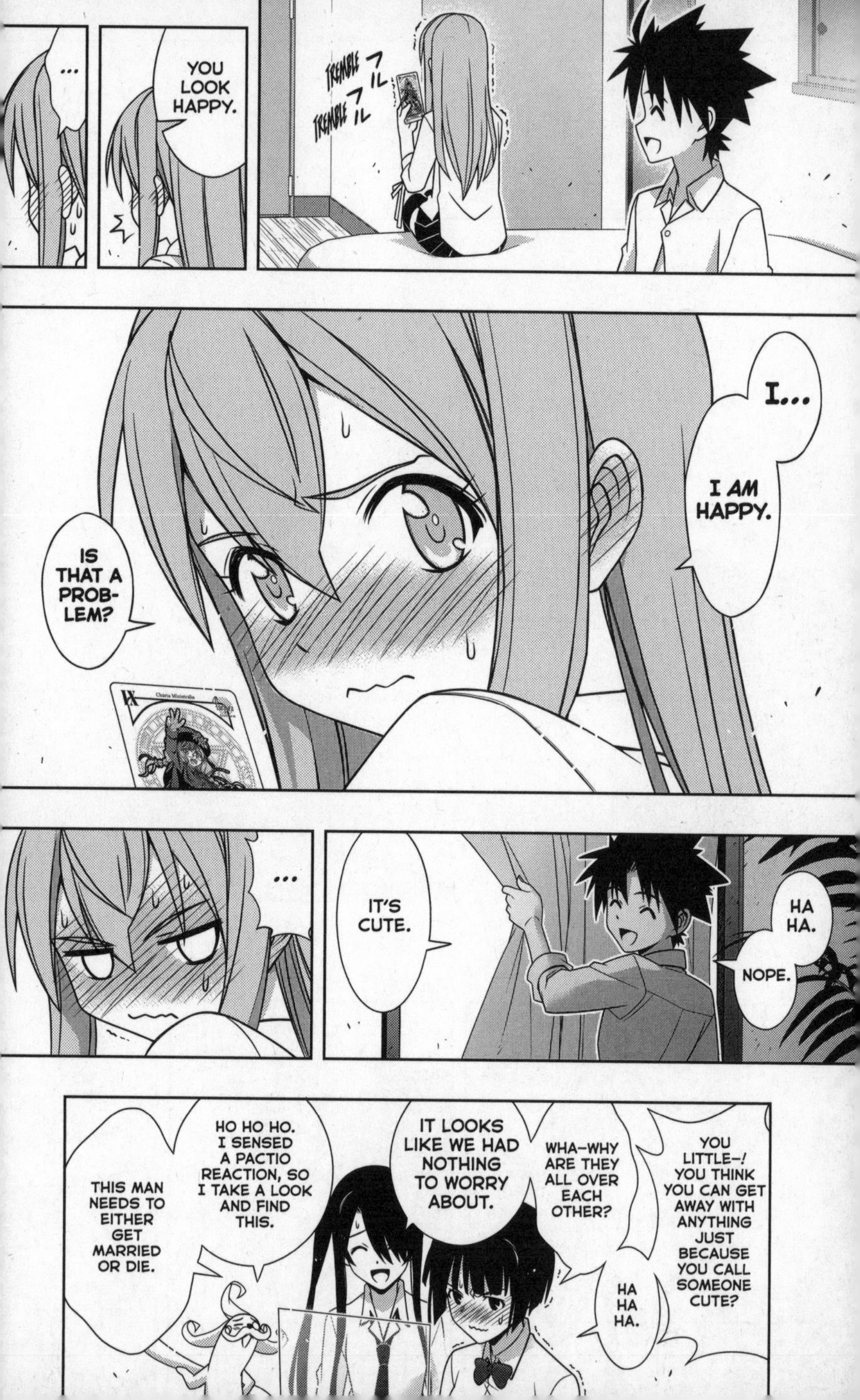
TREMBLE フル
TREMBLE フル
YOU LOOK HAPPY.
...
I...
I AM HAPPY.
IS THAT A PROB-LEM?
HA HA.
NOPE.
IT'S CUTE.
...
YOU LITTLE–! YOU THINK YOU CAN GET AWAY WITH ANYTHING JUST BECAUSE YOU CALL SOMEONE CUTE?
HA HA HA.
WHA–WHY ARE THEY ALL OVER EACH OTHER?
IT LOOKS LIKE WE HAD NOTHING TO WORRY ABOUT.
HO HO HO. I SENSED A PACTIO REACTION, SO I TAKE A LOOK AND FIND THIS.
THIS MAN NEEDS TO EITHER GET MARRIED OR DIE.

UQ HOLDER!

STAFF

Ken Akamatsu

Takashi Takemoto

Kenichi Nakamura

Keiichi Yamashita

Yuri Sasaki

Madoka Akanuma

Thanks to Ran Ayanaga

悠 UQ HOLDER!

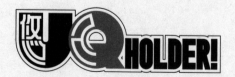

ART GALLERY

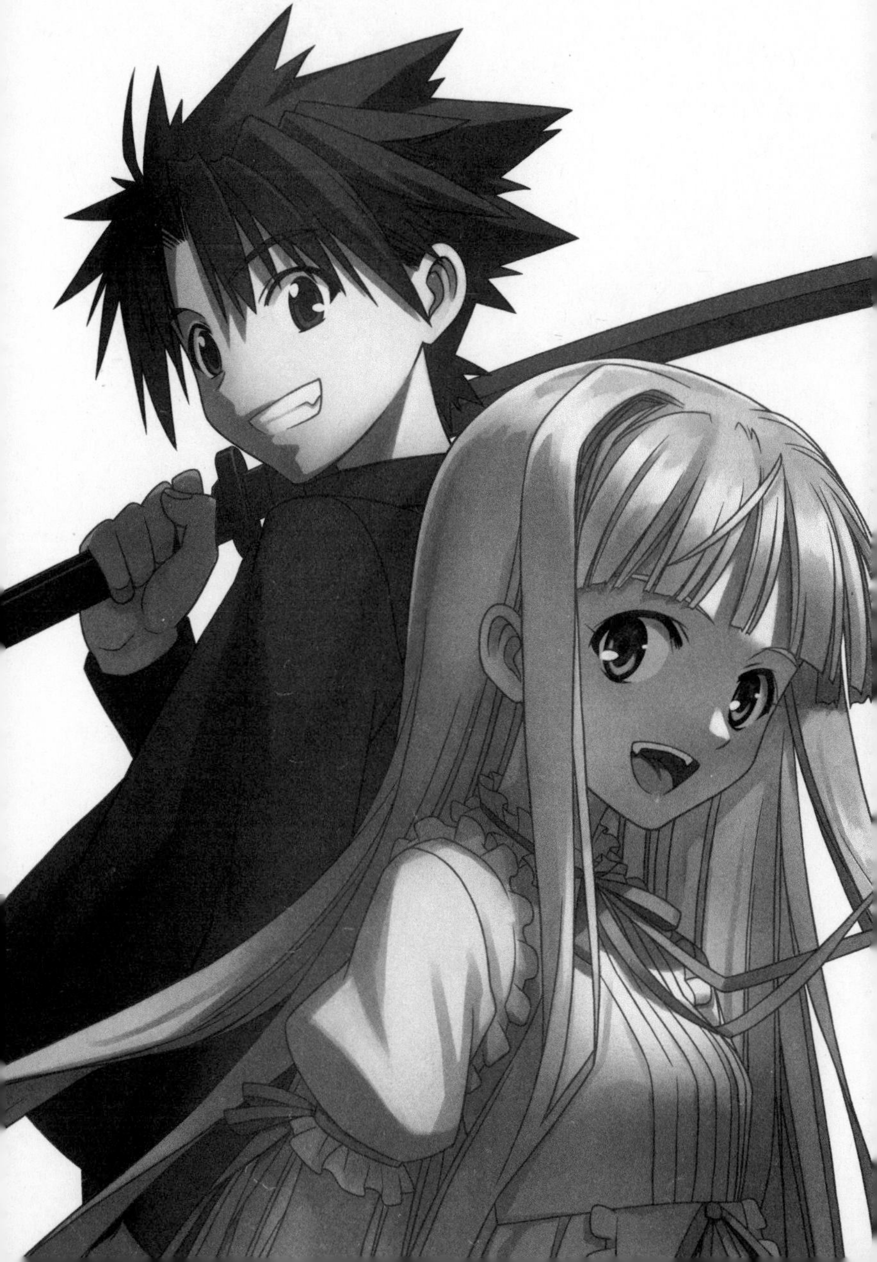

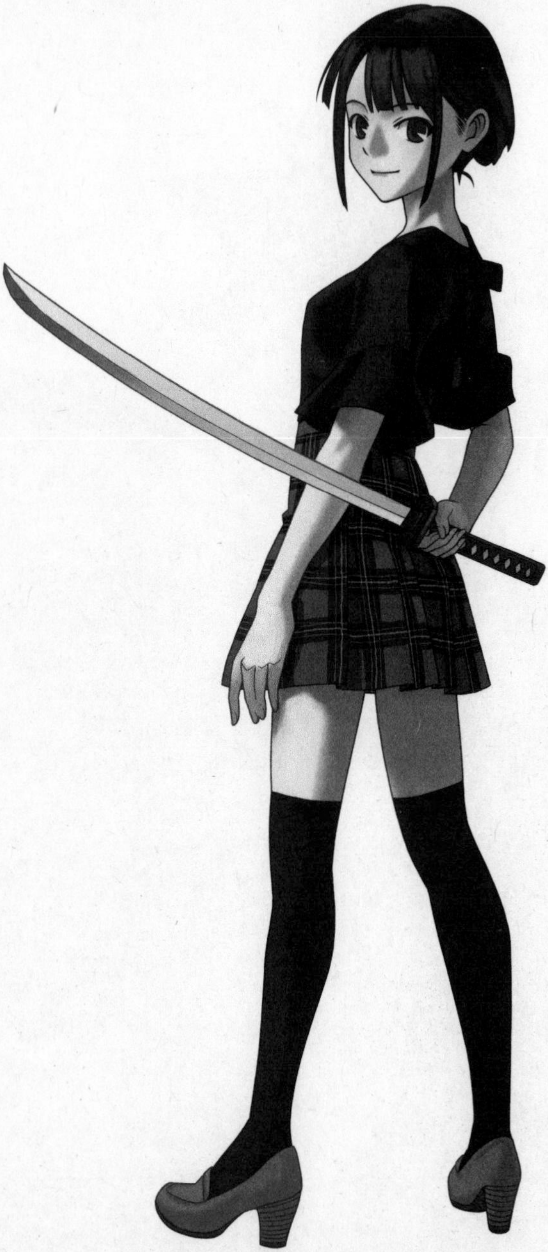

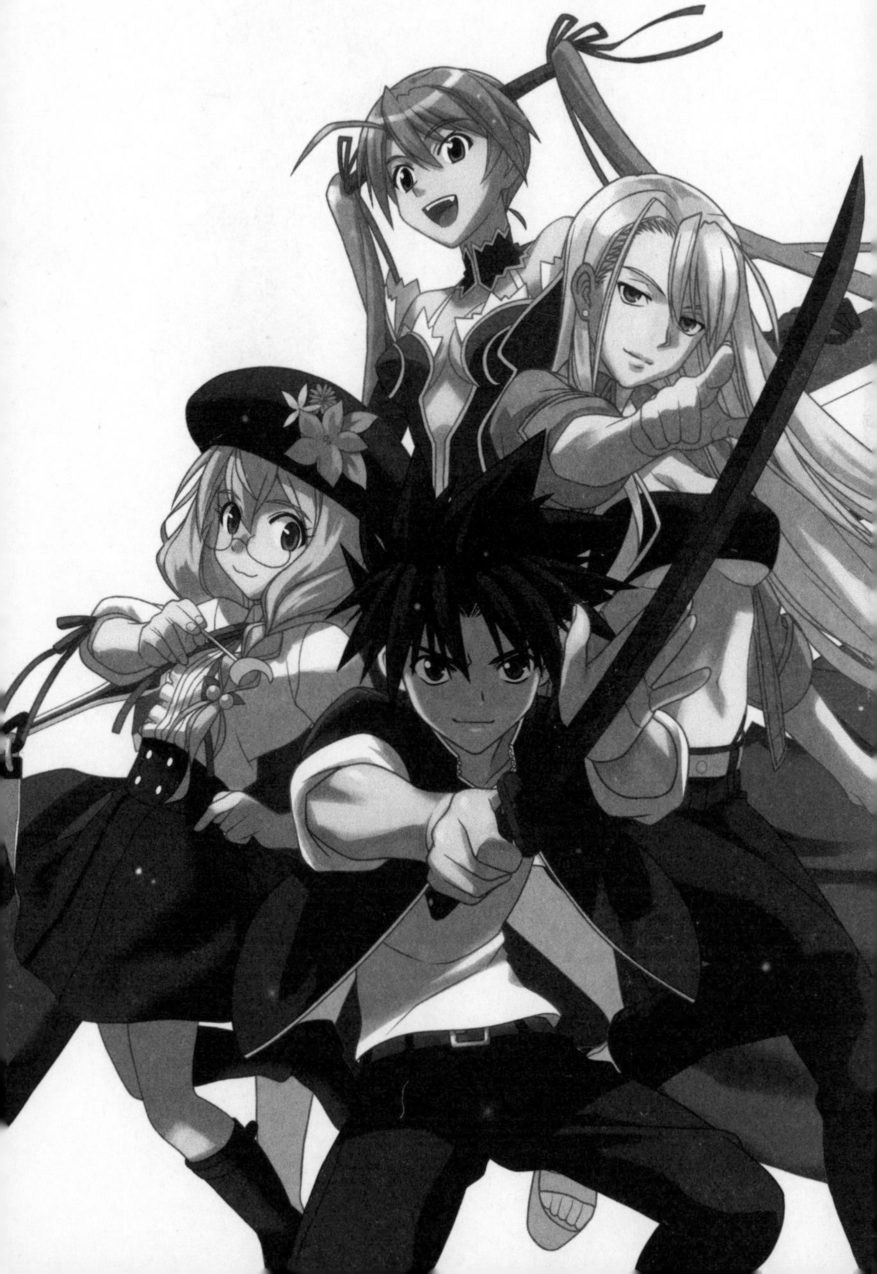

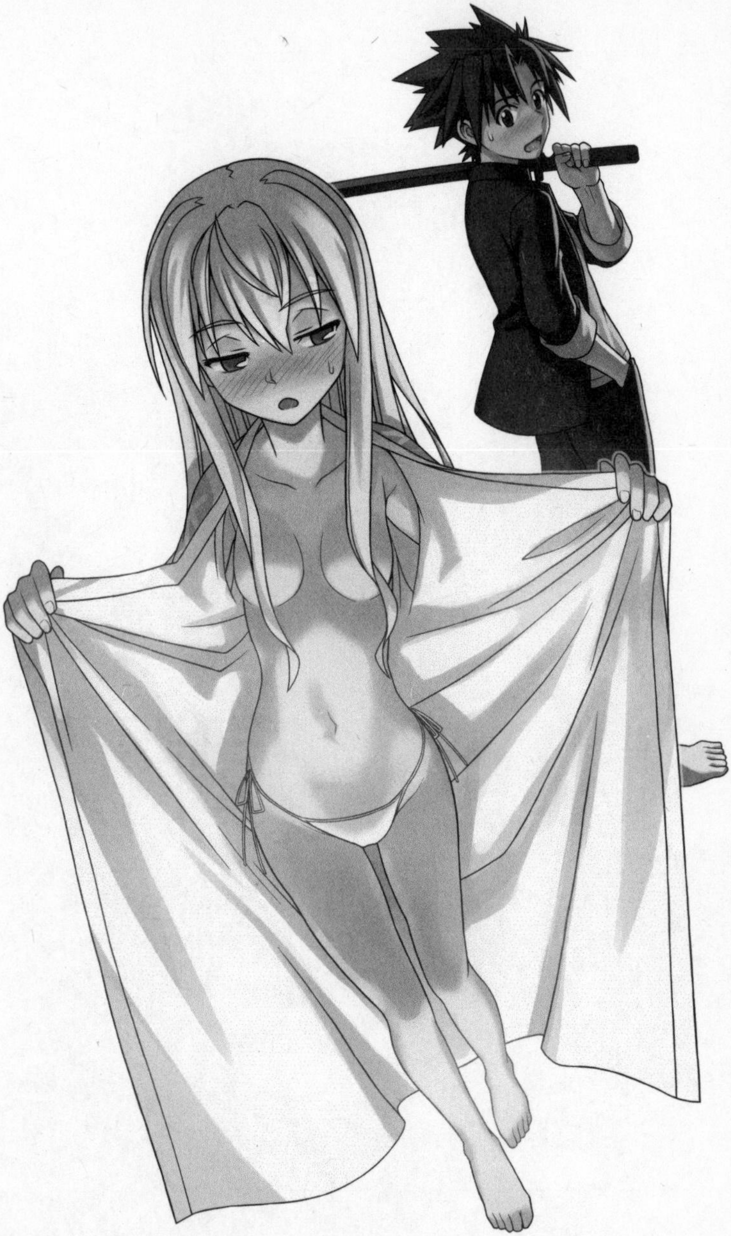

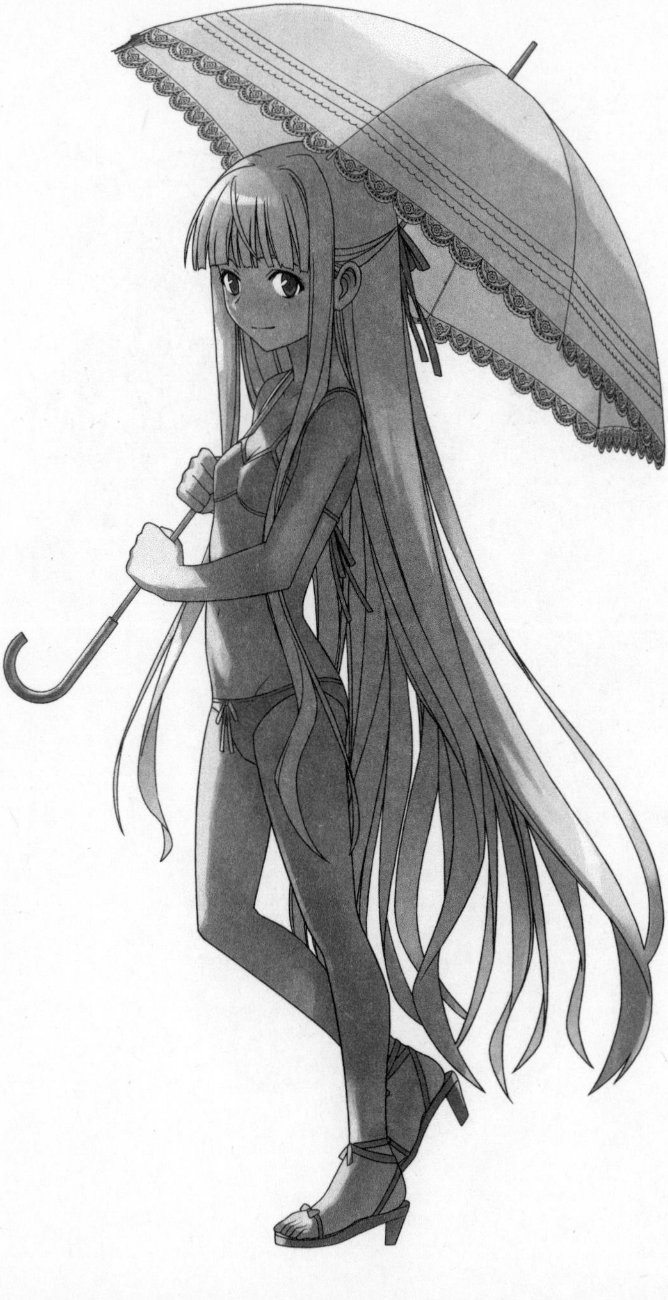

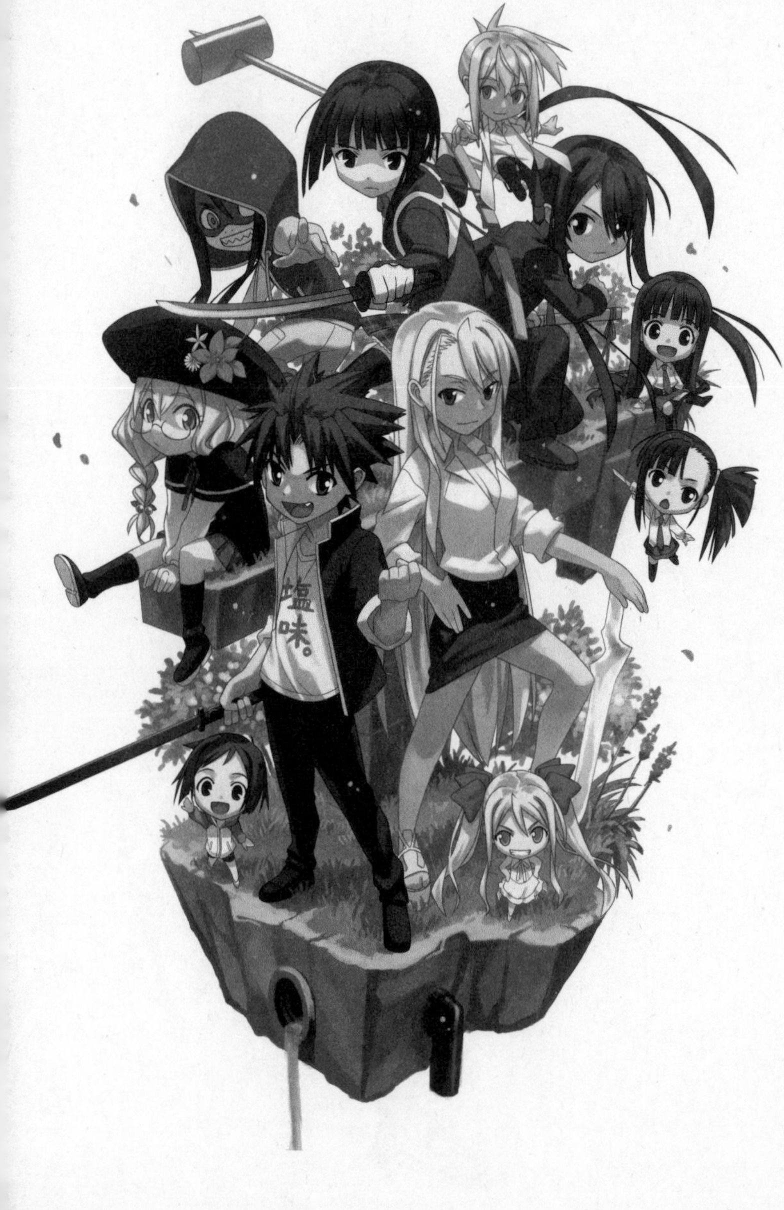
塩味。

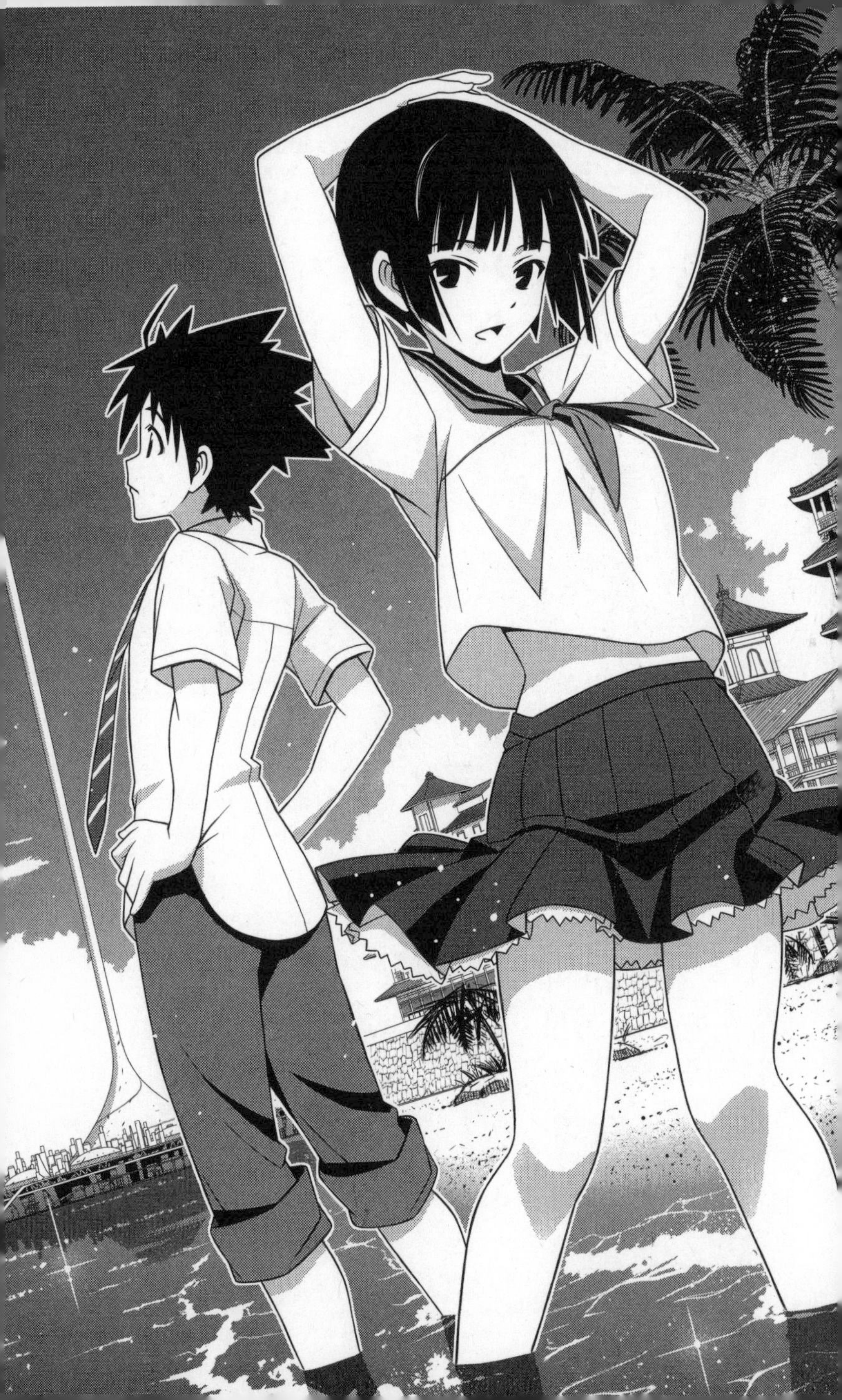

EDENS ZERO
エデンズゼロ

HIRO MASHIMA IS BACK! JOIN THE CREATOR OF *FAIRY TAIL* AS HE TAKES TO THE STARS FOR ANOTHER THRILLING SAGA!

A high-flying space adventure! All the steadfast friendship and wild fighting you've been waiting for...IN SPACE!

At Granbell Kingdom, an abandoned amusement park, Shiki has lived his entire life among machines. But one day, Rebecca and her cat companion Happy appear at the park's front gates. Little do these newcomers know that this is the first human contact Granbell has had in a hundred years! As Shiki stumbles his way into making new friends, his former neighbors stir at an opportunity for a robo-rebellion... And when his old homeland becomes too dangerous, Shiki must join Rebecca and Happy on their spaceship and escape into the boundless cosmos.

KODANSHA COMICS

A Kodansha Comics Trade Paperback Original
UQ HOLDER! 19 copyright © 2019 Ken Akamatsu
English translation copyright © 2020 Ken Akamatsu

Published in the United States by Kodansha Comics, an imprint of Kodansha USA Publishing, LLC, New York.

Publication rights for this English edition arranged through Kodansha Ltd., Tokyo.

First published in Japan in 2019 by Kodansha Ltd., Tokyo.

ISBN 978-1-63236-928-4

Original cover design by Kazuya Sakagami (banjo)

Printed in the United States of America.

www.kodanshacomics.com

9 8 7 6 5 4 3 2 1
Translation: Alethea Nibley & Athena Nibley
Lettering: James Dashiell
Kodansha Comics edition cover design by Phil Balsman

Publisher: Kiichiro Sugawara
Vice president of marketing & publicity: Naho Yamada

Director of publishing services: Ben Applegate
Associate director of operations: Stephen Pakula
Publishing services managing editor: Noelle Webster
Assistant production manager: Emi Lotto